British Investment in
American Railways
1834–1898

WITHDRAWN
UTSA LIBRARIES

BRITISH INVESTMENT IN AMERICAN RAILWAYS

1834–1898

By Dorothy R. Adler

Edited by Muriel E. Hidy

Published for the
Eleutherian Mills–Hagley Foundation

The University Press of Virginia
Charlottesville

THE UNIVERSITY PRESS OF VIRGINIA
Copyright © 1970 by the Eleutherian Mills–Hagley Foundation
First published 1970
Standard Book Number: 8139–0311–4
Library of Congress Catalog Card Number: 79–122437
Printed in the United States of America

Editor's Introduction

IN THE nineteenth century the interregional and international flow of private capital played a significant role in economic development. Dorothy R. Adler addressed herself to an important phase of this subject, the investment by British men and institutions of the United Kingdom in the railroads of the United States. On the one side were the accumulation of savings, the decisions to invest, and the evolving capital market and its institutions; on the other was the multitude of rapidly expanding transportation companies that were seeking funds.

The author was well prepared to undertake her study. Dorothy Fox Richardson, the daughter of Mr. and Mrs. Lawrence Richardson of Cambridge, Massachusetts, was raised in a railroad family. Her father worked for the Boston and Maine Railway Company and was president of the Rutland Railroad Company of Vermont. She received her undergraduate training at Bryn Mawr College in Pennsylvania, earning her B.A. in 1939. She then studied economics at Radcliffe College, Massachusetts, and in February 1943 received her M.A. degree there, after which she had three years of experience as a government economist. On April 27, 1945, she married an economist of English origin, Solomon Adler, and with him went to England in 1950. After receiving her Ph.D. at Cambridge University in 1958, Mrs. Adler was a research fellow at Newnham College and an assistant lecturer in economic history at Cambridge University.[1]

Reviewing Mrs. Adler's work in 1959, Frank Thistlethwaite, the scholar who supervised her study, evaluated the complexity of her subject and her contributions. The time span covered was both a long and a dynamically changing one. Scattered over a vast area of the United States were many different types of railways; they were small and large, built in settled areas and on the frontiers. The pattern of financing that developed was the

[1] Material on Mrs. Adler's life came from records at Radcliffe College, interviews with Dr. Arthur H. Cole and Mr. Lawrence Richardson, and letters from Dr. David Adler, Solomon Adler's brother, to Lawrence Richardson, Nov. 21, 1967, and Dr. David Adler to David T. Gilchrist, Nov. 21, 1967.

result of the decisions of hundreds of men—railroaders, bankers, and investors—inspired by a variety of motives and economic interests. Human and institutional relations were numerous and involved. From this confusing array of data she developed her generalizations.

To quote Thistlethwaite's words:

In short Mrs. Adler has written a first class piece of work of interest to the general, as well as to the economic historian. It is the work of a true historian in the sense that she has rejected the temptation to be too schematic, to force her evidence into a theoretical mould; and instead has gently revealed a pattern which appears to be inherent in the nature of her material. It is clearly written and though she is often tempted to pursue intriguing side-paths she usually manages to return to the high road without loss of direction. It could well be published in its present form; the only question at issue is whether deferring this until she has pursued her researches further, a really major full length study might not emerge[2]

There was not time. Her premature death in March 1963 cut short her plan to complete and publish her work. She had desired to carry the analysis of British capital in the railroads of the United States to 1914 and to the liquidation of British investments during the First World War. Hence, although her revised thesis ends on an incomplete note, given her plans, she has made an important contribution to her chosen subject for most of the long period she had hoped to cover. Especially significant for American readers is the focus; she looks at the flow of capital from the vantage point of the British investor and of the London capital market with its dramatic growth, its distinctive personality, and its ups and downs. Her study of the London capital market is particularly useful.

The complex international economic topic to which Mrs. Adler devoted her careful research involved significant facets of the economic life both of the United Kingdom and of the United States. In the latter country the railroad mileage rose from 23 in 1830 to 9,021 in 1850 and 166,703 in 1890. By the outbreak of the First World War it exceeded 250,000 miles, having reached almost its maximum.[3] In the nineteenth century no other single sector of the economy of the world attracted foreign capital as did the railroads of the United States. In 1910 half of the United Kingdom's portfolio investment abroad (£1,637,684,000 out of £3,191,836,000) was in countries outside of the British Empire. Of this portion, more than 42 percent (£688,078,000) was in the United States, and of this, 85 percent (£586,227,000) was in its railroads.[4]

The impact of the movement of capital was great on the exporting as

[2] Report on Dorothy Adler's thesis to Newnham College, March 24, 1959.

[3] U.S. Bureau of the Census, *Historical Atlas of the United States, Colonial Times to 1957, Statistical Abstract Supplement* (Washington, D.C.: 1960), 427 and 429.

[4] Sir George Paish, "Great Britain's Capital Investments in Individual Colonial and Foreign Countries," *Journal of the Royal Statistical Society*, LXXIV, pt. II (Jan. 1911), 167–87, esp. 176 and 186.

well as on the importing country. Not only did the capital market of the United Kingdom reach a new development, but other sectors of the economic system were also stimulated. Sir George Paish saw "the vast growth of British trade and prosperity" as "largely the result of our investment of capital in other countries." [5] With funds, borrowers could purchase needed capital goods to undertake construction and improvements. Railroads opened up new lands in the United States and attracted an increasing number of settlers, not only from its East to its West but also from abroad. The development of transportation triggered other capital investment. The cumulative effect on growth in terms of the increase of raw materials and foodstuffs produced and exported was dramatic enough for many scholars to consider railroads one of the most dynamic factors in the growth of the American economy.

The relation of export of capital to export of capital goods had particular significance in the case of the iron and steel industry. The credit policies of the Welsh manufacturers of rails, as well as those of bankers, aided railroads in the United States. Some capital arrived in the form of rails. Mrs. Adler included an unusual time series on American imports of British rails, which, it will be noted, brings out the cyclical fluctuations in this trade. She has also pointed up the British investors' interest in developing railroads in coal and iron regions in the United States.

The canvas representing investment in railroads is a very broad one. The safest generalization about sources of capital for railroads in the United States is that the hundreds of railroads got it where and when they could. The pattern depended to some extent on the size of the undertaking, the existing public opinion on government aid to private enterprise, and the conditions of the capital markets, especially as to their confidence in American rails. Although a small enterprise depended on interested local businessmen and their friends, often government aid was important. The help given by towns and counties by bonding themselves rested on the marketability of the bonds rather than on the face value of the issues. States gave comparatively little direct aid, but by taking railroad bonds in exchange for their own more salable ones they played a significant role in some instances in building credit. The federal government's land grants were far more important than its direct aid. [6]

Many facts make it difficult to ascertain the percentage of the investment of capital in railroads in the United States coming from the United Kingdom. First, capitalization in terms of stocks and bonds of a railroad did not always accurately represent actual investment. The figures are

[5] "Great Britain's Capital Investments in Other Lands," *Journal of the Royal Statistical Society*, LXXII, pt. III (Sept. 30, 1909), 1–16, esp. 16.

[6] See Carter Goodrich, *Government Promotion of American Canals and Railroads, 1800–1890* (New York: Columbia University Press, 1960); Robert W. Fogel, *The Union Pacific Railroad: A Case in Premature Enterprise* (Baltimore: Johns Hopkins University Press, 1960).

further complicated by the rapid growth of capitalization of railroads in the United States, their bewildering number, and the many consolidations over time. In 1850 the capitalization of railroads in the United States was little over three hundred million dollars, and in 1890 the figure was about eight billion.[7] In the next quarter of a century the total almost doubled. Even after the many consolidations, some 1,300 companies remained by 1914. The question as to the extent to which capitalization in terms of stocks and bonds actually represented investment in railroads is itself not an easy one to answer.

As Mrs. Adler has pointed out, not all the holdings of American railroad securities by residents of the United Kingdom represented actual capital flow. These investors, along with other owners of stocks and bonds, received not only stock and bond dividends but interest and cash dividends, some of which were reinvested in American railroads. The figure for British holdings of foreign investments thereby was increased, but these actions did not add to actual export of new capital. Reorganizations that resulted in capitalization which either belittled or exaggerated the actual investment in the railroads further obscured the statistical picture.

The situs of the initial marketing of railroad stocks and bonds through capital markets is not, as Mrs. Adler reminds the reader, entirely revealing. The market of flotation was not always the source of savings and investment. Issues floated in New York were often successful only because London firms had previously committed themselves to sell part of the issue abroad, either on commission or at their own risk. On the other hand, securities marketed in London on occasion attracted largely continental European buyers; Dutch and German capital supplied part of the market.

It must be remembered that the size of a loan and its nature did not always reflect its importance to the railroad or its impact on development. A timely short-term loan was often of considerable importance. Such aid enabled a railroad not only to get started but to improve its credit and obtain other capital.

The secondary trading and jobbing of securities already issued have not been ignored by Mrs. Adler. This market had significant psychological effects on the standing of a railroad and its power to effect new issues, quite apart from the profit or loss of the new investor or speculator. Here the reader, who is surprised to note that the Union Pacific and Northern Pacific do not enter into the discussion at the time expected, should be reminded that Mrs. Adler is focusing on the British capital markets. On occasion the stocks and bonds of an American railroad were slow to cross the Atlantic, or they went to continental Europe directly through a New York banker.

It is not the purpose of this volume or of this introduction to dwell on the relation between the export of capital and that of leadership and

[7] *Historical Atlas of the United States,* 428, 429, and 433.

knowledge, but Mrs. Adler supplied here, as in other connections, a challenge to scholars. The exports of control, influence, techniques, and ideas are interesting by-products of capital flow.

The sources of leadership and techniques for railroads in the United States were broad and international. In fact, the flow of ideas was in both directions. Not unimportant in the development of American railroads were the contributions of its military men; frontier work led to explorations, and the experience in organizing men, with the necessary discipline, provided skills later useful in controlling a transportation plant spread over a large area. Codes of organization were developed early in American railroading. Other businesses in the United States contributed able men to fill management positions on railroads. However, the influence, if not full control, of British investors or the bankers representing their interest led to some export of managers along with capital. The outstanding Alexander Mitchell, a Scotsman whose skills were utilized in the Midwest, is one example given by the author. In the case of managers, as in that of the types of investors, Mrs. Adler throws out a challenge for a scholar with a computer as a co-worker.

Editors at times have probably resented the interference of authors, but in the preparation of this book for publication the author has been greatly missed. The reader must bear in mind the fact that Mrs. Adler could not be consulted, and hence amplifications or significant deletions could not be suggested or considered. The aim has been to retain the fruits of her detailed research, the pattern she has evolved, and her thoughtful analysis. Only minor changes in organization have been made to point up her contributions. Some explanatory notes are added for the reader, and a few bibliographical suggestions are included for those who wish to follow certain points further. These editorial additions are enclosed in brackets.

I must take the major responsibility if minor errors have not been avoided or the plan to keep the author's tone has not been accomplished. This editorial task could not have been undertaken without others. At an early stage Richard Overton read the manuscript, and his suggestions are much appreciated. Mrs. Kerin B. Hearn, Publications Assistant, has worked painstakingly to check the footnotes and generally to perform many significant editorial chores. David T. Gilchrist, Director of Publications for the Eleutherian Mills–Hagley Foundation, has contributed from his knowledge of American railroading and editing and has carefully safeguarded the retention of the ideas of the author. New material in the text has been inserted in brackets, even though in some places the ideas grew out of the manuscript itself. It is the hope of all concerned that we have carried through our intention to maintain fully Mrs. Adler's contribution and point of view.

MURIEL E. HIDY

Belmont, Massachusetts
1969

Preface

THE history of British investment in American railways has not previously been systematically studied. It was, in fact, unlikely that this topic would attract attention until the wider field of over-all British foreign investment had been explored. This work, begun by Sir George Paish and Charles Kenneth Hobson, was continued by Leland Hamilton Jenks, Alexander Kirkland Cairncross, and others. Partly as a result of the achievements of these pioneers in the field and partly as a result of interest in all aspects of Britain's balance of payments, a number of students have been led in recent years to undertake detailed studies of particular categories of British overseas investment in the nineteenth century.

The greatest difficulty in dealing with many aspects of British foreign investment in the nineteenth century is the amorphous character of the material. This is particularly true of investment in American railways where Britain supplied only part of the capital and it is impossible readily to identify British holders. The first task, therefore, was to trace the avenues taken by British capital. Because of the length of the period this in itself proved to be a considerable undertaking.

It might be supposed that this task could most easily be approached through analysis of the registry books of the various American railways. However, the bulk of British investment in American railway securities was in bonds rather than in shares, and American railway bonds were usually bearer bonds. This fact facilitated transfer and appears to have been in large measure responsible for the popularity of these securities in Europe. The London market also devised a method by which American railway shares could be freely dealt in without re-registration. Therefore, with a few important exceptions, it is also difficult to identify British holdings of American railway shares. The exceptions are those railways that early paid regular dividends. I hope eventually to do some work on the registry books of railways like the Pennsylvania, the New York Central, the Delaware, Lackawanna and Western, and the Delaware and Hudson.

There is undoubtedly some material on British investment to be found in the files of various American railways, particularly in the correspondence between railway officials and their bankers. The files of some American railways are available, but many are not. Even if all this material were open to research, it is so voluminous that it can be used only when one is sufficiently acquainted with the subject to know for what one is searching. Although I consider this source of information to be of supplementary rather than of primary importance, I also hope to do some work on it in the future, particularly with a view to obtaining further information on the amount of short-term borrowing by various railways that became British favorites.

Some authors of monographs on individual railways have used material contained in the files of various American railway companies. Until recently the number of such monographs was fewer than might be supposed. Since the Second World War, however, there has been a marked increase in their production, partly because many American railways have just completed their first hundred years. They are, however, of very uneven quality and often altogether ignore British investment in the corporations.

The more practical first approach to the subject is through London. The ideal source material, of course, would be the files of the various merchant banking houses that played so active a part in Anglo-American finance. Most of these files are not yet available for the second half of the nineteenth century. Indeed, much of this material was contributed to the scrap paper drive during World War II. I have therefore relied mainly on contemporary newspaper and periodical sources. I have especially leaned on the *Economist* and the *Times,* which are basic to research on the City [the financial district of London], and the *American Railroad Journal* and the *Commercial and Financial Chronicle,* which are basic to any research on American railway history. From one or another of these sources it is possible to get at least a hint, and usually more, of most of the avenues taken by British capital, and these hints can then be followed to other sources.

In spite of the seeming intractability of the mass of raw facts on British investment in American railways, the long period from the 1830's to 1898 can be divided, albeit rather loosely, into three subperiods. In the early period from 1830 to 1861 British investment was largely growth investment undertaken by members of the new industrial middle class, such as ironmasters, textile manufacturers, railway executives, and, with a stretch of the classification, merchant bankers. One of the striking features of the second period, 1861–79, was the flotation of high-interest-bearing American bonds at a discount. The holdings of British investors consequently appreciated steadily in value, and the market for American railway bonds became much wider. Rentier investment [placing of capital largely for the purpose of producing income rather than speculative gains] continued to increase in importance during the last period, 1879–98. At the same time, there was an increase of active British participation in directing American railway affairs.

The main objectives of this thesis were to investigate the mechanisms of investment on one hand and the extent of active British participation on the other. London financiers not only acted through their American alter egos but often maintained direct relationships with American railways, relationships which in some cases were as close as those between American banking houses and American railways. Hence the fact that the increasing quantitative significance of British rentier investment after the Civil War was accompanied by increasingly active British participation in many of the American railways in which British holdings were substantial is only an apparent paradox. This participation included not only direct control but perhaps on occasion covertly exercised influence in the settlement of rate wars.

The subject of British investments in American railways unites two dominant themes of nineteenth-century economic history: the export of British capital and the development of railways in the United States. Of the latter, Sir John H. Clapham said: "If a single national contribution towards the making of the new era had to be selected for its world-wide economic importance, it would probably be this." [1] However conservatively evaluated, the British contribution to this development was vitally important. With the fundamental reservation that market value and total capitalization are two different dimensions, it may be noted that the ratio of the market value of British holdings in American railways to their total capitalization was 15 to 20 percent during the 1890's.

In the nature of the case, my exploration of this vast field must necessarily be preliminary and tentative. There are innumerable problems yet to be solved, such as a more precise quantification of the amount of British investment, the width and depth of the British market for American railway securities, the related problem of the extent to which Continental purchases of American railway securities were negotiated through the City, and most important, the profitability of the investment not only to the syndicates and other market intermediaries but also to the ultimate investor. Railway financing obviously played a key role in the emergence and development of the Anglo-American financial partnership, but some of the interconnections within the City as well as between the City and Wall Street, and between the City and certain American railways, still remain obscure. In particular, why did Borthwick, Wark throw control of the Union Pacific from Charles Francis Adams, Jr., to Jay Gould in November 1890? What was the exact nature of the relationships between the house of Rothschild and the stockbroking houses such as Borthwick,

[1] *An Economic History of Modern Britain* (Cambridge: Cambridge University Press, 1952), II, 213.

Wark and Foster and Braithwaite? What was the precise position of Baring Brothers and Company in relation to the Atchison, Topeka and Santa Fe? I hope in the future to be able to work on some of these problems and in addition to bring the story down to World War I when the larger part of British investment in American railways was liquidated.

DOROTHY R. ADLER

Contents

Tables

British Investment in
American Railways
1834–1898

PART ONE

The Early Years

WHEN Americans began to build railways in the 1830's, it was inevitable that they should look to Europe for aid. In the thirties, the United States had no rolling mills capable of manufacturing railway rails. Although a few mills were established in the forties, their output was insufficient to cope with the demand once the railway boom of the fifties got under way. Only after the Civil War was the American iron industry far enough advanced to produce the bulk of the rails needed by the country's railways. Even at this period the United States was dependent on Europe for part of its supplies in boom years.[1] Funds were needed to purchase them, and these in part came from abroad.

In the early railway age in the United States the domestic capital market was still in its infancy.[2] It was not until the Civil War that an American banker, Jay Cooke, raising funds for the federal government, marketed a large popular loan in the United States.[3] Nonetheless by 1830, the year in which the first section of the Baltimore and Ohio Railroad was opened to Ellicott Mills,[4] a number of Americans had already accumulated fortunes, usually from commercial enterprise. A few could even be called wealthy.[5] It was therefore often possible to raise locally the funds needed to finance the short city-to-city lines such as the chain of roads between

[1] See Table 3 below.

[2] Ellis Paxson Oberholtzer, *Jay Cooke, Financier of the Civil War* (Philadelphia: George W. Jacobs & Co., 1907), 287; see also *Commercial and Financial Chronicle*, XXVIII (March 8, 1879), 244.

[3] [Henrietta Larson, *Jay Cooke, Private Banker* (Cambridge, Mass.: Harvard University Press, 1936), 96 ff.]

[4] Edward Hungerford, *The Story of the Baltimore and Ohio Railroad* (New York: G. P. Putnam's Sons, 1928), 83.

[5] Among the wealthy New Yorkers of the early nineteenth century, the foremost in commerce were John Jacob Astor, Alexander Gracie, and Robert Lenox, the last two being immigrants from Scotland. Robert Greenhalgh Albion, *The Rise of New York Port* [1815–1860] (New York: Charles Scribner's Sons, 1939), 236.

Albany and Buffalo that were consolidated in the 1850's to form the New York Central.[6]

Some of the earliest roads were not merely local in concept, however.[7] Americans have always been quick to adopt new inventions and to adapt them to their particular requirements. From the very beginning they saw in the railways the solution to the problem of communication with the West.[8]

Local finance, either from investors or local government aid, was sufficient to start such ambitious projects as the Baltimore and Ohio, the South Carolina, the New York and Erie Railroad, and the Western Railroad of Massachusetts; but it was often insufficient to carry them to completion.[9] It was necessary on occasion to resort to state aid, often given in the form of state bonds. In return for its railway bonds the corporation received state issues. Since even for them there was not an extensive market in the United States at this time, this exchange of state and railway bonds was in fact a method of inducing the European investor, who favored government issues,[10] to contribute to the construction of early American railways. To provide additional attraction to foreign investors, some American bonds were made payable in sterling.

When the first railway men from the United States arrived in England seeking Welsh iron [11] and British capital, they were fortunate in being able to take advantage of the facilities of an already well-established Anglo-American market. In the eighteenth century London had been the center

[6] The New York Central in 1853 was made up of eleven lines, including the Albany and Schenectady, the Utica and Schenectady, the Syracuse and Utica, the Rochester and Syracuse, and the Buffalo and Rochester. [See Harry H. Pierce, *Railroads of New York: A Study of Government Aid, 1826–1875* (Cambridge, Mass.: Harvard University Press, 1953); Edward Chase Kirkland, *Men, Cities, and Transportation: A Study in New England History, 1820–1900* (Cambridge, Mass.: Harvard University Press, 1948), *passim*, esp. 324–36; and Frank Walker Stevens, *The Beginnings of the New York Central Railroad: A History* (New York: G. P. Putnam's Sons, 1926).]

[7] The railway map of the United States in the 1830's was made up of short lines clustered about the important seaboard towns. It is a mistake to emphasize this fact without drawing attention to the declared ambition of some of these lines to reach the West.

[8] Before the building of railways, canals and plank roads were depended upon to provide communication with the West. The Erie Canal and the Pennsylvania State Works, a system of canals and railways combined, are the best known of these.

[9] When the Baltimore and Ohio was begun its total mileage was expected to be 250 miles, as contrasted with the Albany and Schenectady's 16. *American Railroad Journal,* I (Jan. 1, 1832), 3.

[10] Even the federal government turned to London and Amsterdam to take a large part of its issues prior to the Civil War.

[11] Although not all the rails exported to America were of Welsh manufacture, they were very important.

for commercial as well as for financial relations with America; merchants who did not wish to make the journey to the woolen and cotton districts could make their purchases from the Yorkshire and Manchester manufacturers at their warehouses in the capital. However, with the growth of the cotton industry and its particular orientation toward the United States, Liverpool moved rapidly to the fore in the American trade. Raw cotton from the southern states came into Liverpool, and finished cloth was exported from that port to the United States. The American Chamber of Commerce for the Port of Liverpool, established in 1801, was one of the three senior associations of that city.[12] Indeed, in 1808 Alexander Baring, a partner in the merchant banking house of Baring Brothers and Company, maintained that Liverpool was the principal center of the American trade and that the function of the London houses of such firms as that of his family was merely to act as a banker.[13] Henry Smithers, writing in 1825, described the importance of Liverpool in the American trade in words that stress its position: "The peace, which was signed in 1783, with France, Spain, Holland, and America, was, to all intents and purposes, a treaty of commerce between the latter country and the town of Liverpool; for, of 5,708 vessels, entered inwards, from foreign parts, the last three years, more than one-half were from America." [14]

Eventually most of the merchant houses interested in the American trade found it advantageous to establish branches in Liverpool.[15] Many of the iron companies also opened establishments in that port.[16] Although the

[12] W. O. Henderson, "The American Chamber of Commerce for the Port of Liverpool, 1801–1908," *Transactions of the Historical Society of Lancashire and Cheshire for 1933,* LXXXV (Liverpool: printed for the Society, 1935).

[13] *An Inquiry into the Causes and Consequences of the Orders in Council and an Examination of the Conduct of Great-Britain towards the Neutral Commerce of America* (London: J. M. Richardson, 1808), 7.

[14] *Liverpool: Its Commerce, Statistics, and Institutions* (Liverpool: Thomas Kaye, 1825), 111–12.

[15] The following is a selection from the listing of merchants in *Gore's Directory of Liverpool and Its Environs for 1849* (Liverpool: J. Mawdley, 1849): Baring Brothers; Bird and Gillilan; Borthwick, Barr; Brown, Shipley; Collman and Stolterfoht; Cropper and Newton; John Crosthwaite; Alexander Dennistoun; Dennistoun, Mitchell; Prosper Devaux; Fletcher, Alexander; William Henry Gilliat; Frederick Huth; Leone Levi; John Jardine; Matheson and Scott; Mellor and Eason; Mellors and Russell; Naylor, Todd; Alexander Petrie, Laughland; Rathbone; J. H. Schroeder. Some of these firms had their headquarters in Liverpool, for example, Cropper and Newton and Brown, Shipley [which had grown out of an allied linen-importing house in Baltimore, Maryland]. But many of these firms, for example, Baring Brothers, Devaux, Gilliat, Huth, and Schroeder, were merchant banking houses whose head offices were in London.

[16] The following list is of iron companies maintaining houses in Liverpool in 1849 (*ibid.*): Bailey Brothers; Bowling Co.; British Iron Co.; Carron Co.; Coalbrookdale; Galvanized Iron Co.; Guest and Co.; Low Moor; Mersey Steel and Iron Co.; Pontypool Iron and Tinplate Co.; Netherton Iron Works.

American railway man in search of iron found himself surrounded by persons interested in the American trade as soon as he disembarked at Liverpool,[17] many of these prospective purchasers continued their journey to London. Some transactions in iron were indeed carried through in Liverpool, especially in the 1830's, but the chief houses of most of the merchant bankers were located in London, as were the head sales offices of the ironmasters.[18] Especially in those cases where American railway men hoped to arrange purchase of rails for bonds it was usually necessary to deal with the head office.[19]

Although the rise of Liverpool as an important center was one fundamental change in Anglo-American trade at the beginning of the nineteenth century, the growing importance of the merchant banking houses was another. Houses like those of Barings and of Thomas Wilson had already ceased to act largely on their own account,[20] and after 1815 the functions of these commission and shipping houses in the American trade was still further changed and their importance enhanced.[21] This was at least partly due to the gradual replacement of the direct role of the British merchant in the American trade by the British manufacturer and also by the American importer.[22]

The new generation of American importers that began to rise in the late twenties and thirties initially was made up of men of very little capital, and therefore in need of credit. George Peabody, later the founder of the present-day house of Morgan, Grenfell and Company, Ltd., first arrived in London as the buying partner of Peabody, Riggs and Company of Baltimore, Maryland. This company had been started with a capital of about

[17] When the first line of packets between England and America was established in 1818, Liverpool was its home port. Albion, 13.

[18] In the early part of the nineteenth century the iron-manufacturing firm Guest and Co. maintained its main sales office at Cardiff. In addition, various members of the firm, including Guest himself, traveled to solicit orders. An office was first opened in London in 1837. The Crawshay family's interest in iron began with an iron warehouse in London. John P. Addis, *The Crawshay Dynasty* (Cardiff: University of Wales Press, 1957), chap. 1.

[19] At least in the case of the Guest's Dowlais Iron Co. the bulk of the orders seem to have come through the London rather than through the Liverpool office.

[20] The transition was not complete. Firms that had become largely commission houses might still deal on their own account if a favorable opportunity was offered. The situation was dynamic, and the delimitation of the functions of the various commercial institutions was not precise. Barings even had a finger in shipping and in manufactures. Ralph W. Hidy, *The House of Baring in American Trade and Finance, 1763–1861* (Cambridge, Mass.: Harvard University Press, 1949), 186–89 and 349.

[21] [For an exposition of the functions of the merchant bankers, see Ralph W. Hidy, "The Organization and Functions of Anglo-American Merchant Bankers, 1815–1860," *The Tasks of Economic History, Journal of Economic History*, I (Dec. 1941), 53–66.]

[22] Norman Sydney Buck, *The Development of the Organisation of Anglo-American Trade, 1800–1850* (New Haven: Yale University Press, 1925), 99.

five thousand dollars.[23] Small American importers of this type were able to do a large business on a limited capital base through the use of revolving credits with one of the big merchant banking houses. Thus when Ralston, of A. and G. Ralston of Philadelphia, iron merchants, first approached the Dowlais Iron Company of South Wales in the summer of 1830, he took with him a letter of introduction from Timothy Wiggin, a London merchant banker. This letter authorized Ralston to draw on Wiggin and Company for up to £20,000.[24]

[Several firms competed in the important merchant banking business.] Timothy Wiggin was senior partner of one of the group characterized as the three W's; the other two were George Wildes and Company and Thomas Wilson and Company.[25] Together with Baring Brothers, N. M. Rothschild and Sons, and W. and J. Brown and Company (later Brown, Shipley and Company) of Liverpool, they formed the first rank of Anglo-American houses in the 1830's, although such firms as Lizardi and Company, Morrison, Cryder and Company, Fletcher, Alexander and Company, Frederick Huth and Company, and Reid Irving and Company must also be mentioned.[26] [Some firms concentrating on American business not only included partners from the United States but had in that country an agent or closely associated firm.]

The middle 1830's was an era of great progress and prosperity in the United States. The railway age had just begun, and although it was not yet certain that the promoters of railways would triumph over the advocates of canals, it was abundantly clear that the Americans were determined to build an extensive transportation system. For a number of years western-ers had been pressing for internal improvements. They now found support among businessmen of the various seaboard cities, persons who had a vested interest in widening their market to the West as well as facilitating transportation in the East.

When the last installment of the federal debt, some of which had been held abroad,[27] was paid off in 1834, a wave of optimism swept the country. Europeans were keenly aware of the remarkable event that had taken place across the Atlantic, for in freeing itself from debt, the young United

[23] Muriel Hidy, "George Peabody, Merchant and Financier, 1829–1854" (un-published doctoral thesis, Radcliffe College, 1939), 7.

[24] J. J. Guest to Edward (presumably Hutchins), March 12, 1831, Dowlais Iron Co., Letter Books, Main Series, Glamorgan Public Archives, Cardiff. [The merchant banker often only lent his name; the development of the discount market made it possible to convert time drafts into cash.]

[25] Wiggin, a Manchester merchant, came back from retirement in the 1820's after the failure of Samuel Williams of 13 Finsbury Square, for many years the leading American merchant in London, and paid off half of Williams's obliga-tions. Ralph Hidy, *House of Baring*, 73.

[26] *Ibid.*, 195.

[27] U.S., Department of Commerce, Bureau of the Census, *Historical Statistics of the United States, 1789–1945* (Washington, D.C., 1949), 306; see also Ralph W. Hidy, *House of Baring*, 70 and 501 n.

States had accomplished what no other modern nation had ever done.[28]
Moreover, the establishment in America of a large number of local banks,
in anticipation of the removal of the public deposits from the Bank of the
United States, provided a flood of paper currency. This led to rising prices
that fed the optimism. Americans began to import on a large scale.
Exports, however, did not increase correspondingly, and the resultant
deficit was financed by the merchant bankers and by the discount houses,
which in turn were financed in part by the Bank of England. By 1837, the
bank's advances amounted to over £6 million; it decided to call a halt.[29]

The year 1837 was a year of repentance. The Anglo-American banking
houses were obliged to call on the American merchants for large immediate payments which they could not make. In the United States specie
payment was suspended. In England, several of the merchant bankers
were forced to stop payment. From March 22 until June 2, 1837, the Bank
of England supported the three W's—Wilson, Wildes, and Wiggin—and
W. and J. Brown of Liverpool.[30] When this support was withdrawn from
the three W's, they were forced to suspend and brought down with them a
number of smaller houses: Bell and Grant; Gowan and Marx; Coleman
Lambert; and A. and G. Ralston.[31] The Bank of England continued to help
W. and J. Brown of Liverpool on the guarantee of other merchants.[32] This
first crisis was short and sharp. Imports to the United States almost ceased
for a time, so that the proceeds of its exports were available for liquidating
debts.[33] According to Benjamin R. Curtis, "at the end of the year 1837, our
foreign commercial debt [that of American importers] was nearly paid." [34]

Many now began to think that the reverse of 1837 had been a small and
unimportant affair. Both in the United States and in England the spirit of
optimism quickly revived. The Bank of England kept interest low and
circulation high into the spring of 1839 in spite of a poor harvest in Great
Britain in 1838 and the consequent drain of bullion.[35] The United States
Bank [now operating under a Pennsylvania charter] also encouraged a
return to the conditions of 1835 and 1836. It entered largely into the
purchase of state bonds, into speculations in cotton, and into various other

[28] B. R. Curtis, "Debts of the States," *North American Review,* LVIII (Jan.
1844), 111.

[29] [For a fuller explanation, see Reginald Charles McGrane, *The Panic of 1837*
(Chicago: University of Chicago Press, 1924).]

[30] Muriel Hidy, "George Peabody," 84.

[31] Ralph Hidy, *House of Baring,* 222. It must not, however, be assumed that
these houses all disappeared. Gowan and Marx and A. and G. Ralston were
reconstituted under the same names that they had borne formerly. Gowan and
Marx survived until the 1880's. The 3 W's also reappear. Timothy Wiggin's son
eventually amalgamated the firm with two others to form the London, Asiatic
and American Co., Ltd. See below, p. 74.

[32] Muriel Hidy, "George Peabody," 85–86.

[33] [American short-term debts in Europe dropped from £18 million in March
1837 to £6 million by Sept. Ralph Hidy, *House of Baring,* 535.]

[34] P. 120.   [35] *Morning Chronicle,* Dec. 10, 1841, p. 3.

risky transactions. It should be added in extenuation of the bank's desperate plunge into the negotiation of state securities that it found ready accomplices in the European capitalists who took these bonds almost as freely as if they had been gold and silver.[36]

The indebtedness of the various states of the Union had increased rapidly over the decade of the 1830's. Amounting to a little less than $26 million in 1830, the debt had grown to $172 million by 1838 and reached $231.6 million by 1843. The bulk of this new borrowing took place in the five-year period from 1834 through 1838, with the greatest concentration in the years 1837 and 1838, that is to say, after the banking crisis of 1837.[37]

Not all the states participated in this orgy of deficit spending. Nine states had no debt in 1830 and contracted none during this period. These nine were New Hampshire, Vermont, Rhode Island, Connecticut, New Jersey, Delaware, North Carolina, Wisconsin, and Iowa. A tenth state, Georgia, also did not participate in the borrowing of the mid-1830's.[38] For the other states, the amount of debt as of 1838 is shown in Table 1. At that date approximately one-fourth of total state borrowing was for the construction of railways.

A great part of these state bonds eventually found their way to Europe. Estimates of the amount of these issues held abroad vary from time to time from one-half to three-fourths. Daniel Webster, politician, lawyer, and currently adviser to Barings, put the amount of foreign holdings at $50 million, or approximately three-fourths of the total of $66 million outstanding at the end of 1835.[39] In 1838 Representative Garland, speaking in the United States House of Representatives, stated that half of the

[36] Curtis writes: "During the years of high prices, they had lent their capital on paper which rested only on the exaggerated and unreal values of that period; and an immediate return to specie payments would have shown, that their capital had been very seriously impaired. . . . [Accordingly, the U.S. Bank] at first opposed the resumption of specie payments; and subsequently, when compelled to come into the arrangement, it seems to have adopted the bold measure of attempting to bring back the unnatural state of things which had existed before May, 1837; hoping, that, by means of high prices and unlimited credit, it might be able gradually to withdraw itself from its dangerous position." Pp. 120–21.

[37] B. U. Ratchford, *American State Debts* (Durham, N.C.: Duke University Press, 1941), 79–80; see also U.S., Congress, *House Report 296*, 27th Cong., 3d sess., 1842, pp. 7, 117.

[38] Georgia and North Carolina were kept out of the procession by the bitter political division that existed between the eastern and western parts of these two states. This deadlock was partially broken in North Carolina by the constitution of 1835. The state then prepared to embark on a program of borrowing, but the distribution of federal funds in 1837 and the ensuing depression delayed the move for another decade. In Georgia, the impasse was ended by a series of constitutional amendments beginning in 1833. Ratchford, 87, 103.

[39] Ralph Hidy, *House of Baring*, 316 and 532 n. At this date estimates of the total American indebtedness to Europe varied from £12 million to £20 million.

Table 1. State debts outstanding in 1838 and their purposes (in 1000's of dollars)

State	Banking	Canals	Railroads	Turnpikes	Misc.	Total
Ala.	7,800		3,000			10,800
Ark.	3,000					3,000
Fla.	1,500					1,500
Ill.	3,000	900	7,400		300	11,600
Ind.	1,390	6,750	2,600	1,150		11,890
Ky.	2,000	2,619	350	2,400		7,369
La.	22,950	50	500		235	23,735
Me.					555	555
Md.		5,700	5,500		293	11,493
Mass.			4,290			4,290
Mich.		2,500	2,620		220	5,340
Miss.	7,000					7,000
Mo.	2,500					2,500
N.Y.		13,317	3,788		1,158	18,262
Ohio		6,101				6,101
Pa.		16,580	4,964	2,596	3,167	27,307
S.C.		1,550	2,000		2,204	5,754
Tenn.	3,000	300	3,730	118		7,148
Va.		3,835	2,129	355	343	6,662
Total	54,140	60,202	42,871	6,619	8,475	172,306

SOURCES: B. U. Ratchford, *American State Debts* (Durham, N.C.: Duke University Press, 1941), 88, and U.S., Department of the Interior, *Tenth Census of the United States (1880)* (Washington, D.C., 1884), VII, 526.

states' securities was held in Europe, $86 million out of the total of $172 million.[40] About that time two-thirds of Pennsylvania's state debt of $36 million was reported to be held abroad.[41] In 1843 a House report estimated that of a total of $231.6 million state bonds about $150 million was in foreign ownership.[42]

Although state debt accounted for the greater part of European investment in American securities, the amount of holdings by Europeans in American corporations, banks, and, to a lesser extent, railways was not negligible. Garland's report of 1838 estimated these further holdings at $24 million, principally in banks, while the House report of 1843 called attention to ownership of $28 million in the stock of the United States Bank and $9 million in the securities of the Farmers' Loan and Trust Company, the Commercial Bank of Vicksburg, and New Jersey's Camden and Amboy Railroad.[43]

[40] Margaret Myers, *The New York Money Market* (New York: Columbia University Press, 1931), I, 29–30.

[41] Ratchford, 99.

[42] U.S., Congress, *House Report 296,* 27th Cong., 3d sess., 1842, pp. 7, 117.

[43] The Camden and Amboy floated two loans in London in the 1830's, one for £225,000 and one for £215,000. Interest on these bonds was paid through Palmer, MacKillop and Dent. (See for example, *Economist,* VII [Jan. 27, 1849], the unnumbered page of advertisements opposite p. 85). [The Camden and Amboy bonds are of particular interest, for, as Harry H. Pierce has pointed out,

Nor is this list exhaustive. A number of railroad lines around Philadelphia and several lines in Virginia and North Carolina found a market for their own bonds in London in the 1830's. In the case of the Philadelphia and Reading, perhaps the first American railway to come under English influence, these issues were of substantial amount.[44] Usually, however, they were an investment of $100,000 or $200,000 or even less in a corporation. For example, the agent of the Richmond and Petersburg (Virginia) took to London in 1838 one hundred 6 percent bonds of the company but was able to dispose of only forty-one of these. Since the bonds were of $1,500 denomination, the total obtained was only about $60,000.[45] The Wilmington and Raleigh (North Carolina), another section of the chain of roads running south from Richmond along the Atlantic

---

one lot was issued publicly in London through John Wright & Co. as early as 1834. See Pierce, "Foreign Investment in American Enterprise," in David T. Gilchrist and W. David Lewis (eds.), *Economic Change in the Civil War Era* (Greenville, Del.: Eleutherian Mills-Hagley Foundation, 1965), 41–61.]

[44] On March 1, 1851, approximately one-fourth of the shares of the Philadelphia and Reading were owned by investors in England, a quantity sufficient to gain significant influence in most circumstances, as will be seen from the following tabulation from *American Railroad Journal*, XXIV (March 22, 1851), 181:

Distribution of holdings of Reading shares

(March 1, 1851)

Held by investors in England	21,000
Held by investors in Philadelphia	8,100
Held by investors in New York	8,000
Held by investors in Boston	9,986
Held by brokers in Philadelphia	17,900
Held by brokers in Boston	3,700
Held by brokers in New York	14,510
Total	83,196

The marketing of Philadelphia and Reading securities in England was probably done through Morrison, Cryder and Co., a firm which was dissolved in 1839. Subsequently, John Cryder returned to the United States and tried unsuccessfully to rescue something for the British bondholders out of the Morris Canal and Banking Co.

The supposition that Morrison, Cryder may also have been involved in the original marketing of the bonds of the Philadelphia and Reading is based on the fact that Cryder later served a term as president of the railway, a task which he also undertook in order to aid the British holders. In this mission he was more successful than he had been with the Morris Canal and Banking Co. Muriel Hidy, "George Peabody," 177, 189. The Reading later developed with McCalmont Brothers a close connection that was continued until the 1880's. Indeed, this firm not only controlled the Reading financially but, together with John Gihon and Co. of New York, supplied the presidents of the Reading from within one or the other of these two firms.

[45] Howard Douglas Dozier, *A History of the Atlantic Coast Line Railroad* (Boston: Houghton Mifflin Company, 1920), 40. [See also Carter Goodrich, *Government Promotion of American Canals and Railroads, 1800–1890* (New York: Columbia University Press, 1960), 121 ff. This book gives leads to state and local issues of bonds to aid railroad building from Boston to Mobile.]

coastline, seems to have realized $222,667 from marketing 5 percent bonds in London in the same year.[46] The Richmond, Fredericksburg and Potomac, the line connecting Richmond, Virginia, with Washington, D.C., also appears to have been able to float a loan in London in the thirties.[47]

The subsequent history of the bonds of one Pennsylvania railway is of interest. In July 1841 the Court of Review, Sir J. Cross presiding, heard a case brought by Lieutenant General Vincent Eyre, K.C.S.I., C.B., against the banking house of Biddulph, Wright, and Company. Eyre charged that without his permission the banking firm had substituted £33,000 of the bonds of the Norris-town and Valley Railroad (later the Chester Valley) of Pennsylvania for stock certificates of the Southampton Railway that had been left on deposit with the firm.[48]

There is also evidence that at an early date ironmasters occasionally took securities of American railways in part payment for rails. For example, the British Iron Company received $75,000 in stock of the New York and Erie Railroad on account for rails.[49] It would seem, however, that this mode of payment was less common in the 1830's than it became in the 1850's. There is no specific mention of this practice in letter books of the large Welsh manufacturing firm, the Dowlais Iron Company. However, its chief owner, Sir John Josiah Guest, held some Massachusetts state securities that may have been acquired in payment for rails.[50] As discussed later, even in the fifties this ironmaster's firm was reluctant to barter rails for bonds.

The methods of marketing the flood of American state bonds differed considerably. The states sometimes arranged directly for their sale. More often they turned the bonds over to the enterprises in aid of which the securities were issued. The agents of the corporation then undertook to dispose of them. In some cases the securities were allotted on the basis of bids;[51] in others they were turned over en bloc to a business firm[52] or

[46] *American Railroad Journal,* XXVI (Dec. 3, 1853), 781; see also Dozier, 65. The interest on these bonds was paid in London by Collman and Stolterfoht, and it is probable that they originally issued the loan. *Daily News,* Jan. 3, 1853, p. 7.

[47] Interest on the 6 percent bonds of this road was paid through Thomson, Hankey and Co. *Daily News,* Dec. 27, 1853, p. 7.

[48] Daniel Hardcastle, Jr., *Banks and Bankers* (London: Whittaker and Co., 1842), 261 n.

[49] Edward Harold Mott, *Between the Ocean and the Lakes: The Story of Erie* (New York: John S. Collins, 1899), 329.

[50] R. P. Davis to Mr. Lamphier, Aug. 21, 1838, Dowlais Iron Company, Letter Books, London Series.

[51] Ohio, particularly, preferred to solicit sealed bids rather than to deal through a banking company.

[52] The United States Bank and the Morris Canal and Banking Co. were particularly active in this sphere. The North American Trust and Banking Co. also negotiated American securities in the thirties. This was a New York company, but the greater part of its cash subscriptions seems to have come from England, most of the American subscriptions being in real estate. In spite of the fact that this company's cash subscriptions amounted to only $250,000 (of

individual [53] who undertook to negotiate them. When there were no takers in the United States, the representative of the state or agent of the railway took the securities to Europe himself and hawked them around the several financial centers, especially London and Amsterdam.[54]

There were great differences in the distribution of these securities among investors. Some, such as the Pennsylvania state bonds, were widely taken. Because of the current condition of the capital market, some issues, even of states whose credit was good, hung heavily on the hands of the European houses that had taken the responsibility for marketing them.[55] Some securities found no ready market and temporarily were used as collateral for loans.[56]

Almost all of the Anglo-American houses were actively engaged in the marketing of American securities in these years. Barings eventually achieved control of the bonds of four states, Massachusetts, Ohio, South Carolina, and Maryland,[57] at least in the European market.[58] Rothchilds also was heavily interested in American state bonds. For example, the firm controlled the bulk of the Michigan state securities in Europe,[59] while de

---

which $50,000 was subscribed by Nassau Senior) it did a very large business. For example, it was through this company that Holford took $500,000 in Arkansas bonds. *Morning Chronicle,* Jan. 13, 1842, p. 2. Palmer, MacKillop and Dent was the chief agency of this company. Joseph Dorfman, "A Note on the Interpenetration of Anglo-American Finance, 1837–1841," *Journal of Economic History,* XI (1951), 140–47.

[53] Peabody, for example, was at first the agent for the Maryland state bonds issued in favor of the Chesapeake and Ohio Canal. When in 1839 he was unable to carry through the negotiation of these bonds he relinquished his agency to Barings, which was anxious to get a monopoly of Maryland bonds in Europe. Although the contract was in Barings' name, other capitalists were included, for example, Overend, Gurney & Co. Muriel Hidy, "George Peabody," 164.

[54] The Florida bonds were negotiated in this way. Sidney Walter Martin, *Florida during the Territorial Days* (Athens, Ga.: University of Georgia Press, 1944), 158.

[55] Even the bonds of the state of Massachusetts, issued in favor of the Western Railroad of Massachusetts (now part of the main line of the Boston and Albany), proved unsalable at that time. These had been consigned to Barings to pay for rails in 1838 and 1839. On Jan. 1, 1842, £152,000 of these bonds were still held by Barings. An agreement was made to return these bonds gradually to the United States. Eventually, £50,000 of these were sent to Thomas Wren Ward, American agent of Barings, to sell in New York at the going price. At this sale £10,000 of them were purchased for Barings' account. Ralph Hidy, *House of Baring,* 291 and 547.

[56] The hypothecation of bonds led to some of them being declared void on the grounds that the law authorizing their issue required that they be sold only at par.

[57] At first Barings only controlled the Maryland bonds issued in favor of the Baltimore and Ohio, while George Peabody controlled the bonds issued in favor of the Chesapeake and Ohio Canal. See n. 53 above.

[58] Ralph Hidy, *House of Baring,* 291.

[59] Barings held $100,000 of Michigan bonds, and Elisha Riggs held $250,000, of which he offered George Peabody one third. Aside from this, Rothschilds

Lizardi seems to have occupied a dominant position in respect to Louisiana bonds; interest on several categories of Louisiana bonds were paid through this firm. Palmer, MacKillop and Dent was also engaged in the negotiations of American securities, both state and railway, in this period, as well as in the purchase of rails for American companies. In fact, in the latter business they were accused of unduly favoring the British Iron Company, of which Horsley Palmer was a large shareholder.[60]

For a time after 1839 it was difficult to negotiate American securities in London. In 1841 the period of default and repudiation by states began. Nine states in all defaulted, but the two most famous cases were those of Pennsylvania and Mississippi. The default of Pennsylvania especially aroused indignation since the bonds were held by many investors, and the state's policy was often interpreted as deliberate rather than unavoidable.[61] Many items appeared in London papers and periodicals enumerating Pennsylvania's riches in population, natural resources, industry, and trade. All of these ended with the plaintive refrain that default in the face of such wealth was doubly reprehensible.[62]

Mississippi is one of the three states that not only defaulted on their payments of interest but repudiated their securities, the other two being Florida and Arkansas. There was some justification for the contention of Florida and Arkansas that their securities were illegal. Indeed, Florida was still a territory in the 1830's, therefore under federal control and incapable of issuing legal securities.[63] Arkansas, the bulk of whose bonds were held by Holford and Company,[64] repudiated on the grounds that its bonds had been hypothecated for a fraction of their face value.[65] Mississippi, on the other hand, had received full value for its securities and repudiated in the

---

controlled all the Michigan bonds available in Europe. Muriel Hidy, "George Peabody," 148.

[60] The following quotation is taken from the Dowlais Iron Co.'s correspondence: "These rails are to be manufactured as you like and of any material without the annoyance of an inspector who is only to be employed in passing the Rails when they are ready for shipment either at Cardiff or at the works. We are very anxious to turn out a good article that we may show the Yankees that G. & Co. manufacture is A 1 and that the influence of Mr. Horseley Palmer [sic] should not induce him to give so decided a preference to bad Rails from the British Iron Co. where he is so large a shareholder." R. P. Davis to Thomas Evans, Jan. 1, 1839, Dowlais Iron Co., Letter Books, London Series, 1839.

[61] In the list of American state securities that appeared in the *Economist*, III (Aug. 16, 1845), 783, Pennsylvania occupied first place with a total of $40.5 million. New York was second with $24 million. Indiana was third with $11.6 million, and Ohio and Illinois, each with $10 million, shared fourth place. Later, Pennsylvania still occupied the first place with $41 million, but Ohio had advanced to second place with $19 million, while New York was third with $13.1 million. *Economist*, VII (July 20, 1849), 801.

[62] See, for example, *Economist*, III (April 19, 1845), 366. The Reverend Sydney Smith was especially vociferous in his denunciation of Pennsylvania.

[63] S. W. Martin, 160.   [64] See above, p. 13, n. 52.   [65] Ratchford, 111, 114.

face of a decision by its High Court of Errors and Appeals that found the bonds to be neither illegal nor void.[66]

As a result of these defaults and repudiations the reputation of the United States in Europe, especially in London, fell to what is probably the lowest point in its history. Even the federal government was unable to float a loan in Europe in 1842,[67] not because its own credit was poor, but because it had not assumed the indebtedness of the states.

Nevertheless, the boycott was not complete. The Philadelphia and Reading, for example, was able to float an issue of $2 million in 1843 and a further one for $1.5 million in 1844.[68] The issue of 1843, like those of 1836, was in sterling. The four issues put out between 1844 and 1849 were in dollars.

During these years George Peabody gradually assumed more of the functions of a merchant banker,[69] concentrating on the business of dealing in securities. According to his estimates he bought and sold between 1842 and 1845 over $6 million of depreciated American securities. By May 1848 he could state that over $10 million had passed through his hands in the last five years.[70] Indeed, he appears to have been unrivaled in this field.[71] Nor did Peabody confine his efforts to trading in American securities. He labored hard to raise the prestige of America and Americans in London, writing long letters to the press and joining with other Anglo-American houses in such activities as contributions to the political campaign fund in Maryland to support the Whigs, a party pledged to the payment of that state's debt.[72]

During this period of depression a large amount of American securities were returned to the United States. The New York papers often reported that prices of securities had collapsed under the sale of stocks and bonds on European accounts. This movement reached its peak after the British railway crisis of 1847, when many persons in London were eager to realize on every negotiable asset. In April 1848 the *New York Courier and In-*

[66] As late as 1852 the *Times* (March 26, p. 6) devoted two-thirds of the City Column one day to the sins of Mississippi.

[67] Ralph Hidy, *House of Baring*, 309.

[68] [See Cleona Lewis, *America's Stake in International Investments* (Washington, D.C.: Brookings Institution, 1938), 27.]

[69] In 1845, Peabody severed his connection with the dry goods business. Muriel Hidy, "George Peabody," 135.

[70] *Ibid.*, 270, 271. On May 19, 1848, Peabody wrote to Elisha S. Riggs: "I have the principal controul [*sic*] of the market & buyers and sellers come to me which gives me great advantages. . . . at least Ten Millions of dollars of various American Stocks have passed through my hands within the last 5 years bought or sold by myself. . . . I have always in hand half a Million, but it is now over 2 years since I have borrowed a pound on any American or other security & for the future mean to so manage my business as to avoid it."

[71] Peabody was more successful in speculating in securities than in marketing new issues during this period. *Ibid.*, 343.

[72] *Ibid.*, 282.

quirer reported that "Instead of foreign goods sent here to be sold in order to raise means for Europe, we are receiving back American stocks heretofore held abroad, and now returned upon us." [73] Similarly, in the issue for May 5, 1849, the *Economist* commented, "In the money crisis of 1847 the greater portion of the American stocks held in this country found its way back to the United States." [74] This exodus is the first instance of a phenomenon that was to repeat itself in every crisis of the London money market. [75]

The tide turned in 1847. By then all the defaulted states except Mississippi, [76] Florida, [77] and Arkansas [78] had either resumed the payment of interest on their bonds or reached some compromise agreement with their creditors, [79] and the American correspondent of the *Economist* was able to write: "With the exception of one or two States (Mississippi, Arkansas, and perhaps Florida) . . . we hope never more to hear of repudiation, so long and so justly a reproach to the honour and reputation of the Union." [80]

In 1848 the flight of capital following the political disturbances on the European continent brought to a new peak of popularity there American federal bonds and the securities of some states and cities. [81] Rothschilds, which had wide connections on the Continent, had already entered the market for American federal bonds in 1847, as had George Peabody; [82] but it was 1848 before Barings again became interested in these securities. The particular issue that tempted Barings back into the business of

---

[73] Quoted in the *Economist,* VI (May 6, 1848), 519.

[74] VII (May 5, 1849), 490.   [75] See below, p. 160.

[76] Mississippi is still in default.

[77] After the Civil War the Council of Foreign Bondholders convened a meeting of the Florida bondholders at the request of the fiscal agents of the state, at which it was proposed that settlement be made on the basis of 5 percent in cash and 500 acres of land for each bond. The state of Florida also agreed to attempt to get the banks who had guaranteed the bonds to carry out their guarantees and, if successful in this, to use the funds so obtained to redeem the land warrants. *Times,* Dec. 15, 1871, p. 7. Dent, Palmer and Co. (successors to Palmer, MacKillop and Dent) advised the bondholders to accept this offer. *Ibid.,* Dec. 22, 1871, p. 7.

[78] After the Civil War, in 1869, Arkansas made some sort of settlement on its bonds. *Ibid.,* Oct. 16, 1869, p. 6; April 26, 1874, p. 8; April 28, 1874, p. 10.

[79] Michigan and Indiana compromised on their debts. Pennsylvania, Illinois, Maryland, and Louisiana funded back coupons and resumed payment.

[80] V (Aug. 21, 1847), 955.

[81] *Barings Circular* at the end of 1851 said in retrospect: "The year which has just expired [1851] has been one of regular, but not of very large investments in American stocks; nor could it be expected that the sudden and extraordinary demand produced by the continental events of 1848 should be continued on an equally large scale for many years, unless some fresh stimulus was given to it" (quoted in the *American Railroad Journal,* XXV [Jan. 24, 1852], 57).

[82] *Economist,* VI (April 11, 1848), 380; Ralph Hidy, *House of Baring,* 384; Muriel Hidy, "George Peabody," 292.

negotiating American securities was the federal Mexican War loan of 1848. Over $14 million of this loan of $16 million was bid in by the merchant banking house of Corcoran and Riggs [83] of Washington, D.C., on behalf of itself, Baring Brothers, George Peabody, and others.[84] Aside from the $3 million of these securities that Corcoran took personally to London,[85] Barings and Peabody were responsible for marketing these bonds in the English market.[86] This was the first American loan to achieve popularity in London since 1839.

Beginning in July 1848, the *Economist* reported quite frequently on the enthusiasm with which the federal bonds were received in England.[87] When this enthusiasm was intensified in early 1849 by the first reports of the gold strike in California, the journal felt bound to call a warning:

Turning disappointed from railways, many persons are now looking to the American stocks as a means of profitable investment. The shocks recently given to the public funds of the several nations of Europe, from which those of the United States have been exempted, and the high rate of interest which a scarcity of money has created in the American cities, seem to have created a very exaggerated notion of the value and security of the several funds of the United States. Accordingly, we learn, by the latest arrivals, that large purchases of these have been made on account of persons in this country and on the continent of Europe. . . . It might have been supposed that the character of many of the state and other stocks in America would be a sufficient warning to the monied classes of Europe, but they cannot resist the temptation of a high rate of interest there while it is difficult to employ money here, and the rate of interest is comparatively low.[88]

This warning went largely unheeded. The railway boom that increased America's railway mileage from 5,598 miles in 1847 to 30,626 miles in 1860 had just begun.[89] Thus, although the movement of United States federal and state securities to Europe fell off somewhat after 1848, both because of a decline in the Continental demand [90] and of the scarcity of new governmental issues,[91] railway securities came forward in their stead.

In fact, there seems to have been a period of relative quiet between the

[83] George Washington Riggs of Corcoran and Riggs was the son of Elisha Riggs, who had been George Peabody's partner in Peabody, Riggs and Co., the Baltimore dry goods importing firm. Muriel Hidy, "George Peabody," 8.

[84] *Economist,* VI (July 8, 1848), 769.

[85] *Ibid.,* VI (Sept. 30, 1848), 1126, and (Oct. 28, 1848), 1236.

[86] Muriel Hidy, "George Peabody," 287 ff.

[87] VI (July 15, 1848), 800; (Sept. 30, 1848), 1126; VII (Jan. 20, 1849), 74.

[88] VII (May 5, 1849), 490.

[89] *Historical Statistics of the United States,* 200.

[90] In continental Europe many of the small sales of only $500 or $1,000 were to persons intending to emigrate to the United States and desiring a convenient form in which to transfer their capital. Muriel Hidy, "George Peabody," 293.

[91] American securities were relatively short term: ten, fifteen, or twenty years. Purchasers were therefore unwilling to take those quoted at a premium as the date of redemption drew nearer. The federal bonds issued in 1848 stood at 110¼ in Sept. 1850. *Economist,* VIII (Sept. 7, 1850), 992.

sudden and extraordinary demand for federal and state securities in 1848 and the opening of the London market to the public issue of American railway bonds in 1852. American demand for English iron increased as soon as plans for railway building accelerated in the late 1840's.[92] By 1848 the negotiations for American railways, both for purchases of rails and provision of the necessary short-term credits, had become one of the important functions of a number of the leading Anglo-American houses.[93] The bulk of these purchases was ultimately financed by bonds. These early issues, being the first to reach the market after a long depression, were usually taken up in the United States [94] [where available investment funds were increasing and the New York financial market was developing new capacities]. Some of the bonds purchased by American houses were for the account of European correspondents.[95] These early English investments were usually direct purchases by the investors.

[92] [For an analysis of the methods utilized by merchant bankers in London to finance railroads, see Ralph W. Hidy and Muriel E. Hidy, "Anglo-American Merchant Bankers and the Railroads of the Old Northwest, 1848–1860," *Business History Review*, XXXIV (Summer 1960), 150–69.]

[93] For example, in 1848 Barings; Palmer, MacKillop and Dent; and Frederick Huth were all active in arranging purchases of iron rails. George Peabody began to engage in iron exporting early the next year. Muriel Hidy, "George Peabody," 328.

[94] In the late 1840's money from Boston and other eastern cities went into the buying up and completion of partly finished, bankrupt western roads. The *Economist* (VI [Sept. 23, 1848], 1082), reprinted from the *Boston Courier* the following estimates of Massachusetts capital going into new enterprises but cautioned the reader that since the *Boston Courier* was an organ of the protectionists, these figures should be taken with a grain of salt:

Investment of Massachusetts capital from the beginning of
1846 to the middle of 1848

In factories and manufacturing cities	$13,000,000
Purchase of railroads out of the state	8,000,000
Expansion of old lines of railroads	6,000,000
Construction of new lines of railroad in Massachusetts	7,000,000
Construction of new lines of railroad out of Massachusetts	12,000,000
Boston aqueduct, estimated cost with dead interest, etc.	4,000,000
Stock taken in U.S. loans	7,000,000
Total	$57,000,000

Regardless of the accuracy of these estimates, some Massachusetts capital was going into western roads, for example, the Michigan Central. [The reader will be interested in Arthur M. Johnson and Barry E. Supple, *Boston Capitalists and Western Railroads* (Cambridge, Mass.: Harvard University Press, 1967), chaps. 1–4.]

[95] A large proportion of the bonds issued in this period for the new road-building in Ohio, Indiana and Illinois were convertible bonds which offered the bondholder both security and the right to participate as a shareholder if the road proved to be profitable. Moreover, some of these roads did prove to be profitable, and their bonds were duly converted. The Fourth Report of the Cincinnati, Hamilton and Dayton stated that all the first-mortgage bonds had been con-

The actual financing of most early rail purchases was by short- or intermediate-term credit from the Anglo-American houses rather than by exchange of bonds for iron.[96] However, securities were often taken as collateral for these credits.[97] *Barings Circular* for the end of 1851 read:

The bonds of American railway companies have not yet obtained much currency in the London market, and where investments are desired the orders have been transmitted to the United States.—Capitalists here, although they often take shares in foreign railways, have never seemed to like the debentures at fixed interest of such companies, and even in this country the debentures only of entirely or partially completed and revenue giving lines are selected.[98]

Yet within some months Barings, Rothschilds, and George Peabody were all deeply engaged in the negotiation of American railway securities.[99]

---

verted into stock. *American Railroad Journal*, XXVII (June 10, 1854), 363. Similarly, of $1,675,000 of bonds issued by the Cleveland and Pittsburgh, $304,000 had been converted by 1853. *Ibid.*, XXVI (Feb. 19, 1853), 120. When the Cincinnati, Hamilton and Dayton, and some of the other roads used this device in the early days, it was first-mortgage bonds that were convertible. After convertible bonds became popular they were often issued as junior securities. This was the case of the New York and Erie Railroad.

[96] There are instances of rails being purchased for bonds before 1852. The Cleveland and Pittsburgh, for example, was reported in 1850 to have purchased iron for bonds from a British manufacturer of established reputation, a report which is substantiated by the fact that George Peabody arranged the insurance on the shipment of these rails but did not make the actual purchase. *American Railroad Journal*, XXIII (May 18, 1850), 313, and Muriel Hidy, "George Peabody," 332. The East Tennessee and Georgia was also able to arrange for part payment of its rails in bonds. This contract, which was made in New York with the Bailey Brothers' agent, Raymond and Fullerton, specified a price of $32.75 per ton, of which $22.75 was to be paid in cash, $4 in stock of the railway, and $6 in bonds of the railway. *American Railroad Journal*, XXIII (June 22, 1850), 390, and (Dec. 14, 1850), 786. Also, when the Hartford, Providence and Fishkill purchased rails through George Peabody, its draft was accompanied with securities to be marketed in England. Muriel Hidy, "George Peabody," 317.

More commonly the railway bonds were negotiated in the United States, and the iron was purchased with the proceeds. In 1849, the Nashville and Chattanooga negotiated $300,000 of its 6 percent coupon bonds of $1,000 each in New York at 88⅜ percent with Corcoran and Riggs of Washington, Elisha Riggs of New York, Cammann and Whitehouse of New York, and Charnley and Whiten of Philadelphia. Then V. K. Stevenson, president of the company, proceeded to London to buy rails. *American Railroad Journal*, XXII (Sept. 8, 1849), 563, and Muriel Hidy, "George Peabody," 329.

[97] For example, when George Peabody concluded a joint account arrangement with Chouteau, Merle and Sanford of New York, a firm which was very active in the purchase of rails in this period, it was specified that the limit of securities to be taken as collateral would be $200,000 and that a 10 percent margin would be held. Mrs. Hidy adds, "It is clear that at this time Peabody was unwilling to look to the British market for the sales of such securities." "George Peabody," 333.

[98] Quoted in the *American Railroad Journal*, XXV (Jan. 24, 1852), 57.

[99] Before 1852 Barings had taken in payment for iron only the Baltimore and Ohio's Maryland bonds, although the merchant bankers had purchased $50,000

Indeed, even before Barings and Peabody at length decided to reverse their positions on this business, arrangements had been made for the public issue in London of a number of American railway securities. Of these, those of the Illinois Central are probably the best known.[100] It was also about this time that the ironmasters became more willing to accept payment or part payment for rails in American railroad bonds.[101]

From the beginning of 1852 until the autumn of 1853 the popularity of American railway securities increased almost steadily; then other interruptions occurred. During one month in the summer of 1852 a dispute over fishing rights between the United States and Canada led to a temporary suspension of security business.[102] A more serious event in the late summer and autumn of 1853 was a drain of specie from New York that

---

of Ross County bonds issued in favor of the Marietta and Cincinnati and $25,000 of Panama Railroad bonds on its own account. The first American issue in which they participated was the $3 million, 30 year, 6 percent issue which the Pennsylvania negotiated in the autumn of 1852. Ralph Hidy, *House of Baring*, 408–11.

[100] The first advertisement for American railway bonds in the London daily press seems to have been for the Philadelphia and Reading. This advertisement, which appeared in the *Times* (March 3, 1852, p. 8), was a reprint of an article from the *Philadelphia Gazette* and was an advertisement of the railway itself rather than a direct offer of securities for sale. The earliest advertisement that specifically offered bonds seems to have been that of an anomalous company entitled Belgo-American Atlantic and Mississippi Railway and Emigration Co. Its London agent was Heath and Co., which offered £5 shares and stated its purpose to be to buy land and resell to emigrants and also to construct a railroad from Savannah via Albany, Fort Gaines, Abbeville, Montezuma, Stockton, Ala., and Columbia, Miss., to Natchez. The route selected for the portion in Georgia was circuitous to say the least, and the subsequent history of this concern is obscure. Indeed, the most interesting point about it is that it was a Belgian company, for Belgium was not a country noted for its interest in America or American railways. *Daily News*, April 16, 1852, p. 1.

The first public offering of American railway bonds in London in the 1850's was that of the Illinois Central. It appeared in all the leading newspapers and railway periodicals in June 1852. See, for example, *Economist*, X (June 19, 1852), 696. This was followed within the week by the offer of $3 million of debentures by the New York and Erie. *Ibid.* (June 26, 1852), 724.

[101] The first specific mention of the offer of bonds for rails in the Dowlais Iron Co.'s correspondence is on Jan. 21, 1852, and concerns a proposition by the Columbus, Piqua and Indiana Railway through Robert Harrison to purchase 4,500 tons of rails for half cash, half bonds. George Purnell to Sir John Guest, Jan. 21, 1852, Dowlais Iron Co., Letter Books, London Series. In these papers the subject was discussed in general in 1849. See George Kitson to Sir John Guest, May 3, 1849.

[102] The first mention of dullness in the American market in the summer of 1852 was in the second week of August, and it seems to have passed by the end of August. *Daily News*, Aug. 13, 1852, p. 7; Aug. 18, 1852, p. 7; and Aug. 31, 1852, p. 7. Incidentally, this difficulty in Anglo-American diplomatic relations was also reported to have caused Thomas Baring to cancel a proposed visit to the United States.

resulted in extreme dullness in the New York market; this was reflected in London.[103]

For American securities the year 1854 was an uneven one. By January the price of stocks in the New York market began to improve,[104] but by March political considerations were having an adverse effect on the London market. The outbreak of the Crimean War at the end of March 1854 led to an almost complete suspension of dealings in the American market.[105] Recovery from the setback occasioned by European events had only begun when in July news of a railway scandal erupted. The defalcations by Robert Schuyler on the New York and New Haven and on the Harlem roads in the summer of that year caused a panic on the New York Stock Exchange.[106] There was no corresponding panic in London; the City column of the *Daily News* reported that security holders were not generally alarmed.[107] Nevertheless, there was for some time a feeling of quiet in the market as the English investors awaited further developments.[108] By the autumn of 1854 this atmosphere of suspended animation had begun to pass as the continued depression of prices in New York tempted the English to take advantage of the bargains offered.[109]

Business was variable in the succeeding years. In 1855 and 1856 the tendency on the whole was upwards.[110] On the other hand, 1857 was, almost from the beginning, a year of dull markets.[111] A number of American railways previously popular in England defaulted on their interest payments during the spring.[112] Throughout the summer the situation on the New York Stock Exchange was uncertain and unsatisfactory,[113] but there was no serious panic until the end of August. This was caused by the failure of a company deeply involved in railway finance, the Ohio Life and Trust Company of Ohio.[114]

At first it was hoped that this panic would be confined to the banking business and would pass without spreading to the mercantile commu-

---

[103] *Ibid.,* Sept. 23, 1853, p. 7, for example.   [104] *Ibid.,* Jan. 20, 1854, p. 20.

[105] *Ibid.,* March 31, 1854, p. 7, and June 2, 1854, p. 6.

[106] The report of the overissue of securities by Schuyler was followed by similar reports of overissues by Edward Crane of the Vermont Central.

[107] Aug. 4, 1854, p. 7.   [108] *Ibid.,* Aug. 4, 1854, p. 7; Aug. 25, 1854, p. 6, etc.

[109] *Ibid.,* Sept. 29, 1854, p. 6, and Ralph Hidy, *House of Baring,* 428. There were indeed good bargains to be had in 1854. For example, the Illinois Central 7 percent issue of 1875, which stood around 70 in the autumn of 1854, rose to about 90 at the beginning of 1857. *Daily News,* Nov. 23, 1854, p. 7, and May 1, 1857, p. 7.

[110] Some western roads were already in financial difficulties after 1854, but the British investor continued to take securities of established roads.

[111] *Daily News,* Feb. 13, 1857, p. 7; Feb. 20, 1857, p. 7; Feb. 27, 1857, p. 7; March 6, 1857, p. 7, etc.

[112] *Economist,* XV (May 16, 1857), 541, and (May 23, 1857), 570.

[113] *Ibid.,* XV (June 20, 1857), 682; (June 27, 1857), 705; (July 4, 1857), 736; (Aug. 8, 1857), 877.

[114] *Ibid.* (Sept. 5, 1857), 987.

nity.[115] Just as after the crisis of 1854, the English at first moved in to pick up bargains in depreciated American railway securities.[116] The panic of 1857 was, however, no quickly passing affair. By the end of September the suspension of specie payment had begun. Extensive mercantile failures soon followed. By March 1858 these were estimated to have reached 6,022.[117]

However numerous the difficulties in the rest of the community, the spectacular bankruptcies were those of railways and banking houses. Some of the latter had overextended themselves in financing the new railways of Ohio, Indiana, Illinois, and the surrounding states. Probably the most famous of the banking failures besides that of the Ohio Life and Trust Company were those of Page, Bacon and Company of Saint Louis [118] and of the Western Bank of Scotland.[119] Winslow, Lanier and Company, a New York firm and one of the foremost in negotiating both railway securities and government bonds issued to aid railways, suspended payments temporarily,[120] and George Peabody had to be helped over his difficulties by a loan from the Bank of England.[121] Before recovery from the effects of this crisis was fully made, the Civil War was imminent.

How great was British investment in American railways in the period between 1847 and 1861? The *Bankers' Magazine* estimated that in the four-year period from July 1, 1848, to July 1, 1852, total foreign holdings of American railway securities and of municipal securities issued in favor of railways increased from £12 million to £24 million.[122] This estimate covered only the period before American railway securities began to be issued publicly on the London market, but it was greater than the estimates made a year later by the United States Secretary of the Treasury for all foreign holdings of the same classes of securities [see Table 2].[123]

[115] *Ibid.* (Sept. 19, 1857), 1044.

[116] *Ibid.* (Sept. 26, 1857), 1072: "There is still a disposition to pick up American railway securities at the reduced prices lately established, but quotations in some cases present a further decline, being borne down by the unsettled state of the market in America."

[117] *Ibid.*, XVI (March 6, 1858), 260. This estimate was supplied by Tappan and McKillop, a firm which described itself as a trade protection agency, its business being to provide credit ratings on United States firms, to collect debts, etc.

[118] This firm was especially interested in the Ohio and Mississippi. Wyatt Winton Belcher, *The Economic Rivalry between St. Louis and Chicago, 1850–1880* (New York: Columbia University Press, 1947), 121.

[119] R. H. Campbell, "Edinburgh Bankers and the Western Bank of Scotland," *Scottish Journal of Political Economy*, II (June 1955), 141–42.

[120] *Daily News*, Oct. 22, 1857, p. 6.

[121] *Ibid.*, Nov. 27, 1857, p. 2: "Now that every requisite arrangement has been finally completed, it may be mentioned that Messrs. George Peabody and Co. are the eminent American firm who, to the satisfaction of the whole commercial community, have just been assisted by the Bank of England . . . it is a mere act of justice to the other houses in the trade that the name should be mentioned."

[122] *Bankers' Magazine*, XIII (Feb. 1853), 101.

[123] U.S., Congress, *Senate Executive Document No. 42, 33d Cong., 1st sess.*,

Table 2. American securities owned abroad on June 30, 1853

Issued by	Total outstanding	Foreign owned
United States, stocks	$ 58,205,517	$ 27,000,000
States, stocks	190,718,221	72,931,507
113 towns and cities, bonds	79,352,149	16,462,322
347 counties, bonds	13,928,369	5,000,000
985 banks, stocks	266,724,955	6,688,996
75 insurance companies, stocks	12,829,730	378,172
244 railway companies, stocks	309,893,967	8,244,025
244 railway companies, bonds	170,111,552	43,888,752
16 canal and navigation cos., stocks	35,888,918	554,900
16 canal and navigation cos., bonds	22,130,569	1,967,547
15 miscellaneous companies, stocks	16,425,612	802,720
15 miscellaneous companies, bonds	2,358,323	265,773
Total	$1,178,567,882	$184,184,714

SOURCE: U.S., Congress, *Senate Executive Document 42*, 33d Cong., 2d sess., 1853–54, p. 53, quoted in the *Economist*, XII (March 25, 1854), 316.

However, there seems to be little doubt that the estimates of the Secretary of the Treasury were too low. They were based on actual reports from various companies and governmental units. Although the most important railways and countries were probably included in the survey, there is no indication of the completeness of the various reports. The facts were undoubtedly not all known even to the reporting institutions. Since the inquiry was instigated when the political atmosphere in the United States was hostile to foreigners and foreign capital, it is possible that some railways felt it wise to minimize the extent of foreign holdings reported.[124] [Furthermore, it should be explained that since for ease of transfer brokers in the United States held some securities for foreign owners, the nationality of investors was to some extent quite innocently obscured.]

Two other estimates are informative, if not completely comparable. Winslow, Lanier and Company, with the advantages of deep involvement in flotations in New York, probably could give a more complete estimate of foreign holdings than the report of the Secretary of the Treasury. In fact this firm's estimate was also included in the Senate document. It gave the amount of state bonds held abroad as $110,972,108, as compared to the Secretary of the Treasury's $72,831,507.[125] Samuel Gray Ward, who had

"Report of the Secretary of the U.S. Treasury Dept. in answer to a resolution calling for the amount of Foreign securities held in Europe and other foreign countries on the 30th June, 1853," 1853–54.

[124] This was the era of the Know-Nothing Party, a party which proposed to tax foreign capital. *Daily News*, Feb. 28, 1855, p. 5.

[125] *Economist*, XII (March 25, 1854), 316. See also U.S., Congress, *Senate Executive Document No. 42*, 33d Cong., 1st sess., 1853–54, pp. 5 and 53.

only recently succeeded his father, Thomas Wren Ward, as American agent of the Barings, gave for November 1853 the figure of nearly $70 million (£14 million) for foreign holdings of the United States railway debt.[126] As this included not only railway stocks and bonds but state issues on behalf of railways, it could not be exactly compared with the Secretary of the Treasury's total of $52 million for the railways' corporation stocks and bonds alone.

It seems reasonable to assume that at the beginning of the Civil War, British holdings of American railway securities amounted to around £20 million. This is based on the acceptance of Ward's estimate of £14 million for this debt in the autumn of 1853 and the *Economist's* estimate of £100 million for the total of British investment in the United States at the beginning of 1861.[127]

Although the railway securities did not represent a large proportion of British holdings in the United States, and governmental debt probably accounted for the bulk of the estimated £100 million of British investment, this is not the whole picture.[128] Some of the American municipal bonds as well as those of counties and states were issued to aid railways, and some of these were held abroad. British short-term credits were also significant in aiding American railways and accounted for a portion of the total.

[126] Ralph Hidy, *House of Baring*, 428–29, and 605 n.

[127] *Economist*, XXXIV (Jan. 19, 1861), 71.

[128] According to an article published originally in the *Philadelphia Public Ledger* in late 1859 and widely quoted, an unofficial survey based on the books of the Treasury estimated that two-thirds of the debt of the United States Government was held abroad. An air of verisimilitude was given to this report by the publication of exact figures for the holdings of a number of important persons. For example, Lord Overstone was stated to be the largest single holder with $350,000 of bonds. *Bankers' Magazine*, XX (Jan. 1860), 51. In 1859, the total debt of the United States government amounted to $58,498,000, so that foreign holdings of it can be taken to amount to $40 million.

II

American Railways and
British Rails

EXPORT of rails from Great Britain to the United States was a significant phase of the development of American railways and was closely tied to the export of capital. In November 1853 Samuel G. Ward estimated that half of the European investment of £70 million in American railway bonds and state bonds to aid railways represented securities obtained in return for purchases of British rails.[1] The United States was at that time Britain's best customer for rails, receiving over one-half of the British iron exports for the years 1849 to 1854 [see Table 3].[2] The flood of cheap British rails that poured into the United States after the collapse of the railway boom in the United Kingdom in 1847 for a time had serious repercussions on the infant iron industry of the United States. The dependence of the British iron rail industry on exports to the United States brought about important modifications in the organization of the export market. In particular, it led to the ironmasters' participation in some of the functions earlier performed solely by the merchants and merchant banking firms.

Iron smelting was begun in the American colonies as early as 1643, and at first the process compared favorably both in technique and in capacity with contemporary European manufacture.[3] By the middle of the eighteenth century the American colonies were producing about 20,000 tons of pig iron, bars, and blooms annually. In fact pig iron was an important export from America.[4]

In the three-quarters of a century following the American Revolution, a period of great innovation and expansion in the English iron industry, the United States fell seriously behind. Once the colonies had emerged as

[1] Ralph Hidy, *House of Baring*, 428–29 and 605 n.

[2] It should be noted that total British exports of rails rose very sharply after 1847.

[3] Victor S. Clark, *History of Manufactures in the United States* (New York: McGraw-Hill, 1929), I, 170.

[4] E. D. MacCallum, *The Iron and Steel Industry in the United States* (London: P. S. King & Co., 1931), 21; quotation from Edwin C. Eckel, *Coal Iron and War* (London: George G. Harrap & Co., 1920), 20.

the United States, the Trade and Navigation Acts operated against them. With the disappearance of the export market the industry reverted "from an export-commercial to a neighbourhood or almost homespun stage." [5] Moreover, furnace practice lagged seriously. American ironmasters were reluctant to abandon charcoal. The abundance of timber for fuel led to an understandable prejudice in favor of charcoal iron. A geological fact also had significance: in the older established furnace districts of the East, iron and bituminous coal do not lie adjacent to each other.[6] When charcoal first began to be displaced, it was anthracite rather than bituminous coal that was used in iron making.

[5] V. S. Clark, 221.   [6] Ibid., 412–13.

Table 3. Railroad Iron, 1847–82

Year	Total UK exports (1000's of tons)	UK exports to the US (1000's of tons)	Percentage of UK exports going to US	US production (1000's of tons)
1847	228 [a]	64 [b]	24	
1848	338	162	48	
1849	402	228	57	24
1850	469	n.a. [c]		44
1851	538	n.a.		51
1852	567	n.a.		62
1853	653	410	63	88
1854	616	337	53	108
1855	540	195	36	139

SOURCES: Col. 2: The figures for the years 1847–60 are from *Statistical Abstract for the United Kingdom, 1840–1854,* and from *Statistical Abstract for the United Kingdom, 1855–1869.* The figures for the years after 1860 have been compiled from various trade returns. Col. 3: The figures for the years prior to 1853 have been compiled from various Parliamentary documents. The figures for 1853 and following years have been compiled from various trade returns. Col. 5: The figures for the years 1849–69 are from James M. Swank, *History of the Manufacture of Iron in All Ages* (Philadelphia: American Iron and Steel Association, 1892), 440. The figures for the years after 1869 are from the *United States Statistical Abstract for 1884,* 179, Table 140.

[a] The figures for the years 1847–55 are for bar, bolt, and railroad iron.

[b] The figures for the years 1847–55 are for merchant bar and railroad iron.

[c] Figures for 1850, 1851, and 1852 are not available. Figures for the rail imports of the United States are available, but are not comparable for two reasons: the fiscal years of the two countries do not coincide, and in addition, the United States figures are for rails while the United Kingdom figures given here are for merchant bars and railroad iron. The figures for the rail imports of the United States, virtually all of which came from the United Kingdom, follow: 1849, 69 (in 1000's of tons); 1850, 159; 1851, 226; 1852, 294; 1853, 358; 1854, 339; 1855, 153. Great Britain, *Parliamentary Papers (Accounts and Papers,* LXV, 1874), "Report by Mr. Harriss-Gastrell on the Iron and Steel Industries of the United States."

Table 3 (continued)

Year	Total UK exports (1000's of tons)	UK exports to the US (1000's of tons)	Percentage of UK exports going to US	US production (1000's of tons)
1856	461 [d]	165 [d]	36	180
1857	457	156	34	162
1858	433	30	7	164
1859	528	125	24	195
1860	453	138	30	205
1861	377	28	7	190
1862	325	10	5	214
1863	406	66	14	276
1864	384	108	28	335
1865	330 [e]	56 [e]	17	356
1866	368	103	28	431
1867	458	161	35	460
1868	502	262	52	499
1869	753	295	39	584
1870	897	401	45	553
1871	873 [f]	505 [f]	58	692
1872	853	447	52	892
1873	699	178	25	794
1874	699	91	13	651
1875	490	17	3	707
1876	365	−7 [g]	—	785
1877	413	— [g]	—	682
1878	358	— [g]	—	788
1879	387	43	11	993
1880	604	219	36	1,305
1881	716	290	40	1,645
1882	781 [h]	195 [h]	25	1,507

[d] The figures for the years 1856–64 are for railroad iron only.

[e] The figures for the years 1865–70 are for rails only.

[f] The separate classification of chairs and sleepers was dropped in this year so that figures for the years 1871–81 are for total railroad iron.

[g] Exports in the years 1876, 1877, and 1878 were negligible.

[h] The separate classification of chairs and sleepers was reintroduced in this year.

Railways were eventually to solve two of the most serious problems confronting the American iron industry: the expansion of demand and the opening up of the bituminous coal fields of western Pennsylvania, western Virginia, and Ohio. However, in the 1830's America's iron industry was scattered along the Atlantic seaboard. When in the mid-1840's the high prices of English rails led American ironmasters to make their first venture into the rolling of rails, most of the new mills were set up in the anthracite region of northeastern Pennsylvania. It was 1855 before production of iron with anthracite outstripped production of iron with charcoal in the United States—381,866 tons against 339,922 tons. Production of iron with bituminous coal remained a poor third, the output for that year being only 62,390 tons. Indeed, in iron manufacture bituminous coal did not replace charcoal in second place until 1869 and reached first place only in 1875.[7]

Some observers considered the techniques used in the United States antiquated. Sir Lowthian Bell described the American iron industry in the 1880's as being of a very anomalous character, partly very modern and partly prehistoric.[8] This backwardness of the United States' iron industry led some historians to maintain that the Industrial Revolution in the United States occurred only after the Civil War.[9]

The production of pig iron was not the immediate bottleneck when in the 1830's railway building in the United States began. There were in the country no rolling mills capable of turning out heavy rails.[10] Some cast-iron rails for use on sidings were manufactured locally even in the early 1830's,[11] and some strap rails were rolled at the Tredegar Works in Richmond, Virginia, in 1837;[12] but development was slow.

During the 1840's the domestic manufacture of rails gradually got underway. In 1844 the first American heavy rails were made at the Mount Savage works in Maryland, a rolling mill built the previous year especially for the Maryland and New York Iron and Coal Company. The stock of this corporation was largely held in Europe, and the English stockholders were represented in management by Henry Thomas Weld of New York.[13] A second rolling mill, the Montour Works of Danville, Pennsylvania, was opened in 1845.[14] The next year production began at six more mills: The Boston Iron Company, the New England Company, the Trenton Iron Works, the Phoenixville works of Reeves, Buck and Company, the Great Western Iron Company of Brady's Bend (near Pittsburgh), and the Lackawanna Iron Company.

The impetus leading to the establishment of these first rail mills was the

---

[7] James M. Swank, *History of the Manufacture of Iron in All Ages* (Philadelphia: American Iron and Steel Association, 1892), 376.

[8] In criticism, Bell wrote: "50,000 tons of malleable iron [are] made in a year in the prehistoric ore-hearth, often but little removed in construction from the apparatus used now only by semi-civilised people, and not differing in principle from what is still in use among barbarous nations." Great Britain, *Parliamentary Papers*, XXI (no. 4715, 1886), "Second Report of the Royal Commission Appointed to Inquire into the Depression of Trade and Industry, 1886" [Minutes of Evidence, and Appendix (C-4715), Appendix A, pt. I], 350.

[9] Louis M. Hacker and Benjamin B. Kendrick, *The United States Since 1865* (New York: F. S. Crofts & Co., 1934), 183 ff.

[10] V. S. Clark, 511.   [11] Hungerford, *Baltimore and Ohio*, I, 72.

[12] *American Railroad Journal*, XXII (March 24, 1849), 184. [See also Charles B. Dew, *Ironmaker to the Confederacy: Joseph R. Anderson and the Tredegar Iron Works* (New Haven: Yale University Press, 1966).]

[13] Swank, 434 and 441. See also *Economist*, III (Nov. 15, 1845), 1135.

[14] *Ibid.* The *American Railroad Journal* seems to have been in error when it claimed priority for the Montour Works. XXII (March 24, 1849), 184.

high price of iron in Britain during the railway boom of the 1840's.[15] Quotations of £9 to £12 per ton at Cardiff encouraged a number of mills in the United States to enter into rail production, a business which later proved to be uneconomical.[16] For the time being there was sufficient demand to keep them all rolling. The American correspondent for the *Economist* commented on this situation:

The iron works in Great Britain, having for some time past been so busily engaged in supplying the immense quantities required for making the new lines, and repairing the old ones [in Great Britain], have left the demand here [in the United States] to be supplied by the home manufacturers, who, in consequence, have for a considerable period been up to the head and ears in orders, making bad iron and large profits at the same time.[17]

There are interesting parallels between the situation faced by the early rolling mills in the United States and that of its textile manufacturers at an earlier date. Just as America's infant textile industry got its start during the Napoleonic Wars when normal trade with England was interrupted, so the American iron industry in the 1840's profited by the temporary preoccupation of the English ironmasters with sales at home and their partial withdrawal from the American market. And just as the glut of British textiles pouring into the United States in the 1820's brought distress to America's cotton industry after 1816 [18] and agitation for a protective tariff, so the crack in the price of British rails beginning in the autumn of 1847 [19] contributed to the decimation of the newly mustered

---

[15] The highest price for rails at Cardiff in 1846 was £11.10.0 and the lowest £9.0.0. George Kitson to Lady Charlotte Guest, Sept. 6, 1853, Dowlais Iron Co., Letter Books, London House.

[16] See list of rolling mills from Webster's speech at Faneuil Hall, Boston, Oct. 24, 1848, reprinted in the *Economist*, VI (Nov. 25, 1848), 1326.

[17] V (July 31, 1847), 866.   [18] Albion, 61.

[19] The following rail prices in sterling per ton were asked at Cardiff:

	1846			1847			1848		
Jan.	12	0	0	10	0	0	7	10	0
Feb.	11	0	0	10	0	0	8	0	0
Mar.	11	0	0	9	10	0	7	10	0
Apr.	10	5	0	9	10	0	7	10	0
May	9	15	0	9	5	0	6	5	0
June	10	0	0	8	15	0	6	5	0
July	9	10	0	9	0	0	6	0	0
Aug.	9	10	0	9	0	0	6	0	0
Sept.				9	0	0	6	0	0
Oct.	10	0	0	8	15	0	5	15	0
Nov.	10	0	0	8	0	0	5	15	0
Dec.	10	0	0	7	0	0	5	10	0

Glamorgan, Monmouthshire and Brecon Gazette, Cardiff Advertiser and *Merthyr Guardian* (1846–48). These are the prices given for the last week of each month.

ranks of American rolling mills. At the close of 1847, between sixteen and twenty mills were working full time. By the end of 1848 only four were still in operation: the two mills of Reeves, Buck and Company of Philadelphia (one at Phoenixville and the other at Safe Harbor), the New Jersey works of Peter Cooper and Abram Hewitt, and the Tredegar Works at Richmond, Virginia.

The remaining mills also faced problems. Reeves, Buck and Company were at this time rolling for the Pennsylvania Railroad at a price of $60.50 per ton;[20] Cooper and Hewitt were manufacturing for the Hudson River Railroad at $67.50 per ton;[21] and the Tredegar Works were preparing rails for the Richmond and Danville.[22] The Pennsylvania contract was carried through. Indeed, it would have been difficult for that railroad to go against the interests of the American iron industry, especially since these mills had been constructed specifically to supply its rails;[23] but the Hudson River Railroad's contract was not completed. When the price of English rails, including freight and duty, fell to $40 per ton, this railroad bought out of its commitment to Cooper and Hewitt mills for approximately $50,000, paid in its own bonds.[24]

It was at this time that the American iron manufacturers first came to work in association. Their immediate object was the repeal of the ad valorem tariff of 1846 and the enactment of a stiff specific duty in its place. Daniel Webster worked for this cause: he had entered the lists as early as 1845 and was reported to have received $100,000 from "manufacturers, miners, iron masters, bankers, etc., of Massachusetts, Rhode Island, Connecticut, New York, Pennsylvania, New Jersey and Delaware,"[25] for his efforts.

By 1849 matters were desperate for the American iron industry, and as a result there was a spate of well-organized conventions. Attendance at some of these was not limited to ironmasters, although they were, in fact, very prominent. Peter Cooper of Cooper and Hewitt was president of the New Jersey convention.[26] At the Iron Manufacturers' Convention held in

[20] This contract was for 15,000 tons at a price that was said to be about $10.00 per ton less than the market price at that time on the seaboard. Burgess and Kennedy, *Centennial History of the Pennsylvania Railroad Company, 1846–1946* (Philadelphia: Pennsylvania Railroad Co., 1949), 54.

[21] *American Railroad Journal*, XXII (March 24, 1849), 184.

[22] *Ibid.*, XXIII (March 9, 1850), 147.

[23] The seriousness of the situation from the American iron interests' point of view may be judged by the fact that some Pennsylvania roads did go to England for their iron at this time. The Cumberland Valley Railroad, running through one of the best iron districts of Pennsylvania (but deriving much of its financial support from Baltimore), used English iron when it relaid with heavy rails in 1849. *Ibid.*, XXII (Sept. 1, 1849), 548.

[24] The amount paid by the Hudson River Company to Cooper and Hewitt to terminate the contract was variously reported in the *American Railroad Journal* as $51,000 and $54,000. *Ibid.*, 548 and (Sept. 15, 1849), 584.

[25] *Economist*, V (Jan. 16, 1847), 63.

[26] *American Railroad Journal*, XXII (Nov. 24, 1849), 739.

Pittsburgh in this same year it was proposed that only American iron should be used on the projected transcontinental railway,[27] which had already caught the public fancy.[28]

Even in the South, normally an antiprotectionist section, there was pressure to make use of local resources. Railways in both Virginia and Alabama had hopeful ideas of utilizing rails made from local coal and iron.[29] The Alabama and Tennessee Railroad went so far as to advertise for an ironmaster to set up a rolling mill in Alabama. However, these railways were eventually obliged to contract with Welsh houses.[30]

For ironmasters of the United Kingdom, the years 1849 to 1852 were also hard ones. The well-established, and probably the largest, iron mining and manufacturing firm in Wales, the Dowlais Iron Company, headed by Sir John Josiah Guest, serves as an example. On November 20, 1850, Lady Charlotte Guest, the ironmaster's wife, who was active in the business, wrote in her diary, "For the first time since I married [1833], the accounts of the half year to September have shewn a loss and that a heavy one." [31] A year later, on November 12, 1851, William Purnell wrote from the firm's London office, "We do not know where to find orders for you. The trade gets worse daily." [32] In the same month, when an order for 2,000 tons was received from the United States, Lady Charlotte wrote, describing the reaction of her husband, who was ill at the time: [33] "I thought if the subject were pressing on his mind and he was uneasy about it, it would be best to reassure him, so I told him 2,000 tons had been ordered from America. Then he made me fetch the letter and read part of it to him and said: 'It is the only drop of comfort in the trade for months, and would you keep it from me?' " [34] The price of rails had been hovering around £5 a ton for over three years. In early 1852 the utmost Peabody would give was

[27] Asa Whitney was lecturing in England on the proposed Atlantic and Pacific Railroad in 1851. *Times*, June 11, 1851, p. 5.

[28] *American Railroad Journal*, XXII (Dec. 1, 1849), 752–53.

[29] The railway in Virginia that hoped to use Virginia iron was the Virginia and Tennessee. The second annual report of this company stated that the company had decided to roll its own rails at Lynchburg. *Ibid.*, XXIII (March 9, 1850), 147. But within the year the *American Railroad Journal* reported that sufficient English iron to lay 60 miles of track had been purchased at $42 per ton. *Ibid.* (Sept. 14, 1850), 582. The first contract was made through John Dunlop of Petersburg, the agent for a Welsh house. *Ibid.*, XXII (Sept. 15, 1849), 583. Later, large orders were placed with Guest through Richard Makin. William Purnell to Lady Charlotte Guest, Aug. 21, 1853, Dowlais Iron Co., Letter Books, London House.

[30] The advertisement of the Alabama and Tennessee appeared in the *American Railroad Journal*, XXIII (Sept. 7, 1850), 566. However in the annual report for 1851, an extract of which appeared in the same journal, XXV (May 8, 1852), 292, it was stated that the iron was coming from Wales via Mobile.

[31] Earl of Bessborough (ed.), *Lady Charlotte Guest: Extracts from Her Journal, 1833–1852* (London: John Murray, 1950), 251.

[32] Purnell to William Wood, Nov. 12, 1851, Dowlais Iron Co., Letter Books, London House.

[33] Sir John Guest died at the end of 1852.   [34] Bessborough, 280.

£4.12.6 with six month's credit or £4.10.0 cash.[35] Barings was offering only £4.5.0 a ton for rails of the ⊤ pattern, 48 pounds to the yard.[36]

Throughout this period the United States market was of paramount importance to the British ironmasters. In 1848, 48 percent of British exports of bars and rails went to the United States, and in each of the six years from 1849 through 1854 more than 50 percent.[37] Presumably the greater part of the orders were placed before the upturn in the market in the middle of 1852. American railways thus obtained a very large quantity of rails from the United Kingdom at rock-bottom prices.

In the summer of 1852 the price of rails began to harden.[38] At that time Guest and Company obtained a joint order with Bailey Brothers, a rival ironmaster whose rails were also very popular in the United States, for 130,000 tons of rails for Russia.[39] The worst was over, and orders and prices now increased hand in hand. By the autumn, Guest's firm had plenty of business.[40] Although the members of the firm regretted the sales that they had made to Frederick Huth, a merchant banking house of London and Liverpool, and to Boorman, Johnston, an importing house in New York, at the old price of £6 per ton,[41] they congratulated themselves at being "as well, if not better placed, than most of our neighbours, some of whom have large contracts yet to complete at unremunerative prices." By January 1853 Barings was paying £9.10.0, exactly double what it had been offering ten months previously.[42]

The position of the American ironmasters improved concomitantly with the rise in the price of rails in England. The best indication of this is the construction of plants providing a considerable increase in capacity. New firms were formed. In 1852 the Cambria Company, a joint-stock corporation with a capital of $1 million, was building a works in the heart of the bituminous coal region near Johnstown, Pennsylvania, and was advertising that it was prepared to enter into contracts to deliver railroad iron by the next year.[43] The *American Railroad Journal* reported in 1853 that a smaller company was being formed at Wheeling in western Virginia for

[35] Enclosure with letter from William Purnell to Mr. Walkinshaw, March 18, 1852, Dowlais Iron Co., Letter Books, London House.

[36] William Purnell to Sir John Guest, Feb. 24, 1852, *ibid.*   [37] See Table 3.

[38] In April 1852 Guest was willing to sell at £4.16.6, Cardiff; £5.2.6, Liverpool. William Purnell to Sir John Guest, April 19, 1852, Dowlais Iron Co., Letter Books, London House. In July the price was £6, but it was as yet unclear whether this price would be maintained. Thus, on July 28, 1852, William Purnell wrote: "I believe most of the makers of Iron are so well supplied with orders, that no immediate reduction may be anticipated, nevertheless I should be glad to secure orders to serve us through the winter at £6." *Ibid.*, July 28, 1852.

[39] Bessborough, 288.

[40] George Kitson to Lady Charlotte Guest, Sept. 2, 1852, Dowlais Iron Co., Letter Books, London House.

[41] William Purnell to Lady Charlotte Guest, Oct. 6, 1852, *ibid.*

[42] George Kitson to Lady Charlotte Guest, Jan. 4, 1853, *ibid.*

[43] Simeon Draper was the agent for this company in New York. *American Railroad Journal*, XXV (Dec. 4, 1852), 779.

the purpose of rolling rails.[44] The Dodge County Iron Company of Wisconsin was also expected to be producing 50 tons of rails a day by early 1854.[45] Older rail-rolling companies increased their output. In 1852 the Montour Company was building thirty-two new puddling furnaces and a new rolling mill that was expected to begin operations the next year.[46] By 1854 the United States could boast of sixteen mills capable of rolling heavy rails; [47] some of them were survivors from the pre-1848 boom period, and others were newly erected.[48] It is significant that of the new

[44] The capital of this company was reported to be $100,000. There were two rail-rolling works in Wheeling by 1854, and it is not clear which of the two is referred to here. *Ibid.* (July 9, 1853), 445.

[45] This company was reported to have a capital of $500,000 and to have contracted, before completion, to supply rails to the Milwaukee and LaCrosse at the rate of 50 tons a day on or after March 1, 1854. *Ibid.*, XXVI (Nov. 19, 1853), 745.

[46] *Ibid.* (Feb. 12, 1853), 108.

[47] There were undoubtedly a few other mills besides those listed below. For example, there was said to be one at Hanging Rock, Ohio. *Ibid.* (Oct. 15, 1853), 666.

[48] The *American Railroad Journal*, XXVII (May 6, 1854), 281, reprinted the following table on rail-rolling capacity in the United States in 1854 from an article in the *Philadelphia Record:*

Rail-rolling capacity in the United States in 1854

Mill	Location	Annual capacity (tons)
1. East of the Alleghenies		
Montour	Danville, Pa.	13,000
Rough and Ready	Danville, Pa.	4,000
Lackawanna	Scranton, Pa.	16,000
Phoenix	Phoenixville, Pa.	20,000
Safe Harbor	Safe Harbor, Pa.	15,000
Pottsville Iron Works	Pottsville, Pa.	3,000
Trenton Iron Works	Trenton, N.J.	15,000
Massachusetts Iron Works	Boston, Mass.	15,000
Mount Savage	Maryland	12,000
Tredegar	Richmond, Va.	5,000
Total capacity east of the Alleghenies		118,000
2. West of the Alleghenies		
Great Western Iron Works	Brady's Bend, Pa.	12,000
New Works	Pittsburgh, Pa.	5,000
Washington Rolling Mill	Wheeling, Va.	5,000
Crescent Iron Works	Wheeling, Va.	5,000
New Mill	Portsmouth, Ohio	5,000
Cambria Iron Works	Cambria, Pa.	5,000
Total capacity west of the Alleghenies		37,000
Total capacity of the United States		155,000

works, five were located in the bituminous coal regions and only one in the anthracite area.

By this time the wheel had come full circle. In 1849 the iron manufacturers in the United States had been campaigning for a really protective tariff on iron. Now, railway men were pressing for the free admission of rails. They pointed out that all iron needed for expansion of the railway system had to be purchased abroad because the capacity of American mills was barely sufficient to take care of replacement needs.[49] Attempts to get a bill through Congress favoring railroaders' interests failed, but the campaign continued, including in February 1854 a convention of railway men held in New York.[50]

After 1854 the importance of the American railway demand to the British ironmaster began to decline relatively, although it remained of substantial absolute importance for some years and had occasional spurts at later dates. [To summarize Table 3: In the year 1854, 337,000 tons, 53 percent of the United Kingdom's iron exports, went to the United States, followed by a drop to 195,000 tons, representing 36 percent, in 1855, and 30,000 and only 7 percent in 1858. The partial recovery of the next two years was followed by the dearth of orders during the Civil War. Increased exports later were recorded, with special spurts in boom years of construction, such as 1866 to 1872 and the early 1880's.] However, these were not a portent of better times to come, only the afterglow of what had once been.

Rails from the United Kingdom were highly important to American railroads, especially before the Civil War. In the 1830's Great Britain supplied virtually all the rails used in the United States, which lacked rail-rolling capacity. The first American rolling mills were set up in the 1840's under the protection of the high prices then ruling in England. When, however, British rails again became available at low prices, the United States' infant industry was almost knocked out of the field. In the 1850's and 1860's, the iron industry of the United States became well established on a more economic basis than earlier. Beginning in 1857 the full brunt of cyclical fluctuations fell on imports, until finally they were displaced entirely. The cyclical nature of imports after 1850 stands in sharp contrast to American production, which steadily increased, exceeding imports from the United Kingdom in 1856 and every year thereafter.[51]

It is the selling policies of the British iron manufacturers during the shorter period, 1848 to 1854, that are discussed here. Since the American market was of the utmost importance in those years for the British iron mills specializing in rails, the ironmasters adjusted policies to obtain a large share of this dynamic market. They were not content to rely as

[49] *Ibid.*, XXV (Oct. 9, 1852), 641.

[50] *Ibid.*, XXVII (May 27, 1854), 321. Meanwhile American ironmasters continued to work for the passage of a stiff specific duty on rails, for they feared a recurrence of the late 1840's.

[51] See Table 3.

completely as earlier on orders for exports coming through iron merchants or merchant banking firms and moved into the direct marketing of rails. As a corollary, they also had to participate on a larger scale in the financing of exports. In fact, the organization of the export trade in rails had variety and color.

In the 1830's the rails for American railways came via Liverpool from Staffordshire and Wales, the greater part coming from the latter.[52] Many of these early roads used strap rails, which were in effect only a thin strip of iron nailed to the top of a wooden rail to increase its durability.[53] The New England roads, however, were building more substantially and laid rails of various English types.[54] The most famous rails were those first used by the Camden and Amboy Railroad of New Jersey. Rolled by Guest's Dowlais Iron Company in early 1831,[55] they were invented by the Camden and Amboy's engineer, John Stevens. Eventually these rails became standard in the United States, their distinguishing feature being that they were designed to be spiked directly to the sleepers without the use of chairs.[56]

In the second quarter of the century the British export market in iron was still in its formative stages. Of the iron manufacturers, aside from joint-stock companies such as the British Iron Company, only William Crawshay and Company of Cyfarthfa and Thompson and Forman of Penydarran maintained London houses.[57] Guest's Dowlais Iron Company, in spite of its importance, was still relying for many of its orders on the selling trips by members of the firm.[58]

[52] In 1832 an English paper, *Mercantile*, reported that upwards of 18,000 tons of iron rails had been ordered for American railways in Wales. Since strap rails required only 50 tons to the mile and T rails only 70 tons to the mile, 18,000 tons would have been sufficient for about 300 miles of road. *American Railroad Journal*, I (April 7, 1832), 225.

[53] Even the Baltimore and Ohio used mostly strap rails at first. *Ibid.* (Dec. 15, 1832), 804. So, too, did the South Carolina. *Ibid.*, II (Aug. 24, 1833), 532.

[54] The Boston and Lowell used fish belly rails of the type used on the Liverpool and Manchester. The Boston and Worcester used Clarence rails (called after the Clarence Railway, a line connecting with the Stockton and Darlington) and chairs.

[55] J. J. Guest to Edward Hutchins, Feb. 4, 1831, Dowlais Iron Co., Letter Books, Main Series.

[56] These rails were of rolled iron, 16 feet long, 2⅛ inches wide on the top, 3¼ inches at the bottom, and 3½ inches deep. The neck was ½ inch thick, and the weight was 39⁹⁄₁₆ lbs. per yard. The cost in England was between £7.10.0 and £8 per ton. *American Railroad Journal*, I (Sept. 29, 1832), 626.

[57] An undated list of the ironmasters of South Wales drawn up by Guest refers to Thompson and Forman as a London firm, the iron manufactory in Wales being called the Penydarran Co. Both Thompson and Forman were also interested, along with Samuel Homfray and Richard Fothergill, in the Tredegar works. Similarly, G. and W. Crawshay is listed as of London. Dowlais Iron Co., Letter Books, Main Series, 1831. [In the third generation as ironmasters the Crawshay brothers had different amounts of ownership in the London house and the Cyfarthfa Iron Works in Wales.]

[58] Edward Hutchins, at Newcastle, to John Guest, Aug. 20, 1834, *ibid.*

The American importer, as in the dry goods trade, was becoming more active.[59] Importing firms in the United States often transmitted their orders to the Welsh manufacturers through iron merchants in Liverpool or London. This was not invariably the case: especially in connection with the purchase of rails, the American representatives of various railway companies often felt that it was worth while to make a trip to the iron manufactories. Rails were still a relatively new product; their pattern and make were as yet by no means standard, and the quantities ordered at one time were sufficiently large to make mistakes costly. Thus Gerald Ralston of the iron-importing firm of Philadelphia and later of the Anglo-American merchant house of A. and G. Ralston visited various ironworks of South Wales in 1830.[60] Similarly, John Stevens of the Camden and Amboy traveled to the Dowlais works to supervise personally the rolling of the first Stevens rails.[61] Even when American purchasers of British rails were able to contract directly with iron manufacturers, they were still dependent on the middlemen. They turned to the merchant banking houses for their financing [62] and to iron merchants or brokers in the ports to arrange many of the technical details of export, such as shipping and insurance.[63]

The iron merchants continued to play a marketing role in exports, but they were not the dominant class of businessmen in the trade. In Liverpool, merchant houses such as John Bibby and Sons [64] and Harrison, Ridley and Harrison [65] did handle railway iron, but they were not as important as the merchant banking houses—Baring Brothers and Company, Palmer, MacKillop and Dent, or A. and G. Ralston. It must be

[59] See above, p. 6.

[60] Gerald Ralston to the Dowlais Iron Co., April 4, 1831, Dowlais Iron Co., Letter Books, Main Series. Ralston's career was very similar to that of George Peabody, though on a lesser scale. He began as an iron importer making periodic trips to England but maintaining no office in London. In the middle 1830's he established a house at 21 Tokenhouse Yard and began to act as a merchant banker, purchasing iron and dealing in securities. He was forced to suspend in the crisis of 1837 but recovered and was still in business in the 1850's.

[61] The contract for these Camden and Amboy rails was in Stevens's own name. William Purnell to Mr. Howard, May 22, 1850, *ibid.*, London Series.

[62] When Ralston first went to Dowlais he took with him a letter from Timothy Wiggin authorizing Ralston to draw on Wiggin and Co. for £20,000. Thomas Evans to J. J. Guest, Sept. 29, 1831, *ibid.*, Main Series.

[63] A correspondent to handle these details was necessary because American importers did not always maintain houses in Great Britain. In any case, the details of shipment were difficult, and merchant bankers usually employed someone to handle these for them.

[64] Crawshay, for example, had large dealings with John Bibby and Sons. Addis, 99.

[65] Davis Brooks and Co. of New York dealt with Harrison and Co. R. P. Davis to Thomas Evans, July 5, 1839, Dowlais Iron Co., Letter Books, London House. Incidentally, it was in 1839 that the Dowlais Iron Company undertook its first order directly for a Liverpool merchant. R. P. Davis to Thomas Evans, April 25, 1839, *ibid.* However, according to Addis, Guest had previously dealt through a London iron merchant, Clayston, Chapman and Co. Addis, 98.

emphasized that in the export of rails, unlike the export of merchant iron, the most important institution was the merchant banking house and not the iron merchant. Those merchant firms that survived the critical period of the late 1840's and early 1850's seem to have done so by taking on some of the functions of merchant banking.[66] However, their activities were restricted by the newly aggressive part taken in export marketing by the iron manufacturers.

During the critical years of the late 1840's, the ironmasters moved more actively into export marketing. Some of the firms established offices in Liverpool.[67] These included Bailey Brothers and Guest and Company, the latter of which already had set up an office in London in the late 1830's. A number of the leading ironmasters appointed agents in the United States.[68] Bailey Brothers and Guest and Company seem to have been particularly active in this new form of competition. As a result of its efforts Bailey Brothers' iron became very popular, especially in the South. Fothergill of the Aberdare Company had at least one agent in the United States, Joseph Bramwell. Naylor and Company did not establish an agency but set up its own houses in America, and these eventually were to expand operations to include some security negotiations.[69]

The decision by the large ironmasters to appoint agents in New York was evidence of the desperate state of the iron trade at that time. Prices were then very low, and when an ironmaster authorized an agent in New York to contract for a large amount of iron at low prices, he was, in view of the length of time required to get return mail across the Atlantic, taking a risk of finding his order books filled up with unprofitable orders if and when prices improved. For this reason, Guest's authorizations, especially to the American house of Boorman, Johnston and Company, were for very limited quantities.[70] More generous authorizations were extended to Rich-

[66] This is implicit in A. H. John's account of the marketing of South Wales iron, but is liable to misinterpretation because of the emphasis on the active participation of the iron merchants. *The Industrial Development of South Wales, 1750–1850* (Cardiff: University of Wales Press, 1950), 125. In 1849, both Harrison, Ridley and Harrison and John Bibby and Sons were listed as iron merchants. In addition, Harrison, Ridley and Harrison were already listed as general merchants in 1849. By 1859 John Bibby and Sons were also listed as general merchants. Probably the most important firm that falls into this category is William Bird and Co. This firm also had a house in New York in the 1850's.

[67] See above, p. 5, n. 15, for a list of the iron companies maintaining houses in Liverpool in 1849.

[68] [William Crawshay II preferred not to have agents. See Addis, 120.]

[69] Naylor and Co. was still active in the United States in the 1870's. For example, they took a large part of the bonds of the Mobile and Grand Trunk. *Commercial and Financial Chronicle*, XXX (Feb. 28, 1880), 222. In the 1870's, interest on some short debentures of the Baltimore and Ohio was paid through the related house of Naylor Benzon and Co. *Times*, June 29, 1875.

[70] When prices were low, both Richard Makin and Boorman, Johnston got only very limited authorizations. William Purnell to Lady Charlotte Guest, July 31, 1852, Dowlais Iron Co., Letter Books, London House.

ard Makin, who was the agent for Guest exclusively.[71] Furthermore, the authorization to Makin was continuously renewed, while that to Boorman, Johnston seems to have been closed out at intervals.[72]

Although the iron manufacturers had thus entered into direct competition with their best customers, the merchant banking houses, the latter continued to play an important role in iron exports. Usually the merchant bankers were not sellers of iron but agents acting on commission for the purchasers, the railways. However, on occasion, by agreeing on a price to the American railways before negotiating for rails with an iron company, they acted as speculative sellers. Thus, on September 13, 1849, George Peabody signed a contract with V. K. Stevenson of the Nashville and Chattanooga Railroad Company to supply 10,340 tons of any iron that was equal to the best Welsh iron, at $33 per ton. Then, to fulfill this contract, he purchased iron from the Rhymney Iron Company.[73] In 1851 Peabody made a further excursion into the actual selling of iron by contracting to supply iron to Chouteau, Merle and Sanford, iron merchants, of New York. By this agreement, Chouteau, Merle and Sanford agreed to purchase iron through Peabody while he also would seek orders from railroaders visiting England.[74] Barings continued to participate actively in the marketing of rails during this period. In at least one case, a merchant banking house accepted an authorization to sell iron on behalf of an iron manufacturer: in 1853 Frederick Huth and Company obtained an authorization from Guest to sell 15,000 tons of rails, an authority which Huth and Company transmitted to "their friends Grinnell Minturn of New York." [75]

Nor were the merchant bankers the only people to engage in speculative selling of iron. Ironmasters also commonly contracted for orders that they filled by the purchase of rails from other ironmasters. Thus Guest and Company on occasion rolled for Bailey Brothers and for Thompson and Forman.[76] An order for 3,000 tons from the Cwm Celyn works was declined only because, as George Kitson wrote to the widowed Lady Charlotte Guest, "we thought it would scarcely have your approbation to be working for them." [77] The situation is put most clearly in a letter from William Purnell of the Dowlais Iron Company's London office to Lady Charlotte in 1853: "Rails of Staffordshire make may be had at £8 10s delivered f. o. b.

[71] When prices began to rise in the autumn of 1852 even Makin's authorization was temporarily stopped. George Kitson to Lady Charlotte Guest, Nov. 8, 1852, *ibid.*

[72] William Purnell to Lady Charlotte Guest, Aug. 1, 1853, *ibid.*

[73] Muriel Hidy, "George Peabody," 329, 332.

[74] *Ibid.* [See also Ralph W. Hidy and Muriel E. Hidy, "Anglo-American Merchant Bankers," 150–69, esp. 157–59.]

[75] William Purnell to Lady Charlotte Guest, July 20 and Aug. 1, 1853, Dowlais Iron Co., Letter Books, London House.

[76] In 1851, for example, Guest rolled for Bailey and no brand was stamped on the rails: "neither ours nor theirs." George Kitson to Richard Wood, July 28, 1851, *ibid.*

[77] Kitson to Lady Charlotte Guest, Oct. 27, 1852, *ibid.*

Liverpool. Would it be well to run the risk of purchasing at that rate? You are well aware that our contracts in America bind us to ship G. L. Rails & Altho we might manage to substitute them by other Welsh Rails, it is doubtful whether it could be safely done by shipping Staffordshire ones." [78] Similarly, when the Cincinnati, Hamilton and Dayton Railroad complained that the rails which Guest had supplied to them had proved to be highly defective, the London House wrote to Dowlais to ask whether these rails had been marked GL, Guest, or both and added, "We fear if the Rails complained of should prove to be of our make that our most valuable connexions in the States will be lost to us." [79] Contracts for such auxiliary ironwork as rail chairs were commonly subcontracted, and the profits on such subcontracting were often substantial.

It was not only in the sale of iron that functional differentiation between the ironmasters and the merchant bankers became a little blurred at this period of crisis in the iron trade. The ironmasters also began to take over some of the financing of the trade. In order to make sales, they were sometimes willing to extend short-term credits on their books to American railways and, in some cases, to take bonds in part payment.

Most ironmasters preferred net cash when they were able to get it but were willing to grant credit to get orders. Immediate payment sometimes was offered by the merchant banking houses in order to secure a reduced price. [80] It was also on occasion preferred by railways whose securities were readily marketable, for example, the Great Western of Canada. [81] More usual terms were six, nine, and even twelve months. [82] The Dowlais Iron Company, which unhesitatingly rejected purchasers desiring twelve months' credit in the spring of 1853, was willing to give credits for twelve and eighteen months in the autumn of 1854. [83] Thompson and Forman of Penydarran was also granting long credits of twelve and eighteen months

[78] Purnell to Lady Charlotte Guest, Aug. 16, 1853, *ibid.* A letter from Purnell to Lady Charlotte Guest, July 21, 1852, enclosed a bill from Bailey Brothers for part of an order for rails for Boorman, Johnston which Bailey Brothers had rolled for Guest.

[79] William Purnell to Richard Wood, Nov. 6, 1851, *ibid.* [The origin of the mark GL dated from the partnership of Guest, Lewis & Co.]

[80] In the spring of 1852 Peabody was offering £4.12.6 for six months or £4.10.0 net cash. Barings also was offering £4.10.0 net cash. William Purnell to Mr. Walkinshaw, March 18, 1852, *ibid.*

[81] George Kitson to Lady Charlotte Guest, Nov. 8, 1853, *ibid.*

[82] William Purnell to Lady Charlotte Guest, May 20, 1853, *ibid.*

[83] George Kitson to H. A. Bruce, *ibid.*: "With the sanction of Lady Charlotte Schreiber prior to her marriage [to Charles Schrieber, 1855], we took a contract for the supply of 6000 Tons of Rails for an American Railway at £6 10 per Ton at Cardiff payment by Bills at 12, 15 & 18 months date adding Interest at rate of 7% p. annum. Orders were at the period inconveniently scarce. . . . still so complete a change took place before we got through it that you will readily understand it has been far from advantageous—On referring to the 'Make' of the Works since last May you will trace the order as 'Boody.'" Azariah Boody was the contractor for the Lake Erie, Wabash and Saint Louis, the progenitor of the ill-starred Wabash.

at this time and, as was usual when long credits were given, taking bonds as collateral.[84] This was a real entry into the merchant bankers' sphere.

In spite of the ironmasters' incursion into the marketing of American railway securities in the 1850's, the participation of merchant bankers in the financial aspect of the business remained important. Acceptances and short-term credits were the backbone of the business of houses like Barings.[85] Even George Peabody, who had first reached a significant position in the merchant banking business through large dealings in securities,[86] began to issue short-term credits to American merchants in the forties.[87] [Credits made by merchant bankers continued to run from sixty days, the usual length of bills remitted to cover drafts, to eighteen months. A case of intermediate-term credits is that of the Toledo, Norwalk and Cleveland Railroad Company. On March 1, 1852, it bought through Peabody 1,980 tons of rails at $30 per ton delivered in New York on twelve months' credit. Peabody failed to get the other part of the order, as Barings gave eighteen months' credit to the same railroad for a purchase of 4,000 tons on March 19 and added a loan of $20,000. Although sometimes the merchant banker actually gave cash advances, more often he loaned only his credit, authorizing drafts on his house. The ironmasters usually drew for payments at three, four, or six months and received cash by discounting the acceptance in the London money market. The merchant banker expected the American railroad company to remit funds to meet the obligation when due. Such drafts were important in financing shipments. For illustration, in 1853 iron manufacturers drew on Peabody and Company for more than £400,000. The reservoir of funds awaiting short-term investments at Overend, Gurney and Company and other discount houses made such transactions possible.]

Short-term credits either by merchant bankers or ironmasters to American railways were not always enough to enable ironmasters to obtain orders. Sometimes, as mentioned, the manufacturers had to accept bonds. There had been sales of rails for part payment in bonds as early as the 1830's. From 1840 until 1847 there was virtually no hope of negotiating American bonds in England. The few rails that were exported to the United States were purchased through merchant firms in that country and were financed in the same way as imports of merchant iron: by acceptances on one of the Anglo-American houses.[88] However, as early as 1849,

---

[84] George Kitson to Lady Charlotte Guest, July 17, 1854, *ibid.*

[85] Ralph Hidy, *House of Baring*, 476.

[86] Muriel Hidy, "George Peabody," 184, 223, 309, and 319.

[87] [Hidy and Hidy, "Merchant Bankers," 161–62.]

[88] In the late forties, Guest executed rail orders for America for A. & G. Ralston, who was acting on behalf of its allied iron-importing house in Philadelphia; Boorman, Johnston & Co.; and Erastus Corning. For such rails, credits were often opened in the iron company's favor before the rails were rolled. In 1851 George Kitson wrote to Dowlais to urge the company to hurry with an order for Corning "for the credits opened in our favour for payment of this iron

British iron merchants were anticipating that American railways would attempt on a more general scale to buy iron with bonds. George Kitson wrote to Sir John Guest in May of that year:

I much fear that we must not build our hopes for great things upon America just now for although they are still in want of considerable quantities of rails yet the different companies experience so much difficulty in finding the necessary funds that it is a great drawback to the prosecution of their schemes, They are compelled to pay as much as 18% for money in many instances—so I imagine there will be more propositions to buy rails for Bonds than for cash, As the latter is most unusually scarce in the Country which is attributed to the quantity of corn exported from thence to California.[89]

Bailey Brothers was accepting part payment in bonds as early as 1850,[90] and it is possible that some of the other iron houses were also contracting on these terms. However, there was as yet no real market for American railway securities in London. Even George Peabody, although willing to take American railway bonds as collateral for short-term credits against rail purchases, was not until after 1851 prepared to market a new issue publicly.[91]

The usual practice was to issue new bonds of American railways in New York, Boston, or Philadelphia.[92] The capital market in the United States was developing strength. British purchases of securities were made by the correspondents of European banking houses in these American cities.[93]

---

will expire at the end of the month and it is only *after shipment at Liverpool* that we can reimburse ourselves." Kitson to Richard Wood, July 1, 1851, Dowlais Iron Co., Letter Books, London House. However, by 1848, there were again instances of the representatives of American railways arriving in England to purchase rails. Thus, a letter from William Purnell to Edward Hutchins mentioned that a representative of the Boston Railway Company had been in about the purchase of 7,000 tons of rails. Guest did not succeed in getting this contract, which was awarded elsewhere at £7.10.0. Purnell to Hutchins, Feb. 5, 1848, *ibid.*

[89] Kitson to Guest, May 3, 1849, *ibid.*

[90] In 1850 the East Tennessee and Georgia contracted with Raymond and Fullerton, Bailey Brothers' agent in New York, for rails to be paid for $22.75 in cash, $4 in railway stock, and $6 in railway bonds, or $32.75 per ton. *American Railroad Journal*, XXIII (June 22, 1850), 390; XXIV (Feb. 8, 1851), 91. The Wilmington and Manchester of North Carolina was also able to purchase 7,000 tons of rails from Bailey Brothers for bonds in the spring of 1851. *Ibid.*, XXV (Feb. 21, 1852), 113.

[91] Muriel Hidy, "George Peabody," 333.

[92] The bonds of the states of the Old Northwest (Ohio, Indiana, Illinois, etc.) were mainly marketed in New York. As a result this city began to outdistance its competitors. [See also Muriel Hidy, "The Capital Markets, 1789–1865," in Harold F. Williamson (ed.), *The Growth of the American Economy*, 2d ed. (Englewood Cliffs, N.J.: Prentice-Hall, 1951), 256–77.]

[93] These bonds were often marketed by sealed bids, and the amounts taken by the correspondents of foreign banking houses were often considerable and are sometimes readily identifiable.

Thus, when the Columbus, Piqua and Indiana Railroad Company applied to Guest at the beginning of 1852 for 4,500 tons of rails to be paid for one half in cash and one half in bonds, William Purnell wrote to Sir John Guest: "Were the bonds *good*, they would be saleable in the United States, it would be unwise in us having anything to do with them." [94]

In 1852 the first public issues of American railway bonds were made on the London market, and at the same time the ironmasters became more willing to accept bonds directly in payment for iron. As a result, the price of rails, which for a long time had been hovering around £5 [95] and had fallen even lower in the spring of 1852, began to improve. [96] By December 1852 even Lady Charlotte Guest was considering taking an order for rails to be paid for in bonds, although this was not for an American railway.

While Lady Charlotte appears to have maintained an inflexible position on the question of taking bonds in payment for orders from the United States, other ironmasters were accepting bonds. William Crawshay, for example, secured the contract to supply 10,000 tons of rails for the Illinois Central in the spring of 1853 by consenting to take bonds in payment. [97] He had earlier undertaken a contract for the Wilmington and Weldon [98] of North Carolina on the same basis. [99]

In the face of such competition, it was becoming increasingly difficult for the London House of the Dowlais Iron Company to obtain orders. In the summer of 1853, William Purnell again gently broached the subject to Lady Charlotte in reference to a contract for rails for the Lake Erie, Wabash and Saint Louis:

If we were to contract for supplying the Rails at £9 for ⅔rds Cash and ⅓rd Bonds, it may be the means of locking up £45,000 for an indefinite

[94] Purnell to Guest, Jan. 21, 1852, Dowlais Iron Co., Letter Books, London House. Although Guest seems to have rejected this company it was ultimately able to purchase iron for bonds, for these bonds were known to be held in England in the late 1850's. These bonds were in default in the late 1850's, but the Cleveland and Columbus Railroad, which had endorsed them, eventually paid them off at the original cost to the holders plus accumulated interest at 7 percent; *American Railroad Journal*, XXXIII (Aug. 10, 1860), 746.

[95] The price of rails in Cardiff fell to £5.5.0 in May, 1849, and from then until the summer of 1849 hovered around £5.

[96] Muriel Hidy, "George Peabody," 330.

[97] William Purnell to Lady Charlotte Guest, May 18, 1853, Dowlais Iron Co., Letter Books, London House.

[98] This road was formerly called the Wilmington and Raleigh. See above, p. 11.

[99] William Crawshay was the largest holder in Britain of the bonds of two American railways, the Mobile and Ohio and the Wilmington and Weldon. Addis, 157. The arrangements for the Mobile and Ohio were made through George Peabody, and those bonds not disposed of for iron were ultimately placed privately. *American Railroad Journal*, XXVII (April 1, 1854), 204. English interest in the Wilmington and Weldon dates from the 1830's. In the 1850's new bonds were issued and the road relaid. *American Railroad Journal*, XXIV (Feb. 22, 1851), 123, and XXVI (Dec. 3, 1853), 775.

period, and this with a diminished capital & heavy liabilities to meet I think would be by no means advisable. It is quite true that large profits have in some instances been derived from the sale of Bonds taken in payment for Rails, but that was when they were of a more genuine character and the market less glutted than at present with such species of property.[100]

By September, Purnell was more optimistic: "If it would suit our convenience to lock up capital there are no Bonds issued in the United States I would sooner hold as offering undoubted security than those of the Little Miami, but in the present diminished state of our resources as compared with former times, we dare not look at them." [101] Finally, on October 3, 1853, Kitson was urging Lady Charlotte to accept bonds in payment: "I am inclined to think that the present occasion is perhaps one of the most favourable of that nature that may come before you—as according to all account the Line is a good one and the price it would enable us to secure for the iron would be much beyond that in an ordinary operation." [102]

Two days later, Kitson wrote again, attempting to drive his point home, that unless Lady Charlotte adhered to the "general principle of declining Bonds without reference to the merits of this particular case" she should accept this contract.[103]

There is no doubt that the ironmasters obtained considerably higher prices for their rails when they were prepared to take railway bonds in payment. In December 1852 the Dowlais Iron Company was quoting a price of £10 per ton.[104] At that time Lady Charlotte was considering supplying Thomas Brassey (an enterprising English railway contractor operating in many countries) with a large quantity of rails, and Kitson wrote that he considered that the price would have to be put at £12 per ton, to be paid ¾ in cash and ¼ in shares.[105]

Lady Charlotte Guest's attitude in refusing American securities is understandable on two counts. First, recently widowed, she may have felt herself too inexperienced in the full management of the company to take such risks. Second, the Dowlais Iron Company may have been short of working capital owing to the settlement of Sir John's estate.

Lady Charlotte seems to have stood alone on this matter. Even the Bank of England, which was rolling rails as the owner of a copper company at Cwm Avon near Swansea,[106] was willing to accept bonds in payment for

[100] Purnell to Lady Charlotte Guest, Aug. 20, 1853, Dowlais Iron Co., Letter Books, London House.

[101] *Ibid.*, Sept. 21, 1853.

[102] Kitson to Lady Charlotte Guest, Oct. 3, 1853, *ibid.*

[103] *Ibid.*, Oct. 5, 1853.   [104] *Ibid.*, Dec. 16, 1852.

[105] *Ibid.*, Dec. 25, 1852.

[106] According to Clapham, the Bank of England in 1847 found itself saddled with the Cwm Avon Copper Works in the following way. The bill brokers, Bruce, Buxton & Co., who held some of the bills of the Company of Copper Miners, approached the Bank of England, and the bank advanced £150,000 on the company's debentures to save it from stopping payment. Neither the company

rails. In 1852 the Junction Railroad Company of Ohio (Cleveland to Toledo via Sandusky) negotiated $600,000 of its 7 percent convertible first-mortgage bonds with Chouteau, Merle and Sanford at 80. Chouteau, Merle and Sanford immediately disposed of half of these bonds to an agent [107] acting for the Bank of England in payment for iron presumably from Cwm Avon at $37.50 per ton.[108]

The ironmasters were able to accept bonds for payment because of their accumulation of capital. [For illustration, Sir John Guest was the third generation to be the chief owner of an efficient coal and iron mining and manufacturing works, with only a nominal payment to make for land usage on a 99-year lease.] As early as the 1830's Guest and Company had a considerable amount on loan to the money market. The first reference to this in the Dowlais Company's Letter Books is in the summer of 1839 when Sir John received a letter that commented: "I am sorry to find that you are uneasy about the loan to the Bank of the United States. I believe you are aware that we have a very large cover in their bonds." [109] Nor was this the largest loan made by Guest. Judging by the interest account for the first quarter of 1840 that William Purnell of the London House sent to Dowlais on April 23, 1840,[110] the amount on loan to Overend, Gurney and Company was 50 percent greater than the loan to the United States Bank.

---

nor Bruce, Buxton & Co. was saved, and the Bank of England was left with the copper works on its hands. Clapham says further, "They gave it a world of trouble. Four years later it wanted to get rid of them 'whether at a profit or a loss.'" Clapham also says that the works were taken off their hands the next year (1852) by a new company. Sir John Clapham, *The Bank of England* (Cambridge: Cambridge University Press, 1944), II, 207. Part of the trouble which Clapham says the Bank of England had over Cwm Avon Copper Works may have been due to the attack on them by William Crawshay in a letter that appeared in the *Times*, Dec. 7, 1848, p. 3. Crawshay accused the bank of violating the provisions of their charter by making iron. Cwm Avon was not the only copper company to roll rails at this period.

[107] This agent, a Mr. Illius, had been a partner with Richard Makin in an iron merchant firm in New York that was dissolved in 1851. Makin then became an agent for Guest.

[108] Muriel Hidy, "George Peabody," 338.

[109] R. P. Davis to Guest, Aug. 19, 1839, Dowlais Iron Co., Letter Books, London House.

[110] Purnell to Dowlais Iron Co., April 23, 1840, *ibid.*: "We credit your account with £1909.14.9 for interest received up to the 31 March from the following persons,

Barlow	£ 41	15	3
Hammond	13	0	3
Overend	785	2	4
U.S. Bank	515	8	2
L & W Bank	383	14	1
A & G Ralston	170	14	8
	£1909	14	9"

Moreover, since the total of interest paid to Guest in 1840 was at the rate of over £7,500 a year (£1,900 for the first quarter), the total of his firm's liquid assets at that time was very large. Three months later, Purnell reported to Guest that the firm then had £25,000 with Overend, £20,000 with Glyn, and £10,000 lent to an Australian company.[111] By the autumn of 1852 the amount of the firm's liquid assets had almost doubled.[112] These facts give an idea of the capacity of the ironmasters to absorb bonds. [The Crawshay brothers' position was apparently strong enough to make it possible for their firm to accept bonds, and there were not the restraining factors mentioned in the case of Lady Charlotte's decision.] In 1853, William Crawshay II, the leading brother, alone held £249,099 of American railway bonds, mostly in the Illinois Central, the Canandaigua and Niagara Falls, and the New York and Lake Erie.[113]

These bonds were usually taken not for investment but for payment and as a speculation, with the intention of selling them when the price was favorable. Many were sent to the Continent. Some were sold in the provincial markets.

The assumption of part of the merchant bankers' field of activity by the ironmasters, first, in selling iron and, second, in financing sales of iron both by short-term credits and by the acceptance of bonds in part payment, did not cause any serious difficulties between these two groups. There was enough business for all. Nevertheless, it would have been unreasonable to expect the merchant bankers to undertake to dispose of bonds for the ironmasters. They had their own supplies of American railway bonds to market. It is with this phase of the railroad financing that the next chapter is concerned.

[111] Purnell to Guest, July 23, 1840, *ibid.*

[112] Purnell to Lady Charlotte Guest, Oct. 4, 1852, *ibid.* On Oct. 4, 1852, Guest and Co. had:

Cash balances			
Bank of England	£ 30,304	13	11
London & Westminster	10,000	0	0
Glyn & Co.	15,232	10	0
Total cash	£ 55,537	3	11
Bills in hand	£ 56,624	17	11
Total liquid assets	£112,162	1	10

[113] John, 104.

III

Negotiation of
American Railway Securities
in the City in the 1850's

ALMOST all American railways needed British rails in the early 1850's, but only a small number succeeded in finding sponsors for their bond issues in London. This chapter is concerned chiefly with the few American railways that were so favored.

From the middle 1840's the number of railways in the United States mushroomed, especially in the Old Northwest [1] and in the adjacent state of Kentucky. Most of these lines looked ahead ambitiously to tie-ups with other roads that would one day make them vital sections of great trunk lines. For the time being they were short local lines connecting two or three relatively small towns. They depended for their revenue on moving agricultural and mineral products to a local market or to navigable water transport, such as Lake Erie or the Ohio River.

To assess correctly the merits of any of these hundreds of small roads of the 1850's was no simple matter. It was not hard to foresee that whatever the disasters and disappointments of the start of the preceding decade, these north-central states would shortly become prosperous and populous. It was not so easy to foretell just what would be the pattern of concentration within this area, or just which towns would become the most significant. Cincinnati and Louisville were already well-established river communities looking forward with confidence to ever-increasing importance. [2] Along the shore of Lake Erie there were several towns of some size whose main function was the transshipment of freight bound east over the Erie Canal. [3] In 1850, Chicago had not yet drawn conspicuously ahead of her rivals. Although it was to Chicago that the Michigan Central Railroad Company and the Michigan Southern Railroad Company looked, Cincin-

[1] Ohio, Indiana, Illinois, Michigan, and Wisconsin. [See also "Railroads 100 Years Old, 1945–1955," compiled by Harry L. Eddy (mimeographed, Washington, D.C.: Association of American Railroads, 1948), 1–91. This list includes about 540 railways chartered in the United States between 1845 and 1855 and successful in accomplishing some construction.]

[2] In 1850 the population of Cincinnati was 115,436.

[3] In 1850 Cleveland had a population of 17,034, and Toledo had a population of 3,829.

nati was still the goal of the railway projects of Pennsylvania and Maryland.[4]

In such a rapidly changing situation, wise investment was difficult. Henry Varnum Poor, editor of the *American Railroad Journal*, repeatedly praised the wisdom of German investors in sending to the United States representatives who were able to examine and study the various projects and thus to form "a correct opinion as to their merits, and the value of the securities upon which they are based." [5] Concomitantly, he often berated the English for relying too heavily on the advice of their bankers.[6]

In fact, British investment was not haphazard. It is true that some purchases of American railway bonds by English bankers were made at prices that precluded profitable resale, at least promptly. Furthermore, in the late 1850's a number of the issues of western railways, earlier bought in substantial amounts in London, were in default.[7] The majority of these

[4] The Illinois Central originally had been planned to run from Cairo in the southern tip of Illinois in a northwesterly direction to Galena on the Mississippi, but it had added a branch to Chicago in order to gain the support of this still small but already rapidly growing city. Paul Wallace Gates, *The Illinois Central Railroad and Its Colonization Work* (Cambridge, Mass.: Harvard University Press, 1934), 28–33. Soon the two lines across Michigan—the Michigan Central and the Michigan Southern—also looked to Chicago as a terminus. The Ohio and Indiana was the first Ohio road to turn to Chicago rather than to Cincinnati. *American Railroad Journal*, XXIV (Aug. 9, 1851), 506. The concentration of railways at Chicago enabled it to grow from a population of 29,963 in 1850 to 112,172 in 1860. By 1857 eleven roads (plus branches) with a total of 3,953 miles had their termini at Chicago. Belcher, 68, 71. However, Milwaukee still had hopes of rivaling her neighbor. The Grand Trunk's connection in the U.S., the Detroit and Milwaukee, was intended to give that city a direct communication with the East. Eventually, of course, the Grand Trunk had to build a line into Chicago.

[5] Poor wrote: "The French and German buyers adopt a more sensible course. They follow in the line of safe precedents. All their orders come through responsible American houses. But their precaution is not confined within this limit. They send out to this country competent men, who critically examine all our public works, and study their condition and prospects, until they are enabled to form a correct opinion as to their merits, and the value of the securities upon which they are based." *American Railroad Journal*, XXV (July 3, 1852), 418.

[6] Poor wrote: "The English purchasers on the other hand, pursue an entirely different method. Instead of coming to this country to study the *rationale* of our system, to collect information that shall enable him to discriminate between fictitious and meritorious projects, the purchaser for investment buys of some *London* house, which has brought out an American scheme, in that market." *Ibid.*, XXVI (June 11, 1853), 370.

[7] The Ohio and Pennsylvania, the Ohio and Indiana, and the Fort Wayne lines were consolidated into the Pittsburgh, Fort Wayne and Chicago Rail Road Co. in 1856. This company was obliged to fund its coupons for 1858 and the first half of 1859. The bondholders and the unsecured creditors became restive, and the bondholders threw the company into receivership in Dec. 1859. In the reorganization, in which Samuel J. Tilden was the most active participant, the mortgage bondholders of the old company got new securities of equal rank for the principal and interest of their old securities, the holders of floating debt received

became solid investments after 1861, and those holders who kept their securities eventually did well. For example, the shares of the Illinois Central were quoted at 130 at the beginning of 1881.[8] It is doubtful whether the English investor's policy of relying on the advice of his banker was conspicuously less successful than the German's policy of sending out investigating committees. The London bankers received information from skilled resident agents and special correspondents in the United States, while the German investigators in a foreign country must have been strongly influenced by the configuration of German immigrant communities. Finally, Poor's judgment was not entirely free from bias; perhaps his opinion was prompted by the fact that the Illinois Central had been able to bypass the New York market entirely and to get its funds directly from London.[9]

Many of the securities that were sent to London during the 1850's were portions of larger issues already negotiated in New York or, more rarely, in Boston, Philadelphia, or Baltimore.[10] As the New York market developed, the negotiation of railway securities there was carried out in a variety of ways. A few railways had offices in New York through which they could issue their securities directly in the manner of English railways. Western railways, however, did not usually possess such facilities.[11] They were obliged to entrust their securities to a middleman, either an auctioneer or a banking house.[12]

The banking house [whether acting on commission or on its own account] could select one of several methods to negotiate bonds. It sometimes advertised for sealed bids, usually subject to a minimum price, and allotted the securities accordingly. Sometimes it negotiated the issue pri-

---

new income bonds, and the stockholders received share for share in new securities of the same par value. In 1864 the company began to pay dividends at the annual rate of 10 percent, and in 1869 the line was leased to the Pennsylvania at a rental amounting to 12 percent on the then existing stock or 7 percent on such stock as was increased by stock dividends. Burgess and Kennedy, 176–80, 199. The Chicago and Fond du Lac also underwent reorganization at this time, and Samuel J. Tilden was in charge. It emerged as the Chicago and Northwestern and soon became a gilt-edged investment.

[8] *Times*, Jan. 1, 1881, p. 7. The dividends of the Illinois Central were sometimes quite substantial. Thus, in 1868 it paid a dividend of 5 percent in cash plus 8 percent in stock. *Ibid.*, May 29, 1868, p. 10.

[9] *American Railroad Journal*, XXV (July 3, 1852), 417.

[10] [See also Muriel E. Hidy, "Capital Markets," 266–69, and Fritz Redlich, *The Molding of American Banking Men and Ideas,* History of American Business Leaders, II (New York: Hafner Publishing Co., 1951), Pt. II, Chapter XXI, esp. 343–81.]

[11] The Cincinnati, Hamilton and Dayton, for example, advertised in the autumn of 1853 that the securities of a new issue could be purchased through its office at 62 Liberty Street, New York. *American Railroad Journal*, XXVI (Oct. 22, 1853), 686.

[12] As late as 1853, bonds of the Catawissa, Williamsport and Erie were advertised for sale at the Merchants' Exchange by Wilmerdings and Mount, Auctioneers. *Ibid.* (Feb. 5, 1853), 93.

vately. At times a combination of several methods was used. A purchaser who desired to acquire a large portion for resale abroad on occasion made a private agreement leaving the remainder of the issue to be disposed of to bidders in New York.[13] At other times, after the flotation had been accomplished, a New York banking house merely executed an order for a correspondent in Europe.[14]

Most private banking houses in New York undertook some negotiations of securities for railway companies.[15] However, two firms seem to have been outstanding in this field in the 1850's. The first was Simeon Draper.[16] Draper was originally an auctioneer and for a long time so styled himself.[17] With the growth of the business in western railway securities he attempted to extend his operations to include other functions later characteristic of investment banking. For example, he became treasurer of the Racine, Janesville and Mississippi Rail Road Company.[18] He appears, however, to have expanded too rapidly, for his business failed in 1853.[19]

The other house of great importance in the negotiation of western railway securities was Winslow, Lanier and Company. A comparative newcomer, founded in 1849, it engrossed within a short space of time most of the business of Ohio and Indiana.[20] The firm's interest in this area

[13] This seems, for example, to have been the case with the Ohio Central when the company announced the sale of $450,000 of bonds. *Ibid.*, XXIV (March 1, 1851), 138. The *American Railroad Journal* reported successful bids of only $250,000. *Ibid.*, 136. Subsequently a large portion of these bonds appeared on the London market. The case of the Ohio and Pennsylvania is similar. The road issued $1 million of bonds. Of these $500,000 were sold at auction at the end of 1850. *Ibid.*, XXIII (Dec. 14, 1850), 789. Six months later a further sale of over $500,000 was announced. *Ibid.*, XXIV (June 14, 1851), 377. Shortly thereafter a large issue was also put out in London.

[14] [Like merchandise, stocks and bonds might go through several steps in marketing. These included the issue of securities by railways, the initial flotation into the market by auctioneers or bankers, the sale of portions of the loan in what might be termed wholesaling or jobbing, and then the retail sale to the individual investor.]

[15] There are specific references to sales by Delano, Dunlevy and Co.; Wadsworth and Sheldon; Ketchum, Rogers and Bement; and Cammann, Whitehouse and Co. in the *American Railroad Journal*. Many others also engaged in this business.

[16] On the extent of Draper's operations, see, for example, his advertisement of the security issues negotiated through him which appeared in the *American Railroad Journal*, XXVI (Sept. 10, 1853), 591.

[17] See, for example, Draper's advertisement for the preemptory sale of the bonds of the Buffalo, Corning and New York. *Ibid.*, XXV (April 24, 1852), 269.

[18] *Ibid.*, XXVI (March 19, 1853), 188.   [19] *Ibid.* (Oct. 15, 1853), 666.

[20] [J. F. D. Lanier, *Sketch of the Life of J. F. D. Lanier* (New York, 1870), 18.] Regional specialization was strong, and it was difficult for a company to obtain much business outside its area of special interest. Draper seems to have been exceptional in this. *American Railroad Journal*, XXVI (Sept. 10, 1853), 591. Thus, the bonds of the Galena and Chicago Union were negotiated through Wadsworth and Sheldon, the financial agents of the state of Illinois. *Ibid.* (July 2, 1853), 426.

stemmed from the fact that James Franklin Doughty Lanier was an Indianian. Not only was he a banker of experience,[21] he also was actively involved in railway companies. For example, he undertook the resuscitation of the Madison and Indianapolis, a road which runs north from Madison on the Ohio River to Indianapolis.[22]

It was not, however, houses like Simeon Draper or Winslow, Lanier that made the actual transfer of securities to Europe. The movement of a large portion of an issue abroad was customarily carried out by one of the banking houses in New York that was a correspondent of a London house. Among the more prominent of the purely banking houses [23] were J. G. King and Sons, correspondent of Baring Brothers; [24] August Belmont and Company, agent of the Rothschilds; [25] and Duncan, Sherman and Company, correspondent of George Peabody and Company.[26] James Brown, a brother of William and George Brown of the Liverpool house of Brown, Shipley and Company, had a long-established New York house related to the family's firms in Baltimore and Philadelphia.[27]

In addition, a number of commercial houses transferred smaller quantities of American railway bonds to Europe, mainly to the Continent. The names Carpenter and Vermilye; [28] DeLaunay, Iselin and Clarke; [29] Cammann, Whitehouse; [30] and Moran and Iselin frequently appear in the lists of successful bidders for substantial amounts of issues floated through houses like Simeon Draper and Winslow, Lanier. The Iselins had connec-

[21] Lanier had been associated with Hugh McCulloch (who became Secretary of the Treasury under Lincoln and later a partner of Jay Cooke) in the State Bank of Indiana, the only bank in the Mississippi Valley to weather the crisis of 1837.

[22] Dictionary of American Biography (London: Oxford University Press), X, 600.

[23] Functional differentiation between banking houses, merchant houses, and brokerage houses was very blurred until at least the 1870's. As late as 1875 the Times complained that the term "banker" was used very loosely in New York and that every stockjobber in that city called himself a banker. June 15, 1875, p. 10.

[24] [King & Sons was one of the successor firms to Prime, Ward & King. Barings also bought through other houses, e.g., Ward, Campbell & Co. in which two of the partners were sons of T. W. Ward. The latter was Barings' agent until 1853 when he was succeeded by his son Samuel G. Ward. The latter should not be confused with the bon vivant, Samuel Ward, son of Samuel Ward of Prime, Ward & King. Ralph W. Hidy, House of Baring, 351, 360, 366, 399 and 450.]

[25] Belmont had been in New York as agent for the Rothschilds since 1837.

[26] The partners in this house were Watts Sherman and Alexander Duncan, a Scot. According to Hidy, this house, founded in 1850, applied first to Barings and when Barings refused it, went to Peabody. See Muriel Hidy, "George Peabody," 303.

[27] Bankers' Magazine, XXXII (New York, Dec. 1877), 485.

[28] Later Vermilye and Co.   [29] Later DeLaunay, Iselin and Co.

[30] Circulars of Cammann, Whitehouse; DeLauney, Iselin and Clarke; Marie Kanz; and De Coppet and Co. were quoted regularly in the English press in the 1850's.

tions in Switzerland; the Morans were from Belgium.[31] DeLaunay had business ties with Le Havre.[32] In addition, Philip Speyer and Company of New York was related to Speyer, Ellison and Company of Frankfort; and Meyer and Stucken was the correspondent for Gogel, Koch and Company of the same city.[33] De Coppet and Company, a Swiss firm, was agent for business houses both in France and in Germany.[34]

Negotiated in December 1850, the first portion of Ohio and Pennsylvania bonds is an example of sharing the marketing of an issue. DeLaunay, Iselin and Clarke (Swiss) took $100,000; Moran and Iselin took $50,000, as did J. F. Sanford of Chouteau, Merle and Sanford.[35] A further portion of $500,000 was negotiated privately six months later.[36] Although it is impossible to state definitely, it would seem that a large part of the first offering found its way to the Continent, while the second part, negotiated privately, provided the securities which appeared in London later in the same year.[37]

The important London market showed patterns of selection both as to individual issues and as to the general types of American railway securities it absorbed. From 1848, an increasing number of stocks and a few of the municipal bonds of the older roads in the East found their way to London.[38] With the exception of the Reading, the Erie, the Baltimore and Ohio, and perhaps the Atlantic and St. Lawrence, these purchases do not seem to have constituted a significant portion of the total capital of any individual railway.[39] Nevertheless, amounts that were not insignificant for the period were invested in a number of lines. In Boston the same persons

[31] The Iselins were originally a Swiss family, and Charles Moran was from Belgium. However, it must be emphasized that all these houses, although of Continental orgin, also had connections in London. For example John James Iselin was established in London as an indigo broker in the 1820's but had become a general merchant by the 1840's.

[32] Alfred D. Chandler, Jr., *Henry Varnum Poor: Business Editor, Analyst, and Reformer* (Cambridge, Mass.: Harvard University Press, 1956), 94.

[33] *Ibid.*   [34] *Ibid.* See also *Dictionary of American Biography*, V, 190.

[35] *American Railroad Journal*, XXIII (Dec. 14, 1850), 789.

[36] *Ibid.*, XXIV (June 14, 1851), 377.   [37] See below, pp. 57–58.

[38] Shares were on the whole preferred to bonds at this time.

[39] By 1853, $3 million of the $10 million of Erie's capital stock and $7 million of its indebtedness of $19.2 million were held abroad. Pierce, 6. By 1851 one quarter of the shares of the Philadelphia and Reading were held abroad. *American Railroad Journal*, XXIV (March 22, 1851), 181. Besides marketing the Maryland bonds, issued in favor of the Baltimore and Ohio, Barings arranged for a purchase of 22,000 tons of rails for the line in 1849. Payment for these was made in $566,666.67 of bonds. *Ibid.* (Oct. 25, 1851), 673; see also Ralph Hidy, *House of Baring*, 410. In addition, a further loan of $3.2 million in sterling bonds of Maryland was negotiated through Brown Brothers in 1850. *American Railroad Journal*, XXIV (Jan. 18, 1851), 44. The Atlantic and St. Lawrence is the line from Portland, Maine, to the Canadian border. It provided the Grand Trunk with an outlet to a seaboard port that is open the year around. This road was leased to the Grand Trunk in 1853.

who were at this time buying up substantial amounts of Reading shares were also investing in the Philadelphia, Wilmington and Baltimore. Portions of the securities of both railroads were being passed on to correspondents in London.[40] The *Economist* noted the large amount of the stock of the Philadelphia, Wilmington and Baltimore known to be held in England.[41] There was also some, but not large, participation by British investors in the New York and New Haven [42] as well as the two roads that constituted New York's connections to Albany, the New York and Harlem and the Hudson River.[43]

[Even before public issues of new offerings of American securities in London in 1852 the figures for increased investment of Europeans in United States stocks and bonds were significant.] As mentioned earlier, the *Bankers' Magazine* estimated that in the four years between July 1, 1848, and July 1, 1852, foreign purchases of American railway securities and of municipal bonds issued in favor of American railways amounted to £12 million.[44] In addition, there was an estimated increase of £5.2 million in European holdings of American state bonds, some of which were issued on behalf of railways. However, Continental investment probably outweighed British investment in these four years, and these figures must not be taken as a measure of British holdings alone.[45]

The British market showed a preference for certain types of securities. There is a simple explanation for the fact that the British investor, when he was willing to consider American railway securities, preferred shares to bonds.[46] At that time, both seller and buyer regarded fixed interest bonds

[40] The correspondents of McCalmont Brothers of London were Nathaniel Thayer in Boston and John Gihon in New York. Gihon and Co. and McCalmont Brothers supplied the presidents of the Reading from among the members of their own firms. Thayer was, in 1880, still reported to be the largest single shareholder of the Philadelphia, Wilmington and Baltimore. Burgess and Kennedy, 404.

[41] XII (Oct. 28, 1854), 1182.

[42] *Ibid.* (July 22, 1854), 792, quotation from the *New York Shipping and Commercial List*.

[43] By 1853, $350,000 of the Harlem's total share capital of $8 million, and $150,000 of her total indebtedness of $1.4 million was reported to be held abroad, and almost $1 million of the Hudson River Railroad's total indebtedness of $7.5 million was held abroad. Pierce, 5 and 6; and U.S., Congress, *Senate Executive Document 42*, 33d Cong., 1st sess., 1853–54.

[44] XIII (Feb. 1853), 101.

[45] The boom in American securities in London came after the beginning of public issuance. This started with the offer of securities in the Illinois Central in June 1852. Substantial portions of issues of American railway securities had been put out privately in London before that date. Nevertheless, until this time the Continent was known to be a better market for American securities than London, and it is reported that some of the bonds taken originally by British ironmasters were subsequently transferred to the Continent. Chandler, 97.

[46] *Barings Circular* for the end of 1851, quoted in *American Railroad Journal*, XXV (Jan. 24, 1852), 57. See above, p. 19.

as a temporary financial expedient necessary only to accomplish the completion of a railway. It was confidently expected that these bonds would be paid off once the railway had been brought into operation and that the profits redounding to the shareholders subsequently would be considerable. In fact, several New England roads did reduce their outstanding bonded indebtedness substantially.

However, shares, although giving a voice in management, are risky, and the British investor wanted a measure of security. The memories of 1837–39, when American states had been left with a number of unfinished and revenueless public works, had not been dispelled. The investor therefore was reluctant to buy any shares except those of completed or nearly completed lines. On the other hand, railways in states such as Michigan and Ohio were usually obliged to seek funds from the East and from Europe before they had reached this stage of construction. In particular, they needed money with which to purchase British rails. Some financial device combining the security of a bond with the opportunity to participate in future profits was needed. Convertible bonds provided the answer.

Except for the first and second mortgage bonds of the Erie, an eastern line, all of the American railway bonds that found favor in London in the period before June 1852 were convertible bonds. The 8 percent convertible bonds of the Michigan Central are reported to have been the first of these.[47] If not the first, they were among the first three or four such issues to become current in London.

By the 1850's a greater interest was manifested in American securities in England. Throughout the forties the *Economist*'s listing of American securities included those of only two railway companies, the Camden and Amboy and the Philadephia and Reading,[48] although securities of other roads undoubtedly reached England in this decade. In the winter of 1851–52 interest in American rails was widening sufficiently to elicit comment from the *Daily News:*

The demand for various classes of American state stocks continues, and the appearance of the market is favourable. A limited business has also been done in some of the leading American railway bonds, and more extensive transactions would have been entered into, had the supply been larger. So soon as this want has been met, it is anticipated, judging from the numerous inquiries now made, that an active business will spring up in these bonds, many of which yield a highly remunerative return compared with other classes of investment. Although their introduction into the English market, however, is of recent date, a considerable and increasing business has for a long time been done in them at Hamburg, Amsterdam, Frankfort, and other continental bourses, where American securities are daily increasing in favour. The reason of the preference accorded to these bonds is, that they have coupons attached negotiable in Europe, whilst the dividends on many other United States stocks are payable in America.[49]

[47] *Ibid.*, XXIII (Sept. 1, 1850), 582.
[48] See, for example, III (Jan. 18, 1845), 59.   [49] March 12, 1852, p. 6.

In 1852 the weekly circular of Daniel Bell and Son, American Stock-brokers, London,[50] began to report prices for a number of American railway securities. By the summer this list included the first, second, and 7 percent convertible bonds of the New York and Erie, the 8 percent convertible bonds of the Michigan Central, the first-mortgage convertible bonds of the Ohio and Pennsylvania, and the 7 percent convertible bonds of the Ohio Central.[51] These bonds were not issued publicly in London but were transferred from New York to various London merchant bankers or stock-brokers who, according to the *Railway Times,* dealt them out to the public quietly and by degrees.[52] It is therefore difficult to determine precedence.[53]

But convertible bonds were not enough. Other western states in addition to Ohio and Michigan were anxious to develop railways. A company in Ohio or Michigan was usually able to dispose of enough shares to local individuals and governmental bodies to pay for some construction and was therefore able to offer at least a partly completed line as security for the convertible mortgage bonds it issued to pay for iron. Railways in a still sparsely settled state like Illinois were often obliged to come onto the market for a loan before any construction could be undertaken. In such cases, convertible bonds offered little security beyond that of ordinary shares. Some new financial device was needed to attract investors.

The Illinois Central, together with the Mobile and Ohio, was the first railway to receive a federal land grant.[54] On the basis of this expectation the attention of a group of eastern businessmen [55] was attracted by the

[50] Daniel Bell and Son had been stockbrokers in London since the 1820's. At first the *Post Office Directory of London* listed this firm among British and Foreign Stock Brokers. In the 1840's, however, they were listed as American brokers. Their address from the 1830's onwards was 23 Birchin Lane. The firm disappeared in 1867, but in 1868 a firm called Bell and Co. appeared for the first time. In 1870 this listing was replaced by Daniel Bell, Junior, who continued in business either alone or in partnership until 1879.

[51] *Daily News,* July 9, 1852, p. 7.   [52] April 9, 1852, p. 386.

[53] Bearing 8 percent interest, the entire $2,459,000 issue of convertible bonds of the Michigan Central was sold through Simeon Draper in 1850. *American Railroad Journal,* XXVI (Sept. 10, 1853), 591–92. These bonds may have come onto the market through John Murray Forbes, who on Nov. 28, 1848, wrote to his cousin Paul S. Forbes: "Before getting your note I had renewed R. S. Watson's note with my endorsement at 7% for one year & had lent the rest to the Michigan C. Road for a year at 12% & at the next meeting of Directors they are either to give me the right to take 8% Convertible Bonds at the end of that time or to give me 2½% more interest—meantime they give me as collateral double the amount of 6% Bonds. Depend upon it this is safer and better than Western State Stocks." Quoted in Thomas C. Cochran, *Railroad Leaders, 1845–1890* (Cambridge, Mass.: Harvard University Press, 1953), 327.

[54] Gates, chap. 2.

[55] In particular the group of Bostonians interested in the Michigan Central, including John Murray Forbes, David Neal, George Griswold, and John Thayer, and some New Haven men including Robert Schuyler, Morris Ketchum, Frank-

Illinois Central and through them it eventually found sponsors in London.[56] Moreover, since the attitude in the City was now favorable to American railways, it was decided to offer the securities of this road publicly. In June 1852 the first prospectus for the securities of an American railway appeared in the London press, a prospectus unlike any the London investing public had ever seen.[57] This prospectus offered bonds to the amount of $5 million secured on the land grant and the future railway. In addition a subscription to a $1,000 bond carried with it the right to five shares of $100 each on which a nominal payment of $5 was required.[58] It was strongly implied that no further calls would be made on these shares. Indeed, the prospectus said that "these Shares will thus become an actual bonus, and entitle the holder to a participation in all the profits of the line." [59] In fact, land was not sold as rapidly as anticipated, and later calls were made on the shares until they were finally fully paid up.

In the meantime, although the idea of a land grant was most appealing, as yet few American railways were able to get one; hence, bonds with this collateral did not displace convertible issues.[60] Throughout the 1850's most of the railway bonds offered on the London market were convertible. A few of the established railways of the East were able to issue sterling bonds; on these lower interest could be offered.[61] Occasionally even a new company

lin Haven, and J. W. Alsop. *Ibid.*, 49–50.

[56] The Illinois Central was turned down by Barings and the Rothschilds. *Ibid.*, 70–72. Eventually it was able to get the backing of a syndicate that included Brown, Shipley; Heywood, Kennard; and Devaux and Co. One member of each of these firms plus T. Smith, the deputy-chairman of the North Western Railway, acted as trustees for the mortgage. *Economist*, X (June 5, 1852), 628–29.

[57] This prospectus appeared in the *Economist*, X (June 19, 1852), 696, in *Railway Times*, June 12, 1852, p. 598, and in various other London newspapers and journals.

[58] Providing for these subsequent calls on Illinois shares proved to be a considerable hardship for a number of large holders including Richard Cobden [a liberal member of Parliament.] Elizabeth Hoon Cawley (ed.), *The American Diaries of Richard Cobden* (Princeton, N.J.: Princeton University Press, 1952), 47. The promoters of the company reserved one half of the shares for themselves. However, after 1854 British investors purchased large amounts of these reserved shares. Gates, 76.

[59] *Economist*, X (June 12, 1852), 668.

[60] The securities of the Mobile and Ohio, the southern line that was voted a land grant at the same time as the Illinois Central, also became known in London but they were not issued publicly. As late as 1856 land-grant bonds were still being issued, not alone but in conjunction with shares. Thus the Chicago, St. Paul and Fond du Lac offered, in Dec. 1856, first-mortgage 7 percent land-grant bonds, each bond carrying with it the privilege of taking seven $100 shares at par. *Daily News*, Dec. 29, 1856, p. 1, and Jan. 21, 1857, p. 1.

[61] After its popularity was established, the Michigan Central was able to issue sterling bonds at 6 percent, instead of convertible bonds at 8 percent. The Pennsylvania Railroad made its second mortgage a sterling issue, but the

attempted to market sterling bonds. One of the oddest issues to appear on the London market was that of the 6 percent sterling first-mortgage bonds of the Cincinnati, Logansport and Chicago. Its bonds were convertible either into dollar bonds or shares, but the directors reserved the right to cancel this privilege by payment of £10.[62] Some issues of nonconvertible first-mortgage bonds were also brought forward.[63] However, the usual form of bond offered in London was the convertible one. Indeed, bonds of this type were so popular that somewhat later even the New York Central made convertible an issue of which a portion was intended for the London market.[64]

The bonds of the Illinois Central were among the first American railway bonds put out in London by public issue in the 1850's.[65] When this flotation proved to be a success, other issues immediately followed. Two weeks later, the New York and Erie offered £500,000 of income bonds through Heywood, Kennard, bankers, and Foster and Braithwaite, brokers.[66] In September, £100,000 of 7 percent convertible mortgage bonds of the Marietta and Cincinnati were marketed through the stockbroking firm of Shaw, Cowan and Wilson,[67] while £120,000 of similar securities of the Wilmington and Manchester (North Carolina) were sold through a share-broker named Oliver Lee.[68]

Most issues, however, continued to be sold privately. Evidence of them appears in discussions in the financial columns of the daily press, in quotations in the listings of American railway securities by Daniel Bell and Sons or Edward F. Satterthwaite,[69] and in the appearance of dividend notices in the press.

---

interest was the same as on its first dollar mortgage, 6 percent. The Illinois Central did not issue sterling bonds, but it issued a dollar bond, interest on which was made payable in London at a fixed rate of exchange. This, too, bore 6 percent interest.

[62] *Daily News*, Sept. 6, 1853, p. 1.

[63] For example, the first-mortgage bonds of the New Orleans, Jackson and Great Northern. *Ibid.*, Aug. 21, 1856, p. 1.

[64] *Ibid.*, Nov. 4, 1854, p. 6.

[65] [See pp. 10, 20, for earlier references to public issues of American securities in London. Since Mrs. Adler wrote, Harry H. Pierce has turned up another early example; see his "Foreign Investment in American Enterprise," 41.]

[66] *Economist*, X (June 26, 1852), 724.

[67] *Daily News*, Sept. 4, 1852, p. 7. In regard to this issue it was specifically stated that the half million offered in London had already been taken by New York capitalists and that it was they, not the railway, who were offering the securities in London.

[68] *Ibid.*, Sept. 10, 1852, p. 7.

[69] Edward Satterthwaite's *Circular* began to appear in 1853. There were two Satterthwaites. Clement appears to have founded the firm but shared an office at 38 Throgmorton Street with his brother Edward F. until the late sixties. Then Edward opened an office at 6 Austin-friars, while Clement moved to 30 Throgmorton Street. Correspondence with the descendants of the Satterthwaite family has not revealed its origins, but it is possible that the brothers mentioned were

Most of the British investment in American railways at this time was in the form that is now termed growth investment.[70] The preference of the British investor first for shares, later for convertible bonds, and then for land-grant bonds issued in conjunction with shares is evidence of this.

The rentier investor appears to have evinced little interest in this type of investment. He preferred issues on which he felt sure of a return of 6 percent. Such were federal bonds and the securities of various local governmental bodies and established railways. The large portion of the Pennsylvania Railroad Company bonds handled jointly by Barings and Rothschilds in 1852 probably was taken to sell to this type of investor. The merchant bankers purchased this bond above par in spite of the fact that it bore only 6 percent interest. The bonds sold slowly.[71]

Nor does there seem to have been much short-term trading in American securities at this time. However, there was evidence of one form of speculation for which the British investor was noted throughout the nineteenth century. When there was a panic on Wall Street and bargain prices ruled, he often increased his holdings substantially.[72]

The British investor interested in American railways in the 1850's appears to have concentrated on types of securities that promised the opportunity of profit with the growth of the country. Moreover, the choice of securities to bring out in London, whether by public issue or privately, was made with some shrewdness. Most of them were senior securities of lines that were destined to become parts of the through routes.

It has been mentioned above that the first three western railways whose bonds became current in London were the Michigan Central, the Ohio and Pennsylvania, and the Central Ohio. The Michigan Central provided a connection to Chicago for the New York Central, which connected at Albany with the Western of Massachusetts to Boston and with the Hudson River to New York.[73] The Ohio and Pennsylvania was one of the roads to

---

descended from a Satterthwaite who was a member of the banking firm of Lees, Satterthwaite and Brassey at the end of the 18th and the beginning of the 19th century.

[70] [The reader will want to compare this with Johnson and Supple, esp. chap. 6.]

[71] The interest on the Pennsylvania Railroad bonds, 6 percent, was the same as that on federal bonds of 1848. Both were reported to have been taken at 103.20 percent. [The premium on sterling in New York in 1852 was 6 to 7 percent. Bonds of the Pennsylvania at first were offered at 98. Ralph Hidy, *House of Baring*, 413 and 429.]

[72] *Ibid.*, 428; Gates, 76.

[73] At this time few American railways crossed a state boundary. Charters for railways were granted by the states, not by the federal government, and each state looked to its railways to enrich its own principal city and was jealous in guarding against granting charters to roads that might contribute to the prosperity of a rival state. Thus, Pennsylvania long blocked the path of the Erie across the narrow strip of Pennsylvania that abuts on Lake Erie and divides New York from Ohio. When this connection was finally built under the Franklin Ca-

which the Pennsylvania looked to carry it forward into Ohio.[74] Similarly, the Central Ohio was a continuation of the Baltimore and Ohio from Wheeling on the Ohio River to Columbus, Ohio.[75]

The Marietta and Cincinnati, a line whose bonds were brought out in London in September 1852, was in a strong position since it was being courted by both the Pennsylvania and the Baltimore and Ohio. In 1853 the Pennsylvania Railroad subscribed $750,000 to the stock of the Marietta and Cincinnati to enable it to build a connection from Marietta to Wheeling, where it was hoped that it would be joined to the Pennsylvania.[76] This juncture was not achieved; the Marietta expended all its resources on its main line.[77] Today this road is part of the Baltimore and Ohio Southwestern, but for more than twenty years, from 1860 until the 1880's, it was an independent line largely under British control, control which was achieved by foreclosure on its bonds.[78]

It has already been mentioned that a large amount of the Pennsylvania Railroad's own bonds were taken by Barings and Rothschilds in the autumn of 1852.[79] Before the year was out the bonds of its connection, the Ohio and Indiana, had been introduced to London.[80] Thus, in the first year of popularity of American railways in London, there were sales not only of

---

nal Co. charter, the citizens of Erie rioted. Their ground for indignation was the loss of profits from the transshipment of freight and passengers. The *American Railroad Journal* implied that the Pennsylvania Railroad was involved and warned the railway that it would find itself in an embarrassing position when it next applied to the New York market for funds. The president of the Pennsylvania retaliated by canceling his subscription to the *American Railroad Journal* and by calling it "not American." XXVII (Feb. 18, 1854), 97. Meanwhile, Virginia was blocking the path of the Pennsylvania across the strip of Virginia that separates Pennsylvania from Ohio at Pittsburgh. Burgess and Kennedy, 88.

[74] The Pennsylvania Railroad subscribed to the Ohio and Pennsylvania stock. *Ibid.*, 76.

[75] It seems possible that the Central Ohio, like the Marietta and Cincinnati, was being played off between the Baltimore and Ohio and the Pennsylvania. The first issue of the *Railway Times* that carried a quotation for the Central Ohio also carried an article on a great through line from Philadelphia to Saint Louis. May 15, 1852, pp. 493, 504. Apparently, the Pennsylvania Railroad did not subscribe to stock of the Central Ohio. By 1853, the Central Ohio seems to have been firmly in the Baltimore and Ohio camp, for in that year its bonds were negotiated in Baltimore, rather than in New York as had previously been done. *American Railroad Journal,* XXIV (March 1, 1851), 136, and XXVI (March 12, 1853), 164.

[76] Burgess and Kennedy, 77–79.   [77] *Ibid.*

[78] The pattern of reorganization of the Marietta and Cincinnati was that used commonly later in the post–Civil War period. A London Committee was set up by the London firm of Heseltine and Powell, and London directors were appointed. *American Railroad Journal,* XXXIII (Aug. 11, 1860), 700, and XXXIV (Sept. 28, 1861), 682.

[79] See above, p. 57.

[80] Burgess and Kennedy, 177. The Ohio and Indiana, together with its connection to Pittsburgh on the east, the Ohio and Pennsylvania, and its connection to

Pennsylvania bonds but also of securities of three or four companies implicitly, if not explicitly, endorsed by the Pennsylvania.

Meanwhile, London was also giving support to lines that form the north-south chain along the eastern seaboard. Bonds of the Wilmington and Manchester were issued publicly in September 1852,[81] and about the same time the 7 percent first-mortgage bonds of the Seaboard and Roanoke were put out privately.[82] The British investor's participation in these lines was, of course, a continuation of interest that dated from the 1830's.[83]

The securities discussed above were chosen for consideration because, whether they were issued publicly in London or marketed privately through merchant banking houses, they were all traded, to some extent, on the London market in the 1850's. Moreover, some of the American railway securities known to have been marketed in London at this time but not mentioned in the public press were for lines that occupied strategic geographical positions. Such was the case of the Toledo, Norwalk and Cleveland.[84] Another category of American railway securities was favored by the City—issues of lines leading from Chicago.

Beginning with the Illinois Central, the lines of Illinois completely captured the British investor's imagination. Most probably it was the land grant that was directly responsible for the Illinois Central's immediate success. A mortgage on land not only gave an illusion of absolute security but also hinted at a practical Utopia and was therefore eminently calculated to appeal to such men as Richard Cobden [a liberal member of the House of Commons who was concerned with, among many reforms, obtaining land for the poor].[85]

Chicago on the west, the Fort Wayne, was consolidated into the Pittsburgh, Fort Wayne and Chicago Railroad in 1856. The Fort Wayne is still the Pennsylvania's main line to Chicago.

[81] Of the Wilmington and Manchester's $600,000 bonds, of which $500,000 (£100,000) was offered in London in Sept. 1852, $200,000 was reported to have been paid to Bailey Brothers for 7,000 tons of iron. If the bonds paid to Bailey Brothers for iron were among those sold in London in 1852, this is one of the few cases where bonds paid to an ironmaster were marketed in London. *American Railroad Journal,* XXV (Feb. 21, 1852), 113, and XXVI (Feb. 19, 1853), 118.

[82] Early in 1851 the Seaboard and Roanoke issued $400,000 of bonds. *Ibid.,* XXIV (Feb. 15, 1851), 314. In June of 1851, $250,000 of these were sold in New York. *Ibid.* (June 7, 1851), 360. For the quotation of these bonds, see the *Daily News,* Dec. 31, 1852, p. 7.

[83] See above, p. 11.   [84] Ralph Hidy, *House of Baring,* 428.

[85] Cobden, Sir Joshua Walmsley, and John Bright were already associated in the National Freehold Land Society, a company whose purpose was to purchase large amounts of land to be divided into lots for building purposes. Only land near stations was considered for purchase. *Railway Times,* May 28, 1853, p. 557. See also John Morley, *The Life of Richard Cobden* (London: T. Fisher Unwin, 1896), 360, and 441–42, Morley's report of a conversation with W. S. Lindsay: "'Cobden,' Mr. Lindsay goes on to say, 'viewed his investments in an entirely different light from that in which they would be seen by an ordinary man of business. He thought of the overcrowded cities of Europe, and of the masses of

Moreover, the fact that British banking men were already established in Illinois may have contributed to the ease with which the City accepted this new theater of railway finance.[86] George Smith,[87] a native of Aberdeen, visited Illinois in the early 1830's. He was so impressed that on his return to Scotland he induced some of his friends to join with him in forming the Scottish Illinois Land and Investment Company. After the crisis of 1837 he returned to Chicago to investigate the affairs of the company, and he was convinced that Illinois and the surrounding area would have a brilliant future. He decided to remain and to establish a banking house. Charters for banks were difficult to obtain; so, following the model of the Chicago Marine and Fire Insurance Company, Smith set up the Wisconsin Marine and Fire Insurance Company. In 1857, having accumulated a fortune, he returned to Great Britain, leaving his protégé, Alexander Mitchell, a fellow Scot, to carry on in Wisconsin.[88] Mitchell was to be president of the Chicago and North Western for a short time and for many years president of the Chicago, Milwaukee and St. Paul.

It is probable that the securities of other Illinois roads found their way to London about the same time as those of the Illinois Central. The Galena and Chicago Union [89] is said to have been built with English and Dutch

people who on this side of the Atlantic were seeking, or about to seek, new homes in the far West. His mind surveyed at a glance the vast expanse of rich, unoccupied virgin land in the mighty valley of the Mississippi, through which the Illinois Central ran its course—a valley where millions of people from the old world could find profitable employment. He was aware of the great and rapidly increasing facilities which would enable the intending emigrant to reach this most tempting field at less cost than their fathers could have travelled from Glasgow to London; and for these reasons he came to the conclusion that the demand for the company's land would be both great and immediate. . . . But Cobden was no speculator in the ordinary sense of the word.' "

[86] There was substantial British interest in Illinois in the 1830's. Besides buying bonds, the British investor also participated largely in the Cairo City and Canal Co., which purchased several thousand acres of land and laid out the town of Cairo at the mouth of the Ohio. Originally it was also expected that the state of Illinois would build a railway north from Cairo. However, the English investors refused further financial support in 1840, and all construction came to a halt. Thereupon, the president, D. B. Holbrook, and directors of the Cairo City and Canal Co. incorporated the Great Western Railway Company and again attempted to interest European capital but without success. In 1845 the whole project reverted to the state of Illinois. Howard Gray Brownson, *History of the Illinois Central Railroad to 1870*, University of Illinois Studies in the Social Sciences, IV, nos. 3–4 (Urbana: University of Illinois, 1915), 20–22.

[87] [See Alice E. Smith, *George Smith's Money: A Scottish Investor in America* (Madison, Wis.: State Historical Society of Wisconsin, 1966).]

[88] George William Dowrie, *The Development of Banking in Illinois, 1817–1863*, University of Illinois Studies in the Social Sciences, II, no. 4 (Urbana: University of Illinois, 1913), 129.

[89] Galena is a lead-mining town on the Mississippi River. The Galena and Chicago Union runs east-west across the northern portion of Illinois just below the Wisconsin state line.

capital by English and Dutch engineers.[90] Certainly this road early attracted eastern capital; both William F. Weld of Boston, agent for Thompson & Forman of London, and Erastus Corning, New York iron manufacturer and railroader, were interested in it.[91] The financial structure of this road followed the British pattern, being built with money obtained from sale of shares. Except for a small flotation of 10 percent convertible bonds marketed in 1852,[92] its first issue to come on the market was that of 7 percent mortgage bonds offered through Wadsworth and Sheldon in the summer of 1853;[93] a portion of it was subsequently sold in London by Edward F. Satterthwaite.[94] Because this road was already paying dividends well above 10 percent, it was specifically stated that these bonds were not convertible.[95]

The Galena and Chicago Union became part of the Chicago and North Western. The other road that made up the consolidation under that name was the Chicago, St. Paul and Fond du Lac, itself a merging of the Illinois and Wisconsin (in Illinois) and the Rock River Valley (in Wisconsin).[96]

It is possible that the Rock River Valley also received financial support from London before the Illinois Central. In the autumn of 1850, the *American Railroad Journal* reported:

[90] Robert J. Casey and W. A. S. Douglas, *Pioneer Railroad: The Story of the Chicago and North Western System* (New York: Whittlesey House, McGraw-Hill, 1948), 270. [Irene Neu, *Erastus Corning, Merchant and Financier, 1794–1872* (Ithaca, N.Y.: Cornell University Press, 1960), 84 and *passim.*]

[91] Casey and Douglas, 54.

[92] *American Railroad Journal*, XXVI (April 30, 1853), 281.

[93] *Ibid.* (July 2, 1853), 426. The bonds of 1853, issued to pay for building the third division of the road, totaled $600,000. Moreover, "in order to give these bonds character in the eastern market, and to enable them to be negotiated at a fair price, subscriptions to the amount of $200,000 [of stock] on which the directors promise a dividend of ten per cent until the road was completed," were also solicited. *Ibid.*, XXV (Jan. 10, 1852), 23. In March it was reported that these had all been taken out of the market. *Ibid.* (March 20, 1852), 185.

The cash dividends of the Galena were as follows: 1850, 8%; 1851, 14%; 1852, 20%; 1853, 16%; 1854, 20%; 1855, 10%; 1856, 15%; 1857, 10%; 1858, 4%; 1859, 2%; 1860, 5%. In addition, there was a stock dividend of 10% in 1850 and 12% in 1856. *American Railroad Journal*, XXXIII (Dec. 1, 1860), 1069.

[94] *Railway Times*, June 10, 1854, p. 593. The price at which these 10-year bonds were issued was 82½ plus interest. The road evidently felt that this discount was excessive, for later the *Railway Times* carried a notice that the road had decided to issue to the stockholders, at par, one share for every ten held, in lieu of an issue of further bonds. Nov. 24, 1855, p. 1239.

[95] See n. 94.

[96] The Chicago, St. Paul and Fond du Lac defaulted on its bonds and was sold in 1859 by James Winslow, William A. Booth, and James F. D. Lanier, acting for the bondholders, to Samuel Tilden and Ossian D. Ashley, acting for the railway. It was reorganized as the Chicago and North Western on June 7, 1859. The Chicago and North Western and the Galena and Chicago Union were consolidated in 1864. Casey and Douglas, 80, 121.

The agent of the English capitalists—who have loaned a million or more of dollars, to aid in constructing the proposed railroad from Fond du Lac, down the Rock river valley, to Janesville, and thence to some point on the Galena and Chicago road, arrived at Chicago a few days since on his route to Janesville, with blank bonds to be filled and signed by the officers of the Valley railroad company, immediately after which, the Hon. Robert J. Walker, (ex-Secretary of the Treasury) will take them, and proceed to Europe to close the arrangements for the money.[97]

The editor of the *American Railroad Journal* was skeptical of the truth of this report, but in fact it seems plausible, especially in view of the importance of Scottish bankers in Wisconsin. Moreover, the fact that Robert J. Walker was mentioned as intermediary lends credence to the report; it was he who aided in the negotiations in London for the Illinois Central.[98] In any case, whether or not the negotiations concerning the bonds of the Rock River Valley preceded those for the London issue of the Illinois Central's securities, its bonds were not slow in following those of the Illinois Central onto the London market. They were issued publicly in October 1852.[99]

Regardless of precedence, the Illinois Central was undoubtedly the first Illinois road to catch the public fancy, and immediately bonds of other railways of that state were brought forward. The Michigan Central had taken an early interest in the Illinois Central, over whose tracks it obtained an entrance to Chicago.[100] The Michigan Southern had to seek an alternative connection and accordingly made an alliance with the Chicago and Rock Island. The bonds of this line were among the first Illinois issues to appear in London.

It is somewhat surprising that the advertisements for the bonds of the Chicago and Rock Island stressed the fact that it would form a connection for the Michigan Central [an east-west line] and the Illinois Central,[101] essentially a north-south line. Perhaps the Rock Island was playing the Michigan Central against the Michigan Southern. It seems more likely, however, that this advertisement was an attempt to take advantage of the popularity in London already enjoyed by both the Michigan Central and the Illinois Central, the Michigan Southern being as yet not so well known.[102]

[97] XXIII (Oct. 19, 1850), 663.

[98] *Ibid.*, XXIV (Dec. 13, 1851), 792. Later Robert J. Walker was often mentioned in connection with the Atlantic and Great Western Railway.

[99] *Bankers' Magazine,* XIII (Feb. 1853), 103–12.

[100] On the alliance of the Michigan Central and the Illinois Central, see Gates, 92.

[101] *Daily News,* Jan. 18, 1853, p. 1. The amount of Chicago and Rock Island bonds offered was $400,000, the price £200 per $1,000 bond, or a little less than 89 percent. Masterman, Peters and Co. acted as bankers and Foster and Braithwaite as brokers for the issue.

[102] The financiers interested in the Michigan Southern were largely New Yorkers, whereas the men interested in the Michigan Central were largely

Meanwhile the Michigan Central was also moving ahead to the Mississippi by establishing its connections west of Chicago. Starting from that city, the lines it planned to use were the Chicago and Aurora, the Central Military Tract, and the Northern Cross.[103] Eventually, this chain of roads was consolidated to form the Chicago, Burlington and Quincy. Meanwhile, all these roads were receiving aid from the Michigan Central. The bonds of at least one, the Chicago and Aurora, were known in London by early 1853.[104]

The securities of other Illinois roads also were familiar in England by the early 1850's. These were the Chicago and Alton (then called the Chicago and Mississippi),[105] the Great Western of Illinois,[106] and the Terre Haute and Alton,[107] a road of which the *American Railroad Journal* disapproved as thoroughly as it had of the Illinois Central, and for the same reasons.[108] Thus, starting with the land-grant bonds of the Illinois Central in 1852, the bonds of eight Illinois railways were current in London early in the 1850's. It would seem reasonable to draw the conclusion that the success of the other Illinois lines was attributable in part to the reflected glory of the Illinois Central. But a qualification must be added. Most of these Illinois lines had the backing of established companies like the Michigan Central and were the recognized continuations of them. More-

---

Bostonians. Because the Michigan Southern was one of the earliest Midwestern roads, it is possible that some of its bonds had been finding their way to Europe from at least 1850. However, the first public issue for this road in London was that of the 7 percent first-mortgage bonds of the Northern Indiana. (The two lines were later consolidated into the Michigan Southern and Northern Indiana.) These bonds were issued in April 1854. Adam Spellman was the London agent, and the bonds were also sold through Daniel Bell. *Ibid.*, April 29, 1854, p. 4. Later the bonds were also sold through Edward Satterthwaite. *Railway Times*, June 10, 1854, p. 593. After these two roads were amalgamated their joint bonds, the bonds of the Michigan Southern and Northern Indiana, were marketed in Europe in 1856. *Daily News*, July 26, 1856, p. 7.

[103] These three roads together formed a chain running southwest from Chicago to Quincy on the Mississippi River. From Galesburg, the starting point of the Northern Cross, an alternative line, the Peoria and Oquawka, ran to Burlington, so that the road had in fact two terminal points on the Mississippi. Theodore L. Carlson, *The Illinois Military Tract*, University of Illinois Studies in the Social Sciences, XXXII, no. 2 (Urbana: Unversity of Illinois Press, 1951), 101–3; see also, Richard C. Overton, *Burlington West* (Cambridge, Mass.: Harvard University Press, 1941), 42.

[104] *Daily News*, April 15, 1853, p. 7.

[105] These were 7 percent mortgage bonds, and the amount offered in London was $1 million. *Ibid.*, April 15, 1853, p. 1. This road defaulted on its securities soon after opening, and on application of the bondholders, the road was reorganized as the Chicago, Alton and St. Louis. In due course it became a substantial dividend paying line.

[106] *Ibid.*, May 26, 1855, p. 10. This road is now part of the Wabash.

[107] These were first-mortgage bonds. *Ibid.*, Oct. 13, 1854, p. 7. This road also is now part of the Wabash.

[108] XXV (Dec. 11, 1852), 786.

over, the connection between these lines and the provision of cereals for Europe must not be overlooked.[109]

Cincinnati was falling behind in completing its connections to the Mississippi. The fault was not, however, entirely its own. Just as Pennsylvania did all in its power to ensure that all railways led to Philadelphia, Illinois wanted all railways to lead to Chicago. This midwestern state was therefore reluctant to grant a charter that would facilitate direct connection between Cincinnati and St. Louis.[110] The Ohio and Mississippi, chartered in Ohio and Indiana in the late 1840's, made no progress until 1852 when the entire road was put under contract to the Honorable H. C. Seymour.[111]

Seymour's contract with the Ohio and Mississippi merits a short digression, for it was a forerunner of the type of agreement that was to become common in the post–Civil War period. Before this time the officers of American railways usually exercised personal supervision over the building of their railways, and contracts were let for specific construction.[112] Seymour's contract, on the other hand, was for the entire road. He seems to have undertaken little direct engineering supervision. The work was relet: the entire eastern section to Story, Fuller and Company and the western section to another company.[113] Seymour was free to devote himself

[109] William Lance, *Review of the Commerce of Chicago for 1855,* a pamphlet published by the Chicago, St. Paul and Fond du Lac Railroad Co., 1856. Lance says: "The principal new commercial feature of the year is the appearance in this market of foreign governments, through their agents, as purchasers of grain and produce for direct consignment to Europe. It is not, of course, new or unusual for a portion of western produce to find its way ultimately to European consumers. This has previously been effected through the agency of speculators and middle-men, and has thus far followed the course of trade. It is, however, a new and by no means an unimportant feature to find Europe a customer at our granaries, an operator on our Corn Exchange, and her consumers competing for their shares of bread stuffs and provisions directly at the doors of our western producers."

[110] *American Railroad Journal,* XXIV (Aug. 30, 1851), 557.

[111] *Ibid.* (Oct. 4, 1851), 627, and (Dec. 13, 1851), 796.

[112] Occasionally a contractor undertook to build one section near the beginning of a line and one or two at intervals thereafter. Having completed the first section, he would proceed to those farther along. However, it was not the custom, even on a road like the Erie, to let numerous contiguous sections to one contracting firm. However, there were already several contractors in the United States who were able to undertake the contract for an entire short line or for ironing an entire longer line, that is laying the sleepers and rails on a roadbed that has already been prepared and ballasted. There is at least one precedent for Seymour's contract with the Ohio and Mississippi. This was the Atlantic and St. Lawrence, the American section of a line from Montreal to Portland, Maine, which later became a portion of the Grand Trunk. When Seymour became contractor of the Ohio and Mississippi he had as his chief assistant A. C. Morton, who had previously served as chief engineer under Wood, Black and Company, the contractors for the Atlantic and St. Lawrence. Chandler, 18–19.

[113] *American Railroad Journal,* XXV (Aug. 7, 1852), 508. There was considerable trouble with the contractors for the western section.

to the financial arrangements.[114] The Ohio and Mississippi was not the only line for which he was the financial contractor. He had this relationship with, among other lines, the Louisville and Nashville.[115] This railroad was also able to get substantial financial support in London in the 1850's although its securities were not publicly issued.[116]

It was not Seymour but Professor O. M. Mitchell who traveled to London to make the arrangements with George Peabody for purchases of iron and sales of bonds.[117] Nor was Seymour's death in the summer of 1854 [118] the immediate cause of the difficulties of this road at that time. These were the result of the failure of its St. Louis bankers, Page, Bacon and Company. In turn, this failure may have been partly due to the fact that after the start of the Crimean War it was difficult to raise funds for new American railways in London.[119] Those roads relying heavily on that market were suddenly left with partially finished lines.[120] Both the Marietta and Cincinnati [121] and the Ohio and Mississippi were in this position.[122]

[114] Seymour seems to have formed a brokerage house in New York, Seymour, Morton and Co., through which he marketed the securities which he received in payment for his contracts. *Ibid.*, XXVII (June 24, 1854), 399.

[115] At the time of his death it was reported that Seymour had contracts on hand to the amount of $30 million. *Ibid.*, XXVI (July 30, 1853), 488. [Parenthetically, it should be added that this type of contractor was essentially a financial middleman undertaking the risk of being able to market securities and successfully select building contractors to complete the mileage.]

[116] *Ibid.* (April 23, 1853), 264.   [117] *Ibid.*, 265.

[118] Muriel Hidy, "George Peabody," 349–50. Either for personal reasons or because he felt that the word Mississippi would prejudice the sale of these bonds in London, Peabody preferred to refer to this railway as the Cincinnati and St. Louis. However, it was usually called the Ohio and Mississippi in the London press. This was the last flotation of bonds of an American railway that Peabody undertook for some time. The rails were purchased from William Crawshay, who accepted some bonds in payment.

[119] The revelation that there had been overissues of stock on the New York and Harlem and on the New York and New Haven prolonged the revulsion from American railway securities. For an account of these scandals, see the *Economist*, XII (July 22, 1854), 792.

[120] See, for example, the statement on the Marietta and Cincinnati, *American Railroad Journal*, XXXIV (Sept. 28, 1861), 682.

[121] In spite of the fact that the Marietta and Cincinnati was to have a checkered career, it is doubtful whether the British investors lost much money. On reorganization, bonds issued in 1853 were replaced by a first sterling mortgage. The price of these stood at 122½ in 1882 although the road had been in receivership since 1877, default having been made under the fourth mortgage. *Burdett's Official Intelligence* (London: Effingham Wilson, 1882). At that date Heseltine and Powell, who had represented the bondholders in the reorganization, continued to represent the line in London. Eventually, the Marietta became part of the Baltimore and Ohio Southwestern.

[122] Probably the experience of the British investors with the Ohio and Mississippi was more unpleasant than that with the Marietta, because the Ohio and Mississippi bondholders never found an established house to represent it. Nevertheless, the preferred stock of the Ohio and Mississippi, on which no dividend had been paid since 1876, stood at 115 in 1882. It was thought to be cumulative,

[Shortly before the Crimean War and the economic difficulties of 1854 slowed down the export of European capital, a survey was made that showed both the variety and the concentration of foreign investment in American railways. Incomplete as were the returns for the report of the Secretary of Treasury in 1853, the replies of 222 railways were revealing. Of more than a third of those companies, some securities were held abroad. In more than half of that third the foreign investment per company was $100,000 or higher. The number of corporations in which the foreign interest was $1 million or more had reached only ten. Roughly in order of size of foreign holdings of securities, these ten were the Philadelphia and Reading; New York and Erie; Western of Massachusetts; Pennsylvania; Camden and Amboy; Ohio and Mississippi (Eastern Division); South Carolina; Illinois Central; Baltimore and Ohio; and Belvidere and Delaware.[123] This analysis does not include railways into which foreign investors' funds had flowed through purchase of state, county, and municipal bonds. Furthermore, in some cases the short-term loans to railways were significant both in timing and in amount.]

When after the panic of 1854 London again began to take an interest in American railway securities in 1855 and 1856, attention was concentrated on a few roads such as the Illinois Central, the Michigan Southern, the recently organized New York Central, the Pennsylvania, and others of this class.[124] For each of these favorite roads more than one security issue was now current. Three bond issues of the Illinois Central and five of the Erie were known in London. Whereas dealings in American railway securities had been sporadic in the early 1850's,[125] trading in these favorite issues was now often brisk.[126] A number of these securities recently had been admitted to official quotation on the London Stock Exchange.[127]

---

but there were subsequent difficulties about this. Moreover, there was a long struggle between British bondholders and Robert Garrett of the Baltimore and Ohio. Eventually the Ohio and Mississippi became a part of the Baltimore and Ohio Southwestern. Another Cincinnati road with which the British investor had trouble was the Cincinnati, Logansport and Chicago, a line projected to give Cincinnati a through line to Chicago. Its first-mortgage bonds were put out through Lewis Haslewood, like Daniel Bell a stockbroker who had specialized in American stocks since the 1840's. *Daily News*, Sept. 6, 1853, p. 1. The line was sold on application of the British bondholders in 1860. *American Railroad Journal*, XXIII (May 5, 1860), 382. It eventually became part of the Columbus, Chicago and Indiana Central, and the British bondholders had further trouble with this line in the 1870's; see below, pp. 00–00.

[123] [U.S., Congress, *Senate Executive Document 42*, 33d Cong., 1st sess., 1853–54, 36–47.]

[124] See, for example, Daniel Bell's listing in the *Daily News*, Aug. 10, 1855, p. 7.

[125] In the early 1850's George Peabody warned his friends not to be led astray by brokers' circulars, for there was no real market for American stocks or bonds in Europe. Muriel Hidy, "George Peabody," 344.

[126] In 1857, the *Economist* was commenting weekly on the state of the market for Illinois Central and Erie shares.

[127] *Daily News*, March 9, 1855, p. 7.

The market was deepening, not widening. There was, indeed, an attempt to bring out a few more issues in 1856 and 1857. The New Orleans, Jackson and Great Northern, a line running north from New Orleans along the Mississippi to join eventually with the Illinois Central, issued $2 million of first-mortgage construction bonds through J. Henry Schroeder and Company;[128] the Chicago, St. Paul and Fond du Lac offered $2 million of first-mortgage land-grant bonds through Dodge, Bacon and Company,[129] and the Lake Ontario and Hudson River offered £600,000 of land-grant bonds through Huggins and Rowsell.[130] Barings, in 1856, took $250,000 of the 7 percent first-mortgage bonds of the Hannibal and St. Joseph, a land-grant road in Missouri that formed a continuation of the Chicago, Burlington and Quincy.[131] But these were exceptions. The crisis of 1857 again put a stop to any attempt to start a boom in new American railway issues. On the other hand, it may have intensified speculation in such securities as Illinois Central and Erie shares. Before recovery from this crisis was complete, the Civil War intervened.

In conclusion, almost all British investment in American railway securities in the 1850's was of the type that is now called growth investment. Ordinary shares were at first preferred to bonds. Later, convertible bonds became popular because they offered an added safety. Moreover, land-grant bonds, especially when offered in connection with shares, probably surpassed both these earlier types of security in popularity. Nor must it be supposed that the investment that took place through the City was haphazard. It was concentrated first on those roads that were intended to form part of through lines and second on the railways of Illinois.

The British investor probably made a mistake at the time of the Crimean War in withdrawing support from some new lines that had been depending heavily on British capital. Most of these lines found themselves in trouble after 1854. Even the Illinois Central would have had difficulty surviving without reorganization if it had not been able to make further calls on its shares. Perhaps the City learned from the defaults and reorganizations of these lines that interest in new lines must be on a continuing basis. Only investment in purely rentier securities can be suddenly discontinued without serious consequences to the investor as well as to the enterprise in which he has put his money. In any case, British interest in American railway securities in the years immediately preceding the Civil War narrowed to a handful of lines, but in these favored lines it became increasingly important.

[128] *Economist,* XIV (Aug. 23, 1856), advertisement pages.

[129] *Ibid.,* XV (Jan. 3, 1857), 28. The Fond du Lac was the successor to the Rock River Valley, and thus its issue was not one for a new road.

[130] *Ibid.* (July 4, 1857), 751.

[131] Ralph Hidy, *House of Baring,* 426 and 472.

PART TWO

IV

The 1860's and 1870's

DURING [the two decades of the 1860's and 1870's, British investors in American railways faced the need to adjust to a variety of possibilities and new situations. The author has treated this complex array of decisions in three parts. The first chapter examines the changing character of British investment at a time of uneven but dramatic growth. In the next the relation of the investor to railway management is examined in some detail for two of the railways with a remarkably troubled financial life. The third chapter is concerned with British involvement in related industries in the United States, coal and iron, and some railways emphasizing such freight.]

During the Civil War, new British investment in American railways virtually ceased. After the suspension of specie payments in December 1861, some of the investment built up in earlier years was liquidated,[1] although it is to be doubted whether this realization of British assets was on the scale sometimes assumed.[2] In part, the British investor who had

[1] [See Pierce, 51.]

[2] In discussing the increase of America's foreign liabilities from July 1, 1862, to the close of 1873, the Hon. Edward Young of the U.S. Bureau of Statistics stated that in 1862 no federal securities and about $50 million of state and railway securities were held abroad; quoted in the *Times*, July 25, 1874, p. 10.

Margaret G. Myers, I, 289, gives the figure of $50 million for foreign holdings of rail stocks and bonds in 1866: "By the year 1866 new purchases [of American securities] added to those held abroad before the War, brought the total to approximately 600 millions of dollars. Government bonds accounted for 350 millions, state and municipal bonds for 150 millions and rail stocks and bonds for 50 millions." This estimate of $50 million is highly dubious. In 1860, the United States suddenly found itself with a favorable balance of trade vis-à-vis Great Britain. An atmosphere of suspended animation preceding the Civil War cut off imports just at the time exports of grain from the newly opened lands of the Midwest became large, because of the building of the railways and the invention of McCormick's reaper. A panic occurred on Wall Street due to the fact that the South was taking the proceeds of her discounted cotton bills in specie rather than in bankers' drafts. As a result, the prices of American railway

hitherto been placing capital in American securities now sought other channels of investment. One American railway, however, continued to obtain its financial support from London in the early 1860's. This was the Atlantic and Great Western, a consolidation of three lines in New York, Pennsylvania, and Ohio, which, although begun by Americans,[3] gradually came more and more under European influence. Thomas E. Kennard of the Liverpool banking family was appointed chief engineer.[4] A Spaniard, the Duke of Salamanca,[5] and an Irish-American, James McHenry, became the contractors, and a number of Europeans were elected to the board of directors. Moreover, since the company's bonds were made payable in gold, there was no question about exchange rates.[6] The discovery of oil in the region that the railway traversed provided a lure irresistible even to English businessmen as hardheaded as the railway contractor Sir Morton Peto.[7]

Toward the close of the Civil War it seemed that British capital would soon begin to flow to the United States again. By this time the fact that the United States had a greenback currency was an advantage to the foreign investor; American railway securities that were selling at high prices in New York could be purchased cheaply in terms of sterling. Thus a share of the Illinois Central, a road that was paying 10 percent dividends, could be

securities in New York were depressed below the prices ruling in London. Not only did the British not return securities to New York at this time, they actually increased their holdings, to take advantage of these bargain prices. In an editorial in December 1861, the *Economist* remarked: "Though the trading debts of the North are unusually small, yet the 'securities' of various kinds held in this country, of which the interest is annually payable by the North to us, are as numerous as ever." XIX (Dec. 7, 1861), 1347.

[3] The Atlantic and Great Western was formed by the consolidation of three lines, the Erie and New York City (New York), the Meadville (Pennsylvania), and the Franklin and Warren (Ohio). In the 1850's, A. C. Morton and Henry Doolittle went to London to negotiate the bonds of the line and to obtain rails. They made an arrangement with Henry Gompertz of London, but after the crisis of 1857 he withdrew. Shortly thereafter, James McHenry became interested. At first his commission was simply to furnish cash or bankers' bills to the extent of £193,000 to pay for the purchase of iron. Paul Felton, "The History of the Atlantic and Great Western Railroad Company" (unpublished doctoral thesis, University of Pittsburgh, 1943), 36, 51, 58.

[4] The Liverpool banking house of Heywood, Kennard was one of the earliest supporters of the Atlantic and Great Western. In 1859, Thomas E. Kennard made a trip to the U.S. with C. D. Ward and George Francis Train to inspect the road. On his return he wrote a eulogistic account which was published in the *Daily News*. Soon he was appointed chief engineer of the road. Felton, 53, 65–67, 72.

[5] The Duke of Salamanca, born in Malaga in 1811, was a railway entrepreneur and banker. His full name was José de Salamanca, and the dukedom was created for him. He died in Madrid on Nov. 21, 1883.

[6] See the advertisement for the bonds of the Atlantic and Great Western which appeared in the *Economist*, XVIII (Sept. 22, 1860), 1076.

[7] Peto became interested in this project in 1861 or 1862. Felton, 118–19.

purchased at 54 in London,[8] although it was selling at a premium in New York. *Herapath's Railway and Commercial Gazette* began to feature articles on American railways.[9] The Welsh iron companies anticipated new orders from the United States.[10] Uncertainty about both the American political situation and that country's relations with Britain [11] prevented the development of a boom; but there was some increase in British holdings of American securities during 1865.[12] There were even public issues of the bonds of three American railways in that year. The largest of these issues was for the Atlantic and Great Western.[13]

However, at the end of 1865 there were already portents of disaster. The rumblings in the City increased steadily through the first five months of 1866 and finally culminated in the collapse of the discount house of Overend, Gurney and Company in May. [As will appear in the next chapter, the series of events was of concern to railways ballasted by short-term credit.] [14]

American securities held up fairly well for a time, partly owing to the demand from the Continent,[15] although English demand was also good.[16] In August the *Bullionist* commented that American securities were becom-

[8] *Herapath's Railway and Commercial Gazette*, March 11, 1865, p. 283.

[9] July 22, 1866, p. 782. For example, the author of this article wrote, "This great American railroad is in such good condition that it is almost equal to an English *railway*." The railways which it praises are always the same ones, the New York Central, the Erie, the Atlantic and Great Western, the Pennsylvania, and the Illinois Central.

[10] *Ibid.*, July 15, 1866, p. 760.

[11] Northerners were irate at what they felt to be unjustified support given by Britian to the Confederacy. In Feb. 1865 the *Economist* was already trying to smooth this over by statements such as the following: "For one vessel laden with arms and warlike stores that has entered a southern port, twenty have entered Northern ports. Nine-tenths of the Federal forces have been clothed and armed with British imports. Nine-tenths of the Confederate soldiers who have fallen have been slain by guns made in the United Kingdom." XXIII (Feb. 11, 1865), 160. But the North, still losing shipping to southern privateers, was in no mood to be mollified. Counterirritation sprang up in London after newspapers in the United States published lists of prominent Englishmen, including William E. Gladstone, the editor of the *Times*, and the editor of the *Morning Chronicle*, who had supposedly subscribed to the Confederate loan floated in London by J. Henry Schroeder. See, for example, *Times*, Oct. 6, 1865, p. 7.

[12] *Bullionist*, Jan. 6, 1866, p. 3.   [13] See Appendix I.

[14] [See Wilfred Thomas Cousins King, *History of the London Discount Market* (London: George Routledge & Sons, 1936), 242–51.]

[15] The *Economist*, early in 1866, commented that orders were being constantly received from Germany for investment and that the absorption of stock was consequently large. XXIV (Feb. 18, 1866), 231. The *Bullionist*, in May 1866, anticipated a rapid rise in the price of American securities, as the German and Dutch repossessed the securities earlier sold in fear of war and the possible monetary difficulties. May 19, 1866, p. 585. In Sept. the same journal remarked that the Continental demand for American securities continued unabated. Sept. 1, 1866, p. 978.

[16] *Ibid.*, Aug. 18, 1866, p. 527.

ing a favorite investment. It noted the further import of Illinois Central
securities and of 6 percent federal bonds, redeemable five to twenty years
after issue.[17] The *Commercial History and Review of 1866,* a supplement
to the *Economist,* stated:

American Government Securities greatly increased in favour during the
year, and show an important advance. 5–20 bonds have risen 7 per cent.;
but Erie have declined 10 per cent., and Illinois Central, about 2 per cent.
About *one hundred millions* sterling of American Government securities
are now held in Europe. The Germans and the Dutch are the chief buyers.[18]

However, American securities did not provide a lever to lift the City out
of the paralysis that had attacked it in 1866. In fact, they fell under the
general distrust following the very damaging disclosures about the affairs
of the Atlantic and Great Western early in 1867.[19] By June the *Bullionist*
reported that there had seldom been such a quiet market for American
securities.[20] Only one public issue of a security of a railway in the United
States was attempted in London in 1867: an issue of £200,000 of 6
percent general mortgage bonds of the Pennsylvania was floated at the
end of the year by the London, Asiatic and American Company [21] and by
Foster and Braithwaite.[22]

In 1868, another year of depression in the City, the reputation of
American railway securities as a safe investment received yet another
setback. This was a result of the renewed and intensified outbreak of the
so-called Erie Wars, originating in the struggle for control of that
railway [23] between Daniel Drew, stockbroker, speculator, and sometime
treasurer of the Erie, and Cornelius Vanderbilt, president of the New York
Central.[24] Soon Drew fell out with his associate, Jay Gould, at that time
president of the Erie, and took sides with Vanderbilt.[25] But the basic
alignment continued to be the Erie management on one side and Vanderbilt on the other. From the beginning the latter had the support of a
number of bankers, especially of August Belmont, agent in the United

[17] *Ibid.*   [18] *Economist,* XXV (March 9, 1867), 33.
[19] See below, p. 109 ff.   [20] June 22, 1867, p. 661.
[21] The London, Asiatic and American was an amalgamation of T. Wiggin &
Co. (which had failed in 1837), Thomas Cardsell and Co., and Grey and Coles,
and their correspondents in Liverpool and Bombay. *Economist,* XXIV (Jan. 27,
1866), 101.
[22] *Times,* Dec. 10, 1867, p. 5. Foster and Braithwaite is an old and eminent
firm of stockbrokers.
[23] On the Erie Wars, the *Times* reports were full and of excellent quality. They
were probably written by Joel Cook of Philadelphia. Charles Francis Adams, Jr.,
used the *Times* as a source for his articles, which originally appeared in
various journals and are reprinted in Frederick C. Hicks (ed.), *High Finance in
the Sixties* (New Haven: Yale University Press, 1929). Information from the
librarian of the *Times.*
[24] Besides controlling the New York Central, Vanderbilt had, for some years,
occupied a seat on the Board of Directors of the Erie.
[25] *Times,* March 4, 1868, p. 10; March 30, 1868, p. 9; May 8, 1868, p. 5; Dec.
4, 1868, p. 8.

States of the Rothschilds.[26] Erie securities had been a Rothschild preserve since the 1850's just as Reading securities were that of the McCalmont Brothers.[27]

At first the British investors were only tangentially involved in the Erie, but soon they began to build up their holdings and concern. They were tempted by the low prices of Erie shares during raids of the bears, who sold heavily to drive down prices in the hope of buying low to cover their short position. Alternating higher prices, resulting from the bull movements in the short-term battles of these wars, promised quick profits on security speculations. When Jay Gould revealed that he had been issuing large quantities of new Erie shares to aid him in his stock market manipulations, the British investors immediately moved into action to protect their holdings. From this time the Erie struggle was largely between Jay Gould and the British investors.[28] Gould's rivalry with Vanderbilt was transferred to other spheres.

Nevertheless, in 1869, as the City began to emerge from depression, American railway securities again began to move to London. As early as February the *Economist* reported a large speculative business in American rails both for home buyers and on Continental accounts.[29] But it must be emphasized that London was not yet receptive to loans for the new western railways then being built in the United States. Many of the rails for these roads came from Britain—from Wales, Middlesbrough, and Newcastle—but the bulk of the bonds were marketed on the Continent, particularly in Holland [30] and Germany. In 1868 only three new issues of American railways were brought out in London. In 1869 four new issues were floated. The list lengthened to ten in 1870, but many of these were almost entirely taken up for Continental accounts. It was 1872 before more than twenty new issues were floated in the City; a new boom in public issues of American railway securities had begun in London.

Coming later in the post–Civil War era into the market for new American railway securities, the British avoided investment in some of the more disastrous ventures that attracted so much capital from Amsterdam and Frankfort. In these cities American bankers, like James Lanier of the New York firm of Winslow, Lanier and Company, found a market for dozens of new American securities that London would not touch.[31] Beginning with federal securities immediately after the Civil War, Continental interest had soon spread over into railway securities, and the years 1868 and 1870 were boom years for American railway securities in those markets.

The *Times*, consistently skeptical about all American securities, com-

[26] *Ibid.*, Dec. 4, 1868, p. 8.   [27] Ralph Hidy, *House of Baring*, 410.
[28] See below, pp. 97–98.   [29] XXVII (Feb. 20, 1869), 214.
[30] [See Kornelis Douwe Bosch, *De Nederlandse Beleggingen in de Verenigde Staten* (Amsterdam: Uitgeversmaatschappij Elsevier, 1948), esp. 155, 160, and 161. This gives useful lists.]
[31] Lanier made many trips to Europe after the Civil War. *Dictionary of American Biography*, X, 600–601.

mented disparagingly week after week on the mania for American railway securities that had seized the Frankfort market.[32] Finally, on May 9, 1870, prominent notice was given to an announcement supposedly emanating from the Alderman of Merchants of the Berlin Bourse and released by the North German Consul in New York:

It having come to our knowledge that a yet larger exploration of our markets is contemplated in America and England by the sale of unsound American bonds, as [sic] has hitherto been the case, to the detriment of the public, we are thereby induced to put the community on their guard against the purchase of American bonds, and particularly of American railway mortgage bonds, if they are not guaranteed by the Government of the United States. Notice has been given at the same time to brokers that they should abstain from dealing in such bonds, and that no quotation will be allowed henceforth.[33]

According to the *Times,* this announcement, which had been expected for some time, was finally precipitated by the proposal of Jay Cooke and Company to float $100 million of bonds of the Northern Pacific. The German Consul in New York subsequently denied having made such an announcement.[34] Nevertheless, the boom was soon losing its force.

[During the early 1870's German purchases of American securities showed much irregularity.] At first, speculation was merely diverted from railways to American municipal bonds.[35] The outbreak of the Franco-Prussian War curtailed all foreign investment by Germans and even caused the return of some bonds to New York.[36] A few further American railway issues were brought out late in 1870 and early in 1871.[37] Soon, however, the market was affected by defaults on issues of those American railway bonds, of which substantial amounts were held on the Continent.[38] Early in 1873—six months before the crisis of that year—the list of defaulted American railway securities held on the Continent included:

Alabama and Chattanooga	$ 4,700,000
Fort Wayne, Muncie and Cincinnati	1,800,000
Georgia bonds in aid of the Brunswick and Albany	3,880,000
Des Moines Valley	7,000,000
Peninsular of Michigan	1,800,000
Rockford, Rock Island and St. Louis	9,000,000
	$28,180,000 [39]

[32] See, for example, *Times,* March 19, 1870, p. 10: "People from New York are flocking to Frankfort as to a goldfield." See also *ibid.,* April 20, 1870, p. 7.

[33] *Ibid.,* May 9, 1870, p. 9.   [34] *Ibid.,* May 12, 1870, p. 7.

[35] *Ibid.,* July 4, 1870, p. 7.   [36] *Ibid.,* Oct. 30, 1870, p. 4.

[37] For example, in the autumn of 1871 two new issues were brought out in Frankfort. These were a $3.9 million issue of 6 percent bonds of the Lexington and St. Louis, guaranteed by the Missouri-Pacific, and an issue of $2.5 million of 6 percent bonds of the Buffalo and Philadelphia. *Ibid.,* Oct. 3, 1871, p. 5.

[38] *Ibid.,* Jan. 20, 1871.

[39] *Commercial and Financial Chronicle,* XVI (April 5, 1873), 455.

Then followed defaults on the 8 percent gold bonds of the Saint Joseph and Denver City and on some bonds of the St. Paul and Pacific [40] [a Minnesota line projected from the Mississippi River at Saint Paul to Canada, in which Dutch investors were heavily involved]. Confidence weakened. When the crisis of 1873 struck in the autumn, considerable amounts of American securities were hastily disgorged from France and Germany.[41] Some were returned to New York, and others were bought up in London. Germany ceased to be an important market for American securities. Domestic stocks and European funds were to rule the German bourses for many years.[42]

The Dutch also suffered from overenthusiastic investment in new western American railways. A statement from a Dutch paper, as paraphrased in the *Commercial and Financial Chronicle,* read:

During the last few years upwards of sixty different kinds of American railway securities have been introduced into that little country [Holland] alone. Until lately American railway bonds were the favorite investment in the greater part of Germany and Holland. The news of the various spoliations of the rights of the St. Paul and Pacific bondholders gave rise to a general distrust in all American railway securities; and later, when a crisis was brought about at New York, the panic in Europe became universal.[43]

Continental investors seem to have taken more severe losses than did Americans or the British. By the autumn of 1874, 108 American railways had defaulted on bonds totaling $497,807,660 [See Table 4]. Of this amount it was estimated that $150 million was held abroad. Since total foreign holdings of American railway bonds were then estimated to be about $375 million, it follows that 40 percent of the American railway securities held abroad were in default.[44] Moreover, it would appear that most of the bonds in default were held on the Continent rather than in Britain.

A number of the issues floated or regularly traded in London were in default. The most serious cases were those of the Atlantic and Great Western and of the Erie and its connecting line, the New York, Boston and Montreal. In addition, there were several defaults among the issues offered in London between 1866 and 1872 but taken by Continental rather than by British investors.[45] Default on four issues of bonds of middle western roads carrying a form of guarantee of the Pennsylvania were more serious.[46] One of these issues, that for the Gilman, Clinton and Springfield

[40] *Ibid.*, XVI (May 10, 1873), 627; XVII (Aug. 9, 1873), 189; XVII (Aug. 16, 1873), 220.

[41] *Ibid.*, XVI (June 21, 1873), 819; XVII (Nov. 15, 1873), 654.

[42] *Economist*, XLIX (Aug. 29, 1891), 1113.

[43] XVII (Dec. 6, 1873), 753.   [44] *Ibid.*, XIX (Oct. 10, 1874), 363.

[45] See Table 4.

[46] These guarantees were not unconditional. For example, the guarantee of the bond issue for the Plymouth, Kankakee and Pacific was that the Pennsylvania would work the line at cost turning over all net proceeds to the line. J. Edgar

Table 4. American railway securities, publicly issued in London, in default
in the 1870's

Railway	Year issued	Date of default
Atlantic and Great Western	Various beginning in 1860	1874
* St. Paul and Pacific	Various beginning in 1860's	1873
West Wisconsin	1868, 1873	1875
Chesapeake and Ohio	1868	1873
Alabama and Chattanooga	1869	Before 1873
* St. Joseph and Denver City	1870	1873
* Indianapolis, Bloomington & Western (including the Danville, Urbana, & Bloomington & Pekin)	1870	1874
** Illinois & St. Louis Bridge	1870, 1874	After 1875
Alabama bonds (in aid of Ala. & Chat. Rr.)	1870	Before 1873
* Des Moines Valley	1870	Before 1873
Chicago, Danville & Vincennes	1870	1873
* Oregon and California	1871	1873
Atlantic, Mississippi & Ohio	1871	1874
* Georgia State (in aid of railways)	1871	Before 1873
* Northern Pacific	1872	1874
** Gilman, Clinton & Springfield	1872	1874
Cairo & Vincennes	1872	1874
Plymouth, Kankakee & Pacific	1872	Before 1873
* Arkansas Central	1872	1874
Erie	Various beginning in the 1850's	1875
Burlington, Cedar Rapids & Northern	1872	1873
New York, Boston & Montreal	1873	1874
** Eastern of Massachusetts	1873	After 1875
** New Orleans, Jackson & Great Northern	1856, 1873	After 1875
** Mississippi Central	1873	After 1875
Illinois, Missouri & Texas	1873	1873
Mobile and Ohio	1874	1875
Geneva and Ithaca	1874	1874
St. Louis, Iron Mountain & Southern	1874	1875

* The issues of these roads were mainly taken on Continental account.
** The issues of these roads were protected either by the guarantor or by the issuing house. Thus, the Illinois Central eventually provided for the coupons of the New Orleans, Jackson and Great Northern, the Mississippi Central, and the Gilman, Clinton and Springfield. J. S. Morgan purchased the coupons of the Illinois and St. Louis Bridge and of the St. Louis Tunnel, while Baring Brothers provided for the coupons of the Eastern of Massachusetts.

floated through Morton, Rose and Company, caused little difficulty.[47] However, two other railways ran into real trouble: both the Cairo and Vin-

Thomson, president of the Pennsylvania, and George W. Cass, president of the Fort Wayne, were trustees of the bond issue. *Economist,* XXX (April 6, 1872), 441.

[47] The bonds of the Gilman, Clinton and Springfield were eventually replaced by 1,600 6 percent currency bonds of the Illinois Central secured by a first

cennes, whose securities were put out through J. S. Morgan and Company, and the Plymouth, Kankakee and Pacific, whose bonds were issued through Blyth and Company, were sold at foreclosure in the late seventies.[48] The struggle between the Pennsylvania and the British holders of the bonds of the Columbus, Chicago and Indiana Central (the CC&IC), whose securities apparently were marketed privately in London, was bitter and protracted following defaults in 1874.[49]

When the London market again became receptive to new issues of American railway securities, in the early 1870's, it was on a scale sufficiently large to make up for the cessation of the flow of capital from the Continent. In fact, even when a panic struck in Vienna in the spring of 1873, Americans were complacent:

If this panic had broken out at a time when the capitalists of Vienna were loaded up with our securities, we might have suffered some embarrassment. At that time, moreover, the British market was not opening as promisingly as now for the absorption of American bonds. For all that appears, the London market will take without difficulty such of our securities as have to be thrown over and sold in Germany and Austria. . . . we have lately ceased to depend on German markets for an outlet to our securities.[50]

British investment in American railways continued unabated even after the panic following the failure of Jay Cooke and Company [the banking

mortgage on the Chicago to Springfield division. *Times*, March 21, 1878. Since the issue of Gilman, Clinton and Springfield bonds had been for the amount of £400,000 at 90 percent, this represented a scaling down of approximately 20 percent on the bonds' face value.

[48] The Cairo and Vincennes bonds fell sharply in price after default, standing at 30–40 at the beginning of 1876. In 1880, the railway was sold under foreclosure, purchased for the bondholders for $2 million and reorganized, with J. P. Morgan as the president. The $2 million required to purchase the road was represented in the reorganized company by preferred shares, while the $3.5 million of first-mortgage bonds of the original company was represented by common shares. In 1881 the road was sold to the Wabash, and the common shares were exchanged, share for share, for Wabash common shares which in 1882 stood at 88. The Plymouth, Kankakee and Pacific was sold at foreclosure in 1877.

[49] *Times*, Sept. 15, 1874, p. 4; April 15, 1875, p. 9; and April 16, 1875, p. 11. See also *Commercial and Financial Chronicle*, XXIX (Dec. 27, 1879), 680; XXXVI (Jan. 13, 1883), 55; and (March 24, 1883), 339; and Burgess and Kennedy, 380. The Columbus, Chicago and Indiana Central included the old Cincinnati, Logansport and Chicago, of which the first-mortgage bonds were floated in London in 1850. Starting with default on the first- and second-mortgage bonds of the CC&IC in 1874, there was a troubled history of contention and litigation concerning the Pennsylvania's guarantee and the rights of bondholders. In 1882 the line of the CC&IC was reorganized after a foreclosure sale and separately operated for eight years as the Chicago, St. Louis and Pittsburgh. Then it was merged with the Pittsburgh, Cincinnati, Chicago and St. Louis Railway Co. (the Panhandle). [Mrs. Adler's manuscript had a long discussion from the sources given; this is a summary.]

[50] *Commercial and Financial Chronicle*, XVI (May 17, 1873), 647.

house deeply involved in the railway finance of the St. Paul and Pacific and Northern Pacific] had dried up the flow of investment in the United States. The year 1874 presented a peculiar picture, for the negotiation of American railway bonds went forward with greater ease in London than in New York. Again according to the *Commercial and Financial Chronicle*: "New financial enterprises meet with little encouragement now in this market, and nearly all the railroad loans negotiated this year have been placed in London. It would really appear that for the time being English capitalists have more confidence in the stability of leading American railroads than our own people have." [51]

Negotiations of American securities continued in spite of temporary lulls caused by events that brought American railway issues into disgrace. In 1874 defaults on the Erie were accompanied by rumors of scandal concerning speculations by McHenry and others in the company's securities.[52] Nonetheless, the next year, of the total of £13,998,000 of new issues floated, £8,160,000 were for American railways; [53] and in 1876, of £6,501,000 of new issues, American railway loans accounted for £3,105,000.[54] It must be remembered that all British foreign lending was on a very restricted scale in the years following 1875.

After defaults of the early 1870's and the scandals of the Erie, British investors evinced an interest in a different type of security than earlier. Instead of concentrating on growth investment as they had in the 1850's, they now made their purchases with an eye to security. First-mortgage bonds of well-known established roads were preferred, and the additional safeguard of some kind of guarantee increased the marketability even of these senior securities.

Between the middle of 1876 and 1880 only a handful of public flotations of American railway securities were made on the London market. However, this does not mean that investments in American securities ceased completely. In July 1876 the *Times* reported: "We are told that a steady investment is going on in the better class bonds which are outside the range of speculation, and yield investors more than English securities of the same class." [55] In September the *Times* reported in a similar vein that there continued to be new British investment in American and in Cana-

[51] XIX (Aug. 29, 1874), 211.

[52] The Atlantic and Great Western defaulted early in 1874. Peter H. Watson, president of the Erie during the period when McHenry and Bischoffsheim and Goldschmidt were in virtual control, resigned in the summer of 1874 and was replaced by Hugh Jewett. By this time London holders of Erie securities were already dissatisfied about the financial negotiations of the previous regime, but an out-and-out attack on McHenry and his associates was not made publicly until the spring of 1875. *Times*, May 27, 1875, p. 8.

[53] *Ibid.*, Jan. 24, 1876, p. 7, quotation from *Spackman's Circular*.

[54] *Ibid.*, Jan. 1877, p. 1, quotation from *Spackman's Circular*.

[55] July 27, 1876, p. 6.

dian securities [56] and again, in October, that active buying continued in American rails of the first class.[57] Such investment received a severe shock in late 1876 with news of the financial troubles of the Reading.

At this time there was serious competition among those eastern American railways that relied to a large extent on coal for freight. The Philadelphia and Reading, under the presidency of Franklin Gowen, had been pursuing an aggressive policy of buying up anthracite coal lands and had incurred the enmity of the Pennsylvania. Meanwhile, the Pennsylvania and the Baltimore and Ohio had come into serious conflict over bituminous coal freights from both western Pennsylvania and West Virginia. Moreover, the Pennsylvania had strengthened its position by absorbing the United Canal and Railroad Company of New Jersey (the old Camden and Amboy and other New Jersey railways). The Baltimore and Ohio was in imminent danger of being denied access to New York over these New Jersey roads. Consequently, it had been drawing closer to the Philadelphia and Reading, since, in case of necessity, it could find an alternative route to New York over that line and its associated road, the Central of New Jersey.

Until 1876 the Philadelphia and Reading consistently had paid annual dividends of 10 percent. Then in January 1876 it was unexpectedly announced that the Reading would skip the January dividend entirely and might reduce the one for June.[58] In fact, a dividend was paid in June, but at the same time the Reading, through its agent, McCalmont Brothers, applied to the London market for a new loan of $10 million.[59] In the light of this sequence of events it is not surprising that when, in November 1876, the Reading published a most discouraging annual report on its operations, the reaction in London was immediate and violent.[60]

Three months later, in February 1877, the Central of New Jersey went into receivership.[61] This was followed by a persistent attack on all the coal roads.[62] For a while it seemed that the Reading itself might go under.

[56] Sept. 20, 1876, p. 7. [57] Oct. 31, 1876, p. 8.

[58] *Ibid.*, Jan. 26, 1876, p. 7. [59] *Ibid.*, June 20, 1876, p. 10.

[60] The attitude of the *Times*, which one year previously had lavishly praised the Reading, is evident from the following: "The whole debt, funded or floating, should be stated clearly with its present position and priorities; the relations of the Railway and the Coal Company also want setting forth, and the revenues both as to their amount and as computed between the two companies. Also it is most important that the full truth should be told about the stock operations in which the Directors are accused of having engaged with means that ought to have been otherwise employed in order to keep the shares at a fictitious value. Loan agents incur grave responsibility in maintaining silence when so many fears are excited." Dec. 4, 1876, p. 7.

[61] *Ibid.*, Feb. 28, 1877, p. 10. This loan was put out through Brown, Shipley.

[62] The shares of the Delaware and Hudson fell to 39, those of the Delaware, Lackawanna and Western to 45, those of the Morris and Essex to 63¼, and those of the Reading to 11.

However, it had staunch support from McCalmont Brothers, a firm with which the Reading had had close relations since the late 1840's.[63] In June 1877 a meeting of the share- and bondholders, both of the Reading and of the Perkiomen, was convened by McCalmont Brothers. At this meeting the president of the Reading, Franklin B. Gowen, proposed that for the time being half of the interest coupons on the company's bonds should be funded and that drawings for the sinking fund should be temporarily suspended.[64] A move on the part of some independent bond- and share-holders to set up an investigating committee was effectively scotched.[65] The Reading crash was deferred until the 1880's when the McCalmonts and Gowen fell out over the latter's expansionist policies.

Meanwhile, fright over the Reading report had led to pressure on other American railway securities, especially on those of the Pennsylvania. By June 1877, its shares were quoted at $30.[66] (Like the Philadelphia and Reading, the Pennsylvania had shares with a par value of $50 rather than $100, the usual par value of American railway shares.) The Pennsylvania also called a meeting of its British shareholders. By his address at this meeting the vice-president of the company reportedly did much to allay the shareholders' fears.[67]

Nevertheless, British investors remained wary of American rails for almost a year. In January 1878 the *Commercial and Financial Chronicle* commented that although January was usually a favorable time to nego-tiate new loans, because of the demand for securities in which to reinvest interest and dividends, the activity in investment securities was less than usual.[68] In December 1878 the same journal noted that British investors were sending weekly to New York all kinds of American securities, even bonds of the New York Central. However, the editorial added:

Some make the error that, because our governments have in great part ceased to come, there are no securities in London available for paying bal-ances due us. The truth is, as all know who are familiar with the subject,

---

[63] See above, p. 52, n. 40.

[64] For a report of this meeting at which Thomas W. Powell presided, see the *Times*, June 7, 1877, p. 8.

[65] The Reading had a number of very large shareholders. A letter to the *Times* (Dec. 7, 1876, p. 7), was signed "A Bondholder of over £10,000" and referred to another person who held £100,000 shares. The move to form a share and bondholders protective committee for the Reading was started by Henry Spicer. *Ibid.*, Jan. 25, 1877, p. 6. David Cornfoot became the secretary of the provisional committee which was set up by Spicer, and all interested people were asked to write to him at 5 Royal Exchange Avenue. However, after the meeting was convened by McCalmont, this committee became inactive. *Ibid.*, Feb. 13, 1877, p. 10.

[66] *Times*, June 15, 1877, p. 10, quotation from *McCulloch's Circular*.

[67] *Ibid.*, June 16, 1877, p. 13.

[68] XXVI (Investors Supplement, Jan. 26, 1878), iii.

Europe still holds our evidences of debt in very large amounts, and in moments of semi-panic all that are available will be forced upon us, at least so long as prices on this side are well sustained.[69]

British investment in American railway securities showed changes through the last three years of the decade. It reached a low point in 1877 and 1878. In the next year the City again became interested in speculative investments in American rails. Large blocks of railway shares moved to London and, through London, to the Continent.

Perhaps it is not stretching the facts to draw a parallel between the late 1840's, the late 1860's, and the years 1879–81. Each of these periods was characterized by a speculative movement of British capital into American railway shares. This seems logical, for in each of these periods, the American railways were working up steam for a new period of expansion. It is therefore natural that the speculative interest in the City, which would be the first to reenter the market, should concentrate on the purchase of shares. At the beginning of such an expansion, a greater appreciation can be expected in the price of shares than in the price of bonds. Later, when stories of the capital gains made by the City in American railway shares began to circulate, outside investors would be attracted. Thus, each of these periods of City speculation was followed, sooner or later, by a period in which a large number of American railway bond issues were offered for public subscription.

[To put investment of foreign funds in American railway securities in perspective and to evaluate the estimates made of them, consideration must be given to other aspects of the international movement of goods and of securities. The 1860's was a period of large issues of federal government bonds. The movement of such bonds to and from Europe during the 1860's and 1870's was significant, as were the changes in the balance of payments during this period. The price of railway securities in New York in terms of sterling exercised a stimulus on the demand for American securities.]

According to estimates of the Secretary of the Treasury, who usually erred on the conservative side, the amount of United States government bonds held in Europe declined rapidly in the 1870's. At the beginning of 1870 the total was approximately $1,000 million.[70] Later estimates, usually from the same source, indicate that the debt held abroad had fallen by January 1, 1871, to $845 million;[71] by 1876 to $600 million; and by the

[69] XXVII (Dec. 28, 1878), 663.

[70] This estimate was given by Secretary of the Treasury Sherman in a speech before the Senate on March 2, 1870. It is quoted in the *Economist*, XXXVIII (Oct. 9, 1880), 1171.

[71] This estimate was given by Jay Cooke, McCulloch & Co. It is quoted in Robert Lucas Nash (ed.), *Fenn's Compendium of the English and Foreign Funds* (12th ed.; London: Effingham Wilson, 1876), 470. The full tabulation (from *Times*, March 27, 1871, p. 7) is as follows:

middle of 1878 to $200–$250 million.[72] Moreover, at the beginning of 1879 the frequency of Treasury calls for redemption was intensified; bonds to the extent of $150 million were called in January 1879 alone.[73]

The estimates of the Secretary of Treasury on the repatriation of debt might give the wrong impression. The repatriation of federal debt would appear to be about $400 million in the period between 1870 and 1876 and a further $350–$400 million between 1876 and the middle of 1878. The inference might be drawn that because of their low rates of interest (5, 4½, and 4 percent) only a very small amount of the $853,200,000 of refunding bonds issued by the end of 1878 had been taken up in Europe.[74]

This was not true. In the summer of 1871, bankers in the United Kingdom and on the Continent, who were acting as agents of the United States Treasury in the sale of the New Funded Loan,[75] were notified that, because the balance had been taken up by a group of London bankers,[76] no more of the new 5 percent bonds were available. Moreover, at the beginning of the next year Jay Cooke, McCulloch and Company and also N. M. Rothschild and Sons offered for sale in London $300 million of the new 5 percent loan and $300 million of a new 4½ percent loan.[77] In 1877, when it appeared that Europeans were not purchasing refunding bonds and the

American bonds held in Europe, Jan. 1, 1871

Loan	Total	Held in Europe
Loan of 1858	$ 13,980,000	$ 12,000,000
Loan of 1861	5,032,000	1,000,000
Oregon War Loan	945,000	—
Loan of 1861	68,382,250	40,000,000
5–20 bonds of 1862	383,869,050	360,000,000
Loan of 1863	22,697,600	20,000,000
10–40 bonds of 1864	64,084,250	40,000,000
5–20 bonds of 1864	49,060,900	30,000,000
5–20 bonds of 1865	130,316,000	100,000,000
Consols of 1865	196,433,200	95,000,000
Consols of 1867	255,698,350	125,000,000
Consols of 1868	29,504,750	1,000,000
Total	$1,220,003,350	$824,000,000

In addition, it was stated that of a total of $715 million of inscribed bonds, the greater proportion, $699 million, was held in the United States, so that the grand total of American federal bonds held in Europe was taken to be $845 million.

[72] The figures for 1876 and for 1878 are from a speech by Secretary of the Treasury Sherman at Toledo, Ohio, on Aug. 26, 1878. They are quoted in the *Economist*, XXVIII (Oct. 9, 1880), 1171.

[73] *Commercial and Financial Chronicle*, XXVIII (Feb. 1, 1879), 105.

[74] *Ibid.* (Feb. 1, 1879), 114.

[75] The proceeds of this loan were to be used to call in a portion of the 5–20 bonds.

[76] *Times* (Aug. 12, 1871), 114.   [77] *Times* (Jan. 6, 1872), 7.

Secretary of the Treasury feared that this would result in a drain of gold that would interfere with the planned resumption of specie payments,[78] he made a successful attempt, through a syndicate, to place more of these bonds abroad.[79]

Early in 1879 Treasury calls for the redemption of federal bonds were sufficiently large to cause uneasiness in New York concerning the effect on the exchange rate, but the tension was eased by export of United States government bonds. The exchange rate in New York had been hovering about the specie shipping point in spite of large exports of grain to Europe. Then the market learned with relief that again a foreign syndicate had been formed to market the new federal refunding 4 percent loan in Europe. It consisted of N. M. Rothschild and Sons; J. S. Morgan and Company; Morton, Rose and Company; and Seligman Brothers.[80]

The figures for the United States' balance of trade occasioned doubt as to the Secretary of the Treasury's estimate of debt repatriation. It seems most improbable that the United States was able to repatriate $400 million of federal securities in the six years, 1870 through 1875, a period during which the balance of trade of the United States was adverse and a large sum had to be paid abroad for interest [see Table 5].[81] It is much more likely that the return of these federal bonds was concentrated in the latter part of the decade.

Meanwhile, in the early 1870's the United States was financing the deficit in its balance of payments on current account by sales of railway securities abroad. How great were these sales? For the total of American

[78] The prospectus for this loan announced that Rothschild, Morgan and associates offered bonds of the new U.S. 4 percent fundings issue totaling $700 million (of which $20 million had already been taken up in the United States) at £102 15s for each $500 bond. *Ibid.* (July 13, 1877), 11.

[79] Margaret Myers stated that: "As the date for the resumption of specie payments drew near the treasury began to hoard gold against the redemption of its notes. Gold bonds bearing 4 or 4½ per cent interest were issued at the rate of 5 millions each month during eight months of 1877 through a group of bankers in New York and London. This, with the surplus revenue, gave a coin reserve of 63 millions by the end of the year. During 1878 more bonds were issued and 50 millions of gold obtained in this way was added to the previous reserve. By the day of resumption the total reserve was more than 133 millions in gold coin." I, 362. [See also, Redlich, II, 357–69.]

[80] *Commercial and Financial Chronicle*, XXVIII (Jan. 25, 1879), 79.

[81] For the year ending July 30, 1869, the amount of federal securities held abroad was estimated at $900 million, and the amount of interest due abroad on federal securities for the year amounted to $65 million. *Times,* July 30, 1869, p. 4. In addition there was interest due on railway securities. Thus, David A. Wells put the total of interest due from the United States to Europe at $88 million in 1869. Wells, *Report of Special Commissioner of the Revenue* (1869), xxix, quoted in Charles J. Bullock, John H. Williams, and Rufus S. Tucker, "The Balance of Trade of the United States," *Review of Economic Statistics*, Preliminary Vol. I (1919), 223.

Table 5. United States balance-of-trade position, 1870–89
(in 1000's of dollars)

	A. On merchandise account		B. Total merchandise account including gold and silver	
Year	Export surplus	Import surplus	Export surplus	Import surplus
1865		72,717		14,883
1866		85,952		10,609
1867		101,255		62,457
1868		75,483	4,112	
1869		131,388		94,058
1870		43,186		11,450
1871		77,404		232
1872		182,417		116,284
1873		119,656		56,529
1874	18,877		57,052	
1875		19,562	51,669	
1876	79,644		120,213	
1877	151,152		166,540	
1878	257,814		261,733	
1879	264,661		269,363	
1880	167,684		91,793	
1881	259,712		168,544	
1882	25,902		32,848	
1883	100,658		103,990	
1884	72,816		102,523	
1885	164,663		163,651	
1886	44,089		77,958	
1887	23,863			310
1888		28,002		40,926
1889		2,731	64,948	

SOURCE: *Historical Statistics of the United States, 1789–1945*, 244.

railway securities held abroad in 1869, Margaret Myers gives the figure of $243 million.[82] This estimate seems low, although, of course, the great burst of European investment in American railways came after this date. For the end of 1870 Alexander K. Cairncross gives an estimate of £40 million for British investment in American railways.[83] He emphasizes the fact that this figure represents the market and not the face value of the British investment. His estimate would appear to be more reasonable.

[An understanding of the changes in the British holdings of American railway securities requires a consideration of the type of British investor as well as other influences.] The market value of British investment in American railways has been estimated at approximately £20 million at the beginning of the Civil War. It seems extremely doubtful that liquidation of

[82] Margaret Myers, I, 290.
[83] *Home and Foreign Investment, 1870–1913* (Cambridge: Cambridge University Press, 1953), Table 41, 183.

British holdings in 1862 was on the scale often assumed. A typical British investor of this period held large blocks of securities and looked to long-run appreciation. Moreover, he apparently was not easily panicked at disturbances in foreign financial centers. He was much more likely to sell in times of crisis in London and to sit tight in periods of crisis in the countries in which he invested. Even assuming that as much as one quarter of British investment in American rails was liquidated in 1862, an increase of £25 million in British holdings between 1861 and the end of 1870 is not unlikely. There was some investment in American rails from the end of 1864 to the crisis of 1866. And, most important, as the position of the United States currency improved, the capital gains on these securities were large. Moreover, although the boom in public issues of American railway securities in London did not begin until about 1872, speculative capital seems to have been moving into American rails from the beginning of 1869. Nor must it be forgotten that fairly large amounts of British capital went into the Atlantic and Great Western and into Erie shares during this period.

Accepting Cairncross's figures of £40 million for the market value of British holdings of American railway securities at the end of 1870, the question of the increase in British holdings during the 1870's remains. Margaret Myers gave the estimate of $375 million for the amount of American securities held abroad in 1876, but another source gives that figure for two years earlier, and it appears to be too low for the face value of the investment.[84] It seems more likely that British investment in American railways reached almost £100 million by the end of 1876. During the years 1872 through 1876 there was an extensive movement of British capital into this field. Indeed, the face value of the numerous American railway issues offered publicly in London during the years 1871 through 1876 totaled over £60 million. Of course, part of the securities so offered was taken upon the Continent. Moreover, the actual amount of foreign investment represented by these loans was less than their face value because most American railway bonds were marketed at a discount in this period. On the other hand, a number of issues were handled privately.[85] Although traces of these loans are to be found, it is difficult to determine their amounts.[86]

---

[84] Margaret Myers, I, 290, gives as a source for the figure for 1876 the *New York Journal of Commerce* (Dec. 6, 1911). In fact, this figure appeared in the *Commercial and Financial Chronicle*, XIX (Oct. 10, 1874), 363. There is in the article no indication of the exact date to which this estimate is supposed to refer. However, from the use of this estimate it can be inferred that it is for the face value of foreign holdings of American railway securities.

[85] However, the practice of putting American railway bonds out privately was probably less common in this period than in the 1850's.

[86] Besides issues put out privately, a good example of which is the CC&IC issues discussed above on p. 79, n. 49, London banking houses acquired some issues of American railway bonds as a result of hypothecation. Thus, in 1879

If British investment in American railways at the end of 1876 is taken as £100 million, it may be questioned whether this is also a reasonable estimate for 1879. In that year there was a renewed movement of American railway securities from New York to London.

During the second half of the 1870's the United States exported grain to Europe on an enormous scale; thus, during the six years from 1876 through 1881, it piled up a favorable balance of trade on merchandise account, totaling $1,180,667,000.[87] A large proportion of this favorable balance was offset by the return of federal government securities to the United States. Repeatedly the public press emphasized that the bonds being returned to the United States were government bonds.[88] There was also some repatriation of railway securities to New York; Erie shares figured largely among these.[89] The question to be decided is whether or not the net return of railway securities during the later part of the 1870's was a significant amount.

Beginning in 1878 various American entrepreneurs began to take bankrupt lines in hand and to reorganize and complete them.[90] In some cases British bondholders were doing the same with the American railways into which they had put their money.[91] Regardless of the nationality of these entrepreneurs, reorganization required capital. This was supplied originally by short-term credits.[92] Much of this was obtained in the United States, which currently had idle money available not only in New York [93]

Baring Bros. held $6 million of the bonds of the Illinois Midland, which we learn about only because they became the subject of a lawsuit. *Commercial and Financial Chronicle*, XXIX (Aug. 30, 1879), 225.

[87] If movements of gold and silver are added in, this surplus is slightly lower.

[88] See, for example, the *Times*, Aug. 29, 1878, p. 7; Dec. 28, 1878, p. 4; and Jan. 3, 1879, p. 8.

[89] At first this was thought to be a move on the part of the New Yorkers hostile to the Reconstruction Plan. *Ibid.*, Aug. 22, 1877, p. 7. By 1879 the *Times* thought that New Yorkers must own a controlling majority. March 12, 1879, p. 13. Later in the year it was advising British investors to get rid of these securities while the opportunity presented itself. Nov. 18, 1879, p. 7.

[90] *McCulloch's Circular* said that a class of private bankers, more or less associated with corporate undertakings, together with their wealthy clients, had taken control of a number of railways and were introducing the securities of these rejuvenated and reconstructed railways onto the market. These securities seemed to be going into the hands of permanent investors, and large profits were being made on the transactions by the banking houses and their associates. Quoted in the *Times*, May 30, 1879, p. 7.

[91] See below, pp. 121–39.

[92] American railways during the nineteenth century often initially financed their operations by short-term credits until successful in marketing a bond issue. The fight of British investors to control the contraction of floating debt by the railways in which they invested began in the 1850's with the Illinois Central.

[93] In 1878 the *Times* noted that Americans were taking home bonds but leaving call money in London because of the extreme dullness of the American money market. Sept. 9, 1878, p. 7.

but also in cities like Chicago, where businessmen were making profits from the export of grain.[94] However, in the late 1870's, funds were virtually unlendable in London, although it is possible some credits were obtained there.[95] The repatriation of railway securities was probably not on a large scale and was offset, at least to some extent, by short-term credits from London to American railways and by the small amount of rentier investment that continued throughout this period.[96] It is the author's impression that there was only a small net repatriation of railway securities to America. The figure of £100 million is certainly not too high for the market value of British investment in American railways in 1879.

The total British investment continued to grow. In late 1879 and 1880 arbitrage dealers were already moving large blocks of American railway shares to London.[97] There were also a few new issues in these two years. R. L. Nash gives the figure of £100 million as a minimum estimate of total holdings in 1881, but it would appear that this figure is much too low.[98]

Regardless of the exact total, what were the general characteristics of this new burst of British investment in American railway securities? In particular, in what ways does it differ from the similar boom period of the early 1850's?

For the British investors, several decades were characterized by difficulties that led to new approaches in meeting them. In the 1860's the involvement was with the Atlantic and Great Western and the Erie. Difficulties with these two roads continued through the 1870's, and the proliferation of committees and the conflicts of interest that emerged may go far to explain the readiness with which British investors accepted the "friendly reorganizations" of the 1880's and of the 1890's. The collapse of the Reading in the early 1880's, a collapse that would probably have overtaken the road in the 1870's but for the support of McCalmont Brothers, only served to underline the lessons of the Erie and the Atlantic and Great Western.

[94] *Ibid.*, Oct. 10, 1879, p. 5, quotation from *McCulloch's Circular.*

[95] *Ibid.*, April 18, 1879, p. 6. The supposition that some short-term funds were obtained in London is reinforced by the journeys to London in the late 1870's of the presidents of railways that were becoming known as British favorites. For example, in 1878 H. Victor Newcomb returned from London where he had been engaged in important financial negotiations with Barings concerning the floating debt of the Louisville and Nashville, of which he was the president. In March 1879 Thomas Scott of the Pennsylvania was in London. In July of the same year Alexander Mitchell of the Chicago, Milwaukee and Saint Paul traveled to England. Several other instances can be cited.

[96] Throughout this period there were complaints of the dearth of good investment opportunities in London. Good bonds became so scarce that the *Times* remarked that investors were even beginning to consider taking American refunding 4 percent bonds. *Ibid.*, July 8, 1879, p. 11.

[97] See below, p. 153.

[98] *A Short Inquiry into the Profitable Nature of Our Investments* (3d ed.; London: Effingham Wilson, 1881), 129.

Meanwhile, having avoided investment in the bonds of the new midwestern roads, which were taken in Germany and Holland instead, London began a new boom in American securities in the early 1870's. In this case, the emphasis was on the senior securities of established roads. This may have been partly a virtue of necessity; the reputation of all American railways had been seriously damaged by the Atlantic and Great Western and the Erie scandals, to say nothing of the defaults that were already being made in bond issues taken on the Continent. More important, some of the large Anglo-American houses, such as Morton, Rose [99] and J. S. Morgan,[100] as well as other persons connected with the American market, made a determined and concerted attempt to attract the rentier investor and thus to broaden the market for American railway securities in London.

A number of devices were employed to enhance the attractiveness of American railway securities. All of these were in the nature of guarantees. Guarantees were not new. In the 1850's the Pennsylvania had subscribed to issues of its western connections and appears to have lent them moral support in the flotation of loans in London.[101] The Camden and Amboy went further and actually endorsed $500,000 of bonds for the Belvidere and Delaware Railroad Company in 1853.[102] The Illinois Central guaranteed the first-mortgage bonds of the Peoria and Oquawka.[103]

However, in the 1870's, unconditional guarantees became much more common. The big roads were no longer relying on loose ties with their connections. By consolidations and leases, they were building up the systems that we know today. Under these conditions, guarantees became less dangerous for the guarantor. The Pennsylvania and the Illinois Central also used a form of guarantee based on a traffic agreement, which, though in no sense unconditional, may have appeared so to the British investors.[104]

One new form of guarantee appears to have originated about this time. This was endorsement of bond issues by the merchant banking house through which they were put out. This device was not known in the 1850's, although, on occasion, banking houses did advance funds for the payment of coupons to railways whose bonds they had issued. In any case, it was much less common in the 1850's for a public loan to be floated by a merchant banking house. Banks and a few merchant banking houses occasionally lent their names to American railway issues; [105] but usually

[99] The principal partners in this firm were Levi P. Morton, later U.S. Ambassador to France and, after that, Vice-President of the United States; Sir John Rose, formerly a member of the Macdonald-Cartier ministry in Canada; and Pascoe Du Pré Grenfell.

[100] This house is the successor to George Peabody and Co.

[101] See above, p. 58–59.   [102] Muriel Hidy, "George Peabody," 348.

[103] *Daily News*, Feb. 2, 1858, p. 7.   [104] See above, p. 77, n. 46.

[105] For example, the Erie loan of 1852 was put out in the names of Heywood, Kennard, bankers, and Foster and Braithwaite, stockbrokers, and a loan for the

when a merchant banking house was unable to place bonds privately, it employed a stockbroking firm to do so.[106] Thus, the name of the merchant banking house concerned was seldom publicly connected with the issue, and the merchant banking houses were free from moral responsibility in case of default.

By the 1870's this situation had radically altered. Most American railway securities were now marketed through merchant banking houses,[107] although stockbrokers were often associated with them in the venture. The fact that merchant banking houses were now willing to lend their names to American railway issues may be evidence of a desire to increase marketability of these issues by contributing a reputation of respectability and solidity. Moreover, having once lent their name to an issue, the merchant banking houses may have felt that endorsement added little more to their responsibility yet greatly added to the marketability of a loan.[108] However, not all merchant banking houses endorsed the issues that they marketed. Even Morton, Rose and J. S. Morgan, who took the lead in the use of the endorsement device, did not endorse all the issues they handled. Endorsement was usually reserved for the bonds of established railways.

Chicago and Rock Island was put out by Masterman, Peters, bankers, and Foster and Braithwaite, stockbrokers. *Economist,* X (June 26, 1852), 724; *Daily News,* Jan. 18, 1853, p. 1.

[106] Exceptions to delegating the marketing function to a stockbroking firm are: the loan of the Erie of 1852 for which Brown, Shipley and Heywood, Kennard acted as joint trustees; the loan of the Illinois Central of 1852, which was put out directly by the merchant banking house of Devaux and Co. and for which the trustees were William Brown, M.P. for South Lancashire; J. P. Heywood, of Heywood, Kennard & Co.; T. Smith, Deputy Chairman of the London and North Western Railway; and M. Uzielli of Devaux and Co. *Economist,* X (June 5, 1852), 628–29. In 1856 bonds of the New Orleans, Jackson and Great Northern Railroad Co. were issued by J. Henry Schroeder and Co., agents, and Cazenove and Co., brokers; and bonds of the Chicago, St. Paul and Fond du Lac were put out by Page, Bacon and Co., and William Lance, stockbroker. *Daily News,* Aug. 21, 1856, p. 1, and Dec. 29, 1856, p. 1. And in 1858 an issue for the Raritan and Delaware Bay was put out through Dent, Palmer and Lewis R. Haslewood, stockbroker. *Ibid.,* May 24, 1858, p. 1. However, certain merchant banking houses, such as Barings, Rothchilds, and McCalmonts among others, never allowed their names to appear on a prospectus for an American railway loan.

[107] Rothchilds was the only merchant banking house interested in American railways that was not undertaking the public issue of these loans on the London market in the 1870's.

[108] In some cases an extra charge was made for endorsement. In 1874, a letter to the *Times* complained that the bonds of the Chicago and North Western, which the Railway Share and Trust Co. was offering at £188 per $1,000 bond, could be purchased in New York for £174 per $1,000 bond. The Railway Share and Trust Co. replied that the extra charge was made for their endorsement, which assured that the bonds would be paid in sterling. March 7, 1874, p. 7, and March 24, 1874, p. 13.

Another method of attracting the investor was the establishment of investment trust companies. This device provided the possibility of higher rates of return on American railway securities, while spreading risks. Except for the International Financial Society, which dated from the early 1860's and was set up as a financial company, not an investment trust, the first of these new institutions was the Foreign and Colonial Government Trust established in 1868.[109] This company was very successful and soon had a number of imitators.[110] In 1873 the five trustees of the Foreign and Colonial Government Trust set up the first trust company specifically devoted to investment in American railway securities, the American Investment Trust.[111] It was, in effect, an extention of their field of activity to take advantage of the new interest in American railway securities beginning in 1872.

The number of such trusts soon increased. Within a few weeks of the organization of the American Investment Trust two other groups had brought out the Anglo-American Railroad Mortgage Trust [112] and the Railway Debenture Investment Trust.[113] In April the most famous of all these companies, the Scottish American Investment Trust, was inaugurated.[114] Of all these trusts this was the only one that could appeal to the small investor. All the others issued shares of £100, and their primary purpose must have been the spreading of risk.

Except for the Anglo-American Railroad Mortgage Trust, all these companies were highly successful. The record of the Scottish American was

[109] *Ibid.*, March 20, 1868, p. 10.

[110] By 1872 the *Times* was complaining that the imitation mania that had preceded 1866 was getting under way again. Feb. 22, 1872, p. 7.

[111] The five trustees were: Lord Westbury; Lord Eustace Cecil, M.P.; G. M. W. Sandford, M.P.; G. W. Currie; and Philip Rose. Philip Rose, it should be noted, was not a member of the firm of Morton, Rose and Co. but of a firm of lawyers.

[112] The trustees of the Anglo-American Railroad Mortgage Trust included: Sir Sill John Gibbons, Alderman of London; Sir Charles W. Wentworth Fitzwilliam, M.P.; Andrew Johnston, M.P.; and Richard B. Martin, banker. The certificate holders included Sir Charles E. Lewis, M.P. for Londonderry, and John Cater. The committee in New York included: Philo C. Calhoun, president of the Fourth National Bank; Henry Clews; and William Lamont Taylor, banker. The bankers to the company were Martin & Co., of whom one member was a trustee.

[113] The trustees of the Railway Debenture Investment Trust included: Sir Samuel Laing; Hon. Arthur Kinnaird, M.P.; George Leeman; J. Horatio Lloyd; Philip Rose; Sir Edward Watkin; George Edward Wythes; and Sir William Morris.

[114] The trustees of the Scottish American Investment Trust were: James S. Fleming, cashier of the Royal Bank of Scotland; James Syne, manager, British Linen Co.; W. J. Duncan, manager, National Bank of Scotland; and William Thomas Thomson, manager, Standard Life Assurance Co. [See also, W. Turrentine Jackson, *The Enterprising Scot: Investors in the American West after 1873* (Edinburgh: Edinburgh University Press, 1968), 13 ff.]

outstanding.[115] However, this general success was not merely a matter of careful investment. Most of these companies also engaged in various other financial operations. They not only undertook the flotation of American railway shares but also bought and sold on such short terms that their operations came perilously close to the borderline of speculation. Nevertheless, the investors were highly satisfied with the returns. The trustees also profited, especially from the founders' shares.[116] Moreover, there were also intangible profits. The group of men who made up the trustees of these various companies became a power in the City.

In conclusion, while the bulk of the investment in American railway securities during the early 1870's was concentrated on solid, senior securities, it must not be inferred that Britain was supplying none of the growth capital of which American railways were still in need. This was indeed going on behind the scenes.[117] Just as the surface impression of the 1860's is one of almost frantic speculation, the surface impression of the 1870's is one of solid conservative investment.

The discussion in the two following chapters centers on other aspects of the export of British capital in the decades following 1860. The first one considers the speculative investment in the Atlantic and Great Western and in the Erie. The second deals with a number of American railways where British investment was followed by British active participation.

[115] Various calculations have been made of the returns of the Scottish American Investment Trust since its founding in 1873. Suffice to say that the company's first issue paid a steady 10 percent.

[116] Founders' shares are shares taken at a nominal price, say £5, by a group of persons who guarantee that the capital will be fully subscribed. After the ordinary shareholders have been paid a certain return out of the year's income, founders' shares, which represent only a small investment, are entitled to participate with the ordinary shares in the distribution of the residue.

[117] For example, the city of Glasgow took bonds in the Western Union Railroad, a subsidiary of the Chicago, Milwaukee and St. Paul. *Commercial and Financial Chronicle*, XXX (April 17, 1880), 384.

V

The Erie and
the Atlantic and Great Western

FROM the point of view of the British investor in American railroads, the entire decade of the 1860's was dominated by the Atlantic and Great Western and the Erie [railroads which for some time continued to be a central feature of the American investment market]. This in itself would not be sufficient reason for dealing at length with the rather lurid histories of these companies.[1] However, as Leland H. Jenks has said, "Without McHenry and his road, the story of the finance companies and their crisis would be Hamlet without the King of Denmark." [2] The story of James McHenry's relationships with various British banks and financial companies was complex. Since several of these failed in 1866, his share of responsibility for the financial disaster that overtook the City in that year is equally involved.[3]

The story of the internecine struggle between conflicting British interests on the Erie and the Atlantic and Great Western is no less troubled. Only once or twice is there public record of such a decided split between contending groups of British investors in American railways. The most important occurred over the Philadelphia and Reading Railroad in the early 1880's, when a battle broke out between the company's president,

[1] Among the most famous of the writings on the Erie are Charles Francis Adams, Jr.'s "A Chapter of Erie" and "An Erie Raid," which appeared in the *North American Review*, CIX (July 1869), 30–106, and CXII (April 1871), 241–91. These two articles are reprinted in Hicks. Albert Stickney's article dealing specifically with the difficulties of the Erie's British shareholders was "The Erie Railway and the English Stock," *American Law Review*, VI (Jan. 1872), 230–54. The best history of the Erie is Mott's *Between the Ocean and the Lakes: The Story of Erie*. An account of the struggle by which James McHenry ousted the original American interest and secured control of the Atlantic and Great Western is in Felton.

[2] *The Migration of British Capital to 1875* (New York: Alfred A. Knopf, 1927), 255.

[3] James McHenry was not the only railway financier whose operations contributed to the crisis of 1866. John Watson was actually the first to fail, and four or five others followed.

Franklin Gowen, and its London banker, McCalmont Brothers.[4] Since Gowen was able to rally considerable support among British bond- and shareholders, this altercation also became a public scandal. Backing Gowen against McCalmont, James McHenry was tangentially involved.[5]

After these disastrous battles, the British investors seem to have learned to stand together. Such differences as inevitably arose were smoothed over.[6] The difficulties encountered in satisfying the claims of the various classes of security holders on the Atlantic and Great Western may have accounted, at least in part, for another development: the British investors appear to have welcomed the "friendly reorganizations" of railways characteristic of the late 1880's and early 1890's.

As New York's first through line to the West,[7] the New York and Lake Erie Railroad was an early favorite but soon suffered financial difficulties. Although the road received a grant of $3 million from New York State,[8] it was handicapped from the beginning by precarious finances. The New York and Lake Erie underwent its first reorganization as early as 1845.[9] By 1851, the year of the triumphal opening to Dunkirk on Lake Erie, the line's some 470 miles already carried a floating debt of slightly over $3 million, stock amounting to $6 million, and a bonded debt of $14 million.[10]

It seems likely that some Erie obligations had been finding their way to

[4] McCalmont Bros. had long been intimately connected with the Reading. At first this firm shared this interest with Gihon and Co. of New York. However, in 1857, Gihon and Co. failed. As a result, the president of the Reading, Mr. Tucker of Gihon and Co., resigned and was replaced by a Mr. Cullen, formerly of McCalmont Bros. President Cullen is said to have followed in the footsteps of his predecessor and to have speculated too heavily. When McCalmont Bros. learned of this the firm deposed him and made C. E. Smith president in his place. When Smith resigned, because of ill health, Franklin Gowen, attorney for the Reading, became president. During this period the Reading shares were believed to have been almost entirely held in England, and the firm of McCalmont Bros. was said to hold $12 million of these, while three of the McCalmonts' brothers-in-law were said to hold a further $2 million. S. F. Van Oss, *American Railroads as Investments* (London: Effingham, Wilson and Co., 1893), 317–19.

[5] Since James McHenry was at this time in league with William H. Vanderbilt, it is possible that he had some influence in throwing the weight of Vanderbilt's support to Gowen. On the other hand, McHenry was, by the 1880's, fairly thoroughly discredited, and it is doubtful whether his wishes would have carried much weight. There is no indication that McHenry's action was motivated by enmity for McCalmont Bros.

[6] For example, a dissentient group of British holders of Wabash shares was conciliated. Nevertheless, the story of the Wabash provides another parallel.

[7] The New York Central was not projected as a through line to the West. It was formed by the amalgamation of a number of short local lines.

[8] Mott, 48–51.   [9] *Ibid.*, 79.

[10] The bonded debt consisted of $3 million of mortgage bonds issued in lieu of the state loan of $3 million, a second mortgage of $4 million, an issue of $3.5 million of income bonds put out in 1850, and an issue of $3.5 million of convertible mortgage bonds put out early in 1851. *American Railroad Journal*, XXIV (Feb. 22, 1851), 117.

London from the late 1840's. Ward and Company was reported to have been a successful bidder for a large amount of the income bonds issued in 1850.[11] This was probably in conjunction with Rothschild, since Baring Brothers remained firm in its refusal to undertake the negotiation of any securities of this road.[12]

The first public offering of Erie bonds in London was made in 1852. It was a portion of $2.5 million of the $3.5 million issue negotiated in New York the previous year.[13] Although these were unsecured debenture bonds, an impressive list of backers lent their names to this issue. Heywood, Kennard acted as banker and, together with Brown, Shipley, as trustee. Foster and Braithwaite was the broker. Rothschilds was also reported to be pushing Erie bonds.[14]

From this time on Erie securities were readily taken up in London.[15] Moreover, the railway was only too pleased to oblige with further issues. A third mortgage for $10 million (of which $4 million was reserved to retire the outstanding second mortgage) was floated in 1853.[16] Most of those bonds taken in London were sold privately; but in the summer of 1854 E. F. Satterthwaite was advertising $500,000 of them at 81.[17] It is typical of Erie finance that even while the third-mortgage bonds were being marketed in London, a further loan was being planned in New York. Like the income bonds and the various issues of convertible mortgage bonds, these new ones were unsecured. A sinking fund provision was added to give an appearance of security.[18] [Daniel Drew was elected treasurer in 1854,

[11] This sale took place on May 12, 1850. Ward and Co.'s bids were for $1,250,000 at 90 and $1,250,000 at 85½. All bids above 90 were accepted, and bidders at 90 were awarded two-thirds the amount of the total for which they bid.

[12] Ralph Hidy, *House of Baring,* 410.

[13] The prospectus stated that these bonds were part of an issue of $3.5 million, so they must be part of the issue put out in 1851 and not part of that put out in 1852, which was for $3 million. According to the report of the sales of the first issue of convertible Erie bonds the average price was 90. *American Railroad Journal,* XXIV (March 15, 1851), 168. The report of the sale of the second issue included a long list of bidders; the largest were Ward and Co., with a bid for $1 million, and T. J. Townsend for $800,000. Bidders for $100,000 were fairly numerous. *Ibid.,* XXV (Jan. 17, 1852), 40.

[14] Ralph Hidy, *House of Baring,* 410.

[15] After the first public sale of Erie securities in June 1852, the *Daily News* reprinted the following report from the *New York Tribune:* "It is probable that a further sale of 500,000 dols. of the convertibles of 1862 has been made in London, as a party had an option of that amount at a price below the last quotations. If not sold, a continental house here has made an offer for them equally as good for the owner." Aug. 31, 1852, p. 7.

[16] *American Railroad Journal,* XXVI (March 19, 1853), 177–82.

[17] *Railway Times,* June 10, 1854, p. 593.

[18] This loan was for $4 million. Subscriptions could be paid one half in the income bonds issued in 1850 and due in 1855. These bonds were advertised for sale in the *American Railroad Journal,* XXVII (Oct. 28, 1854), 685, and on Feb. 1, 1855, the *Railway Times* reported that they had been taken at 80.

largely as a result of having endorsed $980,000 of the Erie's paper.] [19]

A large part of the unsecured Erie bonds held by the British were eventually exchanged for bonds of the fourth and fifth mortgages. Charles Moran, a New York broker who was voted president of the Erie in 1857 largely because of his success in raising funds abroad,[20] traveled to London in 1858 to negotiate a fourth mortgage. The British and Continental holders of unsecured Erie loans, anxious about the company's financial position, exacted the right to subscribe to the fourth-mortgage bonds, one half in unsecured bonds and one half in cash. In addition, they insisted on the right to convert the remainder of their unsecured bonds (to an amount not to exceed $3 million) into a fifth mortgage.[21] The advantage to the foreign holders was considerable. Although it would seem that only $1,253,000 of unsecured bonds were exchanged into fifth-mortgage bonds, these were all held in Europe, and it was under this mortgage that the Erie soon was foreclosed and reorganized.[22]

The New York and Lake Erie Railroad emerged from its second reorganization as the Erie Railway in December 1861, and throughout the Civil War its career was relatively prosperous and unmarred by scandal. Potentially, the situation was explosive, for the reorganization did not displace Daniel Drew, who had been manipulating Erie securities, from his official position as treasurer.[23] Moreover, Cornelius Vanderbilt had become a director of the line just before the reorganization.

The struggles over the Erie, for all their lunatic aspect so well brought out in Charles Francis Adams's "Chapter of Erie" and "An Erie Raid," were not as completely irrational as might appear. They were partly a struggle for the control of the railway traffic of New York.[24] [In 1867 Cornelius Vanderbilt, already president of the two roads from New York to Albany (the Harlem Railroad and the Hudson River Railroad) gained control of

[19] [See Mott, 115. See also Julius Grodinsky, *Jay Gould, His Business Career, 1867–1892* (Philadelphia: University of Pennsylvania Press, 1957), 27 ff., esp. 28–29.]

[20] Charles Moran and L. von Hoffman (Von Hoffman was the New York house with which the London Erie Shareholders' Committee dealt in the late 1860's) were elected to the Erie's Board of Directors out of deference to the foreign holders in late 1854. *American Railroad Journal*, XXVII (Oct. 14, 1854), 648.

[21] Mott, 127–29. The total of this loan was $6 million. Since $3 million of the unsecured bonds could be funded into a fourth and $3 million into a fifth mortgage, $4 million of unsecured bonds were thus left unprovided for. When the Erie was foreclosed in 1859, the amount of unexchanged, unsecured bonds plus the interest due on them amounted to $7,825,150.

[22] *Ibid.*, 135. The purchasers of the Erie were the unsecured bondholders, who became preference shareholders in the new company, and the common shareholders assented to the reorganization within six months.

[23] *Ibid.*, 115.

[24] [For an account of the rivalry of railways, read Grodinsky, 38–49 and 58, and Alvin F. Harlow's *The Road of the Century* (New York: Creative Age Press, 1947), 191–95.]

the New York Central long led by Erastus Corning. Vanderbilt became president of the consolidated road, renamed the New York Central and Hudson River Railroad, which, like the Erie, ran from New York to Lake Erie.] [25] He apparently wanted control of the Erie to reinforce his railroads' position. It was the way in which the wars were fought out, on the stock exchange, in the law courts, in the New York State Legislature, and on the railways themselves, that provided the bizarre aspects that captured the public's imagination.

On Wall Street, Vanderbilt was able to rally the support of a number of foreign bankers, particularly August Belmont, agent of the Rothschilds. The British were building up their holdings of Erie shares at the low prices resulting from bear raids.[26] To some extent this persistent buying from London may have obscured the effect of the railroad's new large issue of shares. Early in 1868 it was suspected that Daniel Drew, Jay Gould [a stockbroker and speculator who had joined the Erie as a director in 1867], and [his associate and soon fellow director] James Fisk had been manipulating the market with shares obtained by converting convertible bonds acquired in payment of supposed loans to the railway.[27] On October 26, 1868, a committee of the stock exchange questioned Gould [recently elected president of the railway]. Only then, when he admitted that the Erie common stock had been increased from $11 million (110,000 shares) to $39.5 million (395,000 shares), did outsiders gain any idea of the extent of his operations.[28]

August Belmont immediately filed a suit charging Gould and Fisk with the illegal creation of 58,000 shares.[29] Gould, getting wind of this development, arranged for the railway to be put into receivership. Belmont's suit bogged down in the welter of injunctions and cross injunctions, suits and countersuits characteristic of the struggle for the Erie. What the courts were not able to accomplish, the New York Stock Exchange did. Belmont and Drew persuaded its Board of Brokers to pass a resolution not to deal in

[25] Vanderbilt got his start in steamboats. He purchased railroad stock and starting in 1857 got control of his first railway, the New York and Harlem Railroad. He then took over the Hudson River Railroad. [See Neu, 182–85, and Wheaton J. Lane, *Commodore Vanderbilt: An Epic of the Steam Age* (New York: Alfred A. Knopf, 1942), 184–259.]

[26] Erie shares amounted to 111,000 on its reorganization in 1861. By Oct. 26, 1868, they had been increased to 395,000. According to the annual report of Sept. 30, 1869, the total of common stock was then $78,536,910 (approximately 785,000 shares). Mott, 136, 163, 176. Of the 785,000 shares outstanding on Sept. 30, 1869, the British were estimated to hold 450,000. Stickney, 237.

[27] Early in 1868 Vanderbilt was threatening to get an order to seize the Erie to prevent Jay Gould from converting more convertible bonds. At this point Drew, Gould, and Fisk fled to New Jersey. *Times*, March 20, 1868, p. 9.

[28] Mott, 163. At this interview Gould not only admitted the conversion of $5 million of convertible bonds, bringing the total of stock outstanding to $39.5 million, but said that construction on the Erie might necessitate further operations of this nature.

[29] *Times*, Dec. 4, 1869, p. 8 (from Philadelphia, Nov. 20, 1868).

Erie shares after January 30, 1869, unless the registry books were deposited in the safekeeping of a reputable bank.[30] Gould was forced to capitulate, and the books were deposited with the Farmers' Loan and Trust Company.

British shareholders now determined on the establishment of a Shareholders' Protective Committee to fight Gould at the next Erie elections.[31] At first the attitude of the Erie board toward this move was one of contempt. The shareholders' first meeting was in May 1869; the next month they appointed a London Committee to represent them.[32] Although the revelation that more than $50 million of the Erie's stock was in foreign hands must have come as a shock to Gould, he contrived to turn this situation to his advantage. It enabled him to use the threat of British control to get the New York State Legislature to pass a number of laws.[33] Among them was the Classification Act. It provided that, in order to give continuity to the Erie's management, the directors elected at the next meeting should be classified into five groups, only one-fifth to retire in any one year.[34] Meanwhile, in order to prevent the British shareholders' representatives from voting at the next meeting, the Erie board announced that since the London Committee of the shareholders had stamped shares to show that an assessment of one shilling had been paid, these shares had been defaced and were not legal. Therefore, none of them could be transferred into the name of the Shareholders' Protective Committee, and none of them could be voted.[35]

[30] [Daniel Drew had defected from his associates in 1868. Mott, 155.]

[31] The first meeting of residents of Great Britain interested in the Erie was in May 1869, and those attending included: William Brown, Lichfield; C. Borthwick, Austinfriars, London; Thomas Thomasson, Glasgow; H. J. Trotter, Bishop Auckland; J. S. Stett, Liverpool; Henry Rawson, Manchester; A. G. Dallas, London; and James Watson, Glasgow. At this meeting it was decided that all who wished to cooperate should send their names to J. Denman, 5 Austinfriars. *Times,* May 10, 1869, p. 7.

[32] In June a London Committee representing shareholders was appointed. It consisted of Henri Bischoffsheim, Robert A. Heath, and E. F. Satterthwaite. It was decided that an assessment of one shilling per share should be paid, and that Glyn, Mills would be the banker for receiving this assessment. *Ibid.,* June 19, 1869, p. 12. Thus, the powers of the City took over what began as a movement by smaller firms and investors.

[33] Stickney, 239. In May 1869 Gould got the New York Legislature to pass an act providing that no officer, director, or stockholder of the New York Central, the Hudson River, or the New York and Harlem could be an officer of the Erie. The act requiring all officers of the New York railways to be residents of New York had been passed previously. In fact, Gould did not rely entirely on persuasion of the New York Legislature, nor did Vanderbilt, but Gould was supposed to be more adept at its manipulation than Vanderbilt.

[34] The Classification Act was passed in May 1869.

[35] *Times,* Oct. 18, 1869, p. 5. John Swann, the representative of the Erie Shareholders' Protective Committee, attended this meeting but was unable to vote because the shares had not been transferred into the name of Heath and Raphael. Swann, a graduate of Oxford, later served as president of the Alabama

The representatives in New York of the London Committee concentrated their efforts on two objectives; the repeal of the Classification Act and the transfer of shares deposited with the London Committee to Heath and Raphael to act with power of attorney.[36] As a first installment, 60,000 British-owned shares were sent to the Erie office for transfer. Gould countered by having a receiver appointed for these shares;[37] the matter was soon straightened out by their return to L von Hoffmann and Company, the depositary for the London Committee.

However, when these 60,000 shares were examined, it was discovered that half of them had been canceled.[38] Moreover, Gould had issued new certificates in their place in order to further his stock market operations, which had been held in check since his deposit of the Erie books with the Farmers' Loan and Trust Company.[39] The attention of the London Committee representatives was now diverted to the task of securing replacement of these shares. Gould volunteered to do so provided that he was allowed to issue 30,000 additional shares.[40] The London representatives maintained that he should be compelled to enter the market and purchase shares at the prevailing price.[41] Indignation in London reached a high pitch. The Erie Shareholders' Protective Committee had found it impossible to dislodge Gould by using orthodox methods.

Just at this time the Atlantic and Great Western, which had been leased to the Erie in 1869, was finally wrested from Gould's control as discussed below. James McHenry was the hero of the hour. He had fought Gould and won, and had succeeded where the London Committee of Erie stockholders had failed.[42] In October 1871 James McHenry had returned to London from New York. Shortly afterward, Henri Bischoffsheim [partner in Bischoffsheim and Goldschmidt, specialists in railway securities] resigned from the London Committee for Erie investors and joined McHenry. The latter inserted an advertisement in the press asking Erie shareholders to transfer their shares from the London Committee to him.[43] James McHenry had decided to take over the Erie.

The relationship of James McHenry and the Atlantic and Great Western

---

Great Southern. He was also active in the interests of the British investors on other American railways.

[36] At the beginning of 1870, 105,000 shares deposited with the London Committee had been sent to Devon, Hoffman and Co. in New York for registration in the name of Heath and Raphael, and a further 84,000 were being prepared to be sent from London. *Ibid.*, Feb. 9, 1870, p. 10.

[37] *Ibid.*, June 28, 1870, p. 10.   [38] Stickney, 247.

[39] Gould and Fisk had used these 30,000 shares to convert more convertible bonds and had sold the shares on the market.

[40] *Times*, July 20, 1871, p. 7.

[41] *Ibid.*, Aug. 22, 1871, p. 8. In fact, however, Gould ultimately got a decision that since the shares had been used to convert convertible bonds, they were legally issued, and that it was therefore legal for a further 30,000 of shares to be issued. Stickney, 247.

[42] *Times*, Dec. 11, 1871, p. 7; see below, pp. 112–13.

[43] *Ibid.*, Dec. 13, 1871, p. 7; Dec. 20, 1871, p. 7.

is the background for the later history of the Erie and its security holders. McHenry was the son of an Irish poet and novelist who emigrated to the United States in 1817. In his youth, McHenry returned to the British Isles, set up as a grain merchant in Liverpool and, in spite of an early bankruptcy, quickly gained a place for himself. In the 1840's he was credited with having suggested to Sir Robert Peel the possibility of importing corn from the United States to relieve the Irish famine.[44]

McHenry's first connection with the Atlantic and Great Western came in the late 1850's, when he was commissioned to purchase the rails for the road.[45] This appointment seems to have been conditioned on his getting the support of the Duke of Salamanca and other Spanish bankers.[46] H. W. Kennard of the Liverpool banking house Heywood, Kennard and Company was also involved in the Atlantic and Great Western from its earliest days. McHenry seems to have become the real promoter behind the railway, and the first issue of the company's bonds sent to England was consigned to him.[47] In September 1860 the £200,000 of 7 percent first-mortgage bonds on the New York section of the road were advertised in London.[48] The prospectus announced Worthy S. Streator and José de Salamanca as the contractors of the company[49] and Thomas W. Kennard, a member of the Liverpool banking family, as chief engineer. Three London brokers and one broker in Frankfort were named,[50] as were several banks and bankers: the Bank of England, the Bank of London, I. Barned and Company of

[44] *Ibid.*, June 1, 1891, p. 7. McHenry was born in 1817 or the next year. He died in London in 1891.

[45] McHenry was to purchase the iron, furnishing £193,000 in cash or bankers' bills for the purpose. Felton, 58.

[46] The Atlantic and Great Western was originally three roads, the Erie and New York City (in New York), the Meadville (in Pennsylvania), and the Franklin and Warren (in Ohio). A. C. Morton, contractor of the Erie and New York City, and Henry Doolittle, contractor for the Meadville, traveled to London in 1856 to sell the bonds of the road and to purchase iron. They made a tentative agreement with Henry Gompertz (Wertheim and Gompertz). After the crisis of 1857 Gompertz withdrew, as did A. C. Morton and Samuel Hallet, who had also been involved in the early negotiations. James McHenry, together with C. L. Ward (of the Ohio section), Henry Doolittle (of the Pennsylvania section), H. W. Kennard, George Francis Train (a Boston eccentric who is credited with having constructed the first street railway in England, that in Birkenhead), and Beverly Tucker (the U.S. Consul in Liverpool), traveled to Paris. There negotiations were carried through with Leon Lillo, Salamanca's banker. The reason for approaching Salamanca appears to have been that the railway was to run through a tract of Pennsylvania land belonging to Queen Christina of Spain. She had obtained it in settlement of claims against the Bank of the United States. Felton, 1–67.

[47] The bonds were shipped to the trustees, John Goddard and Benjamin Moran (not to be confused with Charles Moran of the Erie), in care of James McHenry, Liverpool. *Ibid.*, 91.

[48] *Times*, Sept. 27, 1860, p. 5.

[49] It is doubtful that Salamanca ever went to the United States.

[50] The brokers in London were Heseltine and Powell, E. F. Satterthwaite, and Hope, Dodgson; in Frankfort, Phillip Nicholas Schmidt.

Liverpool, M. L. Cuarda of Paris, and Phillip Nicholas Schmidt of Frankfort. In particular, the Bank of London guaranteed the first four coupons of the railway's bonds.[51]

In spite of opposition from the Pennsylvania Railroad and its representative in London, T. Wiggin and Company, McHenry was now riding high. He seems to have obtained the United States Naval Agency in London about this time.[52] More important, he soon was able to rally to his support the great railroad builder, Sir Morton Peto, apparently as both a financial participant and an active associate.[53]

Soon new bonds were authorized. Divisional bonds were issued on both the Ohio and the Pennsylvania sections of the line. The discovery of oil in 1860 on the Pennsylvania part of the line appeared to justify all expenditure. Second-mortgage bonds were also authorized. These, however, were not sold to the public but were used as collateral for the bank advances to which McHenry was addicted. [The impact of the Civil War on this, as on other new railroads, was to hinder the sale of bonds; floating short-term debt met the exigencies.]

By the end of 1864 McHenry's credit was stretched to the utmost.[54] He decided on another public issue. Accordingly, three-year debentures bearing 8 percent interest were advertised for sale.[55] These were guaranteed by the Consolidated Bank.[56] The committee of the stock exchange expressed doubt about McHenry's authority to issue this form of security. It asked for a delay of six weeks to determine the legal status of the issue.[57] Public doubts were also aroused by the rumors that the Atlantic and Great Western was a financiers' railway.

In these circumstances offense appeared to be the best defense: the prospectus for the new debentures boasted that this road was unusual in that it had been largely built by big financiers. The public had not been asked to subscribe until the road was completed and ready for full operation.[58]

---

[51] See advertisement in the *Times,* Sept. 27, 1860, p. 5; and Felton, 73. According to Felton, Prescott Grote and Co. of London and I. Barned and Co. of Liverpool also guaranteed the coupons on these securities for two years.

[52] *Ibid.,* 94.

[53] *Ibid.,* 118–19; compare A. W. Currie, *The Grand Trunk Railway of Canada* (Toronto: University of Toronto Press, 1957), 102. Currie states that the Atlantic and Great Western was owned by Sir Morton Peto, one of the original contractors of the Grand Trunk. This seems to be an overstatement, although Peto had agreed in 1862 to some sort of partnership with McHenry.

[54] In 1864, the Bank of London was attempting to reduce the amount of its advances to McHenry.

[55] The prospectus appeared in the *Times,* Dec. 17, 1864, p. 4.

[56] This bank was a consolidation of Heywood, Kennard and Co.; the Bank of Manchester; and Hankey and Co.

[57] *Ibid.,* Jan. 10, 1865, p. 7. This matter was straightened out and a settling day was set. *Ibid.,* Feb. 18, 1865, p. 10.

[58] The prospectus even stated that of the total funded debt of the line amounting to £3,600,100, only £1,755,070 was held by the public.

It was now urgent to arouse the investing public's interest in the Atlantic and Great Western. The time seemed auspicious. In 1865 the credit of the federal government was high and American railway securities were beginning to reappear on European markets. Sir Morton Peto therefore organized a triumphal tour of inspection of the Atlantic and Great Western. He was accompanied by an impressive group of men: Senor Leon Lillo, the Parisian banker; E. F. Satterthwaite, a London stockbroker; T. W. Kinnaird, M.P.; Robert Cooper Lee Bevan of the banking house of Barclay, Bevan and Company; and J. Forbes of the London, Chatham and Dover Railway. On his return to England, Peto published a large volume, *The Resources and Prospects of America,* a work of general interest in which the Atlantic and Great Western was accorded discreet mention.[59]

Nor was Sir Morton Peto's contribution to the Atlantic and Great Western limited to his pocketbook and his pen. Organizing ability is more typical of a great contractor than literary talent. While on this trip he evolved an ambitious plan for making the Atlantic and Great Western into a great through trunk line. In the West, connections were to be made with various roads in Ohio and Indiana, notably the Cleveland, Columbus and Cincinnati and the Ohio and Mississippi, in which the British already had a substantial interest.[60] Connections to the Atlantic seaboard on the east were to be made over the Catawissa and the Philadelphia and Reading, a road closely associated with the London merchant banking firm of McCalmont Brothers. New York was to be reached by means of the Morris and Essex Railroad. There were also plans for linking the Atlantic and Great Western with the British-controlled Canadian lines, especially the Grand Trunk.[61] A subsidiary steamship line from Philadelphia to Liverpool was proposed to complete the connection with England.[62] The first step in the implementation of this scheme was taken by the leasing of the Catawissa.

Planning systems of this extent was a new phenomenon in the United States. So far, eastern roads like the Pennsylvania and the New York Central had been content to rely on rather loose agreements with their western connections.[63] Sir Morton Peto was one of the first entrepreneurs to consider the consolidation of a single system reaching from the Mississippi to the Atlantic seaboard that would transcend several state bounda-

[59] London: Alexander Strahan, 1866.   [60] See above, p. 64 ff.

[61] A link between the Atlantic and Great Western and the Grand Trunk was finally brought about. In 1871 the Grand Trunk built the International Bridge at Buffalo to enable it to exchange freight with the New York Central and the Atlantic and Great Western. Currie, 102.

[62] For a full account of the details of Sir Morton Peto's plans see the *Times,* Nov. 24, 1865, p. 6; Jan. 27, 1866, p. 9.

[63] This was partly because of uncertainty regarding the financial stability of these roads. The Pennsylvania was already acquiring, by consolidation and lease, lines within Pennsylvania, and other companies were also building up their systems within their own states. It was the connections to the West that were loosely controlled.

ries and be under unified management. It is probable that the genesis of this major innovation was inspired by Peto's international and, more especially, Canadian experience in building extensive systems.

The reaction in the United States, particularly of the Pennsylvania Railroad, to the projected system was one of opposition. Immediately, the Pennsylvania and its leased line, the Philadelphia and Erie,[64] applied to the Pennsylvania Supreme Court for an injunction to prevent the Catawissa from crossing the Philadelphia and Erie's tracks. This prevented the building of a line by the Catawissa, a road lying east of the Philadelphia and Erie, to join the Atlantic and Great Western, a line lying to the west of the Philadelphia and Erie.[65]

In arguing the case before Pennsylvania's Supreme Court the lawyers of the Pennsylvania relied mainly on two points: the traffic from the West would be diverted away from Philadelphia, and this new amalgamation would form a powerful alien influence in the state. It is therefore not surprising that the Supreme Court's decision was in favor of the Pennsylvania Railroad.[66]

The Atlantic and Great Western declared that it would take the matter to the Supreme Court of the United States.[67] Also, rumors of an agreement between the Pennsylvania and the Atlantic and Great Western were already in the air.[68] However, by the spring of 1866 holders of the Atlantic and Great Western's securities, alarmed by the disclosures of the finances of the railway, were no longer in a mood to advance the capital necessary for the additional building to implement the ambitious plan. By the summer, when the suit was finally decided on appeal in favor of the Atlantic and Great Western, the project was already dead.[69] Sir Morton Peto had failed, and the Atlantic and Great Western was very shaky.

Sir Morton Peto did not succeed in bringing to life his magnificent conception of a through line from St. Louis to New York and Pennsylvania, but he had accomplished one thing. He had awakened roads like the Pennsylvania to the necessity of protecting their hitherto loosely controlled connections to the West.[70] Moreover, Jay Gould apparently did not think of building up a vast system until after he became associated with James McHenry. It can be assumed that the idea was James McHenry's, and therefore came originally, perhaps, from Sir Morton Peto. Nor does the chain end here. Gould's first move in building up his through line was an attempt to lease the Columbus, Chicago and Indiana Central, a step that quickly brought him afoul of the Pennsylvania. That company had lapsed

[64] The Pennsylvania leased the Philadelphia and Erie for 999 years in 1862. Burgess and Kennedy, 156.

[65] These hearings began on Jan. 15, 1866. See report in the *Times,* Feb. 5, 1866, p. 7.

[66] *Ibid.,* March 20, 1866, p. 5.   [67] *Ibid.*

[68] *Ibid.*   [69] *Ibid.,* July 13, 1866, p. 7.

[70] *American Railroad Journal,* XXXIX (Jan. 27, 1866), 81.

back into its old ways after Sir Morton Peto disappeared from the field, but it was now forced into action.[71] Meanwhile the lease of the Atlantic and Great Western to the Erie alerted Vanderbilt, who had previously been concentrating on controlling traffic into New York, to the danger that the western connections of the New York Central might be absorbed by rival lines.[72]

The whole movement that transformed the Pennsylvania, the Erie, and the New York Central from lines contained within the borders of one state into trunk lines was accomplished within a year. Gould's first move to control the CC&IC took place early in 1869, and by September of the same year all three trunk lines were through to Chicago.[73]

The consequences of Sir Morton Peto's ambitious plans for the Atlantic and Great Western have taken the story of this line several years beyond the crisis of 1866,[74] which was important in the history of the company. At that date the financial problems of John Watson and Company, a firm of British railway contractors, touched off a spark that was to lead to the suspension of Overend, Gurney and Company and the crisis of May 1866. In particular, much was to be revealed about the Atlantic and Great Western.

The repercussions of Watson's difficulties put pressure on the Joint Stock Discount Company. On January 31, 1866, at a stormy meeting of this company something of James McHenry's involvement was disclosed. The first advance by the Joint Stock Discount Company on the collateral of railway securities in 1864 had been made not to John Watson but to James McHenry.[75] The discount company had made an advance to him on the collateral of second-mortgage bonds of the Atlantic and Great Western taken at 45 percent.

McHenry was then still solvent, and a brave face was put on the matter. The vice-chairman of the Joint Stock Discount Company maintained that

---

[71] Gould first attempted to get control of the CC&IC. In this he was easily bested by the Pennsylvania. He next bought up the stock of the Fort Wayne, which the Pennsylvania, after consolidating its control of the CC&IC, had been ill-advised enough to let go. The Pennsylvania, however, quickly persuaded the Pennsylvania Legislature to pass an act that provided that only one-fifth of the board of directors of the Fort Wayne should retire in any one year. (It was possibly from this move by the Pennsylvania that Gould derived the idea for the Classification Act which he used against the British shareholders in the autumn of the same year.) Thus, Gould's control of the shares of the Fort Wayne availed him nothing, for before the next election of the Fort Wayne, the Pennsylvania had arranged to lease the road. *Times,* Feb. 16, 1869, p. 6; June 2, 1869, p. 6; and June 14, 1869, p. 10. See also, Mott, 176.

[72] Mott, 174.   [73] *Times,* Sept. 14, 1869, p. 5.   [74] [See King, 240 ff.]

[75] At this meeting of the board of the Joint Stock Discount Co., it was announced that the company would not only be unable to pay a dividend but would have to make a further call of £5 on the shares. This announcement provoked a stormy attack on the directors. *Bankers' Magazine,* XXVI (March 1866), 335–50.

he would be glad to give 70 for the bonds.[76] However, he refused to name the amount of Atlantic and Great Western bonds held by his company.

This revelation was troublesome to the Atlantic and Great Western. At the next meeting of its Board of Control,[77] which had been set up in 1865 at the time of the consolidation of the railway's three divisions, McHenry faced hostile questioning. He stated that he had placed only £41,000 of securities with the Joint Stock Company and that subsequently £30,000 had been returned. He also denied categorically that any bonds had been issued at a reduced price to any discount company.[78] In fact, however, years later among the £919,281 railway securities still hopefully held by the Joint Stock Company were £240,000 of the Atlantic and Great Western Railway.[79]

After the first revelations in 1866 about the Joint Stock Company, confidence in similar institutions ebbed lower and lower. As early as March the *Times*, taking fright at the mounting tension in the City, reversed its usual Cassandra role to plead that the public reaction against finance shares was unreasonable, that even the Joint Stock Discount Company was perfectly safe, and that finance companies had a legal right to make long-term investment and to undertake agencies.[80]

It was too late to stem the tide. The position of many such companies was not sound. A long step down toward the crash of Overend, Gurney took place on April 19 when Barned's Banking Company, Ltd., of Liverpool suspended before the completion of its first year of existence as a limited liability company. As in the case of Overend, Gurney, the assumption of

[76] *Ibid.*, 339.

[77] The members of the Board of Control besides Sir S. Morton Peto and Joseph Robinson, deputy chairman of the Ebbw Vale Co., Ltd., were S. Goodson, M.P., and W. Fenton, respectively chairman and deputy chairman of the Great Eastern Railway of Great Britain.

[78] *Times*, March 30, 1866, p. 5.

[79] *Bankers' Magazine*, XXXI (June 1871), 534. Of the Atlantic and Great Western Railway securities, £120,000 were common shares that were sold for £21,000 in 1872–73. *Ibid.*, XXXIII (June 1873), 547. £60,000 were preferred shares, and £60,000 were third-mortgage bonds. The liquidators of the Joint Stock Co. held onto the third-mortgage bonds too long. Nevertheless they were able to realize £7,800 on these. *Ibid.*, XXXV (July 1875), 595. Since the Atlantic and Great Western had been reorganized twice between 1866 and 1871, it is difficult to determine the amount of original investment or loans by the Joint Stock Discount Co. that these securities represented. Furthermore, the report by the liquidators of the Joint Stock Discount Co. to the general meeting of the stockholders on May 19, 1874, revealed that there were still considerable outstanding claims against other companies in liquidation. One of these proved to be the International Contract Co., which was also involved in McHenry's affairs. In fact, it seems to have borne the same relation to McHenry that the Imperial Mercantile Credit Association bore to Peto and the Contract Corporation bore to John Watson. *Ibid.*, XXXIV (July 1874), 549.

[80] March 12, 1866, p. 7.

the form of a limited liability company may have permitted this bank to work its way a little deeper into insolvency. It was already involved in foreign railway financing, particularly with James McHenry and the Atlantic and Great Western.[81]

Barned's was one of McHenry's oldest creditors. His debts to this bank went back at least to 1862 and probably to before 1860.[82] At the time of its failure, however, he was not among its largest debtors. In 1866 a debt of McHenry and the Atlantic and Great Western Railway of only £126,000 had been transferred from the earlier bank organization to its new limited liability company. Against this was held the security of acceptances.[83]

Barned's was also held liable to the Bank of London for £160,000 because it had guaranteed a credit extended to McHenry. The facts of this case were involved. In 1864 the Bank of London had wished to terminate its credit of £200,000 to McHenry. Therefore, in November it arranged for the Imperial Mercantile Credit Association (of which Peto was the principal shareholder) to open a credit for McHenry for that sum on the guarantee of Barned's.[84] In February 1866 the credit was reduced by £40,000. After the failure of all three companies, the Imperial Mercantile Credit Association, Barned's, and the Bank of London, an investigation disclosed that the Imperial Mercantile Credit Association had made no actual cash advance to McHenry. For advances to him, it had immediately

[81] According to the *Times*, April 20, 1866, p. 12: "The failure of Barned's Banking Company produced a very painful feeling to-day, from the extent to which it confirms the growing impression on the part of the public that it is difficult to place confidence anywhere. It cannot be too strongly enforced that banks and discount companies can never fail except through gross and culpable mismanagement. There is no security in the world like that of a sound commercial bill of exchange, and it is only of such securities that the mass of assets of any respectable bank or discount company should be found to consist. . . . People may fancy that it is difficult for a bank or discount company to get business in the midst of the general competition without incurring special risks. . . . But there is not an atom weight in either of these pleas. The trade of the country has of late years increased with such extraordinary strides that there is ample legitimate business for all existing establishments."

[82] I. Barned and Co. was one of the five banks listed on the prospectus for the first-mortgage bonds of the New York section of the Atlantic and Great Western issued in 1860.

[83] These acceptances were J. H. Levita's for £100,000, given in July 1865, due on May 29, 1867, and one of Leon Lillo for £15,000, given in 1865 in exchange for £39,000 in promissory notes of the Atlantic and Great Western. Lillo's acceptance fell due in 1866 and was dishonored.

[84] The case of Barned's brought out another aspect of the financial machinations that led to the crisis of 1866—the complex interrelationships by which various financial and banking companies made a little credit go a long way and liabilities appear on their books as assets. *Bankers' Magazine*, XXVI (June 1866), 683; (Dec. 1866), 1384–85, and XXVII (Dec. 1867), 1162; XXIX (Dec. 1869), 1219–23; XXXII (Dec. 1872), 1018.

reimbursed itself by drawing on the Bank of London for the same amount. The bank's books no longer showed this particular transaction as an advance to McHenry, but as one to the Imperial Mercantile Credit Association. The purpose seems to have been simply not to show the extent of credit extended by the Bank of London to McHenry.[85]

The desire to minimize the advances to the railroad man on the books of the Bank of London is not surprising. After this bank went into liquidation in July 1866, the committee to investigate its affairs reported that the bank held a "large unsecured claim of the bank on the Atlantic and Great Western Railway, estimated to amount to upwards of £500,000, of the value of which it is difficult at the present time to form any reliable opinion." [86]

The Bank of London in turn brought down the Consolidated Bank. Just before closing, the Bank of London had made an extraordinary arrangement with the Consolidated Bank; the latter undertook to protect the current and deposit accounts of the former.[87] This move, which amounted to according one class of creditors a privileged position, raised a hue and cry in the City. No one could understand what had induced the directors of the Consolidated Bank [88] to ally itself with an institution known to be shaky by an agreement of such a dubious nature. The *Bankers' Magazine* attributed the policy to a fit of insanity on the part of the Consolidated Bank.[89] Indeed, within a few days, it too was forced to suspend because of an injunction taken out by the holders of acceptances of the Bank of London.[90] It was then disclosed that the Consolidated Bank also had made advances to James McHenry. These, however, amounted to only £105,000 on collateral of £140,000 in debentures issued in 1865. The Consolidated Bank reopened and was able to carry on successfully. The loan to McHenry was written off in 1870.

The story of the advances made to McHenry by various companies that failed in 1866 is not yet completed. When the firm of Peto and Betts failed in May, its books showed unsecured advances to McHenry amounting to £227,000, as well as £104,000 covered by the Atlantic and Great Western securities.[91] Although it is possible that the Imperial Mercantile Association, which was under Peto's control, also made advances to McHenry, no information about this company became public. After this Association failed, Sir William Jackson, a friend of Sir Morton Peto, worked for four years to straighten out the company's affairs, meanwhile refusing to divulge any information about its security holdings. He was successful,

[85] *Ibid.*, XXXII (Dec. 1872), 1018.   [86] *Ibid.*, XXVII (July 1867), 706.
[87] *Times*, May 24, 1866, p. 7.
[88] The Consolidated Bank, it should be remembered, was formed by an amalgamation of the Bank of Manchester; Heywood, Kennard; and Hankey and Co.
[89] *Bankers' Magazine*, XXVI (June 1866), 766–67.
[90] *Times*, May 29, 1866, p. 10   [91] *Economist*, XXIV (June 16, 1866), 699.

and the company eventually was reconstituted as the Imperial Credit Company.[92]

The International Contract Company also avoided mentioning McHenry as long as possible, though it was well known that he had been a very large shareholder. On November 28, 1870, its official liquidator finally reported that claims against McHenry amounted to £268,000, of which £115,000 was on the account of the Atlantic and Great Western Railway.[93]

Not including an insignificant £18,000 that the Oriental Financial Corporation had advanced to McHenry,[94] and estimating the advances from the Joint Stock Discount Company, the Bank of London, and the International Contract Company at a minimum, McHenry had obtained from the six companies mentioned credits of more than £1,200,000.[95] It is amazing that it was possible to operate on such a scale and in such a manner. McHenry himself admitted late in 1864 that out of the Atlantic and Great Western's total funded debt of £3,600,100, only £1,755,070 was held by the public.[96] After the debacle, he left England to await settlement with his creditors.

The day of reckoning had not yet arrived for the Atlantic and Great Western, but it was growing nearer. Throughout the autumn of 1866 rumors that the line was unsound became increasingly persistent. At the general meeting of the company in March 1867 a committee of investigation was appointed.[97] To make a personal survey of the property, represen-

---

[92] *Bankers' Magazine,* XXVI (June 1866), 762–64; (July 1866), 887–91; XXX (Aug. 1870), 722–31; (Oct. 1870), 888–90.

[93] In reporting that the claims of the International Contract Co. amounted to £268,000, the official liquidator said: "For £115,000 of this latter sum, and £11,367.10s., the amount of certain bills in my possession arising out of transactions with the Atlantic and Great Western Railway, on which Mr. McHenry's name does not appear, that railway company is liable to the International Contract Company. Mr. McHenry disputes the company's claim against him, but accepting his mode of computing it, its amount must exceed £200,000. Mr. McHenry's inspectors are now distributing to his creditors debenture bonds of the Atlantic and Great Western Railway £ for £ upon the amount of their debts, and to a similar payment this Company is entitled. I do not attempt to assess the value of this asset." *Ibid.,* XXXI (Jan. 1871), 50–51.

[94] In 1864 the Oriental Financial Corporation accepted £100,000 of accommodation bills for James McHenry. These were renewed from time to time, and £82,000 was eventually paid off or provided for. Information about this transaction comes from a law suit which the Oriental Financial Corporation brought to prevent Overend, Gurney, the company with whom McHenry discounted £10,000 of the remaining bills, from suing it. *Ibid.,* XXXII (Feb. 1872), 95.

[95] In computing this total the author took the advances of the Joint Stock Discount Co. at a minimum sum of £500,000, the estimate given at the time of the Bank of London's failure, rather than at the sum of £754,696 which, together with interest, was the amount due fom McHenry to the Bank of London in 1869. *Ibid.,* XXIX (March 1869), 297.

[96] In the prospectus for the Certificates of Debenture issued in Dec. 1864.

[97] This committee included: Sir William Russell, M.P.; T. Cave, M.P.;

tatives were sent to the United States. These included two members of the committee, Thomas Cave, M.P., and F. W. Oewel of Amsterdam,[98] accompanied by the son of the engineer, Richard Trevethick, added on the recommendation of the railway builder, Thomas Brassey.[99] Meanwhile, the London committee, with the support of the trustees of the various mortgages, procured the appointment of a receiver, General Robert B. Potter, in order to protect the road against hostile action by individual creditors.[100] This was not long in materializing. The very day that the announcement of a receiver appeared in the *Times,* a meeting of dissentient divisional bondholders opposed to the committee of investigation was convened. However, Sir William Russell, M.P., chairman of the London Committee, attended the dissentient meeting and was able to persuade his audience to defer action and to join with the London Committee.[101]

By October, the representatives of the London Committee who had visited the United States had returned. Trevethick's report concluded that the road was worth more than the total of the divisional mortgages but not as much as the full amount of the claims against it.[102] It was proposed that only divisional bondholders were to continue to receive interest in cash.[103] Disapproving of this suggestion, some holders of debenture certificates felt that their best course would be to realize immediately on the securities deposited with the Bank of England as collateral for that issue.[104] They appointed another committee [105] and, at first, refused to be placated.[106] Their persistence resulted in the London Committee settling with them.[107]

J. Fildes, M.P., Manchester; and Crawshay Bailey, ironmaster, representing respectively divisional bonds, consolidated bonds, debenture certificates, and unsecured creditors. On the nomination of the General Exchange Committee for Public Stocks of Amsterdam, F. W. Oewel was added to the committee. *Times,* March 5, 1867, p. 5, and March 16, 1867, p. 10.

[98] *Ibid.,* Oct. 23, 1867, p. 5.   [99] *Ibid.,* April 3, 1867, p. 12.

[100] *Ibid.,* April 2, 1867, p. 10.   [101] *Ibid.,* April 3, 1867, p. 12.

[102] *Ibid.,* Oct. 4, 1867, p. 5.

[103] Holders of the consolidated bonds and certificates of debenture were to receive interest in noncumulative preference shares, which were to be taken from the already authorized common shares and would not represent any addition to total capitalization. Other creditors were to receive interest in similar second-preference shares. *Ibid.*

[104] This collateral seems to have consisted of $5,236,000 of divisional bonds and $14,541,150 of common stock of the Atlantic and Great Western Railway, plus $931,000 of the shares of the New Lisbon and Oil Creek Railroad. *Ibid.,* July 25, 1868, p. 10.

[105] This committee consisted of non-City persons: a Mr. Lawes of Rothampstead, holder of bonds to the amount of £85,000; E. L. J. Ridsdale, £6,000; a Mr. Wallace, £7,000; and Major Gordon, £10,000. W. T. Huxley was the secretary.

[106] Instead this committee filed a bill in chancery to compel the trustees for the certificates of debenture to realize on their security. *Ibid.,* April 7, 1868, p. 6.

[107] They were offered for one half of their bonds: divisional bonds in trust with the Bank of England, $5,236,000, and £133,290 cash (in exchange for

Terms were negotiated for taking the road out of receivership and placing it under the control of a board of directors in London.[108]

Meanwhile, creditors of James McHenry, representing £2.4 million out of a total of £3.6 million, had agreed to a compromise with him. He was able to return from Paris to London,[109] and apparently to a warm welcome from the London Committee.

During his enforced absence from London, McHenry had gone to New York and had seen Jay Gould. Although Gould already had admitted to the large increases in the Erie stock, he was able to obtain a lease of the entire line of the Atlantic and Great Western to the Erie on December 10, 1868.[110] This move did not have the unanimous consent of the London board of directors,[111] but for the time being James McHenry appears to have labored under the delusion that he could manage Gould as easily as he had persuaded other financial tycoons. Indeed, he stated that the Atlantic and Great Western had reason to be grateful to the Erie; the latter advanced the $1.6 million necessary to pay off the receiver's liabilities and release the Atlantic and Great Western from receivership.[112]

All was not well. The dissentient debenture bondholders of the Atlantic and Great Western again threatened trouble. Moreover, the British holders of Erie were also beginning to be interested in McHenry's railway. In May 1869, when S. L. M. Barlow of New York, a lawyer for the representatives of the British shareholders of the Erie, was in London, the *Railway News* published a significant correspondence. It detailed the steps proposed to place the interests of the holders of the Atlantic and Great Western

---

bonds of the Erie and Niagara and of the New Lisbon and Oil Creek Railroad). For the other half they were offered: income bonds bearing 5 percent interest, the interest on which was payable in income bonds bearing 7 percent. Alternatively they were offered £280,000 in cash. For overdue coupons on their divisional bonds they were offered income bonds to the amount of $1,171,000. *Ibid.*, July 25, 1868, p. 10.

[108] The members of the board of directors were: S. Laing, M.P., chairman; Sir William Russell, M.P., vice-chairman; J. Fildes, M.P. of Manchester; E. F. Satterthwaite, stockbroker; F. W. Oewel of Amsterdam; E. L. J. Ridsdale, of the Debenture Holders' Committee; and J. Everett. *Ibid.*, July 28, 1868, p. 8.

[109] The report of the Bank of London's negotiations with McHenry in Paris shows that this bank held equipment bonds of the Atlantic and Great Western Railway, a novel class of security. D. Chadwick and J. C. Chadwick of the Bank of London seem to have prepared the draft scheme by which McHenry undertook to pay his unsecured creditors by installments. *Bankers' Magazine*, XXIX (March 1869), 297 ff. One creditor for the paltry sum of £5,000 was still threatening to take out a summons in bankruptcy in June 1868, but in fact bankruptcy proceedings were avoided. *Times*, June 4, 1868, p. 7.

[110] *Ibid.*, Dec. 24, 1868, p. 7.

[111] Mr. Ridsdale's committee was now revived because the Erie objected to the issuance of the income bonds needed to complete the settlement between the debenture Certificate Holders' Committee and the London Board of Control.

[112] *Times*, Feb. 18, 1869, p. 7.

securities under Barlow.[113] At a meeting, J. S. Morgan and Company [114] consented to act as depositary for securities of Atlantic and Great Western,[115] and yet another committee was appointed, headed by Mr. Chadwick of the Bank of London.[116]

Meanwhile, McHenry briefly continued to work with Gould. It was even rumored that Gould had promised McHenry a seat on the Erie board of directors.[117] This came to naught. A few days before the lease money from the Erie was due to the Atlantic and Great Western, Gould secured his own appointment as receiver of the latter line.[118]

McHenry now suddenly threw his support to Chadwick's committee, and suits were begun to free the Atlantic and Great Western from its lease.[119] This was not a simple matter: suits had to be started in each of the three states, New York, Pennsylvania, and Ohio. As each section of road was freed, the trustees for the bondholders came into control. When all had finally been released, McHenry announced his "Official Scheme of Reorganisation." There was only token opposition. Mr. Oewel of Amsterdam, who had been associated with Mr. Ridsdale's dissentient Committee of Divisional Bondholders, announced a rival scheme; this was quickly scotched as an "Erie" proposal, an effective epithet although probably untrue.[120]

This was the heyday of McHenry's comeback. Even the *Times* came to his support. Bischoffsheim and Goldschmidt now became European agents for the Atlantic and Great Western. In 1871 two issues of reorganization stock were made, each of £400,000.[121] These were the last issues to be

[113] This is a significant change of alliance. The *Railway News* had previously been thought to be in McHenry's pocket. Nevertheless, serious charges of having accepted money from McHenry were later brought against the editor of the *Railway News*.

[114] Throughout this period, J. S. Morgan was the London representative of the Erie.

[115] *Times,* May 15, 1869, p. 7. At this time, even before the trouble with Gould over the 60,000 English shares, shareholders refused to deposit their certificates with Morgan unless needed in legal proceedings. *Ibid.,* June 23, 1869, p. 10.

[116] The committee representing some holders of securities of the Atlantic and Great Western included: D. Chadwick, M.P.; Mr. Hastings; Rev. Watkins; Mr. Brown; Mr. Thomas (Bristol); Mr. Thorpe; Mr. Bickley; Mr. T. Matthews; Mr. J. B. Matthews; Rev. Dr. Haycroft; Mr. Curtler; and Mr. A. Grierson (Darlington). Mr. Ridsdale's committee, which had by now become the Committee of Divisional Bondholders, alone refused to join Mr. Chadwick's committee. *Ibid.,* Nov. 6, 1869, p. 12.

[117] *Ibid.,* Oct. 18, 1869, p. 5.   [118] *Ibid.,* Nov. 27, 1869, p. 10.

[119] *Ibid.,* Feb. 23, 1870, p. 10.

[120] *Ibid.,* May 25, 1870, p. 10, and May 28, 1870, p. 10.

[121] This was not stock in the sense of ordinary stock. It was convertible into the first general mortgage bonds of the newly reorganized, but as yet not repossessed, company. (Gould refused to give up possession of the Atlantic and Great Western for some time after the issuance of court orders requiring him to do so.)

floated on the Atlantic and Great Western itself for a long time. Later bonds were secured on various leased lines. One lot of leased lines rental trust bonds was brought out in 1872 and another in 1873. An issue of 8 percent Western Extension bonds was made in 1873 and a further one of 7 percent Western Extension bonds, guaranteed by the Erie, in 1874. Equipment for the line was provided under a separate organization, the United States Rolling Stock Company.[122] With dismemberment of the Atlantic and Great Western in the 1880's, the legacy of this complicated financial structure was the appointment of a series of London Committees and a small, completely British railway.[123] In the meantime these various issues provided an effective method of diverting revenue from the Atlantic and Great Western.

When in late 1871 Bischoffsheim resigned from the Erie Shareholders' Protective Committee and joined James McHenry, the two had little difficulty in winning over the remaining three members of the committee. Even the *Times* was now pro-McHenry, and it lost no opportunity to refer to the policies of the original committee as ineffectual. In fact, McHenry's policy, apparently carried out largely through General Daniel E. Sickles, former American Minister to Spain, was simple; he is reported to have bribed all the members of Gould's board of directors.[124]

Jay Gould was removed from the presidency of the Erie in March 1872. The question remained as to which group would gain control. The influence of the Atlantic and Great Western on the first temporary post-Gould board was strong. The board included Watts Sherman, of the New York banking house of Duncan, Sherman,[125] correspondent of J. S. Morgan and Company, although this London merchant banking house was replaced as the financial agent of the Erie in Europe by Bischoffsheim and Goldschmidt. McHenry's Erie Shareholders' Protective Committee now resigned on the grounds that this railway was at last in responsible hands. The three American members of this committee became representatives of the Erie in London.[126]

In the meantime there were still threats of opposition. These came from the original London Erie Shareholders' Protective Committee and from W.

[122] This device was not original. A similar organization called the United Kingdom Rolling Stock Co. had been organized in the late 1860's to provide rolling stock for Irish railways.

[123] The Shenango Railway and Mercer Coal Co., Ltd. The directors of this line in 1882 were Sir Henry W. Tyler, M.P.; Sir C. L. Lewis; and Captain D. Galton. *Burdett's Official Intelligence,* 1882.

[124] Mott, 182–200.

[125] Duncan, Sherman & Co., a correspondent of J. S. Morgan and Co., had been supporting Mr. Chadwick's committee from its inception. Besides Watts Sherman, other members of this temporary board were General McClellan, president of the Atlantic and Great Western, Charles Day, secretary of the Atlantic and Great Western, and Colonel Stebbins, ex-president of the Atlantic and Great Western.

[126] These three men were Wetmore Cryder, E. H. Green, and Gilson Homan.

B. Clerke, the president of the New York Stock Exchange. As a result there was a wild scramble for Erie shares in the spring of 1872. None of the parties held sufficient shares to control the coming elections.[127] During the resulting struggle for shares, European ownership of the Erie increased from around 60 to almost 100 percent. On March 16, 1872, the gross turnover of Erie shares in Frankfort alone was reported to have reached 300,000.[128] Nine days later the price of Erie shares had risen to 67½.[129] Gould was rumored to have made a fortune out of his own downfall.[130]

In spite of persistent reports that there would be difficulties over the Erie's July election in 1872, it went off quietly. The anticipation of trouble probably arose because Thomas Scott of the Pennsylvania was said to be casting eyes at the Erie,[131] and because of the division in London between two groups of security holders, Bischoffsheim and McHenry on the one side and those represented by Heath and Raphael on the other. Although the Atlantic and Great Western interest was not heavily represented on the new board, the new directors were not hostile to McHenry.[132] Some compromise evidently had been reached, and McHenry had made concessions to the original Erie Shareholders' Protective Committee. In particular, the Atlantic and Great Western was not leased to the Erie, as McHenry would have liked. The arrangement between the Erie and the Atlantic and Great Western remained for some time a loose one; the two roads simply agreed to prorate their earnings.[133]

By the middle of 1873, however, it was believed that McHenry was the master of the Erie as well as of the Atlantic and Great Western. Thus, the *Times* blandly reported that the McHenry-Bischoffsheim ticket for the board of directors had been elected.[134] Meanwhile, in spite of the fact that Bischoffsheim and Goldschmidt had negotiated several loans for the Erie

[127] The act of the New York Legislature repealing the Classification Act (April 20, 1872) provided that a new election for the board of directors of the Erie should be held on July 10, 1872. Mott, 203. This repeal was obtained by the representatives of the original Erie Shareholders' Protective Committee, especially Frank Southmayd of New York and John Swann of London, mentioned below. *Times*, April 1, 1872, p. 8. Moreover, Swann was reported to have stated that Bischoffsheim and McHenry had approved this move. *Ibid.*, April 3, 1872, p. 6.

[128] In March it was thought that of the total of 865,269 of Erie common shares outstanding, Jay Gould held 120,000; Bischoffsheim and McHenry, 60,000; the American party headed by W. B. Clerke, 210,000; and Heath and Raphael, 300,000. *Ibid.* McHenry voted proxies for 250,000 shares. *Ibid.*, April 3, 1872, p. 6, and July 25, 1872, p. 4.

[129] *Ibid.*, April 11, 1872, p. 12.   [130] *Ibid.*

[131] See, for example, *ibid.*, May 17, 1872, p. 6.

[132] For example, Bischoffsheim and Goldschmidt remained the financial representatives of the company in Europe.

[133] It was not until June 25, 1874, that the Atlantic and Great Western was again leased to the Erie. Mott, 227.

[134] July 10, 1873, p. 7.

in the course of 1872 and early 1873,[135] the Erie's financial position had become desperate. In the summer of 1873, its president, Peter H. Watson (elected in 1872),[136] made a trip to London hoping to negotiate yet another loan. At a meeting in the City on September 25, Watson explained that a further $35 million would be needed to put the Erie into good shape and that it would be best to spend the money as rapidly as possible instead of scraping along from day to day. He also defended McHenry and Bischoffsheim and, in reply to criticism, said that the success of the Erie was entirely due to their efforts.[137] Nevertheless, Bischoffsheim now fell into the background, and McHenry, the specialist in desperate finance, once more came to the fore. It was he, under the guise of the London Banking Association, Ltd., who brought out the first bonds of the New Erie mortgage.[138]

Criticism of the Erie had again been gathering strength. A committee of

[135] Three loans were brought out by Bischoffsheim and Goldschmidt during 1872 and 1873:

Date	Type	Amount	Price
June 1872	7% convertible	£6 m. (£4,710,000 reserved)	92
Feb. 1873	7% convertible	$10 m.	82
March 1873	7% 1st mortgage on the N.Y., Boston and Montreal	$6,250,000	80

There was considerable criticism of the first and third issues. *Times*, Oct. 10, 1872, p. 8, and Mott, 220. It should be noted that the first issue was partly to reimburse Bischoffsheim and Goldschmidt for an advance of $4 million which they made to the Erie shortly after Gould was ousted from office. The second issue seems to have been relatively straightforward. But the third, that for the New York, Boston and Montreal, is unpleasantly reminiscent of the Gould days. This was a line newly formed by the amalgamation of existing lines, gaps between which were to be constructed out of the money raised. In fact, no construction was ever done, the existing lines were already heavily mortgaged, and the bondholders ended with nothing. The trustees later told the Council of Foreign Bondholders that they had never seen the prospectus and that they had used the money in accordance with the trust deed, which, according to the *Times*, "is understood to mean paying themselves for claims on the original undertakings which it was proposed to consolidate." Sept. 22, 1875, p. 6, and Sept. 25, 1875, p. 4.

[136] Watson was born in England but went to the United States at the age of 20. Mott, 469.

[137] J. Fildes, M.P., of Manchester presided at this meeting, which was held on Sept. 25, 1873. *Times*, Sept. 26, 1873, p. 4.

[138] The total of this issue was to be £8 million of which £2 million was reserved. A first portion of £3 million of these second consolidated bonds (7 percent sterling) was offered by the London Banking Association Ltd. in March 1874 at 78. *Ibid.*, March 7, 1874, p. 6.

the New York State Legislature had investigated the road in 1873,[139] and a further investigation was threatened. In April matters came to a head when the former auditor of the line, a man named S. H. Dunan,[140] made public serious charges of the Erie's insolvency. President Watson's resignation was now imminent,[141] and the Atlantic and Great Western was quickly leased to the Erie.[142]

At first it was thought that Thomas Scott of the Pennsylvania would succeed Watson, holding this position concurrently with his post on the Pennsylvania. However, his associates were opposed; at that time the Pennsylvania was being investigated by a committee of shareholders.[143] Moreover, the company was engaged in a rate war with the Baltimore and Ohio, and the proposed presidency surely would have aroused opposition in that quarter. Scott therefore withdrew, and Hugh Jewett, a former official of the Pennsylvania, acceptable also to vice-president John King, Jr., of the Baltimore and Ohio, was chosen.[144] However, default was now inevitable.

The Atlantic and Great Western went into receivership before the year was out.[145] The Erie struggled on for another year. But it, too, was forced into receivership in 1875.[146] Again there arose a welter of committees.

McHenry was never accorded any recognition by the new Erie Committee, but he fought to continue his influence.[147] During 1877 he attempted to form an opposition party with Sir Charles Whetham as his chief supporter.[148] By this time, however, all the power of the City was ranged

---

[139] One of the purposes of this investigation was to determine whether the dividend of 3½ percent on the preferred stock and 1 percent on the common stock of the Erie had been earned. The committee was unable to decide on this point, and the Erie was allowed to pay the dividends. Mott, 219–21, and *Times*, June 4, 1874, p. 6.

[140] *Times* reports this name as Disman. April 30, 1874, p. 12.

[141] *Ibid.*, April 30, 1874, p. 5, and June 10, 1874, p. 10.

[142] Mott, 227, and *Times*, June 26, 1874, p. 7.

[143] Burgess and Kennedy, 314 ff.

[144] *Times*, June 10, 1874, p. 10; June 17, 1874, p. 7; and June 24, 1874, p. 9.

[145] *Ibid.*, Dec. 10, 1874, p. 4, and Dec. 23, 1874, p. 7.

[146] *Ibid.*, June 15, 1875, p. 10.

[147] *Ibid.*, Dec. 20, 1875, p. 7. The members of the Erie Committee were: Sir Edward Watkin, chairman; Cecil Beadon; B. Whitworth, M. P.; Henry Rawson; J. M. Douglas; W. Weir; J. C. Conybeare; Philip Rose; J. K. Cross, M.P.; J. Westlake; P. MacLagan, M.P.;—Leeming; G. Smith; A. H. Moncur; O. G. Miller; and Robert Fleming. This is one of the first appearances of Robert Fleming on a shareholders' committee. Fleming was the secretary of the Scottish American Investment Trust and was important in negotiations on American railway securities after 1880. A temporary committee consisting of Charles Morrison, Whitworth, Wiley, and Sir Cecil Beadon preceded this committee. *Ibid.*, July 6, 1875, p. 10.

[148] A meeting, presided over by Whetham, expressed opposition to the reconstruction of the Erie. This seems to have been abortive. *Ibid.*, May 10, 1877, p. 10.

against him.[149] He therefore decided to throw his support to William H. Vanderbilt, the son of the Erie's old enemy. But even with somewhat conditional reciprocal support from Vanderbilt, McHenry was unable to exercise much interference except in regard to the Cleveland, Columbus, Cincinnati and Indianapolis.[150]

When the Atlantic and Great Western went into receivership in 1874, McHenry immediately announced an "Official Scheme of Reorganisation."[151] There was, of course, difficulty with the first-mortgage bond-holders,[152] who wished to foreclose. Nevertheless the committee representing the group[153] was still dealing with McHenry through E. F. Satterthwaite early in 1876.[154] At this point a new group composed mainly of members of the investment trust section of the City decided to take over. In January 1876 a meeting that began as one for the first-mortgage bondholders changed into one for bond- and shareholders of every class of security under the chairmanship of C. E. Lewis, M.P.[155] He, Sir G. Balfour, M.P., and the Rev. J. Lockington Bates were appointed trustees of the Atlantic and Great Western with the object of meeting with the Erie shareholders and working out a new lease of the Atlantic and Great Western to the Erie.

[149] In fact, the Erie Committee had instituted proceedings in three cases; one each against McHenry and Bischoffsheim and the London Banking Association, Ltd., *Ibid.,* June 26, 1876, p. 8.

[150] In 1881, Vanderbilt of the New York Central was struggling with Hugh Jewett of the Erie for possession of the CCC&I. A large number of the shares of this company were in the hands of the London Trustees of the Western Extension Certificates of the Atlantic and Great Western (Sir George Balfour, George Herring, and H. Wollaston Blake). They decided to vote for Vanderbilt's nominees. Jewett got an injunction to prevent these persons from voting, but the shares which they represented were instead voted by Vanderbilt himself. Meanwhile, McHenry obtained an order which tied up the use of the 11,000 shares of the CCC&I in Jewett's hands. *Economist,* XXXIX (Oct. 22, 1881), 1315, and (Nov. 12, 1881), 1405. Indeed, McHenry was still interfering with the Erie in the CCC&I in the mid-1880's.

[151] For the provisions of this scheme, see *Times,* May 25, 1875, p. 10.

[152] See, for example, *ibid.,* May 19, 1875, p. 6.

[153] This committee, none of whom except Conybeare seem to be City men, included: J. C. Conybeare, chairman; G. F. Rait; Rev. J. Lockington Bates; F. B. Forwood; T. Shelmerdine; J. Caw, Jr.; J. Wilson, Jr.; T. P. Gaskell; and M. O'Shaughnessy.

[154] At a meeting of this committee in Jan. 1876, a report by Rev. J. Lockington Bates was circulated. Bates's report stated that the Atlantic and Great Western had cost $100 million but was not worth $20 million and that most of its value depended on its leased lines. *Ibid.,* Jan. 15, 1876, p. 7. A Mr. Adams then said that the committee should have nothing to do with anything emanating from Westminster Chambers, implying that Bates was in league with McHenry. Bates explained that the reason for going along with McHenry (they had coalesced with McHenry) was that then all matters in dispute would be referred to Mr. Satterthwaite as arbitrator. *Ibid.,* Jan. 22, 1876, p. 7.

[155] C. E. Lewis and G. Balfour were members of what the *Economist* called the ring of investment trust directors.

These trustees seem to have maintained some sort of relationship with McHenry [156] without being under his control. For four years this committee operated the line,[157] but it had no delegated functions and no legal power to manage the road or to commence action against anyone. It was not even officially appointed, although it had the backing of holders of $47 million out of a total of $55 million of the bonds. It carried on from day to day without funds or credit, always facing the possibility of an adverse foreclosure by the trustees of the first-mortgage bonds of the Ohio section.[158]

At last, in 1879, the trustees seemed near their objective, a lease of the Atlantic and Great Western to the Erie.[159] At this point, McHenry came out in open opposition. He convened a meeting at which Thomas Cave, M.P., was chairman, and an impressive committee was nominated.[160] Unfortunately, at least some proposed members of this committee had not been previously consulted as to their willingness to serve, and several refused membership.[161]

In fact, another group—Sir Henry W. Tyler, Sir Charles Young, and Captain Douglas Galton—seems to have been perfecting a scheme of its own. It was in many respects similar to that of James McHenry, but in this case designed to benefit not him but the Grand Trunk. Entailed was the reconstruction of the road without foreclosure and without lease to the Erie.[162] Sir Henry Tyler was by now the president of the Grank Trunk.[163] It was for his company's advantage that the Atlantic and Great Western was to be operated.

---

[156] McHenry still held a large amount of the shares of the company, but his relationship with the trustees of the Atlantic and Great Western was an uneasy one, and in due course McHenry brought suit against them to recover for expenses he had incurred during the early days of the receivership.

[157] The leased lines rental trusts and the Western Extension were run under their own trustees during this period.

[158] *Times*, March 1, 1879, p. 1. Letters were written denying membership on the committee by several men.

[159] Bates and Lewis had been to the United States in 1879 to discuss a lease with Hugh Jewett of the Erie, and an agreement had been reached. However, the consent of the security holders was needed to perfect this lease. *Ibid.*

[160] *Ibid.*, March 13, 1879, p. 7. The committee appointed in 1879 included: Professor Henry Fawcett; F. Mowatt; Lord Robert Montagu, M.P.; Lord Bury; Sir Henry Tyler; Sir C. Young; Lord Kinnaird; Mr. Shepperd; Mr. MacDougall; and James McHenry.

[161] *Ibid.*, March 18, 1879, p. 11. For denials by various nominees, see *ibid.*, March 14, 1879, p. 6, and March 20, 1879, p. 7.

[162] *Ibid.*, April 28, 1879, p. 9.

[163] Tyler was president of the Grand Trunk from 1876 to 1882. Currie, 138–60. Tyler carried the old trustees, General Sir George Balfour, Charles E. Lewis, and Rev. J. Lockington Bates, with him in the end. A "Revised Official Scheme of Reorganisation" was now issued. Trustees certificates for prior lien bonds to the amount of £500,000 (of an authorized £1.6 million) were put out to meet the interest on the Ohio mortgage and other expenses. E. F. Satterthwaite acted as broker for the trustees. *Times*, Aug. 15, 1879, pp. 11, 13.

The Atlantic and Great Western now disappeared from the stock exchange listing and was replaced by the New York, Pennsylvania and Ohio. This road struggled on for a number of years. Finally, in 1883, when Tyler had ceased to be president of the Grand Trunk after that company had found other allies, the Atlantic and Great Western again was leased to the Erie.[164]

Two contemporary comments serve to close this chapter. One is from the *Times* on the occasion of Sir John Swinburne's report on the leased lines rental trusts of the Atlantic and Great Western in 1875: "Interests cross and conflict with each other, and powers are divided, mixed up, or overridden in a way that renders the whole subject hopelessly bewildering to an outsider; but one purpose is always clear, that money should be made by promoters, and one effect is always visible—wreck and ruin." [165] The other appeared in the *Economist* at the time of the lease of the Atlantic and Great Western to the Erie in 1883. This journal wrote of the Atlantic and Great Western: "[It] has been leased and reorganised, and again leased and reorganised, and put up to auction, and has passed into the hands of receivers more times than we can remember since the three sections were consolidated in 1865; but what, the bondholders may well ask, has been the good of it all?" [166]

The British investor undoubtedly lost money on the Atlantic and Great Western, and probably some on the Erie. However, in both cases, it is difficult to estimate the total. The usual figure given at the time was £10 million to £20 million. However, the claim that the loss on the Atlantic and Great Western alone was at least £10 million is based on a comparison between the value of the physical assets of the road and the total face value of the securities issued.[167] In fact, the securities of this line were never floated at face value but more often at about half of that amount. The claim of a substantial loss on the Erie is equally difficult to verify. It depends entirely on one's estimate of the astuteness of City speculators. If they bought only on bear raids, their losses were probably not great. In so far as they aided Vanderbilt in trying to corner the market, they probably lost.[168]

[164] This was on May 1, 1883. *Burdett's Official Intelligence*, 1884.

[165] June 18, 1875, p. 8.   [166] XL (Nov. 4, 1882), 1367.

[167] The Revised Official Scheme of Reorganisation of the Atlantic and Great Western in 1875 estimated the value of the assets of the road at $40,082,229 against a total of outstanding securities of $99,089,700. *Times*, Sept. 10, 1875, p. 2.

[168] It is perhaps apposite to quote here a statement from the *Investor's Review* of 1892: "Perhaps more money has been made on the Stock Exchange out of 'Erie shares' alone than out of any half-dozen other prominent speculative securities in the list. But much of this money which the market has made has been lost by the public." I (Jan. 1892), 21. The British public would not appear to have been concerned in this case. Therefore, if the City speculated as astutely as it was reputed to have done, the profits it made were not at the British public's expense.

Finally, did the British investors learn anything from these losses? Perhaps they learned not to trust financial wizards like McHenry to run at a distance railways in which they were investors. During the Erie troubles the British investor had had some experience in working with and through Americans and seems to have learned that, in so far as it was not practicable to send men out from Britain, it was necessary to build up a group of Americans to whom some of the responsibility could safely be delegated. Despite difficulties which McCalmont Brothers were to have with their appointee, Franklin Gowen, the president of the Reading, it was this pattern of control that became important again in the 1880's.

VI

The Attraction of Coal and Iron

IN SPITE of the experience with the Erie, British investors continued to evince an interest in American rails in the 1870's. Writing in the first year of the decade, when the export capital from Great Britain was relatively low, the *Times* conservatively estimated that normally $20 million to $30 million annually was invested by the British in American enterprises.[1] Merchant banking houses, investment trust companies, and even banks continued to provide some growth capital for American railways. [The involvement went beyond short-term loans and purchase of stocks and bonds in railways. Some capital went into related American industries, such as iron and coal. Furthermore for these mining companies, as in the case of a few railways, the export of capital was accompanied on occasion by the export of business skills or at least strong advice from Great Britain.]

Some British subjects played a variety of direct roles in American railways during this period. A number of British contractors were working in the United States. Many of these were small operators who undertook only subcontracts.[2] A few were more important.[3] In 1873 an English firm agreed to build a new tunnel for the Delaware, Lackawanna and Western.[4]

[1] May 19, 1870, p. 7. The report stated that the large purchases of American securities which were being made on the Continent would not do much more than make up for what the British were not investing that year.

[2] Such men were often emigrants who probably settled in the United States.

[3] For example, in 1873 H. V. and H. W. Poor made arrangements in England for the construction of the Selma and Guy "by parties who are to take up our bonds and pay us." Chandler, *Poor*, 232. The Mobile and Alabama Grand Trunk also appears to have been undertaken by a group of British capitalists. W. P. B. Stockman, C.E., was associated with this group. Great Britain, *Parliamentary Papers* (*Accounts and Papers*, LXXIV, 1876), "Report of H.M. Consul Cridland, 1875," 430.

[4] With the exception of C. P. Huntington, Americans do not seem to have taken readily to work on tunnels. [American railways were often built cheaply, and later when funds were available they were rebuilt using more tunnels.] None of the early railways that required extensive tunneling were completed

Some British engineers became interested in American projects. One of them was John Collinson, mentioned later in connection with the Atlantic, Mississippi and Ohio, the predecessor of the Norfolk and Western. An engineer named William Wilson undertook to build the Little Rock Bridge.[5]

One group of British businessmen, although not directly connected with railroading, was to have a great influence on British investment in American railways. These were men who were interested in coal and iron. Among them Thomas Whitwell, a Quaker ironmaster from Stockton-on-Tees, must be accorded preeminence.[6] Together with several of his relatives, members of the Pease family of Darlington, he was the first Englishman to consider setting up an English iron company in the Tennessee-Alabama area.

British interest in coal and iron deposits in the United States stemmed at least from the 1830's.[7] Most of the early efforts were abortive. Many

---

before the Civil War. The Hoosac Tunnel on the Troy and Greenfield Railroad of Massachusetts, begun in 1854, was finally completed in 1876. It was built by a Canadian contractor, Shanley and Company, whose engineer was a Dane named Wederkerich. N. H. Egleston, "The Story of the Hoosac Tunnel," *Atlantic Monthly*, XLIX (March 1882), 289–304. The tunneling on the Virginia Central (now the Chesapeake and Ohio) was also completed after the Civil War by C. P. Huntington, who already had considerable experience in this type of work while building the Central Pacific. The railway from South Carolina to Louisville and Cincinnati, chartered in 1835 as the Louisville, Cincinnati and Charleston, was another road that required extensive tunneling. It was not completed until 1908. Meanwhile, its name, having been changed several times, was the Carolina, Clinchfield and Ohio. This road, usually called the Clinchfield, was finally built by Americans, although it was heavily dependent on British capital. General John Wilder, who became an important ironmaster in Tennessee after the Civil War, obtained funds for this line from Barings in 1888. W. W. Way, Jr., *The Clinchfield Railroad* (Chapel Hill: University of North Carolina Press, 1931), 69. Way fails to point out that Barings was interested in this line before that date. In 1880 Barings announced the payment of interest on various bonds of the Louisville, Cincinnati and South Carolina, including some secured by deed of trust of 1868. *Times*, July 30, 1880, p. 11. The Hudson River Tunnel by which the Pennsylvania Railroad reached New York was built by a British engineering firm, Thomas Costain and Co., with British funds.

[5] *Times*, Oct. 24, 1874, p. 6.

[6] After an early apprenticeship in the locomotive-building shops of Alfred Kitching of Darlington, Thomas Whitwell entered the engineering establishment of Robert Stephenson and Co. In 1859, having completed his apprenticeship he went into partnership with his brother William as an ironsmelter at South Stockton. Unfortunately, in the late 1870's, when only 40 years old, he was killed by an explosion while he was examining a faulty furnace in his works at Thornaby. William Thomlinson (ed.) *Thomas Whitwell* (Middlesbrough and Stocton: "Gazette" Office, 1879). Extracts from this memoir were sent to the author by a member of the family, Mrs. Amelia Eliza Wallis of Darlington.

[7] For example, the Pennsylvania Bituminous Coal, Iron and Timber Co., the Hazleton Coal Co., and the Lehigh Coal and Mining Co. Jenks, *Migration of British Capital*, 361.

years passed before production of bituminous coal became important. In the meantime, during the long depression of the American iron trade in the late 1840's, even the largely British-owned Maryland and New York Iron and Coal Company, whose Mount Savage Works rolled the first heavy rails in the United States, encountered financial difficulties. As a result, in the early 1850's,[8] these works were sold to a group of Americans including John Murray Forbes and Erastus Corning. A fresh start was made by the British in 1860 with the formation of the Great Kanawha Company to develop 85,000 acres of coal, iron, and timber lands in Putnam County in western Virginia.[9] The outbreak of the Civil War was to delay the extension of this interest to a later period. By 1873, however, one of the most noteworthy developments in the coal and iron industry of the United States was the extensive investment by British capitalists in mining properties, especially in Virginia and West Virginia.[10]

Although British interest in the coal and iron fields of western Virginia started before the Civil War, that in the coal and iron areas of Tennessee and Alabama only began in the post-bellum period. Sir Charles Lyell had visited this region on his second trip to the United States, in the late 1840's, and had reported favorably on the quality of the mineral deposits.[11] At that time Alabama was still predominantly a cotton-growing state with its population concentrated in the southern lowlands. In the hill region to the north transportation was deficient and labor scarce.

However, after the Civil War, Alabama and Tennessee were eager to attract capital. The findings of geological surveys were used in advertisements in northern and European papers. *De Bow's Review* carried numerous articles extolling the coal and iron deposits of the South. One of these quoted the following from a Montgomery, Alabama, newspaper:

Why do not such influential publications as the New York *Mercantile Journal* aid in bringing these lands prominently before the public? Many of them, at the North, profess the best feelings for the welfare of the South. They could not do the South a better service than to inform the capitalists and manufacturers of their section of the manifold inducements we can present to such of them as may be looking for profitable fields of investment and actual settlement.[12]

---

[8] See the advertisement in the *American Railroad Journal*, XXII (Jan. 6, 1849), 11.

[9] *Times*, Nov. 16, 1860, p. 7. The directors of the Great Kanawha Co. included: Sir Henry Potter, Bart.; William Berry; George Gamble; Samuel Lees; Mayor-General G. R. Pemberton; James Roberts; Alexander Shand; and Charles Whetham.

[10] This investment in coal and iron lands, especially in Virginia and West Virginia, was not by individuals, as formerly, but by companies. *Commercial and Financial Chronicle*, XVII (Aug. 16, 1873), 209.

[11] Lyell, *A Second Visit to the United States* (London: John Murray, 1849), I, 80–82.

[12] Nov. 1867, p. 490.

These pleas did not go unheeded. In 1867, General John Thomas Wilder, a former Union officer who had fought in the area around Chattanooga, returned to the South to establish the Roane Iron Works. Within three years he had extended his operations to include a rail-rolling mill at Chattanooga, and before two decades had passed he was very powerful in the iron trade of this district. Wilder later extended his activities to Johnson City, Tennessee, and by the late 1880's he had amassed a considerable fortune.[13]

In 1872 a Quaker group from the Cleveland district of northeastern England arrived in the South to assess the possibilities of production there. These English ironmasters had hoped to be able to purchase land in Alabama, but they found that the title to coal and iron lands there was in dispute, owing to the claims of holders of the state bonds that had been issued in London and on the Continent.[14] The ironmasters finally settled on a tract of land just over the border in Tennessee.[15] Returning to England, they organized the Southern States Coal, Iron and Land Company, Ltd., to carry out their project in Tennessee.[16] In that state they had purchased almost 180,000 acres (120,000 acres of brown hematite land, 1,400 acres of red hematite land, 55,000 acres of coal land, and 2,500 acres of township land). They founded a town called South Pittsburg, and later at least two other towns were started in the neighborhood, one called Cleveland and the other bearing the name of Whitwell in honor of the leader, Thomas Whitwell. After his death in 1878 the other directors found it difficult to continue this enterprise, and in the early 1880's the firm was amalgamated with the Tennessee Coal, Iron and Railroad Company, a corporation formed in 1881 as a successor to an earlier one.[17]

[13] Wilder was influential in the building of the Charleston, Cincinnati and Chicago, a predecessor of the Carolina, Clinchfield and Ohio, and by his own account lost $750,000 in the debacle that overtook that road after Barings was forced to withdraw its support in 1890. Way, 86.

[14] See below, p. 125 ff.

[15] *The Hill Country of Alabama, U.S.A.* (printed by E. and F. N. Spon for the English Committee of the Alabama 8 percent Gold State Bonds of 1870, 1878).

[16] The directors of the English company, the Southern States Coal, Iron and Land Co., Ltd., were: Thomas Whitwell, ironmaster (William Whitwell and Co.), Thornaby Ironworks, Stockton-on-Tees; Henry Fell Pease, J.P., coal owner, Brinburn, Darlington; William Barrett, managing director, Norton Iron Co., Ltd., Stockton-on-Tees; Edwin Lucas Pease, Bushel Hill, Darlington; William Henry Hewlett, Wigan Coal and Iron Co., Ltd., Wigan; Henry Barrett, iron and brass founder, Beech Street, London; Joshua Stagg Byers, J.P., timber and lead merchant and director of Stockton Iron Furnace Co., Ltd., Stockton; William Ramwell, solicitor, Bolton.

[17] The antecedent firm to the Tennessee Coal, Iron and Railroad Co. was the Sewanee Mining Co. *Commercial and Financial Chronicle*, XLIV (Feb. 19, 1887), 245. The Tennessee Coal, Iron and Railroad Co. eventually became outstanding in the production of steel rails by the open hearth method and provided severe competition for the United States Steel Corporation, which took it over in 1907.

When in 1873 Sir I. Lowthian Bell made his first trip to the Alabama coal and iron fields, he, too, was favorably impressed by their potentialities. On his return to England he read a paper before the Iron and Steel Institute in which he said: "The comparatively underdeveloped resources of Tennessee, Georgia, and Albama . . . will, as I have already indicated, prove a match for any part of the world in the production of cheap iron . . . there seems every reason for believing that pig-iron can now be laid down in the Southern States . . . at little above one half the cost of that made in the North." [18]

What were the reasons for such an overwhelming response by British ironmasters to the appeal of the southern states? A number of iron areas in the United Kingdom were running into difficulties, either because of the exhaustion of known resources, the uncertainty of finding new ones,[19] or because the presence of phosphorus in their ore rendered it unsuitable for use in the early Bessemer converters, currently revolutionizing the industry. Furthermore, it was now clear that the United States was committed to a high protective tariff. The end of the large export trade in rails to the United States was in sight. British interest in the possibilities of production in America was serious; one member of the British Embassy at Washington was assigned to investigate most of the iron and steel districts of the United States.[20]

The existence of excellent coal and iron deposits in Alabama eventually had a great influence on the holders of bonds of the Alabama and Chattanooga Railroad and of the Alabama state securities issued in its support. However, when in 1869 and 1870 these bonds were brought out in London, coal and iron were not the immediate factors determining the investment. The British and Continental investors bought these bonds without any idea that they might become actively involved in the running of the railway. Their immediate interest was only the excellent rate of return offered on promising securities.

There was, indeed, no reason to anticipate default on these bonds.

[18] "Notes of a Visit to Coal- and Iron-Mines and Ironworks in the United States," *Journal of the Iron and Steel Institute*, 1875, pp. 141–42.

[19] In particular, there seemed to be doubt about the new resources of iron ore in Scotland. Indeed, one of the first British-owned iron companies to commence production in the United States in the post–Civil War period was the Glasgow Port Washington Iron and Coal Co. The company erected two blast furnaces in the Hanging Rock district of Ohio and was producing American Scotch pig iron in 1872. All its officers were brought from Scotland. *Engineering*, XVIII (Sept. 25, 1874), 253. Unfortunately there was some difficulty about this company's finances. The report of a committee of inquiry in the 1880's revealed that the property, which was purchased for £35,000 plus £1,000 expenses, had been transferred to the company for £71,000. *Economist*, XXXIX (June 18, 1881), 767.

[20] Great Britain, *Parliamentary Papers* (*Accounts and Papers*, LXV, 1874, Commercial No. 18), "Report by Mr. Harriss-Gastrell on the Iron and Steel Industries of the United States," 131–816.

Alabama's credit was high. Not only had it never defaulted on obligations in the ante-bellum period, it had even managed throughout most of the Civil War to pay the interest on Alabama bonds held abroad.[21] Moreover, Alabama had very good connections in the City. J. Henry Schroeder and Company, the London merchant banking house through which the Confederacy had floated the Cotton Loan of 1863,[22] was the state's agent in London, while a member of the Schroeder family, H. A. Schroeder, had been for many years a resident active in the business affairs of Mobile.[23]

Unfortunately the Alabama and Chattanooga was incorporated and controlled by minor financial wizards who were lesser editions of Jay Gould.[24] Chief among these were Daniel M. Stanton and John C. Stanton, New England brothers.[25] Arriving in Alabama in 1869, they bought up the stocks and bonds of two small pre–Civil War railways, the North-East and South-West Alabama Railroad and the Wills Valley Railroad. They then

[21] Council of Foreign Bondholders, *First Report of the Alabama and Chattanooga Railroad, "First Mortgage Indorsed Bonds of 1869," and 8% State Gold Bonds of 1870* (London, July 1875). In 1861 the amount of Alabama state bonds held in London was $1,336,000. When after the Civil War, Governor Patton took office, one year's interest was due on these bonds. This back interest was then paid in bonds. In 1867 a further $648,000 of 5 percent bonds was issued in London and in 1870 another $688,000 of 6 percent bonds. These bonds were in addition to the $2 million of 8 percent gold ones issued in aid of the Alabama and Chattanooga Railroad.

[22] The original interest of J. Henry Schroeder was sugar, and its trade was mainly with the West Indies. Later cotton also became a major interest of the firm.

[23] H. A. Schroeder was the president in Mobile at least from the 1850's to the middle 1870's. In the 1850's he became a director of one of the southern railways. In 1875 he retired from the presidency of the Southern Bank of Alabama in Mobile. *Bankers' Magazine*, XXIX (New York, Jan. 1875), 561.

[24] Such "entrepreneurs" were at work in Georgia, South Carolina, and North Carolina. In fact, these are the true carpetbaggers of whom the South complained so loudly. The South charged the carpetbaggers with defrauding the southern states of enormous amounts of bonds and leaving them with debts that were a burden to taxpayers for years. A recent study has shown that the amount of state bonds issued to southern railways during the Reconstruction period was not greater than the amounts issued in the preceding and succeeding periods. On the other hand, there undoubtedly were cases of individual piracy. By a strange coincidence the Stantons of Alabama and Hannibal I. Kimball, the archpirate of Georgia, emulated Jay Gould by building opera houses, presumably with railway funds. When charges were brought against Kimball in 1874 he returned to Atlanta to defend himself, but no indictment was ever brought. John F. Stover, *The Railroads of the South, 1865–1900* (Chapel Hill: University of North Carolina Press, 1955), 81–92.

[25] The board of directors of the Alabama and Chattanooga in May 1871 included: Daniel M. Stanton, president, Boston; John C. Stanton, general superintendent, Boston; Lewis Rice, Boston; Samuel Wheeler, Boston; A. C. Lippitt, Conn.; F. B. Loomis, Conn.; W. P. Rathburn, Chattanooga; A. Bingham, Alabama; and C. A. Miller, New York Central.

incorporated the Alabama and Chattanooga, transferring their two railways to this new corporation for payment in its stock. [The plan was to
complete 295 miles from Meridian, Mississippi, to Chattanooga.] Next
they sought state endorsement for the bonds of this new corporation at the
rate of $12,000 per mile.[26] Endorsement was obtained, and the bonds were
negotiated with two New York houses, Soutter and Company and Henry
Clews and Company,[27] through which they were transferred to London.
Later the Stantons also persuaded the state to issue $2 million of state
bonds in aid of the railway.

All of this was perfectly straightforward, and no criticism would have
arisen if the interest had been paid on the railway's bonds. However,
default was first made on interest due January 1871.[28] The state of
Alabama recognized its responsibility and paid the coupons. Moreover, the
state took possession of the railway [which had somewhat less than 240
miles in operation] but then did not know what to do with it. Alabama
tried to sell the line, but the only potential buyer was Daniel Stanton, who
was unable to raise enough money to complete the purchase.[29] A little later
there were rumors that a party of American bondholders was preparing to
take over the road.[30] The British bondholders approved of this move, but it
did not materialize.[31] On February 21, 1873, the state legislature authorized the issue of $1.5 million of 8 percent currency bonds to fund the
overdue coupons, but the governor appears to have used these bonds for

[26] Later this was increased to $16,000 per mile, which was not excessive.
However, there seems to have been a second mortgage for $9,000 per mile. Great
Britain, *Parliamentary Papers* (*Accounts and Papers*, LXXV, 1875), "Report by
H.M. Consul Cridland for the years 1873 and 1874," 430.

[27] Henry Clews was English-born and educated. His house, Henry Clews and
Co. in New York, was the financial agent for Alabama and Georgia. Stover says
that Clews was honest. Stover, 62. The report of H.M. Consul Cridland implies
the opposite: "The financial transactions with H. Clews and Company are
anomalous. Money was borrowed of that firm from time to time by Governor
Lewis, commencing about the 1st of January, 1873, amounting to between
300,000 and 400,000 dol. The amount appears to have been reduced by payments to 299,660 dol. 20c. on the 10th day of July, 1873, as shown by an
account current rendered on that day." Great Britain, *Parliamentary Papers*
(*Accounts and Papers*, LXXIV, 1876), "Commercial Report by H.M. Consul
Cridland at Mobile, 1875," 529.

[28] *Times*, Jan. 10, 1871, p. 7; Jan. 13, 1871, p. 5; Feb. 28, 1871, p. 10.

[29] Council of Foreign Bondholders, *First Report*. See also, *Times*, Jan. 1, 1873,
p. 7.

[30] At this point bondholders were asked to deposit their bonds with the
Bondholders' Committee, which included: E. F. Satterthwaite; T. Sandeman;
George Webb Medley; General Vaughan, C.B.; E. P. Moriarty; Mr. Engelhardt;
and Augustus Abraham. About $2,700,000 of first-mortgage endorsed bonds
were deposited. Council of Foreign Bondholders, *First Report*. It was also at this
time that the Council of Foreign Bondholders was asked to intervene. *Times*,
Jan. 23, 1873, p. 7.

[31] Council of Foreign Bondholders, *First Report*.

other purposes.[32] Then, in 1874, Abraham Murdoch, president of the Mobile and Ohio, and A. F. Elliot, a partner in the banking house of Duncan, Sherman and Company, were appointed to replace the original receivers.[33] By this time, some of the British bondholders decided to try to take over the railway.[34] Within the year this became the official policy of the Bondholders' Committee and of the Council of Foreign Bondholders.

There were two difficulties. The first was the Stantons. Having lost control of the railway to the state when the railway defaulted on the state-endorsed bonds, they had contrived to secure appointment as trustees for the first-mortgage bondholders, the very group to whom their interests were opposed.[35] Later, they succeeded in securing appointment as receivers replacing the incumbents, Murdoch and Elliot. The second barrier was the large amount of receivers' certificates, which had to be reduced.

In 1874 the bondholders had secured the eminent American economist, David A. Wells,[36] to represent them, and the solution of these problems was left to him. Accordingly, in 1875 Wells negotiated what appeared to be a very favorable settlement. He arranged for the purchase of the railway for $1.2 million, subject only to certain liens, costs, and charges. The price was payable in the endorsed bonds and overdue coupons of the Alabama and Chattanooga Railroad. Wells also obtained an agreement for Alabama to issue $1 million state bonds bearing 2 percent to replace the railway bonds with state endorsement.[37]

Something went wrong. The bondholders either would not or could not raise the £160,000 needed to clear the title to the railway.[38] The company therefore reverted to the local creditors. At this point, Emile Erlanger and Company, the firm through which the bonds had been marketed on the Continent, reappeared in the negotiations. In 1877 John Swann, representing this firm,[39] bought the road from the local creditors for $1,480,090 and

[32] *Times*, March 15, 1873, p. 6.

[33] Council of Foreign Bondholders, *First Report*.

[34] Among those who were in favor of taking the road over were Francis Bennock, Sir Philip Rose, and T. Sandeman. *Times*, Aug. 6, 1874, p. 10.

[35] The Stantons were able to accomplish this because Governor Patton had been replaced by a governor friendly to them. Having secured appointment as trustees, the Stantons proposed to buy the railway for the bondholders and to run it themselves. However, David A. Wells, who was now representing the bondholders, managed to get a decision from the U.S. Circuit Court to the effect that trustees could not buy for bondholders except by their especial consent. *Ibid.*, June 1, 1874, p. 9; June 2, 1874, p. 11; July 30, 1874, p. 6.

[36] Wells, a member of the faculty of Harvard University, was a free trader.

[37] *Final Report of the Committee Appointed to Act in Conjunction with the Council of Foreign Bondholders, Alabama and Chattanooga "First Mortgage Bonds of 1869"* (London, 1875).

[38] At a meeting of the Alabama and Chattanooga bondholders in July 1876, Roger Eykyn, the chairman of the English Committee, reported that only one quarter or £40,000 of the money needed to redeem the property in the United States had been raised. *Times*, July 3, 1876, p. 9.

[39] *Commercial and Financial Chronicle*, XXVII (July 27, 1878), 85.

reorganized it as the Alabama Great Southern, a task which Erlanger stated the firm had undertaken in the path of duty.[40] [The railway later was added to the roads controlled by a British holding corporation, the Alabama, New Orleans, Texas and Pacific Junction Railway Company, registered in England in 1881.] [41]

Meanwhile, the settlement of the 8 percent Alabama bonds, issued in aid of the Alabama and Chattanooga, had been negotiated separately. A land grant figured prominently in the advertisements for the endorsed bonds of the Alabama and Chattanooga.[42] Later it was revealed that while the railway had, indeed, obtained a land grant, these lands formed no part of the security for the endorsed bonds. Moreover, during the railway's period of bankruptcy, Alabama secured the return of these lands by proceedings in chancery. The governor of the state made several attempts to dispose of them both in the United States and in Europe. The Committee of Bondholders of the Alabama 8 percent Gold Bonds [43] wanted to secure these lands in settlement of their claim against the state. Accordingly, the Council of Foreign Bondholders dispatched a representative to Alabama.[44] He was able to arrange the exchange of these bonds for 500,000 acres of land.[45] However, the actual transfer was delayed for some years because Alabama demanded, before giving up the land to the committee, reimbursement for the interest it had already paid.[46] In 1882 the

[40] In a circular to the bondholders of the Alabama and Chattanooga, Erlanger announced that a new company, the Alabama Great Southern, would be formed with the following capital structure: 6% 1st-mortgage bonds, $1,750,000; 6% preferred shares, £156,600 (15,660 shares of £10); ordinary shares, £1,566,000 (156,660 shares of £10). The circular further stated that Erlanger and Co. would take up the purchase money in 1st mortgage bonds, and in preferred and ordinary shares. Bondholders of the old Alabama and Chattanooga were asked to subscribe to the preferred shares on terms equivalent to an assessment of 10 percent of their holdings. *Ibid.*, XXV (Aug. 25, 1877), 186. The exact terms on which bonds and overdue coupons of the old company were exchanged for securities of the new are not stated. (It is to be presumed that they were represented by ordinary shares.)

[41] [Stover; and Lewis, 104.]

[42] *Economist*, XXVII (Aug. 21, 1869), 987. The advertisement specifically stated that these bonds were a first mortgage on 300 miles of road and 1,900,800 acres of land.

[43] In 1878 this committee included: Augustus B. Abraham, chairman; Roger Eykyn; George Webb Medley; George Buck, Jr., secretary; Charles Schiff; and J. M. Coventry. Except for Coventry and the secretary of the committee, all of these men were members of the committee of 8 percent endorsed bonds of the Alabama and Chattanooga and after the formation of the Alabama Great Southern became directors of that road.

[44] This was T. W. Snagge of the Middle Temple and the Council of Foreign Bondholders.

[45] Council of Foreign Bondholders, *Final Report*.

[46] *Ibid.* In Dec. 1879, the committee asked that bonds and overdue coupons be deposited and that an assessment of £2 per bond be paid. *Times*, Dec. 18, 1879, p. 6.

Alabama Coal, Iron, Land and Colonisation Co., Ltd., was organized.[47] Control of this company rested with the same people as that of the Alabama Great Southern. Moreover, it proved to be a good investment and was still British owned at the beginning of the Second World War.[48]

In the 1880's the Alabama Great Southern was not content to remain a short local line. The *First Report* of the Council of Foreign Bondholders on this railway stressed the fact that the road would have to depend on minerals if it were to get sufficient traffic to sustain it, but it also suggested the Alabama Great Southern could be built up into an essential part of a beeline route from Washington to New Orleans by connecting to other lines. The most important of these were the Atlantic, Mississippi and Ohio (now the Norfolk and Western) and the East Tennessee, Virginia and Georgia. In fact, as discussed later, British investors did unsuccessfully attempt to implement this suggestion by gaining control of the Atlantic, Mississippi and Ohio. Moreover, the East Tennessee refused to cooperate with either the Alabama Great Southern or the Atlantic, Mississippi and Ohio.

Nevertheless, the Alabama Great Southern persisted in its ambitions. The Cincinnati Southern, a line built and owned by the city of Cincinnati, was leased.[49] The Vicksburg and Meridian and the Vicksburg, Shreveport and Pacific were purchased. The New Orleans and Northeastern was constructed.[50] A determined attempt was made to wrest the Memphis and Charleston from its lease to the East Tennessee.[51] Thus, in one way or another, the less-than-300-mile line earlier named the Alabama and Chattanooga was built up into the great Erlanger system, extending from Cincinnati in the North to New Orleans in the South and from Texas in the West to Georgia in the East. In spite of its size, this system was not immediately successful,[52] not because of poor management but because its

[47] After the formation of the Alabama Coal, Iron, Land and Colonisation Co., only 1,405 of 2,000 bonds had been deposited; at this time the committee advised holders that they must either come in or "they must hereafter surrender their bonds in person or by their own agents to the Governor of the State of Alabama." *Economist*, XL (May 6, 1882), 546, and (Feb. 11, 1882), 177.

[48] The Alabama Coal, Iron, Land and Colonisation Co., Ltd., paid a 25 percent dividend in 1909, and in 1917 it paid 75 percent plus a 50 percent bonus [these were in part the gradual liquidation of its holdings]. Lewis, 83.

[49] The Cincinnati Southern was leased in Oct. 1881 by the Cincinnati, New Orleans and Texas Pacific, an operating company.

[50] All these companies (except the Alabama Great Southern which had an English as well as an American incorporation) were controlled by a British limited liability company, the Alabama, New Orleans, Texas and Pacific Junction. *Commercial and Financial Chronicle*, XXXVII (Oct. 20, 1883), 424.

[51] *Ibid.*, XXXVI (Jan. 20, 1883), 81.

[52] The Alabama Great Southern, for example, had to pass its dividend in 1885. *Economist*, XLIII (May 23, 1885), 639. Later in the same year the Alabama, New Orleans, Texas and Pacific Junction announced that neither the New Orleans and Northeastern nor the Vicksburg, Shreveport and Pacific had earned

territory was not yet developed.[53] Later the company became more prosperous.

Of all American railways, the Alabama Great Southern was undoubtedly the most completely British. It was British owned, British managed, and largely British built. Nevertheless, even this line was not completely British. Some American investment, dating from before the days of British control, remained in the various lines composing the system. Moreover, although the top officers were at first sent out from London,[54] they were shortly replaced from a group of American railway men whom British investors regarded as their protégés.[55] But, the Alabama Great Southern was completely owned by a British company supported by Erlanger and Company, a merchant banking house that by now was also domiciled in London.[56]

In 1916 the Alabama Great Southern and the New Orleans and Northeastern were sold to J. P. Morgan and became part of the main line of the Southern Railway,[57] the beeline route from Washington to New Orleans that the British investors had hoped to build when they first considered taking over the line. The holding company of the system, the Alabama, New Orleans, Texas and Pacific Junction Railroad Company, then became the Sterling Trust Company, Limited. British interest in this company was sold in 1924.

The Atlantic, Mississippi and Ohio Railroad was one of the roads out of which the British investors in the Alabama and Chattanooga originally hoped to form a through line from Washington to New Orleans. It ran

---

or paid their interest during the preceding two years; the holding company therefore proposed that these two roads should issue securities to reimburse it for this amount. *Ibid.* (Sept. 19, 1885), 1149. (Later the company was reorganized.)

[53] Of these railroads an article in the *Times* commented: "Altogether, the showing they make is a very poor one, and their prospects are far from encouraging, for the country they traverse requires much development before substantial earnings can be obtained. The lesson taught is the foolishness of investing in American railways on the strength of an apparently good "English" management, when the property itself is of so extremely poor a character." *Economist*, XLIV (May 29, 1886), 684. It must be remembered that the South was soon to begin to develop, especially in the production of iron and steel.

[54] John Swann, mentioned in connection with the Erie, was sent out from London to manage the Alabama Great Southern. He later served on other American railways where British interest was strong. Eventually he retired to Stockbridge, Mass., where the descendants of the family still live.

[55] Swann was followed by Frank Bond, who served on the Reading, on the Texas-Pacific, on the Alabama Great Southern, and later on the Chicago, Milwaukee and St. Paul. All of these roads were British dominated. Bond's tour of duty on the Texas-Pacific coincided with Robert Fleming's fight with Jay Gould over this line.

[56] Erlangers established a branch in London in 1870. R. J. Truptil, *British Banks and the London Money Market* (London: Jonathan Cape, 1936), 149.

[57] Lewis, 104 [and cf. Stover, 202, 246 and 281 fn.].

from Norfolk on the Atlantic seaboard to Bristol, a town half in Virginia and half in Tennessee.[58] At first glance this road's inclusion in a chapter entitled "The Attraction of Coal and Iron" might seem inappropriate. The Atlantic, Mississippi and Ohio lies in the southern, and purely agricultural, part of Virginia, and its great importance from the 1850's to the 1880's was derived from the fact that it was that state's only connection to the West.[59] Nevertheless, after its reorganization as the Norfolk and Western, it became a coaler par excellence and remains so today.

In the pre–Civil War period the line from Norfolk to Bristol was made up of three independent railways.[60] Shortly after the war, William Mahone, a former Confederate general who was a railway official in civilian life, consolidated these three roads into one through line by 1870.[61] Mahone had contacts in London. Many of these were probably derived from his work as president of the Virginian and North Carolina Immigration and Colonization Society, an organization founded after the Civil War to encourage the immigration of white labor to replace slave labor.[62] It is not clear whether there was any connection between this society and the visit of an enterprising British engineer, John Collinson, to Mahone in the summer of 1871. Collinson's purpose, to secure contracts from American

[58] At the time of its consolidation, the Atlantic, Mississippi and Ohio was reputed to be the longest continuous road in the U.S.

[59] The only gap in the Alleghenies through which a railway could be run without extensive tunneling was at Bristol. Virginia's other line to the West, the Virginia Central, also started to build track to the West further to the north. This route, however, required tunneling, and therefore the Virginia Central made little progress. It was only after the Civil War, when C.P. Huntington took over and reorganized it as the Chesapeake and Ohio, that it was completed.

[60] The three lines that were consolidated to form the Atlantic, Mississippi and Ohio were the Norfolk and Petersburg, the South Side Railroad (running from Petersburg to Lynchburg), and the Virginia and Tennessee Railroad. All three got their rails from Britain in the pre–Civil War period. Moreover, bonds of the Virginia and Tennessee, the longest and most important of the three, were known in London in the 1850's. Chandler, *Poor,* 68. These securities were mentioned in *Daniel Bell's Circular* in the 1850's.

[61] Mahone became president of the Norfolk and Petersburg in 1860, just before the Civil War, and returned to this line immediately after the war. He became president of the South Side in 1865. The directors of the Virginia and Tennessee opposed his plan for consolidation, and he was obliged to buy up the stock in order to gain control; by 1867 he was president of that railway too. Nelson Morehouse Blake, *William Mahone of Virginia* (Richmond: Garrett & Massie, 1935), 81.

[62] In the immediate post–Civil War period, most southern states were eager to encourage immigration from Europe, particularly of Germans and Scandinavians. Emigration agents were dispatched to various European cities. Nevertheless, few immigrants chose the South as a place to settle. Half-hearted attempts were made in the South to blame the agents of northern and western states for discouraging potential immigrants from going south. The main difficulty, as even the South realized, was that the counterattraction of western land was too strong. *De Bow's Review,* April–May 1866, p. 352.

railways for the purchase of iron and the negotiation of bonds,[63] resulted in agreement with Mahone.[64]

On returning to London, Collinson did not find the task he had undertaken easy. He not only had difficulty obtaining iron, but in negotiating the bonds he also encountered opposition from the Pennsylvania Railroad, at that time engaged in building up its railway holdings in the South.[65] Nevertheless, the bonds were brought out through the Union Bank of London in October 1871, and a number were sold.[66] Some, however, remained unsold in 1873 and were eventually taken to Amsterdam.[67]

On January 1, 1874, the Atlantic, Mississippi and Ohio defaulted. [Panic, depression, and poor revenues led to difficulties with British bondholders.] At first it appeared that arrangements for funding would be possible. Mahone traveled to London in October 1875.[68] At a meeting the following January presided over by Judah P. Benjamin, Q.C., the former Confederate Secretary for War, Mahone's proposals were approved.[69] Nevertheless, three months later the London Committee [70] broke with Mahone.[71]

It is impossible to say whether the quarrel with Mahone was trumped up by Collinson as an excuse for taking over the railway. The Alabama and

[63] Collinson was also involved in the negotiation in London of the bonds of the West Wisconsin. *Bullionist,* June 27, 1868. He also negotiated the Florida bonds issued in aid of the Jacksonville, Pensacola and Mobile. *Commercial and Financial Chronicle,* XVII (Sept. 6, 1873), 323.

[64] Blake, 121 n.

[65] The Pennsylvania was using the Southern Railway Security Company in these operations. Burgess and Kennedy, 279–80; Stover, 99 ff. Regarding opposition from the Pennsylvania, Collinson wrote to Mahone on Sept. 15, 1871: "A very influential friend of mine in the London Stock Exchange called me today, and presented a return to me which had just been brought over from America. It is a loan for $10,000,000 Norfolk & Great Western Railroad Bonds, $6,000,000 of which are guaranteed by the Pennsylvania Railroad Company. Negotiations had already been opened with a Paris house, but cooperation was desired here. I have managed to secure some delay, and hope to postpone the matter until after our issue." Quoted in Blake, 122 n. In view of the Pennsylvania's acknowledged activity in this area in the 1870's there seems no reason to doubt the authenticity of Collinson's report.

[66] Collinson took 9,500 7 percent first-mortgate gold bonds of $1,000 each at 68. Most of these were taken in London.

[67] Blake, 125.   [68] *Ibid.,* 128.   [69] *Times,* Jan. 7, 1876, p. 6.

[70] This London Committee included: Captain Henry Tyler, R.E.; J. C. Gooden; C. W. Lomer; Robert Monckton; T. E. Grassie; P. Myburgh; Hon. John Robertson; W. Brown; Henry Tredway; George Clarkson; J. L. Hale; and J. Collinson. None of the men seem to have been members of the great Anglo-American banking houses. From the point of view of British interest in American railways, Tyler was the most important among them and even he was an outsider. He started as a member of the office of the Railway Commissioner of the Board of Trade and from there worked his way into the management of various roads in which British interest was strong.

[71] *Times,* March 6, 1876, p. 6.

Chattanooga bondholders had already decided to take possession of that line in Alabama and were, no doubt, seeking railway connections. Moreover, some large bondholders still favored Mahone in 1876,[72] and Collinson had difficulty in getting the committee's support for his plan.[73] On the other hand, Mahone was determined to run the railway his own way with little regard to the rights or opinions of the bondholders.[74]

As in the case of the Alabama and Chattanooga, the foreclosure of the Atlantic, Mississippi and Ohio was difficult. Collinson had staunch support from Henry Tyler, the president of the Grank Trunk, who also controlled the Atlantic and Great Western in the late 1870's and early 1880's. But some powers in the City were averse to having the A.M.&O. joined to the Alabama to form a great through line. Barings, for example, had an association with the Louisville and Nashville, which hoped for connections with the A.M.&O. and was a competitor of the Alabama. Therefore, when Frederick J. Kimball,[75] the representative of E. W. Clark and Company,

[72] Hale, reported to be a very large bondholder, was strongly opposed to Collinson's plan. As late as 1878, he was still attending meetings to try to forestall foreclosure. *Ibid.*, June 20, 1878, p. 7.

[73] The meeting in March 1876 was a stormy one. Collinson finally threatened to resign if the committee persisted in resisting his demands.

[74] The main point at issue between Mahone and the London Committee was the disposition of $4 million of bonds authorized to be issued on the Cumberland Gap branch of the A.M.&O. When the Virginia Assembly authorized the formation of the A.M.&O., it included, along with the three predecessor roads making up the main line from Norfolk to Bristol, a fourth line. Chartered but as yet unbuilt, this line was planned to run from the main line near Bristol through the Cumberland Gap into Kentucky. Part of the agreement between General Mahone and the London Committee was that $4 million of these bonds would be deposited in London to prevent their being misappropriated to meeting the running expenses of the main line. After Mahone returned to Virginia he wrote to Collinson that he would be able to deposit only $3.5 million of these bonds instead of $4 million as originally agreed. He also wrote that he was unable to pay even half of the coupon due in April, as had also been agreed. It was on receipt of this communication that a meeting of March 1876 was called and the committee decided to abandon Mahone. Mahone's biographer says that there is no doubt that Mahone would have been able to pull through if the London Committee had continued to support him and quotes a letter from Mahone to H. H. Riddleberger: "The British went back on us. I made a settlement with them of all our matters, and while we were earnestly at work to carry it out, they broke it up and went secretly at work. They propose to seize the property in derogation of the rights of interest of all other parties. They cooly [*sic*] propose to wipe all interest but their own and the Divisional Bondholders, and these latter, they would hold as Creditors in their mercy." Blake, 129. Mahone's running of the line was so autocratic that it was said locally that A.M.&O. stood for "All Mine and Otelia's," Otelia being Mahone's wife. Joseph T. Lambie, *From Mine to Market: The History of Coal Transportation on the Norfolk and Western Railway* (New York: New York University Press, 1954), 5.

[75] Kimball was president of the Norfolk and Western for many years. Earlier he had served two years in the various British railway shops, mostly those of the London and Northwestern in the late 1860's. Lambie, 7, 20.

one of the largest private banking houses in Philadelphia,[76] arrived in London to arrange for the sale of the A.M.&O., he was able to find considerable support among those London houses that had long been established in the financing of American railways.[77] Nevertheless, Collinson was not yet defeated.

The London Committee proceeded with plans for the purchase of the A.M.&O. at foreclosure, issuing £260,000 of its own certificates to obtain funds. John Collinson and Captain Douglas Galton, the Railway Commissioner of the Board of Trade in the 1850's, once Tyler's superior and now his closest associate, went to Virginia to attend the foreclosure sale. After a number of postponements it took place on February 10, 1881. Although E. W. Clark and Company outbid John Collinson, he was not immediately replaced as the London agent of the railway. In 1881 the A.M.&O. became the Norfolk and Western Railroad Company, but Vivian, Gray and Company, the London house with which this road was henceforth associated, did not become the London representatives of the line until 1883.[78]

Whereas Collinson's chief aim probably had been to make the A.M.&O. into part of a beeline from Washington to New Orleans, E. W. Clark was primarily interested in coal. Nevertheless, even after the A.M.&O. had become the Norfolk and Western, it still sought western connections, especially with the East Tennessee. When the latter road proved uncooperative,[79] the Norfolk and Western turned more and more to the mountains of Virginia and the coal traffic. British interest in these coal lands, especially in the Kanawha field, dating from before the Civil War,[80] became more extensive.

Collinson had wanted to turn the A.M.&O. into a completely British line

---

[76] Clarence Clark, the senior partner, was a director of the Louisville and Nashville at this time.

[77] Erlanger and Co. was still a newcomer to London at that time. The London houses supporting Clark and Co. were: Foster and Braithwaite; Heseltine and Powell; Vivian, Gray; B. G. Goldsmid; John Taylor; Walker Russel; Herbert Wagg and Campbell; Thomas Nicholls; Clews and Lichtenstadt; F. L. Slous; Haes and Sons; L. Messel; Gowan and Marx; and T. E. Twycross. The London houses named held a total of about $1.5 million of the line's second-mortgage bonds, issued at 95 and bearing interest at 6 percent. In 1880 these firms addressed a letter to the Purchasing Committee of the A.M.&O. Published in the *Times*, it read in part: "In holding these certificates [the certificates of the Purchasing Committee] we do not wish to be understood to acquiesce either in the scheme proposed by your committee or in your subsequent proceedings, but that, on the contrary, we shall hold ourselves at liberty to represent our views before the Court if and whenever necessary." *Times*, March 3, 1880, p. 11. [See also Lambie, 6–8.]

[78] *Lambie*, 8.

[79] Although there was some British investment in the East Tennessee and the road later had British directors, this line did not cooperate with either the Alabama Southern, or the Norfolk and Western. Its ally was the Richmond and Danville.

[80] See above, p. 123.

on the pattern of the Alabama. The relationship between the Norfolk and Western and the London house of Vivian, Gray was more like that between the Chicago, Milwaukee and St. Paul, under the presidency of Alexander Mitchell, and its British supporters. The American president of the Norfolk and Western was in constant communication with Vivian, Gray, whose wishes were always respected. All financing was done through Vivian, Gray and associates acceptable to them. This house was also a party to profitable investment in related projects such as coal lands.[81] In return the London bankers undertook to support the securities of the line in the London market. Thus, the Norfolk and Western, like the Chicago, Milwaukee and St. Paul, came to be known in the City as a "cliqued" road.[82] Its London banking house was, in effect, a silent partner in all its operations, and outside operators could not influence the price of its securities.

Not only in the South did coal and iron play an important part in influencing the direction of British investment in American railways. Location of coal, iron, and other minerals was one of the factors uppermost in the minds of General William Palmer, an American Quaker, and his English associate, William Bell,[83] in deciding to build the Denver and Rio Grande.[84] The railway was only one part of the project. The founders

---

[81] The house of Heseltine and Powell was also sometimes associated with the financing of the Norfolk and Western. T. W. Powell was associated with Vivian, Gray in raising the capital for the Flat Top Coal Land Co. [an enterprise originated by E. W. Clark of E. W. Clark and Co. of Philadelphia, but which got much of its capital in England]. Later Robert Fleming, who had not yet founded a house in London, was also counted among the friends of this road. He was associated with Vivian, Gray in the sale of the railway's preferred shares in 1891. He also arranged a syndicate to buy control of the Scioto Valley in 1880. The price for the Scioto and New England was $3 million paid in preferred shares of the Norfolk and Western. *Economist*, XLVIII (June 21, 1890), 801. Good relations were also maintained with the Dutch house of A. A. H. Boissevain (Blake, Boissevain in London). Lambie, 38, 130–31.

[82] *Economist*, XLIV (July 3, 1886), 839.

[83] William Bell was the son of a London physician and a graduate of Cambridge. He traveled with Palmer on a trip of exploration through the West during which the idea of the Denver and Rio Grande was evolved. Subsequently he became the president of the North and South Construction Co., the contracting company that built the road. (The North and South Construction Co. was replaced by the Union Contract Co. of which Charles S. Hinchman was president; William Palmer was secretary of both companies.) Bell also served for a time as vice-president of the railway. It was undoubtedly through Bell that Maurice Kingsley, son of Charles Kingsley [author of *Westward Ho!*], became interested in the development of the Denver and Rio Grande. Young Kingsley was for a time an official of the company formed for the development of the town of Colorado Springs.

[84] [See Richard C. Overton, *Gulf to Rockies: The Heritage of the Fort Worth and Denver-Colorado and Southern Railways* (Austin: University of Texas Press, 1953), and Robert G. Athearn, *Rebel of the Rockies* (New Haven: Yale University Press, 1962), esp. 11–16.]

of the Denver and Rio Grande planned a new colony, designed to attract middle-class emigrants both from the East and from Britain.[85] In addition, a residential town was established at Colorado Springs and an industrial town at Pueblo. To carry out these enterprises, three organizations were separately incorporated: the railway, the land company, and the industrial company.[86] However, their securities were marketed jointly, and subscription to one carried with it the right to subscribe to the others.[87]

In spite of its strong London connections and the fact that many of its securities were marketed there and in Holland in the early 1870's, the Denver and Rio Grande did not at first maintain a close relationship with any particular London firm. Its primary banking connections were in Philadelphia, and coupons of the British-held securities were paid through various London houses on instruction from Philadelphia.[88]

Like many other American railways, this company found itself burdened with a large floating debt in the late 1870's. Arrangements for funding this obligation were made in New York with a syndicate, including foreign bankers. Shortly thereafter the Denver and Rio Grande was leased to the Atchison, Topeka and Santa Fe.[89] Indeed, the lease followed so closely after the funding that it is difficult to resist the inference that

[85] Greeley, Colorado, not Colorado Springs, was the pioneer colony founded with an eye to the encouragement of middle-class immigration to this area. Later, in the 1870's, Thomas Hughes, author of *Tom Brown's School Days*, also became active in this movement. Hughes bought a track of land in Tennessee near the line of the Cincinnati Southern and founded a town called Rugby, Tennessee. The difficulty with these colonies, as the *Times* pointed out, was that they could not hope to remain British but were bound to be eventually absorbed. Sept. 18, 1880, p. 6. The middle-class immigrant preferred to settle in the United States rather than Australia or New Zealand because he could return home to Britain quickly. New Zealand would have been preferable if it could have been towed around the world and anchored near Bermuda. The United States was preferable to Canada because it was felt that Canadian soil was inferior. Thomas Hughes, *Rugby, Tennessee* (London: Macmillan and Co., 1881).

[86] The three main companies were the Denver and Rio Grande Railway, the Central Colorado Improvement Co., and the Southern Coal and Iron Co., plus a number of their subsidiary companies. The Central Colorado Improvement Co. had a subsidiary company that was directly responsible for the building of Colorado Springs.

[87] George L. Anderson, *General William J. Palmer: A Decade of Colorado Railroad Building*, Colorado College Publication, General Series no. 209, Studies Series no. 22 (Colorado Springs, 1936), 119. This proliferation of companies led to a very complex financing. Thus, in 1879, the Coal and Iron Co. held $135,000 of the 5-year 6 percent coupon certificates of the Central Colorado Improvement Co., which in turn owned $1,040,000 of the 7 percent gold bonds of the Denver and Rio Grande Railway. *Commercial and Financial Chronicle*, XXX (April 3, 1880), 357.

[88] Coupons were paid by J. S. Morgan and Company in 1872; *Times* and by Samuel Montagu in 1876. *Times*, April 22, 1872, p. 4, and April 21, 1876, p. 6.

[89] *Commercial and Financial Chronicle*, XXVII (Sept. 21, 1878), 203; (Sept. 28, 1878), 331; and (Dec. 7, 1878), 603.

the two events were closely connected causally.[90] General Palmer now lost control,[91] and the railway, blocked by the Atchison from building south to the Rio Grande, had to turn west and to rely more completely on mineral traffic.

However, as a result of this new financing, securities of the Denver and Rio Grande became very popular in London. Ordinary shares, as well as bonds, were transferred to London in large quantities in the early 1880's, and after the road again found itself in financial difficulties in the middle 1880's, it came under the control of a London Committee. This development is discussed in a later chapter.

The Alabama Great Southern, the Norfolk and Western, and the Denver and Rio Grande were not the only American railways dependent largely on coal and iron traffic to find favor with British investors. They are not even the only American railways of this type that became largely British owned.[92] The Philadelphia and Reading, one of the earliest roads in which British interest became predominant, is an anthracite-carrying road. In addition, a number of smaller "coalers" came under British control. For example, the Shenango and Allegheny, a short line that resulted from the rationalization of the leased lines trusts of the Atlantic and Great Western, was also a coal road.

In the period after 1879 British interest in coal and iron areas in all parts of the United States was destined to become even more extensive. British companies were formed to exploit coal areas adjacent to many American railways. The Central Pacific Coal and Coke Company, Ltd., is a

[90] This impression is strengthened by the following letter from John Murray Forbes of Boston to Charles J. Paine, a director of the Chicago, Burlington and Quincy, Sept. 27, 1878: "There is room for a compromise perhaps a capitulation on the part of the D.&R. [Denver and Rio Grande] and A.&T. [Atchison, Topeka and Santa Fe] which would be good for both. From what I gather great irritation personally prevails which makes a danger that they may renew their alliance with Jay Gould, which I think is not their natural alliance.

It occurred to me that if you could take your gun and come out to shoot Elk or blacktail in the South Park while I am here you would naturally be thrown into social intercourse with Bill Palmer and others which might lead to a renewal of friendly relations. I have nothing definite to base this upon and perhaps it partly grows out of a desire to see you in this splendid country." Cochran, 336.

[91] Palmer retained control of the Denver and Rio Grande Western. He also continued to be active in the Mexican National, the line originally planned to carry the Denver and Rio Grande south from the Mexican border to Mexico City. This line was built in the 1880's with financial support from Matheson and Co. of London.

[92] American and British creditors of the Utica, Ithaca & Elmira reached a compromise by which the British assumed the American claim and the Americans withdrew. The railway was then turned over to Daniel A. Lindley and Edward K. Goodnow, representing the British bondholders, at a nominal price of $50,000, the British agreeing to equip and complete it. *Commercial and Financial Chronicle*, XXVI (May 4, 1878), 445.

good example.[93] In the South, particularly, there were extensive British holdings both in Virginia and in the Tennessee-Alabama area dominated by the Tennessee Coal, Iron and Railroad Company.[94]

[93] *Ibid.*, XXIX (Aug. 9, 1879), 137.

[94] Examples are numerous, but perhaps the North Alabama Development Co., Ltd., is representative. This company was connected with the Birmingham, Sheffield and Tennessee River Railway Co., a road which was British controlled. Its object was to purchase coal and iron ore properties in northern Alabama adjacent to this line. Contracts were made in advance with the Tennessee Coal, Iron and Railroad Co. that ensured the North Alabama Co. a market for all its iron ore output. *Economist*, XLVIII (March 8, 1890), 304–5.

PART THREE

VII

The Organization of the Market for American Securities in London, 1879–1898

THE 1880's was the first decade in which American railway securities gained substantial popularity in London. The base of this popularity had been laid in the period from the close of the Civil War to 1879, in spite of the difficulties with the Erie, the Atlantic and Great Western, the Philadelphia and Reading, and a handful of smaller companies. From 1872 to 1876, large amounts of senior securities of established roads had been purchased that not only yielded higher rates of return than other securities traded in London but also appreciated steadily in price. Substantial capital gains were made.[1] In the late 1870's the United States began to emerge from the long depression following the Jay Cooke crisis of 1873.[2] The prices of American railway securities again rose in New York, and London anticipated another boom in American rails. The organization of the London market for American securities had been changing significantly since the Civil War.

Foremost in importance were the great international merchant banking firms.[3] Seven of these financial houses, with their associated firms in the United States, dominated the Anglo-American financial scene. Three of these houses, J. S. Morgan (Drexel, Morgan of New York);[4] Brown,

---

[1] Cairncross, Table 53, 229.

[2] The immediate cause of the crisis that took place in the autumn of 1873 was the failure of the house of Jay Cooke and Co., but, as has already been pointed out, defaults by the newer railways of the South and West had mounted up earlier.

[3] The author chose to use the term international instead of Anglo-American because firms like Rothschilds and Philip Speyer were regarded in New York at that time as foreign banking houses.

[4] J. S. Morgan and Co. was the successor firm to George Peabody and Co. The house of Drexel, Morgan was comparatively new in 1879. When J. P. Morgan, the son of J. S. Morgan, returned to New York to enter the banking business there, he first became a partner in Dabney, Morgan and Co. On the dissolution of this house, Drexel, Morgan was formed. Drexel and Co. of Philadelphia was an old established firm.

Shipley (Brown Brothers of New York); [5] and Morton, Rose (Morton, Bliss of New York), [6] were of American origin. A fourth, Baring Brothers, was of English origin. [7] This firm differed from the first three in that not until 1891 was a house bearing the family name established in New York. [8] For many years it had depended on its American agent, T. W. Ward, and later his son Samuel G. Ward, who was joined by his brother, George Cabot Ward. Barings had been increasing its dependence on selected correspondents. [9] After Samuel G. Ward's retirement the London house announced in a circular that it would divide its business between the agency of Baring, Magoun of New York and Kidder, Peabody of Boston. [10]

The remaining three firms were of Continental origin, with associates in New York. [11] They were N. M. Rothschild (August Belmont and Company in New York); [12] Seligman Brothers (J. and W. Seligman and Company of New York); [13] and Speyer Brothers (Philip Speyer and Company of New York). [14] Rothschilds was established in London in the early nineteenth century and perhaps should be included, with Barings, as a house of English origin. Seligmans and Speyers were comparative newcomers to London, both firms having established houses in England in the 1860's.

The merchant banking firms in the United States had been junior

[5] Brown, Shipley (originally W. & J. Brown) was founded in Liverpool in association with the Brown family firm, already active in Baltimore, which had been founded by an Irishman. An office was later opened in London in 1863, and the Liverpool house was closed in 1889.

[6] Levi P. Morton, Sir John Rose, and Pascoe Du Pré Grenfell were the principal members of Morton, Rose. Levi P. Morton and George Bliss were the principal members of Morton, Bliss. The firm was eventually amalgamated with the Guaranty Trust Co. of New York.

[7] The Baring family was of Continental origin. Baring migrated from Bremen, Germany, to Exeter, England, in 1717. Truptil, 138. [See also Hidy, *House of Baring*, 429, 492 n.] Barings had close connections with the United States from the end of the eighteenth century. Both Alexander and Henry Baring married Americans. Two Americans, Joshua Bates and Russell Sturgis, were partners in the firm for many years.

[8] The partners in Baring, Magoun and Co. were Alexander Baring, formerly of Kennedy, Tod and Co., New York, and George Magoun, formerly of Kidder, Peabody and Co.

[9] Hidy, *House of Baring*, 421–22 and 482.

[10] *Economist*, XLIX (May 2, 1891), 577.

[11] [See Barry E. Supple, "A Business Elite: German-Jewish Financiers in Nineteenth-Century New York," *Business History Review*, XXXI (Summer 1957), 143–78.]

[12] August Belmont was also of Continental origin.

[13] Like the Rothschilds, the Seligman family came from Germany and was prolific enough to supply partners for houses in all the financial capitals. In the latter respect, the Seligmans also resembled the Brown family of Brown, Shipley.

[14] The parent firm was Lazard Speyer-Ellissen of Frankfort. Philip Speyer had a comparatively small house in New York in the 1850's; the London house was not established until the 1860's, but it became powerful by the 1880's.

associates in the 1850's. After the Civil War they grew in strength and approached a position of equality to their older counterparts in London.[15] To a greater and greater extent, American houses became more like partners and were able to initiate action instead of merely functioning as agents.[16] In the 1870's the syndicates for funding the federal debt gave a number of these houses considerable experience in working together, and they also acted for other houses. This collaboration was not an entirely new development,[17] but the amounts of securities involved were now very large.[18] These new syndicates were of an informal continuing nature; the same houses formed the backbone of many syndicates.[19] The pattern of operation, evolved in connection with federal bonds, served for the flotation of large new railway issues [20] and for the reorganizations that were such a striking feature of the late 1880's and most of the 1890's.

These great merchant banking houses maintained close ties with a number of American railways. It was precisely the combination of these characteristics, a transatlantic partnership, the ability to work together, and the maintenance of close and continuing relationships with a number of American railways, that distinguished the seven dominant houses.

A number of smaller houses, including several of American origin, worked closely with the main houses. The once powerful firm of Jay Cooke, McCulloch dwindled and was transformed into Melville, Evans and

[15] In the three instances of Barings, the Morgans, and Rothschilds, the London house was the senior firm. Morton, Rose and Morton, Bliss were founded within a short time of each other, but the American house was slightly older. Moreover, both Levi P. Morton and George Bliss had been established in New York separately before the formation of Morton, Bliss. In the case of Seligmans and Speyers, the Continental houses were older.

[16] In one syndicate for the negotiation of the 4½ percent U.S. loan, Morton, Bliss represented the United States Trust Co.; the Merchants' Bank; the American Exchange Bank; the Third National Bank; Kuhn, Loeb and Co.; and Winslow, Lanier and Co. [For refunding syndicates of the federal debt, see Redlich, II, 365–69.]

[17] Thus, when the bonds of the Marietta and Cincinnati were offered in London in 1852, it was stated that they had already been taken by a group of New York capitalists who had transferred the bonds to London. *Daily News,* Sept. 4, 1852, p. 7.

[18] At the beginning of 1872, $300 million of the U.S. 5 percent loan and a further $300 million of the U.S. 4½ percent loan were offered by Jay Cooke, McCulloch, and Rothschild, acting for a syndicate. *Times,* Jan. 6, 1872, p. 7.

[19] The syndicate, which acted for the U.S. government in selling 4 percent federal bonds abroad in 1879, included Rothschilds; Morgans; Morton, Rose; and Seligmans. *Commercial and Financial Chronicle,* XXVIII (Jan. 25, 1879), 79. Speyer and Co. acted with various members of this syndicate in negotiation of railway bonds in the early 1880's. It would appear that Brown, Shipley and Barings remained aloof from these early syndicates, but they too joined in on the Philadelphia and Reading reorganization issues. *Economist,* XLV (Sept. 10, 1887), 1157.

[20] For example, the flotation of $40 million of the bonds of the Northern Pacific Railway in 1881. *Economist,* XXXVIII (Dec. 4, 1880), 1426.

Company.[21] It continued in business but was not of outstanding importance in the market for American railway securities in this period.

Some New England firms played significant roles. One smaller American firm, Blake Brothers of Boston, gained importance. Its origin was as Gilmore, Blake and Ward, a correspondent of Barings that specialized in securities.[22] For a time it had a close relationship with George Peabody.[23] Moreover, by the 1880's, the firm acquired strong Dutch connections, as is attested by the admission of A. A. H. Boissevain to Blake's own London house in 1886.[24] Blake Brothers of New York and Boston (Blake, Boissevain of London) worked closely with Speyer Brothers, the latter taking the lead. The principal interest of these firms was railways, such as the Union Pacific and the Chicago, Milwaukee and St. Paul. Another Boston firm that was ultimately to become important was Lee, Higginson and Company.[25] It began as a stock brokerage firm in 1848 and had a close relationship with John Murray Forbes [a leading Boston investor in western railroads]. Although Henry Lee Higginson made many trips to London during the last quarter of the nineteenth century, a house was not established there until near the end of the period.

Some British stockbroking firms were also closely associated with the seven great London houses, although they acted independently on occasion. Among these Borthwick, Wark;[26] Foster and Braithwaite; and E. F. Satterthwaite and Company were preeminent.[27]

In addition to the great houses and their satellites, there was a comparatively independent group. These houses acted together in much the same

[21] *Times*, Sept. 25, 1873, p. 5.

[22] Ralph Hidy, *House of Baring*, 399 [and 448–49]. [The Blake firm had several names as partners changed. In the early 1850's it was Blake, Ward and Co. with George Baty Blake and George Cabot Ward, son of T. W. Ward, Barings' agent in Boston. Blake, Howe and Co. was its name in 1853.]

[23] Muriel Hidy, "George Peabody," 316.

[24] *Economist*, XLVI (Jan. 7, 1888), 19. Before this time, Blake Brothers of London consisted of Francis Blake and Emil Heineman. Heineman set up his own firm in 1886 and also became important in the negotiation of American securities. The partners in Blake, Boissevain were Stanton Blake, A. A. H. Boissevain and F. B. Blake, and the firm was termed general merchants. However, Blake Brothers had had Dutch connections before this time. In 1879 the agency of the Nederlandsche-Maatschpiij was divided between Blake Brothers and Carter, Hawley and Co.

[25] Lee, Higginson and Co. was founded by John C. Lee of Salem and George Higginson of Boston. Bliss Perry, *Life and Letters of Henry Lee Higginson* (Boston: Atlantic Monthly Press, 1921), 268.

[26] The principal partners of Borthwick, Wark in 1887 were John Wark, Herbert Charles Mayhew, Thomas Rutledge Denman, and Charles Stewart Makery.

[27] Satterthwaite did not always confine his operations to the brokerage business, as is shown by his bankruptcy in 1894. Moreover, it appears that to a greater extent than Foster and Braithwaite he acted independently of the large houses.

way as did the big syndicates. Several of the firms making up the nucleus of this group were merchant houses. One was J. K. Gilliat and Company of London (Maitland, Phelps in New York [28] in which George Coppell, an Englishman, was a partner). When the Denver and Rio Grande came under the control of a London Committee led by Gilliat and Company, George Coppell became the chairman of the railway's board of directors. Other houses were Robert Benson and Company,[29] Pothonier and Company,[30] and Rathbone Brothers.[31]

Several important firms in this group were referred to as stockbroking firms, although, as far as investment banking activities were concerned, the distinction between the smaller merchant houses and the larger stockbroking firms was becoming tenuous, not only in New York but also in London. Of the larger stockbroking firms connected with this group, Heseltine and Powell was undoubtedly the oldest. This firm was for many years the representative of the British bondholders of the Marietta and Cincinnati. Moreover, in the 1880's T. W. Powell became the London representative of the Pennsylvania.[32] Vivian, Gray and Company, another stockbroking firm, commanded a significant position, particularly through its connections with the Norfolk and Western.

Robert Fleming of Dundee, another member of this group, was neither a merchant nor a stockbroker.[33] He eventually founded a merchant banking

[28] Gilliat and Co. was a very old firm, dating back to the eighteenth century. The name became J. K. Gilliat and Co. in the middle of the nineteenth century. In the 1880's the head of the firm was John Saunders Gilliat, a son of J. K. Gilliat. J. S. Gilliat became a member of the Court of the Bank of England in the 1880's and governor in 1884. He died in 1912.

[29] Robert Benson and Co., representative of the Illinois Central from the middle of the 1850's, failed after the death of its senior partner in 1875. *Times*, Jan. 13, 1875, p. 6, and June 18, 1875, p. 8. Within a few months Robert Benson's son, also called Robert, entered into a partnership with J. W. Cross to carry on his father's business in American securities. *Ibid.*, Sept. 20, 1875, p. 6. The name Robert Benson and Co. was resumed in the 1880's.

[30] Pothonier and Co. was originally engaged in the grain trade, particularly from Alexandria. The member of the firm often mentioned in connection with American rails is Sligo de Pothonier.

[31] Rathbone Brothers was originally a Liverpool house that also maintained a New York branch.

[32] T. Wiggin (later the London, Asiatic and American Co.) represented the Pennsylvania for many years; when this house failed, its liquidator, F. Boykett, took over this function. Later he was replaced by T. W. Powell. The Heseltine family was also an old City family. An A. R. Heseltine was listed as a stockbroker of Capel Court in the 1820's.

[33] Fleming was born in Dundee in 1845 and in his youth became a clerk in the jute firm of Baxter and Co., which had large investments in American railways. In the early 1870's the Baxters sent Fleming to the United States in connection with these investments. While on this trip Fleming was so impressed by the prospects of the United States and of its railways that on his return he founded the Scottish American Investment Trust. Thereafter he devoted all his time to American railway investments.

house bearing his name,[34] but during the 1880's and 1890's his primary connection was with Scottish investment trusts.[35] During the last quarter of the nineteenth century he was a person of considerable importance in the annals of British investment in American railways.

Some evidence that these houses worked together is shown by the case of the Denver and Rio Grande. The London Protective Committee, set up immediately after this company's default in 1884, was formed and dominated by J. K. Gilliat and Company.[36] Yet the delegates whom this committee sent to the United States were Robert Fleming, Sligo de Pothonier, and Dillwyn Parrish.[37] Moreover, Robert Fleming was a member of the later London Committee by which this road was controlled in the late 1880's.[38]

There is also evidence of cooperation among these various firms on the Norfolk and Western, whose representatives in London were Vivian, Gray and Company.[39] Robert Fleming sat on the Norfolk's board of directors for many years,[40] while T. W. Powell was associated in the financing of the Flat Top Coal Company, an enterprise formed to develop the coal lands

[34] Toward the close of the nineteenth century, Fleming opened an office in London to facilitate his operations. He did not establish the house of Robert Fleming and Co. until 1909. Nevertheless, even before this house's inception, his operations in American railway securities were very large. Thus, from 1901 to 1909, Fleming's participations in American securities amounted to approximately $34 million, of which the larger amounts were as follows:

Kansas City Street Railway 5 percent bonds	$ 1,400,000
Pennsylvania Shares (through Kuhn, Loeb)	2,000,000
Union Pacific 5 percent notes at 98½ percent	1,100,000
Lake Shore 4 percent bonds at 96	1,000,000
Wisconsin Central Duluth 4 percent bonds	1,000,000
Union Pacific 4 percent bonds at 90 percent	2,500,000
Atchison, Topeka and Santa Fe 5 percent bonds	3,000,000
Kansas City, Fort Scott and Gulf 4 percent bonds	1,193,000
Caroline Clinchfield 5 percent bonds	1,000,000
Western Pacific 5 percent bonds	1,000,000
Chicago Great Western Railway Syndicate	2,200,000
Others (approx.)	16,500,000
Total	$33,893,000

This information was supplied from the files of the company to the author by Major Philip Fleming, son of Robert Fleming, in a letter dated Jan. 29, 1958.

[35] J. S. Kennedy & Co. (later Kennedy, Tod and Co.) was the correspondent of the Scottish American Investment Trust in New York, but Kuhn, Loeb & Co. often appeared in association with Fleming and, indeed, with other members of this group.

[36] *Economist*, XLII (Dec. 13, 1884), 1521.

[37] *Commercial and Financial Chronicle*, XL (Feb. 7, 1885), 181.

[38] *Burdett's Official Intelligence* (1885). The complete London Protective Committee concerned with the Denver and Rio Grande was: Howard Gilliat, chairman; H. J. Chinnery; T. Collier; and Robert Fleming. The inclusion of H. J. Chinnery of Chinnery Brothers should be noted and included in this group.

[39] See above, pp. 135–36.   [40] Lambie, 74.

along the railway's line. George Coppell was called in to advise the railway on its finances in 1895.[41]

Similarly, although Robert Benson and Company took the lead in the Chicago Great Western,[42] the Gilliats and William Lidderdale [43] of Rathbone and Company were also interested in this road.[44] Moreover, in the early 1900's, Robert Fleming was also a member of the syndicate formed for the flotation of this company's securities.[45] With the exception of William Lidderdale, the names enumerated above appeared in different combinations time and again in connection with the American railway securities. These firms seldom appeared in connection with the railways in which any of the great houses had an established interest, although there were exceptions.[46]

Whenever the London market evinced great interest in American railway securities and large numbers of new issues were being brought forward, a number of houses that did not ordinarily float American railway securities were attracted to them. In the 1880's Matheson and Company, the parent firm of Jardine, Matheson, the leading British firm in the China trade, became interested in the Mexican National; [47] Dent, Palmer, another China firm, which had been active much earlier in the flotation of American railway securities, also undertook one issue in the late 1880's. This issue was the first-mortgage bonds of the Cleveland and Canton, a

[41] *Ibid.,* 148.

[42] The Chicago Great Western was formed in 1892 by amalgamation of the Minnesota and Northwestern and the Chicago, St. Paul and Kansas City.

[43] Lidderdale began his commercial career in Heath and Co. in 1847. Later he moved to Rathbone Brothers and represented that firm in New York from 1857 to 1863. In 1864 he became a Rathbone partner. Later he became a director of the Bank of England and was governor of the bank at the time of the Baring crisis.

[44] Both Gilliat and William Lidderdale were members of the original London Finance Committee of the Chicago Great Western which included: Rt. Hon. William Lidderdale, A. F. Wallace, H. Gilliat, A. Gray, and C. Sligo de Pothonier. Robert Benson and Co. was the agent of the Chicago, Great Western. *Burdett's Official Intelligence* (1893).

[45] See above, p. 148, n. 34.

[46] Especially after the Baring crisis, various members of the group given above were associated with Baring roads, the Atchison, Topeka and Santa Fe, for example.

[47] *Economist,* XL (July 8, 1882), 848. The bonds of the Mexican National were issued in 1882. The Committee on the Mexican National also included many of the group of smaller merchant houses: Matheson; Thomas Collier; Robert Fleming; William Grantham, M.P.; Everett Gray (of Vivian, Gray & Co.); Joseph G. Price (of the English Association of American Bond and Share Holders); L. Messel; C. Sligo de Pothonier; A. G. Renshaw; Edward Wagg (of Herbert Wagg & Co.); and Dillwyn Parrish (associated with Scottish investments trusts). It may be that Matheson and Co.'s interest in the Mexican National, a narrow-gauge road originally planned as a continuation of the Denver and Rio Grande to Mexico City, was connected with silver for trade with China.

narrow-gauge road in Ohio.[48] William Russell and Company, an American firm in the China trade, put out an issue for the Railroad Equipment Company.[49] In October 1888 C. J. Hambro floated two issues of American railway bonds.[50]

From the point of view of American railways, the establishment of a close and continuous relationship with a financial middleman was unquestionably highly desirable. The association might be with a wealthy merchant or merchant banking house or with a stockbroking firm that had close connections with one of them. Such a house was able to supply short-term credits for which it would ultimately be reimbursed when the market became favorable for a flotation of an issue of bonds. Such accommodation was particularly valuable for American railways because of their predilection for financing construction by running up vast floating debts.[51] As long as the railway could count on its bankers for support, all was well. Failure to obtain financial assistance generally brought trouble, in the form either of a change of management or of default on obligations.[52]

The merchant firms and the larger stockbroking firms were not the only

[48] The issue of the Cleveland and Canton was for $2 million of first-mortgage bonds at 97½ percent. The money was needed to change the line from narrow gauge to standard gauge. *Economist*, XLVI (Jan. 28, 1888), 110.

[49] The issue of the Railroad Equipment Co. was for $1 million of 6 percent car trust bonds. Russell and Co. advertised themselves as of New York, China, and London. *Ibid.*, XLI (Feb. 17, 1883), 208.

[50] These two issues were $1 million for the Marietta and North Georgia and $1.5 million for the Knoxville, Cumberland Gap and Louisville. *Burdett's Official Intelligence* (1893).

[51] [A study of mortgages shows that to safeguard investors a clause was often inserted stating that bonds would be issued to a certain number per completed and equipped mile on certification of that accomplishment. Since bond issue then must await construction, short-term loans were essential.]

[52] As early as 1839 the Baltimore and Ohio had established a close relationship with Barings. Since American securities were unsalable in London at that time, Barings advanced the credit to purchase iron for building toward Harper's Ferry, taking £720,000 of Maryland bonds as security. Ralph Hidy, *House of Baring,* 281. Similarly, in the 1870's J. P. Morgan bought an issue of Baltimore and Ohio bonds outright since the market was unfavorable for sale to investors. In the case of the Illinois and St. Louis Bridge, when the company was unable to meet its interest in Oct. 1874, a loan was negotiated with J. S. Morgan. Further loans were made in 1875 and eventually the trustees, J. P. Morgan and Solon Humphreys, took over. *Commercial and Financial Chronicle,* XX (June 5, 1875), 545. Thus, one often runs across statements in the financial press that certain issues of American railway bonds in London would not affect the foreign exchange since the proceeds long ago had been transferred to the United States.

Professor Edward C. Kirkland told the author that Charles Francis Adams, Jr., attributed his removal from the presidency of the Union Pacific to the fact that he had been unable to make arrangements with Barings for that railway's floating debt. Trottman also stated that it was failure to deal with the floating debt of the Union Pacific that brought about Adams's defeat. Nelson Trottman, *History of the Union Pacific* (New York: Ronald Press Co., 1923), 241.

agencies to issue American railway securities. As mentioned, many of the investment trust companies did not rely solely on the income yields of investments for earnings. Some also floated American railway bonds. The Railway Share Investment Trust,[53] headed for many years by Sir Samuel Laing, formerly Finance Minister for India,[54] seems to have had much the same relationship with the railways whose securities it floated as did some of the merchant houses. So deeply was this trust engaged in financing [55] that toward the end of the 1890's it announced that it would seek reorganization in order to participate in the syndicates.[56] Thus American railways were sometimes able to establish a continuing relationship with investment trust companies, advantageous both to the railway and to British investors.

Establishment of a close relationship was not usually the case when the bonds came onto the market through one of the Johnny-come-lately firms that always clung about the edges of a boom. These firms varied considerably in type. Some were suspect organizations like the Co-operative Credit Bank, which disposed of a number of bonds of the Keokuk and Kansas City before the arrest of its partners.[57] Some were firms founded by eminently respectable outsiders such as Bernard Cracroft,[58] the Cambridge alumnus who commissioned Robert Giffen's work on American railways in the 1870's,[59] or S. F. Van Oss, the one-time editor of the *Journal of Finance*

[53] There were two organizations, the Railway Debenture Investment Trust and the Railway Share Investment Trust Co., both under the same management.

[54] Sir Samuel Laing (1812–1897), B.A., Cambridge University, where he was Second Wrangler and second Smith's Prizeman, began his career as secretary to the Railway Department of the Board of Trade. Later he was Financial Secretary of the Treasury and then Finance Minister for India.

[55] There were damaging revelations about the Railway Share Investment Trust's financial operations in 1884, but the matter was smoothed over. *Economist*, XLIV (July 10, 1886), 857.

[56] The *Economist* remarked that the Railway Share Investment Trust did not publish lists of its securities, but that a list was known to consist mainly of American railway securities, many of which were highly speculative and fluctuating. *Ibid.*, XLVI (Nov. 10, 1888), 1410.

[57] *Times*, Nov. 5, 1875, p. 5, and Jan. 25, 1876, p. 7. Even reputable firms like Brooks and Co. (whose sole proprietor for many years was Sir William Cunliffe Brooks) occasionally undertook a very suspicious issue. In 1886 this house inserted a most peculiar prospectus in the *Times*, which announced the issue of $5 million of first-mortgage gold 6 percent bonds of the Eastern and Western Air Line Railway Co. The advertisement carried a list of trustees in the United Kingdom including Sir Francis Wyatt, Sir John Robert Heron-Maxwell, W. Leatham Bright of Tyler and Bright, and Arthur Sperling. Sir Charles Bright, M. Inst. C.E., was named as a consulting engineer. The proposed road was to run from New York to Chicago. *Ibid.*, July 5, 1886, p. 13.

[58] Cracroft failed soon after the publication of Giffen's work, which was but one in an impressive series entitled *Sir Cracroft's Investment Tracts*.

[59] Sir Robert Giffen, *American Railways as Investments* (London: Edward Stanford, 1873).

and author of *American Railroads as Investments*.[60] Whether these firms failed or were successful, they were not in a position to protect the holders of bonds marketed through them.

Another group responsible for the introduction of considerable quantities of American railway bonds onto the London market in this period were the arbitrageurs.[61] As early as the 1830's firms like Brown, Shipley and George Peabody, among others, had employed this means of settling balances during times when American securities were in demand in London.[62] In 1860, the *Bankers' Magazine* remarked that foreign exchange was ordinarily regulated by the transfer of securities. In the 1880's the *Economist* again noted that movement of securities settled the exchange.[63] But the movement of American railway shares to London in the period from 1879 to 1881, although undoubtedly carried on in a manner that would not unnecessarily upset the exchange rate, was much more than a mere mechanism for the short-term balancing of the exchanges. By the end of 1879 the spectacular rise in the price of some American railway securities from that of the depressed middle 1870's had reawakened the interest of the speculative element in the City. It was hard to resist temptation in the face of an unexampled rise that more than doubled the price of many railway shares in the course of one year.[64]

In the late 1870's, if not earlier, the very scale of British investment in America provided a partly autonomous impetus to its further growth. After 1865 substantial holdings in federal obligations yielded a steady flow of interest. Considerable capital gains were also made. Furthermore, taking as base the estimate of £100 million for the total of British holdings of American railway securities at the end of 1879,[65] the annual yield of this class of securities could not have been less than £5 million and was probably more. With the growing enthusiasm for American rails, a large part of the current annual earnings on British investments in the United States was reinvested in additional railway securities. Even in depression years some interest and dividends were ploughed back. Moreover, by the

[60] London: Effingham Wilson and Co., 1893.

[61] The leading firm of arbitrageurs in New York was Osborn & Co. [Arbitrageurs were dealers taking advantage of the difference in prices in various national markets to buy and sell items that go to make up the balance of payments, including securities and coupons.]

[62] Muriel Hidy, "George Peabody," 263.

[63] *Economist*, XLI (July 14, 1883), 818.

[64] Nash, *Profitable Nature of Investments* (2d ed.), 46–50. In particular, Nash mentions that the shares of the Union Pacific that were admitted to quotation on the London Stock Exchange in Dec. 1878 had appreciated $27 during 1879. Assuming that the shares were purchased at the price that they commanded at the time of their introduction, the yield to the purchaser, dividend plus capital gain, amounted to 45 percent.

[65] See above, p. 88.

end of the period annual interest and dividends on American rails may have totaled £16 million.[66] The investment of current earnings accounted for a large part of the increase in British holdings of American rails over this period.

The London and New York security markets were so big and their interconnections so intimate that large gross movements between them were frequent, particularly in times of panic. Therefore, it would be erroneous to attempt to infer net movements over time from panic sales. The fact that crises in one market did not necessarily coincide with crises in the other intensified gross movements. But panic liquidation was often succeeded by repurchase in the following months, and the net change was probably relatively small.

Finally, prices of American rails were affected by the weather and crop reports in the United Kingdom [as well as those in the United States]. Since Cobden's day the connection between American railways and food for Europe had been apparent. After the United States' bumper harvest in the late 1870's, the connection between bad harvest in Europe and profits for American railways also came to be widely known. Thus, good weather in the United Kingdom might mean a flat market for American rails in London.

The first new development of the period from 1879 through 1898 was the introduction onto the London market of the shares of a number of American railways, of which a dozen or so were destined to become favorites. Before 1878 the shares of only six American railways had been quoted and actively traded in London, namely those of the Erie, the Illinois Central, the New York Central, the Pennsylvania, the Philadelphia and Reading, and the Central of New Jersey, an affiliated line of the Reading.[67] Except for the shares of the Central of New Jersey, all of these had been known and traded in London since the 1850's. Speculative interest in the late 1860's had been concentrated on Erie shares, and the burst of investment from 1872 to 1875 had been confined to senior securities. From 1879, for the first time, the market for American shares, and particularly for speculative shares, began to widen.

Surprisingly enough, the first new American shares to attain quotation on the London Stock Exchange were those of a Jay Gould road, the Union Pacific. At the time of their introduction these shares were paying dividends and commanding a fair price. However, they were not investment securities, and their British purchasers did not regard them as such. Jay Gould had not reformed.[68] He had merely devised a more orthodox tech-

[66] This is based on information from the Inland Revenue and from Somerset House. Nathaniel T. Bacon, "American International Indebtedness," *Yale Review*, Nov. 1900, pp. 265–85.

[67] See, for example, the listing given in the *Times* each day.

[68] For a short time the *Economist* seems to have fallen into this error. Thus in

nique of milking the market. Having bought up the nondividend shares of the Union Pacific at the bargain price of 30 during the depression of the 1870's, he gained control of the board of directors. Once control was firmly established, he arranged for the dividends to be resumed. As the holder of 190,000 shares he was quickly able to recoup a part of his initial investment. Moreover, due to the resumption of dividends the shares began to appreciate in value. In 1879 he was able to dispose of a block of 100,000 at a price reported to be between 70 and 75.[69] Presumably it was a part of this block that appeared on the London market in 1879. But if the British investor took these shares in any quantity, he probably did so to hold them only for a short time in order to make capital gains. When the Union Pacific ceased paying dividends in 1884, British holdings were small. After this date, when these shares became primarily speculative, British holdings began to increase [see Table 6].[70]

Table 6. Distribution of Union Pacific shares
by ownership, 1884–91

Year	U.K.	Holland	Total Foreign	Mass.	N.Y.
1884	13,289	31,675	51,748	238,268	263,065
1885	29,567	42,075	76,997	228,630	244,197
1886	82,616	53,785	142,332	208,601	203,084
1887	62,546	51,355	118,272	201,882	239,736
1888	67,745	60,713	132,479	197,773	210,789
1889	110,876	55,805	171,003	157,905	233,218
1890	153,089	39,935	199,836	150,148	218,567
1891	185,220	22,481	214,418	149,257	203,350

SOURCE: *Economist*, L (May 14, 1892), 630.

For over a year after the Union Pacific's admission to quotation in 1878 there were no others. The year 1880 marked a radical departure in that a number of American railways were admitted to quote on the London Stock Exchange. Nevertheless, of these, only the shares of the St. Louis and San Francisco were really speculative.[71] The shares of two of these roads, the

the *Commercial History and Review of 1879,* p. 39, the editors said that Gould was no longer a stock operator but had become a leading railway capitalist and manager. [Cf. Grodinsky.]

[69] *Commercial and Financial Chronicle,* XXVIII (Feb. 22, 1879), 200.

[70] The *Economist* censured the British investor for buying the Union Pacific shares after they had become speculative. It would seem equally pertinent to congratulate him for shrewdness in preferring other investments when the Union Pacific shares commanded an investment price and for treating them as they deserved, as purely speculative. L (May 14, 1892), 630.

[71] J. and E. J. Seligman were among the directors of the St. Louis and San Francisco. These men were also two of the founders of the Anglo-Californian

Ohio and Mississippi and the Saint Louis Tunnel and Railroad Company, were the product of reorganizations and represented previous British investment in American railway bonds.[72] The shares of two others were investment securities.[73] The most spectacular transaction in American railway securities in 1880 was unquestionably of an investment character. J. S. Morgan sold 250,000 shares of the New York Central Railroad, previously held by the Vanderbilt family.[74] Since Morgan was reported to have paid 120 for these shares, this transaction alone probably represented a transfer of about £6 million to the United States.[75]

In the middle of 1880, other speculative shares began to appear in London. Among the first were those of the Central Pacific and of the New York, Ontario and Western.[76]

The shares of five of the eight American railways admitted to quotation in 1881 were frankly speculative.[77] Henceforth, until they were displaced in part by the Kaffirs [South African investments], American railway shares were a favorite form of speculation.[78] In almost every succeeding year the shares of one or two new American railways were introduced to

---

Bank. *Commercial and Financial Chronicle*, XXVIII (March 8, 1879), 253; Nash, *Profitable Nature of Investments* (2d ed.), 49.

[72] The first and second preferred shares of the St. Louis Bridge and Tunnel Company were admitted to quotation in April 1880. *Times*, April 17, 1880, p. 9. The ordinary and preferred stock of the Ohio and Mississippi was admitted to quote in May 1880. *Ibid.*, May 1, 1880, p. 9.

[73] These were the shares of the Cleveland and Pittsburgh, which were guaranteed a dividend of 7 percent by the Pennsylvania and the shares of the Delaware and Hudson.

[74] *Times*, Nov. 22, 1879, p. 5, and Nov. 27, 1879, p. 9. [For the American side of the marketing of these New York Central securities, see Redlich, II, 383.]

[75] These New York Central shares were offered by J. S. Morgan in Jan. 1880 at a price of $137.50 or £27.3.0. *Times*, Jan. 20, 1880, p. 5. A letter signed "Rip Van Winkle" in the *Times* the next day stated that Vanderbilt had sold the shares to Morgan at 120. *Ibid.*, Jan. 21, 1880, p. 6. The estimate of £6 million is a minimum based on the price reputedly paid to Vanderbilt. It makes no allowance for the commission of Drexel, Morgan of New York.

[76] *Ibid.*, Nov. 16, 1880, p. 7; Nov. 17, 1880, p. 7; Nov. 18, 1880, p. 7; Nov. 19, 1880, p. 7; Nov. 23, 1880, p. 7; Nov. 24, 1880, p. 7; Nov. 25, 1880, p. 7.

[77] The eight American railways whose shares were admitted to quote in 1881 were: Cairo and Vincennes; Central Pacific; Chicago, Milwaukee and St. Paul; Denver and Rio Grande; Lake Shore and Michigan Southern; Louisville and Nashville; New York, Ontario and Western; and Wabash. The shares of the Cairo and Vincennes were the result of a reorganization and those of the Lake Shore and Michigan Southern were investment securities comparable with the shares of the New York Central or of the Pennsylvania. Those of the Chicago, Milwaukee and St. Paul were on the border line. However, the other five were undoubtedly speculative. Thus the Louisville and Nashville had paid a stock dividend of 80 in 1880, and the price had risen well over 100, a position which could obviously not be maintained.

[78] Kaffirs, of course, did not replace American rails (Yankees as they were now coming to be called) permanently but were able to do so at times.

London.[79] But no year rivaled 1881 in the introduction of so many speculative favorites.

The manner in which most American railway shares were introduced onto the London market differed radically from the way in which bonds were sold. With the exception of the 250,000 shares of the New York Central, stocks were not marketed by one of the usual issuing agencies. Occasionally, shares were purchased from American railway offices in London. Most commonly, they were brought to London in large blocks by arbitrage dealers or by jobbers.[80] The consequent anonymity about their introduction at first aroused great indignation in the *Times*.[81]

As with the Union Pacific, many of these shares were held only for a short time for in-and-out trading. Nevertheless, those of some lines, the Denver and Rio Grande, the New York, Ontario and Western, the Oregon and California, and the Wabash, found long-term holders in the United Kingdom. Therefore, when these roads got into financial difficulties in the middle 1880's, they all came under some form of British influence. To generalize, in the period from 1879 to 1881, a large number of American railway shares were introduced to London, and many of these shares

[79] Further shares admitted to quotation on the London Stock Exchange in this period included:

Railway	Year admitted
Norfolk and Western	1882
Oregon and California	1882
Missouri, Kansas and Texas	1885
Pittsburgh, Fort Wayne and Chicago	1885
East Tennessee, Virginia and Georgia	1887
Saint Louis, Arkansas and Texas	1887
Delaware and Bound Brook	1888
New York, Susquehanna and Western (pref.)	1888
North Pennsylvania	1888
Wheeling and Lake Erie	1889
St. Paul, Minneapolis and Manitoba	1890
Baltimore and Ohio Southwestern	1890
Cleveland, Columbus, Cincinnati and Indianapolis	1891
Chesapeake and Ohio	1891
St. Louis and Southwestern	1891
Atchison, Topeka and Santa Fe	1892
Chicago Great Western	1893
Southern Railway	1894
Northern Pacific	1897
Kansas City, Pittsburg and Gulf	1897
Great Northern Railway (U.S.A.)	1897

[80] For example, in the summer of 1880 the *Times* observed that large quantities of United States railway securities had been imported by jobbers who had not yet succeeded in selling them to the public. Aug. 14, 1880, p. 11.

[81] The *Times* particularly disapproved the introduction of the shares of the Central Pacific and of the New York, Ontario and Western in 1880. Every prospectus, the *Times* said, should bear its sponsor's name.

became favorite objects of speculation. At the same time, investment securities were also finding their way to London, and a few issues of new railways were floated there.[82]

The movement to London of American railway shares ceased temporarily toward the end of 1881. A fairly large quantity in the hands of speculative City holders was appparently returned to New York in the years from 1882 to 1885. The fight between President Gowen and McCalmont Brothers over the Philadelphia and Reading and the revelations of new financial difficulties on the Nypano (Atlantic and Great Western) [83] probably would not by themselves have gone far to shake confidence. But rate wars on passengers and freight had broken out.[84] [Even more important the United States and its railways were suffering a reaction from the boom years at the start of the decade.] To some extent, also, London might have been showing foresight.

Rentier and growth investment, both largely in the form of bond purchases, continued to go forward throughout 1883. Although the amounts involved were becoming increasingly difficult to pinpoint because of the operations of the syndicates,[85] the quantities were undoubtedly more than sufficient to offset sale of shares back to the United States.

There might have been some liquidation in one year. Although the depression of the mid-1880's was not as serious as that of 1873 or of

[82] An example of this type of railway is the Galveston and Eagle Pass and Air Line Railway, which offered $2 million of first-mortgage bonds in Nov. 1882. The name of a member of Gladstone's Government, Sir C. Rivers Wilson, appeared on the prospectus. However, after questions in the House of Commons, Wilson was obliged to resign. *Economist*, XL (Nov. 11, 1882), 1411. The New York, Texas and Mexican, a road which, in spite of its name, is a short line confined to Texas, is another railway of this type. It issued £600,000 of 6 percent first-mortgage bonds in London in 1882. *Ibid.* (April 22, 1882), 482.

[83] The report of Allport Swarbrick on the Nypano in late 1882 was described by the *Economist* as "a depressing document." (Nov. 4, 1882), 1367.

[84] So far these wars had been largely confined to the eastern trunk lines, the Erie and the New York Central; the Pennsylvania and the Baltimore and Ohio; and the various anthracite coal lines. The wars now threatened to extend to the West.

[85] In Dec. 1882, the *Commercial and Financial Chronicle* reported that the first-mortgage bonds of the New York, West Shore and Buffalo (an affiliate of the New York, Ontario and Western) had been negotiated by Winslow, Lanier for a powerful syndicate of foreign and American bankers and that $15 million cash would be thus provided for the construction of the line. XXXV (Dec. 2, 1882), 638. Yet these bonds were not publicly issued in London. Similarly, when E. F. Winslow, president of the St. Louis and San Fancisco, returned from Europe early in 1883, it was reported that the syndicate which took the first $2.5 million of the general mortgage bonds had an option on a further $2.5 million. It was also reported that a large sale of the land of this railway had been made to Scottish settlers. *Ibid.*, XXXVI (March 17, 1883), 301, and (April 21, 1883), 445. But again there was no public issue of these securities. Finally, in the same year $3 million of the collateral trust loan of the Union Pacific was taken in Europe. *Ibid.* (April 28, 1883), 467.

1890–93, it nevertheless occasioned financial difficulties for a number of American railways, including several in which British interest was large. Many securities moved from Europe to New York in this year, whereas on similar occasions in the past European holders had not only protected their holdings but had even enlarged them.[86]

The crisis of the mid-1880's had passed by the summer of 1885, and British investment in American railways revived until the so-called Baring crisis of 1890. In an ever-increasing stream British capital poured into American railways through the purchase of every type of security. The market began to widen perceptibly. Investment was made not only in favorite securities quoted on the London Stock Exchange but also in classes of stocks and bonds of which the greater part was held in the United States. In addition to the tables of stock exchange quotations and the price lists of these securities in New York,[87] the *Economist* began to carry a table of quotations for American rails not listed but extensively held in the United Kingdom.[88] British investment in some of these lines, such as the Mobile and Ohio, the Chicago and Alton, or the South Carolina, dated from the 1850's. Many were first-mortgage bonds; all were senior securities likely to appeal to the conservative investor. With a few exceptions, such as the securities of the Texas-Pacific, the road over which Robert Fleming was struggling with Jay Gould in 1886,[89] all these securities commanded substantial prices. Indeed, in 1886, the *Economist* stated:

Now, it has been more or less a canon with investors, that if you wanted to leaven your holdings of secure English stocks so as to increase your

[86] *Ibid.*, XXXVIII (Feb. 2, 1884), 127.

[87] This was the listing of A. P. Turner and Co.

[88] The list of securities of American railways extensively held in the United Kingdom but not listed on the Stock Exchange is set forth in Appendix II.

[89] The Texas-Pacific went into the hands of receivers in Dec. 1885. The Philadelphia interest in this road was organized into a committee called the Wistar Committee (after I. J. Wistar, who was its chairman). This committee, according to the *Commercial and Financial Chronicle*, was a Gould creation, and the plan that it evolved was very unfavorable to the bondholders of the Rio Grande Division. A meeting of the bondholders of the Rio Grande Division of this road was then called at the office of A. M. Kidder and Co. of New York. A few months later, a meeting of the London bondholders of the Rio Grande Division appointed a committee made up of Benjamin Newgass, Robert Fleming, and Joseph Price, representing holders of $4 million of bonds. Fleming was assigned to proceed to the United States. His plan was to buy up a controlling interest in the consolidated bonds of the Texas-Pacific and thus to upset the plans of the Wistar Committee to freeze out the Rio Grande Division and to turn the reorganized road over to Gould's Missouri Pacific. Together with Drexel, Morgan and Kuhn, Loeb, he, therefore, offered to buy all bonds offered at 96. Finally, there was a compromise between the Wistar Committee and the Fleming-Olcott Committee as a result of which Fleming's plan of reorganization was substantially accepted. *Commercial and Financial Chronicle*, XLI (Dec. 19, 1885), 714; XLII (Jan. 9, 1886), 61; (April 24, 1886), 519; (May 1, 1886), 550; XLIII (July 3, 1886), 12; (July 17, 1886), 73; (Aug. 7, 1886), 163.

total income without serious risk, you could not do better than invest in good American bonds, which were cheaper, and practically as safe as our debenture stocks. There has been a good deal of buying of this sort during late years, and under its influence, the prices of good bonds have been steadily going up, until they have now reached a point at which it almost pays as well to purchase Home debenture stocks.[90]

There is only one proviso to be added. Purchases of American railway shares were important only in the early part of this boom. Just as the move into American railway shares beginning in 1879 slowed down by 1881, so the similar boom in American railway shares starting in the middle of 1885,[91] reportedly in part a result of the optimism generated by the sale of the West Shore to the New York Central,[92] petered out by the end of 1887. Shares taken in the expectation that they would soon begin to pay dividends failed to reach the dividend paying list.[93] The rate wars continued. In general the situation of American railways was not one to inspire confidence in the holders of equity securities. But in spite of these facts, large amounts of new capital continued to be invested in American railway bonds. Moreover, British holdings were now large enough to produce very substantial amounts of dividends and interest for reinvestment.

When speculation did begin to turn again to the United States toward the end of 1889, it assumed a new form. A new boom in investment trust companies had started in 1888. Companies such as the Railway Debenture Trust Company and the American Investment Trust increased their capital. So many new investment companies [94] sprang up that competition for certain classes of securities, among them some American securities, was intense. Railway stocks and bonds probably did not make up the bulk of these companies' investments. A substantial movement of British capital into American industrial enterprise occurred. The three largest fields of British interest in American enterprise were brewing, meat packing, and milling.[95] Meat packing and milling, directly related to the export of

[90] XLII (May 5, 1886), 616.

[91] The large expansion of trade then taking place also influenced this new move into shares. *Ibid.,* XLIV (April 7, 1888), 438–39.

[92] See below, p. 179 ff. This is the famous sale made on board Morgan's yacht, the *Corsair.*

[93] Fewer American railways whose shares were favorites with British investors paid dividends in 1885 and 1886 than in 1884.

[94] The Morgans, Barings, and a number of other prominent merchant banking firms remained aloof from these large new agglomerations. Brown, Shipley, however, together with its affiliated house in New York, participated in more than one investment company. On the whole, it may be ventured as a generalization that the lists of New York participants were more impressive than those of London. Besides the Scottish members, the London lists were made up largely of stockbrokers and of the members of the investment trust rings. The lists of the directors and founders of three of these trusts are set forth in Appendix III.

[95] Among the granaries taken over were the Chicago and North West Granaries. *Economist,* XLVII (Oct. 26, 1889), 1367. An even more important venture was the purchase of a number of firms that were consolidated into the Pillsbury

American farm produce, were reasonable extensions of British interest in American land and cattle companies and, indirectly, in railways. But there were also excursions into other fields, including cotton thread and photographic supplies. In this new type of investment the British investor was offered securities of the British holding company, not the American operating company. This procedure had already been used in a number of cases, notably that of the Alabama Great Southern Railway. British interest in other fields came to an end temporarily with the so-called Baring crisis in the autumn of 1890.

There is one more point to be made about British investment in American railways in the late 1880's. British financiers were again assisting in building largely British-owned roads in the United States. In addition to the roads that properly formed part of Canadian trunk lines, such as the Minneapolis, Sault Ste. Marie and Atlantic,[96] there were also roads like the Chicago Great Western and a number of lines in the South.[97] There was at least a difference of degree from the days of James McHenry. The British retained some financial controls while construction and operation were entrusted to Americans in whom they had confidence.[98]

After the Baring crisis of 1890, which arose in part from the large quantity of foreign securities underwritten in London,[99] the price of American rails collapsed following enforced realizations. The settlement of stock market accounts of late October 1890 was anticipated with trepidation.[100] In particular there were fears for one brokerage firm that had sold to speculators the option of "putting" on them no less than 500,000 shares, the equivalent nominally of £10 million.[101] Large parcels of this firm's holdings of Union Pacific shares were distributed at judiciously chosen

---

Washburn Flour Mills, Ltd. *Ibid.* (Nov. 2, 1889), 1400. Its establishment was directly connected with British interest in American railways, for some grain and flour from Minneapolis went to the seaboard over the new system of British-controlled roads that had just been formed, namely, the Minneapolis, Sault Ste. Marie and Atlantic (later the Minneapolis, St. Paul and Sault Ste. Marie), running from Minneapolis to the Canadian border at the Sault Ste. Marie, the Canadian Pacific and the New York, Ontario and Western. The meat-packing concerns that were British-owned at this time were the Chicago Junction Railway and Union Stock Yards Co., Fowler Brothers, the Chicago Packing and Provision Co., and the International Packing and Provision Co., Ltd.

[96] At this time it was said that the main line of the Canadian Pacific ran from Minneapolis to New York.

[97] For example, the Birmingham, Sheffield and Tennessee River and the Cape Fear and Yadkin.

[98] A. B. Stickney was the president of the Chicago Great Western.

[99] [See King, 301–8. This crisis of 1890 was associated with the house of Barings, which had undertaken to sell large quantities of South American securities.]

[100] *Economist,* XLVIII (Oct. 11, 1890), 1287.

[101] *Ibid.* (Oct. 25, 1890), 1351. There is a presumption that this firm was Benjamin Newgass & Co., since its conversion into a limited liability company occurred at the same time as that of Baring Brothers. Stockbroking firms and merchant banking firms were ordinarily partnerships.

times in mid-week, and the danger hanging over the market was averted.[102] Americans purchased the shares. The Union Pacific shares sold in London were reported to have been taken up by Vanderbilt and the Missouri Pacific shares by Jay Gould.[103] Nor were these the only large blocks of British-owned securities sold to Americans at this time. British control of the Denver and Rio Grande was reported to have been sold to George Jay Gould, the son of Jay Gould.[104] Moreover, there were large sales of the shares of the Minnesota and Northwestern, one of the constituent lines of the Chicago Great Western.[105] Indeed, a few months later the New York correspondent of the *Economist* estimated that at least $100 million of American securities had been sold to New York in the last two months of 1890 to obtain funds needed to meet South American demands.[106] [For a short time even the sound house of Baring Brothers, solvent but lacking liquid assets, had to seek aid from the Bank of England.]

The Baring crisis passed away, the bank rate fell back to 2½ percent the following July, prices of American securities began to improve, and it seemed as if there might be another revival of British interest. Although interest in investment securities soon sprang up again, the anticipated speculative boom did not mature. Early in 1892, there were again substantial foreign sales of American railway shares to New York, and the correspondent of the *Economist* in that American city estimated that 150,000 shares had been returned from London. This alone is not significant, since British investors had been withdrawing their capital from shares and moving into more conservative securities for some time. But the same writer added that vast amounts of bonds and investment securities that did not figure in the public transactions [107] were also flowing to New York.[108]

What happened in this period is crucial for the estimation of the total amount of British investment in American railway securities. It is there-

[102] *Ibid.*, 1366.   [103] *Ibid.*, 1360.

[104] According to his biographer, General Palmer, who had retained control of the Denver and Rio Grande Western after he lost control of the parent road, had about this time opened negotiations with George Coppell, representing the foreign stockholders, for the sale of the Rio Grande Western to the Denver and Rio Grande. Fisher says further: "At first Mr. [George Foster] Peabody dealt with Mr. Coppell, but after the latter's death the negotiations were carried on on behalf of the D.&R.G. by Mr. Schiff, a director, and it was with his firm, Kuhn, Loeb & Co., that Mr. Peabody concluded the sale of the construction company's holdings in the R.G.W. and in the Utah Fuel Company. While these negotiations were going on, and unknown either to Mr. Schiff or to Mr. Peabody, George Jay Gould had acquired from the foreign holders a controlling interest of the stock of the D.&R.G." John S. Fisher, *A Builder of the West: The Life of General William Jackson Palmer* (Caldwell, Idaho: Caxton Printers, 1939), 302–3.

[105] The Chicago Great Western's report for the year following the Baring crisis stated that whereas three-fourths of the shares had previously been held abroad, three-fourths were now held in the United States.

[106] XLIX (March 14, 1891), 342.

[107] That is to say, securities of the type listed in Appendix II.

[108] L (March 5, 1892), 320–21.

fore necessary to consider what was going on in the United States at this time.

At the beginning of 1892 the growing agitation over bimetallism in the United States, which would have changed the relationship of gold and silver, had an impact on the monetary situation and aroused fears in Europe. The election of Grover Cleveland, a Democrat, not only reinforced these fears but inspired concern over possible changes in tariff policy that would adversely affect American industry. Moreover, the United States was now experiencing great labor unrest. In the field of railway finance, the Atchison, Topeka and Santa Fe was forced to undergo a second reorganization, only four years after the first. In addition, there was new concern over the Reading, now pursuing an expansionist policy reminiscent of the Gowen era.

Although there was probably no significant *net* repatriation of American railway securities held abroad from the beginning of 1890 to the end of 1891, there was possibly a small net repatriation in 1892. Since, in contradistinction to the late 1870's, the great mass of American securities held in Europe were not federal but railway obligations, repatriation on any scale, whether gross or net, necessarily involved some American repurchase of railway securities.

In May 1893 there was a panic on Wall Street that did not seriously involve the European investor. Net purchases on European accounts were made immediately after the panic,[109] but this movement was not sustained. The European investor seems to have been apathetic to the attractions of net purchase. The Reading, the Erie, and the Northern Pacific were all in receivership. Nor had the troubles of the Atchison yet been straightened out. The British investor had become inured to the temporary difficulties of most of these roads. Financial problems within the roads influenced him less than the generally unsatisfactory economic situation in the United States. Nevertheless, there were no significant withdrawals of British capital during 1893.

The year 1894 was equally unfavorable for the United States, and there was probably some net repatriation. America had been in a state of subacute crisis for a long time. The market for American securities in London was not much better and was virtually stagnated after 1891. Over and over again the professionals unsuccessfully tried to get a boom started, many ruining their own fortunes in the process. John Taylor, a stockbroker who had been prominent in a number of the American railway reorganizations including the first of the Reading, was declared a defaulter in April 1891.[110] In 1894, E. F. Satterthwaite and Company not only failed for a large amount but also was barred from the stock exchange after admitting that the firm had been pledging clients' securities.[111]

[109] *Ibid.*, LI (May 20, 1893), 603 and 610.
[110] *Ibid.*, XLIX (April 4, 1891), 433.
[111] When Satterthwaite and Co. protested that this practice of pledging clients'

In 1895 prices of American securities began to improve. On numerous occasions, especially during the first half of the year, London was again a purchaser on Wall Street.[112] Nevertheless, uncertainty over the United States' policy on silver continued to disturb the market for American rails.[113] In the summer of 1895, the exchange position of the United States became so unfavorable that it was necessary to form a syndicate to protect the gold reserves of the United States Treasury. On behalf of this syndicate J. P. Morgan made a trip to London and arranged the sale there of $101,970,000 of American bonds. Of these slightly less than one third were United States government obligations; the bulk of the remainder were railway issues.[114] In an interview with the press, Morgan attributed

---

securities was common on the Stock Exchange, its downfall was completed. *Ibid.*, LII (Jan. 27, 1894), 120, and (Feb. 17, 1894), 204–5.

[112] See, for example, *ibid.*, LIII (March 30, 1895), 427; (April 6, 1895), 458; (April 20, 1895), 510; etc.

[113] *Ibid.*, (May 11, 1895), 620. Some of the speculative interest that had previously been concentrated on American rails was transferred to the South African market. Nevertheless, speculation was considerably reduced at this time, which accounted for the inactivity of the City. (The *Economist* estimated that three-quarters of the ordinary business of the Stock Exchange was purely speculative. LII [April 7, 1894], 418.)

[114] The list of securities marketed by the bond syndicate in 1895 is as follows:

United States 4's	$ 32,500,000
New York Central debentures	3,500,000
Wabash refunding bonds	8,500,000
Minneapolis and St. Louis 5's	2,000,000
Southern bonds	1,750,000
Chesapeake & Ohio 4½'s	1,250,000
Missouri, Kansas & Texas	750,000
Manhattan 4's	8,500,000
New York Central shares	4,750,000
City of Chicago 4's	2,750,000
Cleveland & Marietta 4½'s	1,250,000
Terminal of St. Louis consol.	4,500,000
Allegheny Valley 4's	5,000,000
City of Toronto 3½'s	300,000
Twin City Rapid Transit pref.	870,000
New York, Ontario & Western 4's	500,000
Minneapolis Western bonds	500,000
Pennsylvania Railroad	5,000,000
Other bonds, estimate	6,000,000
Other shares, estimate	2,500,000
Lehigh Coal 5's	6,800,000
Lynn and Boston $	2,500,000
	————————
Total	$101,970,000

From *Economist*, LIII (Aug. 3, 1895), 1022, quotation from the New York *Journal of Commerce*.

There was considerable criticism of this new bond syndicate in the United States. This was in part because Lazard Frères, a firm prominently identified

the pressure on the United States exchange rate not to withdrawal of capital by foreigners, but to their failure to purchase securities while the currency policy of the United States remained unsettled.[115]

In spite of the efforts of the bond syndicate, the pressure on the exchange rate continued. A crisis over relations with Venezuela threatened a rupture between the United States and the United Kingdom, and a crisis in the Kaffir market led to the throwing over of American securities.[116] Nonetheless, while there were large gross movements into and out of railway securities during this year, it would not appear that there was any net repatriation of railway securities.

Although in 1896 the Baltimore and Ohio, which had hitherto consistently paid high dividends, had financial difficulties,[117] the low point had now been turned. Matters began to improve. Just as at the end of the 1870's, this improvement was not immediately apparent. Even the election of William McKinley, a Republican President, did not appear to have an appreciable effect on the American market in London; it continued to be dull throughout 1897. Nevertheless, a number of reorganization issues were marketed in London during these years.[118] The flow of investment, in addition to reinvestment of interest and dividends, resumed.[119]

Another development merits attention. The friendly reorganizations[120] that came to be common on American railways had a direct bearing on the

------

with the syndicate, took $2.5 million of gold for export at a time when the syndicate's aim was to protect the U.S. Treasury gold reserve. *Ibid.* (Sept. 28, 1895), 1275-77.

[115] *Ibid.* (Sept. 28, 1895), 1275.

[116] The New York correspondent of the *Economist* in reporting this phenomenon produced the recurring figure of 100,000 shares for London's sales during this crisis.

[117] This did not affect British holders substantially since in March J. S. Morgan; Brown, Shipley; and Baring Brothers, Ltd., announced that they had agreed to cooperate to protect the British holders of securities issued through their houses. *Burdett's Official Intelligence* (1897). On the other hand, the *Economist* commented on this announcement: "In many instances, however, the protection thus accorded to English holders of American railroad securities has been a very costly piece of business, and has materially added to the losses which the general proprietary bodies have had to sustain. Of course, we do not expect issuing houses to work for nothing, but there is a moral responsibility attaching to their position which should weigh with them, and induce them to use their best endeavours in the protection of the interests which they have helped to create, without reference to the fees to which their services may entitle them. And when these services are volunteered, there is all the more reason why their cost should be kept within moderate limits." LIV (March 7, 1896), 295.

[118] *Ibid.* (May 30, 1896), 699.

[119] Although speculation remained quiescent, Fleming and his associates were again pursuing a forward-looking policy.

[120] The term "friendly reorganization" is used to denote reorganization by agreement and compromise between the various classes of security holders as opposed to reorganization by foreclosure and sale.

amount of British holdings. The object of these reorganizations was to satisfy major classes of security holders, and the net result was always a considerable increase in the total capitalization of the railway under reorganization. In some cases senior mortgages were left undisturbed. In others, holders were asked to accept a reduced rate of interest. They were compensated for this by receiving a sufficient additional quantity of income bonds or preference shares [121] to bring their total income in good years up to that received at the old rate of interest. Junior securities were usually downgraded but increased in quantity. Owners of equities were asked to pay an assessment, and additional securities were issued to represent this payment. All these devices increased the total capitalization of the railway under reorganization, since all of the securities of the old company were kept alive and additional new ones were issued. It has often been suggested that this method of adjustment was directly responsible for the fact that so many railways had to undergo not one but two reorganizations. But in spite of criticism,[122] friendly reorganization was usually employed in the 1880's and 1890's. The financial structure of American railways had become too complex to permit foreclosure and sale.

The imposing list of new American railway securities admitted to quotation in some years might give the impression that large amounts of new British capital were pouring into the United States. In fact, some of these new listings occurred in years when there were several reorganizations and merely reflected these adjustments. Only in so far as they included funded interest can they be said to represent new British investment. However, after the depression of the 1890's, some of the income bonds and preference shares received by the senior security holders began to appreciate in value, so that capital gains were made. The plans of reorganization of two railways with relatively simple financial structures are set forth in Appendix IV.

A most difficult task is the evaluation of the amount of British investment in American railways. There are three estimates that may be relevant. The first is the figure, conceptually perhaps the most interesting, for the amount that British investors actually paid for their holdings. No estimates of this amount are available, and there are good reasons for this lacuna.[123] The only information available even for securities that were

[121] These income bonds and preference shares were not cumulative. They received income if currently earned.

[122] See, for example, *Economist,* LII (Feb. 3, 1894), 140.

[123] Global surveys of the balance of payments, such as those of Hobson, Cairncross, and Albert Imlah for the United Kingdom and of Bullock for the United States, throw only incidental light on the bilateral balance of payments on capital account between the United States and the United Kingdom. It should be noted that their estimates of the capital item are admittedly at least partly residual and therefore doubly conjectural. In addition, there are significant divergences between the various estimates. Bullock assumes that the total of United States railway securities quoted in London in 1883 was roughly

publicly issued in London is the selling price to the public. This was sometimes widely divergent from the price at which the marketing house itself acquired them. In addition, large amounts of securities were privately sold, and on these information is very sporadic. Finally, even in the earliest period, large quantities of American railway securities for British investment were purchased in New York, and the prices paid are unknown. As the British market for investment securities widened in the 1880's more and more securities were acquired in this way. Moreover, many of these securities were frequently transferred back and forth across the Atlantic.[124]

The second possible figure is that for the face value of British holdings of American railway securities. This figure is not particularly helpful in this period. Most American railway shares stood at considerably less than par, while many senior securities commanded premium prices. Moreover, face value conceals capital gains and losses and gives a false impression of total value when there has been a large number of reorganizations.[125]

The figure of the market value of British holdings is selected here, although there are also difficulties with this concept and the tentative nature of these estimates must be stressed. American railway shares in particular were subject to wide fluctuations not only over the course of the cycle but in erratic bull and bear movements. It is easier to deal with the course of the prices of American railway bonds over this period. Except when a railway was in default, the prices of these securities appreciated relatively continuously, so that those who had purchased early were able to make sizable capital gains. Capital appreciation is, of course, included in the estimates for the market value of British holdings.

There are a few estimates of the market value of British holdings of American railway securities before the turn of the twentieth century. Nash gave a figure of £100 million for the year 1881.[126] This figure is certainly much too conservative. The market value of British holdings of American securities must have reached this total by 1876, and there is no reason to suppose that it had fallen by 1879. Since British investors greatly in-

----

equivalent to total *foreign* investment in American railway securities made in that year. Bullock, Williams, and Tucker, 225. [See also Albert Imlah, "British Balance of Payments and Export of Capital, 1816–1913," *Economic History Review,* 2d ser., V (1952), 208–39.]

[124] In estimating the amount invested over a long period of time, there is also the additional problem of allowing for changes in the value of money.

[125] In the discussion on Sir George Paish's paper before the Royal Statistical Society in Dec. 1910, Lord Keynes implied that British investors had sustained considerable capital losses on American railway securities, but as Sir George pointed out, he ignored capital gains. Paish, "Great Britain's Capital Investments in Individual Colonial and Foreign Countries," *Journal of the Royal Statistical Society,* LXXIV, pt. II (Jan. 1911), 196–97.

[126] *Profitable Nature of Investments* (3d ed.), 129.

creased their holdings of American railway securities from 1879 through 1881, and since there was significant capital appreciation on securities already held, an estimate of £160 million is much more reasonable for the latter date. The plausibility of this estimate is increased by the fact that with the development of boom conditions, investors became less willing to hold federal bonds, and some capital was transferred from these lower interest-bearing securities into American rails.

From 1882 until the middle of 1885 the flow of British capital into American railway securities was curtailed. To some extent British holders of the more speculative varieties were liquidating. On the other hand, in more conservative securities, whose prices were relatively steady, investment held up well enough to more than offset disinvestment by speculative holders. Moreover, in the latter half of 1885, British interest in American railways again became strong, and prices, particularly of shares, began to rise.

At the end of 1885, the market value of British investment in American rails must have amounted to at least £200 million, even taking into account capital losses taken on the shares of some American railways. This figure is conservative and may be judged too low when compared with Cairncross's figure of £300 million for total British investment in the United States at the end of 1885.[127] The switch from federal obligations to rails had been more or less completed by this time,[128] and the latter now constituted the bulk of American obligations held abroad.

Cairncross also estimates that in the five years from 1886 through 1890, British investment in American rails increased by another £100 million. On this basis, total holdings would have amounted to £300 million at the time of the Baring crisis. In view of the exceptionally great activity throughout these years and of the *Economist*'s estimate of £250 million for British holdings of United States railway securities for the end of 1887,[129] the actual increase was probably somewhat greater. However, there was panic liquidation after the Baring crisis, and low prices ruled at the end of the year. Taking all these factors into consideration, £300 million is probably a reasonable estimate for market value of British holdings of American rails at the end of 1890.

The panic liquidation following the Baring crisis was largely made up in a recovery that started in the autumn of 1891, spurred by a bumper harvest in the United States. But the period from the beginning of 1892 until the end of 1895 is more controversial. Charles J. Bullock stated that there was net repatriation of securities to the United States amounting to

[127] Cairncross, 182–83.
[128] There may also have been some net repatriation of federal securities from 1882 to 1885. In any case, by 1885, European holdings of federal securities had been much reduced.
[129] *Economist*, XLVI (Jan. 7, 1888), 5.

$60 million a year in each of the five years from 1891 through 1896.[130] This statement is somewhat difficult to accept. There was certainly no net repatriation in 1891. It is possible that there was some small repatriation in 1892 and again in 1894. It is extremely doubtful if there was net repatriation in 1893 or 1895. The year 1893 was a panic year in New York, not in London, and in 1895 the bond syndicate made extensive sales in London. Such disinvestment as occurred in 1893 and 1895 was more than offset by investment both of new capital and of accruing interest and dividends.[131] The dominant impression of these years is that it was the absence of customary active participation by the British investor rather than liquidation that was most distressing to Wall Street. Furthermore, it must be remembered that panic sales moved both ways. In predominantly British crises, such as that of the Barings, British holders unloaded at whatever prices securities would bring and were forced to take capital losses. But in the New York crisis of 1893, the British investor was a buyer, although this was partly for relatively short-term gains. On balance, therefore, the total of British holdings by the end of 1895 was probably little different from that at the end of 1890. An estimate of £300 million appears reasonable.

Allowing for new investment and for some capital appreciation, total British holdings of American railway securities had probably risen to £350 million by the end of 1898. This estimate is somewhat less than Nathaniel T. Bacon's figure for the same year. Bacon worked with information obtained from the Inland Revenue, taking incomes declared by British subjects under Schedule D and estimating the proportion of this income obtained from the United States. This estimate was based on information from Somerset House on payments for estate duty. After making an apparently liberal allowance of 33⅓ percent for evasion and distributed profits, Bacon arrived at a figure of $100 million for the amount of income derived by citizens of the United Kingdom from the United States in 1898. He then capitalized this figure on the basis of an estimated rate of return of 4 percent and arrived at $2,500 million for the market value of all British capital invested in the United States. Bacon also stated that the

[130] Bullock derives this conclusion from movements in the balance of trade and from a controversy in the *Commercial and Financial Chronicle*. Bullock, Williams, and Tucker, 226; and *Commercial and Financial Chronicle*, LX (March 30, 1895), 542–44; (April 13, 1895), 630–32; and (May 4, 1895), 769–72. In fact, the balance-of-trade data do not support this sweeping conclusion. In 1890 the balance of trade favorable to the United States amounted to $86,690,000; in 1891, $112,528,000; in 1892, $216,277,000; in 1893, $86,314,000; in 1894, $278,840,000; and in 1895, $132,736,000. *Historical Statistics of the United States*, 244. Only in two years, 1892 and 1894, was the balance of trade abnormally favorable to the United States. Of course, the United States normally had a favorable balance of trade to cover its deficit on invisible items in the balance of payments on current account.

[131] Some investment of interest was enforced both by coupon funding and by reorganization.

vast mass of this investment was in railway securities. Thus, on the basis of his figure, British investment in American railways in 1898 would be at least £400 million. However, he adds that there is a margin of error in his estimates of not more than 25 percent.[132]

Looking ahead, Bacon's estimates would appear to be reconcilable with those of Sir George Paish in 1909.[133] The biggest capital gains in many American railway securities were yet to come, and a large amount of new investment was made starting from at least 1905.

[132] Pp. 265–85.

[133] Paish, "Great Britain's Capital Investments in Other Lands," *Journal of the Royal Statistical Society,* LXXII, pt. III (Sept. 30, 1909), 465–95; "Great Britain's Capital Investments in Individual Colonial and Foreign Countries," *ibid.,* LXXIV, pt. II (Jan. 1911), 167–200; and *Statist Supplement* (Feb. 1914).

VIII

Protection of British Investment

THE average Englishman is not called "John Bull" without reason. In the nineteenth century the bulldog quality of perseverance was applied no less to his financial operations than to other aspects of his life. He was not inclined to take losses lightly. Even when prospects for a favorable settlement were remote, as in the case of Confederate bonds, hope died slowly. Losses were never forgotten. Sydney Smith's outcries in the early 1840's against the state of Pennsylvania are still remembered, yet Pennsylvania was in default for only a few years, and all dishonored coupons were ultimately paid.

This is not the whole story, and by itself gives a false impression of the character of the British investor. It is true that he howled loudly over each fresh default. On the other hand he was also prepared to do something about it. As this chapter will show, he was in the end uncommonly able to turn what appeared to be a loss into a substantial gain. Moreover, he was prepared to vary his preventive and remedial measures to suit individual cases. The British investor used not one but many different formulas to protect his investments in American railways.

A number of these formulas were evolved before the 1880's, and of them one proved most effective. This pattern of control was the establishment of a close and continuing relationship between an American railway and a British financial house.[1] By this method the British house became, in effect, a silent partner in the operation of the railway. Sometimes, as in the case of the Philadelphia and Reading, the British house actually owned a controlling amount of the shares.[2] This, however, was not necessarily the case. Control of the purse strings was often enough to accomplish substantially the same effect. Barings did not own a majority of the shares of the

---

[1] In the early period, the British house was usually a merchant banking house. Later, it was sometimes a stockbroking firm like Vivian, Gray or an individual like Robert Fleming.

[2] McCalmont's sold its interest in the Philadelphia and Reading in the 1880's. When Hugh McCalmont died in 1887 he left a fortune unrivaled even by J. S. Morgan.

Baltimore and Ohio or of the Eastern of Massachusetts. Since these roads relied on Barings almost entirely for their financing, the London house was able to influence policy on some points. This was particularly so in relation to the expansion of mileage, a policy of fundamental importance to American railways in the nineteenth century.[3]

When control was based on the banker-railroad relationship, there was always the possibility of the railway finding another banker. After 1875, the Baltimore and Ohio did indeed establish relationships with other banking houses, notably J. P. Morgan and Company [4] and Brown, Shipley and Company.[5] Control through stock ownership could also be upset unless the financial house held an absolute majority of the shares. For example, when McCalmont Brothers and its appointee, Franklin Gowen, had a difference of opinion, the banker's control proved inadequate;[6] in the early 1880's an election of directors was swung by a block of Reading shares recently purchased by William H. Vanderbilt [Cornelius Vanderbilt's son and principal heir] and voted for Gowen. Thus, both variants of this type of control depended for stability on mutual understanding between members of the British house and the American managers of the railway.

In spite of difficulties of this nature, a close and continuing relationship was in many ways the most effective form of control, except for outright ownership. During the period after 1879, examples multiplied. The Norfolk and Western's relationship with Vivian, Gray and Company has already been mentioned. The Louisville and Nashville is another example that falls into this category.[7] The Atchison, Topeka and Santa Fe may also be included, although in this case primary control was by the American

[3] The occupation of new territory was one of the major forms of innovation by American railways in the nineteenth century. Cochran, 147–48.

[4] J. S. Morgan first marketed a loan for the Baltimore and Ohio in 1877. This issue of £1.6 million of 5 percent sterling bonds on the Chicago Division was purchased outright early in 1877 but not sold until Dec. when the market was more favorable to new issues. *Times*, Sept. 3, 1877, p. 7, and Dec. 5, 1877, p. 7. Jenks errs in saying that Speyer Brothers put out an issue for the Baltimore and Ohio in London in 1872. Jenks, *Migration of British Capital*, 268 n. The issue put out by Speyer Brothers was for the Baltimore and Potomac. However, some short promissory notes of this line were taken by Frederick Banbury and Co. and Naylor Benzon in the middle 1870's.

[5] Brown, Shipley had long been associated with the Baltimore and Ohio, since the Brown family came from Baltimore, but did not float a loan for this road until 1833. *Commercial and Financial Chronicle*, XXXVI (April 14, 1883), 411.

[6] According to a report in early 1882 on the bitterly contested Reading election, 215,385 votes of which over 120,000 belonged personally to the McCalmonts, had been promised to Frank Bond and 183,508 votes had been promised to Gowen. William H. Vanderbilt therefore held the casting vote. *Economist*, XL (Jan. 14, 1882), 50.

[7] Both Barings and Rothschilds had interests in the Louisville and Nashville. In the 1890's, 75 percent of its shares were held abroad. William Z. Ripley, *Railroads: Finance and Organization* (London: Longmans, Green and Co., 1915), 5.

house, Kidder, Peabody, while Barings, the London house, participated indirectly.[8]

The existence of a banker-railroad relationship usually insured smoothing over of the American railway's financial difficulties. The road could ordinarily count on short-term finance, even during periods when the market was not receptive to new issues. Moreover, the British investor usually was assured of strong representation when reorganization became necessary. These reorganizations were often, although not always, relatively free from conflict. That of the Reading was difficult and prolonged; by the time the company collapsed it was no longer under McCalmont's control.[9] There were complaints that the reorganization of the Atchison in the late 1880's favored shareholders over bondholders because the controlling houses held large quantities of shares.[10]

The second device employed by British investors to safeguard their investment was the creation of protective committees. This device was of very early origin. A Spanish Bondholders' Committee was formed in 1827.[11] One of the first instances of the use of such a committee in dealing with American railways was the London Committee of the Shareholders of the Illinois Central, organized in the 1850's.[12] But whereas the early committees formed in connection with various South American loans were, according to Jenks, relatively ineffectual, the London Committee of the Illinois Central accomplished its purpose.

Immediately after the formation of the committee for the Illinois Central, James Caird, M.P., was dispatched to Illinois to investigate the line and to confer with the management.[13] On receiving a favorable report

---

[8] Barings also held shares in the Atchison. Thus, in Sept. 1883, it was reported that the firm bought $2 million of shares. *Commercial and Financial Chronicle*, XXXVII (Sept. 8, 1883), 245–46.

[9] The Reading reorganization was carried out under a syndicate consisting of the big houses, Morgans; Barings; Brown, Shipley; and Rothschilds. *Economist*, XLVI (June 2, 1888), 707. It had been in receivership from June 2, 1884, until Jan. 2, 1888. It was to undergo another reorganization in the 1890's.

[10] *Ibid.*, XLVII (Oct. 19, 1889), 1330, and (Nov. 2, 1889), 1405. After the second Atchison reorganization in the early 1890's, Barings was alleged to have forced the Colorado Midland onto the Atchison in order to relieve a clique of its friends, including some members of the board of the Bank of England, who were heavily involved in the securities of the Colorado. *Investor's Review* (Dec. 1894), 350–51. Even when the railway undergoing reorganization was closely identified with a particular London house, a committee was sometimes formed. The Atchison committee for the reorganization in the late 1880's included: C. E. Bretherton; Cecil W. Boyle; W. M. Chinnery; Walter Scrimgeour; F. L. Govett; Robert H. C. Harrison; A. Haes; A. Brenner; Granville Farquahar; Alexander Henderson; and Joseph Price.

[11] Jenks, *Migration of British Capital*, 121.

[12] *Economist*, XVI (Sept. 4, 1858), 991.

[13] *Ibid.* Caird was not the only shareholder of the Illinois Central to visit Illinois. Richard Cobden also made a tour of inspection of this road. In 1856

from Caird, the shareholders decided that it would be in their best interests to continue to support the Illinois Central. Before agreeing to do so, however, they exacted certain concessions from the management. One was the retirement of the floating debt of the railway. The second was the regular publication of information on traffic and earnings.[14] From this time on, quarterly traffic and earnings reports appeared in many London journals and newspapers.

Even in the 1850's the London Committee of the Illinois Central was not an isolated phenomenon.[15] All these committees were short-lived and were dissolved as soon as the emergency with which they had been formed to cope had been overcome.[16] The committees organized in the post–Civil War period for the protection of various classes of security holders of the Erie and of the Atlantic and Great Western were also of a temporary nature. These two roads might well have benefited from continuing surveillance.

In this respect there was a definite change after 1879. Some of the London committees in the 1880's were permanent or semi-permanent bodies. Their purpose was no longer simply to protect the security holders in times of emergency but also to continue an interest in and an influence on the railway.

Good examples of this new type of committee were those used in connection with the New York, Ontario and Western and with the Denver and Rio Grande. The London Committee for the Ontario was organized under the auspices of the English Association of American Bond and Share Holders, established in 1884. This was a shareholders' committee; at that date this railway had no funded indebtedness.[17] The Committee for the Denver and Rio Grande, formed by J. K. Gilliat and Company when the railroad defaulted on its bonds in 1882, was originally a bondholders' committee.[18] However, in the summer of 1885 the English Association of American Bond and Share Holders took up the cause of the shareholders

---

Benjamin F. Johnson, a clerk employed in the Illinois Central office, wrote: "Honorables, lords, and members of Parliament are so plentiful here these days that I keep a copy of *Burke's Peerage* and the *Blue Book* on the same shelf as the *English Dictionary* and other books of ready reference." Quoted in Carlton J. Corliss, *Main Line of Mid-America* (New York: Creative Age Press, 1950), 66.

[14] *Economist*, XVII (Nov. 19, 1859), 1299.

[15] A London committee was established for the reorganization of the Marietta and Cincinnati, for example.

[16] The London Committee of the Illinois Central was dissolved in 1860 after two years of existence. *American Railroad Journal*, XXXIII (May 19, 1860), 430.

[17] Both the English Association of American Bond and Share Holders and the New York, Ontario and Western will be considered in some detail later in this chapter.

[18] The bonds of the Denver and Rio Grande had been marketed in London privately. Two issues were involved, consolidated bonds and first-mortgage bonds. Default was made on the first-mortgage bonds in the autumn of 1884, the consolidated bonds having defaulted in 1882.

of the Rio Grande.[19] These investors had been without a champion, because their shares, like most American shares, had not been floated in London through a merchant house or an established stockbroker but had been introduced onto the market by jobbers and arbitrageurs. However, the move by the English Association of American Bond and Share Holders was not aggressive but defensive.[20] Although there were some motions of bargaining,[21] agreement was soon reached, and the shareholders' committee was fused with Gilliat's bondholders' committee.

The settling of the affairs of the Rio Grande was accomplished with remarkable dispatch. Agreement on the form of reorganization was reached in 1885, and on July 12, 1886, the road was sold at foreclosure. The 7 percent first-mortgage bonds were unaffected by the ensuing reorganization. On the consolidated bonds[22] the interest was reduced to 4 percent, but the holders also received 5 percent noncumulative preferred shares. General mortgage bonds[23] and car trust certificates were also transformed into preferred shares, which holders of common stock received to represent their assessment.[24] Shareholders also received share for share in new common stock.[25] Most important, holders of preferred shares were given the right to elect two-thirds of the board of directors for a period of five years, and as a result George Coppell became chairman of the board. The British investors, however, did not rely completely on control through this board. The London Committee was not dissolved.[26] Although it was probably formed originally as an emergency measure, it now evolved into an instrument of continuing control; specifically its assent was required for the authorization of any new indebtedness.

Although the committee for the investors in the Rio Grande was the first

[19] In 1883 it was reported that $17 million of the common stock of the Rio Grande, of which $33 million was outstanding (1882), was held in Europe. *Commercial and Financial Chronicle*, XXXVII (Sept. 29, 1883), 342.

[20] This committee for stockholders of the Denver and Rio Grande was set up at a meeting on May 28, 1885, after the publication of the plan of reorganization of the Rio Grande. Its members were G. Herring, J. T. Davies, J. Grant Maclean, and Joseph Price. *Economist*, XLIII (May 30, 1885), 671.

[21] In July the shareholders' committee announced that it could not agree to the terms of the reorganization that the bondholders' committee had arranged. *Ibid.* (July 4, 1885), 822.

[22] To the beginning of 1886, $10,650,000 of the consolidated bonds of the Denver and Rio Grande had been deposited with the London Committee, and $8,255,000 had been deposited with the committees in New York and in Amsterdam. The total of this issue at the beginning of 1885 was $19,740,000. *Burdett's Official Intelligence* (1885, 1886).

[23] In Oct. 1883 general mortgage bonds of the Denver and Rio Grande were issued to shareholders in connection with an issue of shares. For $750 holders received one $1,000 5 percent general mortgage bond and $1,000 in shares. *Ibid.* (1885).

[24] The assessment was $6.

[25] For details of the reorganization see *Burdett's Official Intelligence* (1886).

[26] The London Committee for the Denver and Rio Grande now consisted of Howard Gilliat, chairman; H. J. Chinnery; T. Collier; and Robert Fleming.

one of its kind, it was related to similar procedures in other instances. In the case of the Alabama Great Southern, a number of the members of the bondholders' committee eventually became directors of the Alabama Great Southern Railway Company, Limited. In the case of various auxiliary companies of the Atlantic and Great Western, some trustees controlled the railway's assets for a number of years. Only a few companies were ever completely controlled by the method of a continuing committee.[27] The Ontario has already been mentioned. The Wabash eventually came under such a long-lived London Committee.[28] So, too, did the Chicago Great Western, although this company belongs more properly in the group of railways in which British influence depended upon control of the financing of the line from the very beginning.

Part of the control exercised by the British investor over the Denver and Rio Grande depended on the membership of the board. An Englishman, George Coppell, was chairman of the board of directors, and a majority of its other members were also elected by the preferred shareholders. This third method of protecting British investment by securing seats for the representatives of British bondholders on the board of directors also dates from the 1850's. After the reorganization of the Marietta and Cincinnati, three British subjects became members of the railway's board.[29] This method of control was not always possible. Many states had laws requiring all members of railway boards to be residents of the state. Nevertheless, in most railways in which a large amount of British capital was invested some members of the board of directors were elected in conformity with the wishes of the British investors. The fact that the Pennsylvania did not agree to British participation on its board of directors was a cause of complaint by the London press for many years. The Pennsylvania consistently paid high dividends, but British investors felt that they were depend-

[27] Joseph Price may have been responsible for this type of continuing committee. It emerged shortly after the setting up of the English Association for American Bond and Share Holders of which he was the managing director. Furthermore, Price was associated with a number of the roads that eventually came under this form of control. He had served as an official on an American railway for a number of years before returning to London and setting up the English Association. According to the reputation of Price in the Association, which is still functioning, he was a man of forceful character who overawed his subordinates.

[28] On Nov. 19, 1890, at a meeting of the British bond and shareholders of the Wabash, which had emerged from the reorganization of the Wabash, St. Louis and Pacific Railway Co., resolutions were passed for the purpose of exercising efficient control over the management of the railway. It was decided that the debentures and shares be deposited with the committee and that the certificates of the committee would be placed in the market as substitutes. The committee included: Evelyn Heseltine, J. Blyth, C. E. Bretherton, H. Chinnery, W. Vivian, D. Marks, H. Paxton, Joseph Price, and A. Wagg.

[29] The British members of this board were E. W. Fernie, T. W. Powell, and William Ferguson. Heseltine and Powell were the representatives of the Marietta and Cincinnati in London. *American Railroad Journal*, XXXIII (Aug. 11, 1860), 700.

ent for these dividends on the favor of the railway's management, which they termed "autocratic." [30]

The safeguarding of British investment by British representation among the directors was occasionally the only method of control exercised. Thus, part of the agreement on the Texas-Pacific reorganization was that the first post-reorganization board of directors be approved by Jacob Schiff, a partner of Kuhn, Loeb; Charles M. McGhee; and Robert Fleming (a man devoted to British investors' interest who for this board and other purposes is reported to have made seventy trips to the United States). [31] Similarly, after the reorganization of the East Tennessee, Virginia and Georgia, Fleming became a member of its board. [32]

But there were obvious difficulties in relying solely on this method. Attendance by British residents at board meetings in the United States must have been necessarily occasional. Moreover, when British investors were represented on the boards of American railways by American residents, ideally there needed to be some organization in Britain to consider the policy which its American representatives would favor.

A fourth method of protecting British interests was by foreclosing a mortgage, taking over the property, and developing it. It appears to have been used for the first time in the case of the Alabama Great Southern. This was, however, not the first time that an American railway had been sold on the application of the British bondholders. [33] Nor was it the first time that the British investors had considered taking over a railway and completing it themselves. [34] Dutch and German investors who held large

---

[30] Although foreign ownership of the Pennsylvania rose from 7.37 percent in 1871 to 29.83 percent in 1881 and 47.46 percent in 1888, no representative of foreign shareholders was allowed to sit on the board. The *Economist* in an editorial entitled "The Greatest Railway Company in the World" complained: "But as to its future, that is largely with President Roberts; and even if the English shareholders desired a larger voice in the managment, they could not get it." XLII (March 22, 1884), 352–53. Nevertheless, the Pennsylvania management kept constantly in touch with its British share and bondholders. So, also, did the New York Central. Chauncey Depew was known as Vanderbilt's ambassador to the British investor.

[31] *Commercial and Financial Chronicle*, XLIII (Aug. 14, 1886), 191. Here is another instance of association between Fleming and Kuhn, Loeb.

[32] *Ibid.* (July 3, 1886), 22.

[33] For example, the Cincinnati, Logansport and Chicago was sold on application of the British bondholders in 1860, the purchasers being Pierre Chouteau, F. C. Gebhard, U. A. Murdock, John H. Thompson, and Henry Morgan. *American Railroad Journal*, XXXIII (May 5, 1860), 382.

[34] In the late 1850's the land-grant bonds of a railway named the Hudson River and Lake Ontario were marketed in London. The road soon defaulted, and it was proposed that the British investors should take it over and complete it. When in 1859 Richard Cobden made his second trip to the United States, he was commissioned by interested British parties to investigate the advisability of undertaking this task. Cobden returned an unfavorable report. Cawley, 195 n. In 1860 the line was sold at foreclosure, and a new company was formed to complete the line. A number of the members of this new company were reported

quantities of bonds in the new western lines in the early 1870's also adopted this expedient.[35] Nevertheless, it was a solution that necessitated great organization and was only used in rare cases. More commonly, an agreement was reached by which the railway was sold for the benefit of the foreign bondholders; they furnished the funds for the completion of the line but entrusted the carrying through of the plans to Americans.

The four methods of protecting investment so far discussed continued to be used during the 1880's and 1890's.[36] Three of them originated in the 1850's, and one, the taking over of the railways, was first used in the late 1870's. In addition, a number of new devices, or new variants of older devices, evolved.

When in 1879 large blocks of American railway shares started to be transferred to London by jobbers and arbitrage dealers, a number of difficulties arose. Most American railway bonds were bearer bonds, but American railway shares were technically registered. When these shares were brought to London, they were registered in the name of the arbitrage dealer or jobber who had imported them. Moreover, it was not easy for the British purchaser to effect transfer into his own name. Since few American railways maintained registry offices in London,[37] the share certificates had to be returned to the relevant railway's registry office in the United States for transfer. Few purchasers troubled to do this, and the stock exchange evolved a method by which these technically registered shares passed from hand to hand as freely as bearer bonds. Most American railway shares bore on their back a blank transfer form. It became a recognized custom in London for a registered owner to sign this transfer form but leave the name of the transferee blank. The certificates were then bought and sold freely.[38] Dividends could be collected on these shares,

---

[35] to be British. *American Railroad Journal*, XXXIII (Sept. 29, 1860), 870. Nevertheless, even this was not a completely British road. The only road which fell into that category was the Detroit and Milwaukee.

[35] The Brunswick and Albany was sold at foreclosure, purchased on behalf of the German bondholders and taken over. This was with the object of connecting with the British Alabama Great Southern.

[36] The taking over of railways was only done in the 1880's in cases like the Birmingham, Sheffield and Tennessee River where the British bondholders had a representative in the United States to act for them. Alfred Parrish of Philadelphia became president of the line while Dillwyn Parrish was the representative of the British bondholders.

[37] Several American railways had maintained registry offices in London in the 1850's, but by the 1880's even the shares of the Pennsylvania and the Illinois Central had to be returned to the United States to effect a change in registration. *Economist*, XLII (Sept. 20, 1884), 1139.

[38] This custom was not called into question until the late 1880's, when a case was heard before Judge Manisty involving the ownership of some Pennsylvania Railroad shares. The relevant part of the decision was: "If the right of suing upon an instrument does not appear upon the face of it to be extended beyond a particular individual, no usage of trade, however extensive, will confer upon it the character of negotiability." Reported in the *Journal of the Institute of Bankers*, X (April 1889), 192.

but they could not be voted.[39] Thus, many shareholders were in a very awkward position when an American railway, whose shares were circulating in large quantities in London registered in the name of a dealer, defaulted on its bonds and a reorganization was threatened.

The methodical Dutch already had perfected a method of dealing with this difficulty. No American railway securities were negotiable, as such, on the Amsterdam Bourse. In order to make the bonds or shares of an American railway negotiable, the owners had to deposit certificates of ownership with an official deposit agency. This agency held all actual American bonds and shares in its own vaults and issued its own certificates in their stead.[40]

A group of members of the London Stock Exchange sought to establish a similar agency in London.[41] On October 3, 1884, at the first meeting held in the stock exchange to consider this proposal, those present, mostly stockbrokers, appear to have intended to make this new agency a part of the stock exchange. Between the date of this meeting and the establishment of an incorporated company, the English Association of American Bond and Share Holders,[42] considerable opposition appears to have arisen in some undetermined quarter. One piece of evidence that points to this conclusion is the fact that a number of the important firms represented at the first meeting were not represented on the first board of directors of the English Association.[43] Secondly, the stock exchange persistently refused to list the shares of this new company.[44]

---

[39] Until the shares were transferred, the original owner retained the right to vote them and sometimes did so.

[40] A study of Dutch investments in American railways would therefore be much easier than a study of British investment since the amount and distribution of Dutch holdings was accurately known. This method of dealing with American railway securities also enabled the Dutch to move quickly in time of emergency, and they were able to secure a number of concessions from American railways in which Dutch holdings were large. [See Bosch, 136 ff.]

[41] The provisional committee appointed at the meeting of a group of members of the stock exchange on Oct. 3, 1884, included: H. J. Chinnery of Chinnery Brothers; J. M. Douglas; J. H. Hutchinson; H. C. Mayhew of Borthwick, Wark and Company; L. Messel of Messel and Company; F. H. Milbank; T. W. Powell of Heseltine and Powell; G. Russell of E. F. Satterthwaite and Co.; S. Scott; W. Vivian of Vivian, Gray and Company; William Trotter; and Joseph Price.

[42] Like its counterpart, the Council of Foreign Bondholders, the English Association is an incorporated company. It is not competitive with the Council of Foreign Bondholders, which deals only with the obligations of governmental bodies. The Council of Foreign Bondholders worked on the bonds of the Alabama and Chattanooga only because they were guaranteed by the state of Alabama.

[43] None of the representatives of the big stockbrokers of the American market were represented on the board of directors of the Association of American Bond and Stock Holders.

[44] Eventually, in the late 1880's the stock exchange was obliged to establish a registry agency within the stock exchange. However, this agency did not accept

Opinions differ as to the reasons for the opposition. Joseph Price, the guiding spirit of the English Association, attributed this opposition to the vested interests; many firms, making good revenues out of such clerical operations as the payment of coupons on American bonds and of the dividends on American shares, feared the loss of such business.[45] Apparently, there was also some apprehension that this association might, like the investment trusts, sooner or later start to issue American securities despite the fact that it was specifically forbidden to encroach in this manner on the functions of stock exchange members. A more likely explanation is that no specific encroachment was feared, but that even at the beginning the great houses and the big stockbrokers foresaw that this association might become very powerful.[46] In particular, it might become an active participant in representing American security holders in reorganizations.

If this were so, the great houses and the stockbrokers were right. The English Association was seldom called upon to represent British bondholders. The houses through which the relevant issues had been floated continued to perform this function.[47] On the other hand, the association was able to form committees to represent the shareholders of various American railways and to negotiate with the various bondholders' committees on behalf of the shareholders. These investors might otherwise have been without representation except by dissentient and rather powerless committees.

A second method of protecting British investment in American railways appeared for the first time in the 1880's. The backing of London Committees was used by the great Anglo-American houses, headed by J. P. Morgan, to attempt to control both competitive building and rate cutting on the part of various American railways.

Probably the most famous "deal" in all American railway history is that which was arranged between the Pennsylvania and the New York Central in the course of a cruise on J. P. Morgan's yacht *Corsair* one early July day in 1885. Both roads had been violently competing. The New York Central,

---

American securities for deposit and did not issue its own certificates in their place. It only undertook the responsibility of sending the certificates back to the United States for transfer at the registry office of the pertinent railway.

[45] Report of the English Association of American Bond and Share Holders in the *Economist*, XLV (April 16, 1887), 498.

[46] In Oct. 1885, the *Economist* said: "We should not like, for instance, to see a shareholders' association controlling the management of our English railways. Such an arrangement might remedy some existing abuses, but it would certainly lead to the creation of other and still greater abuses." XLIII (Oct. 17, 1885), 1270.

[47] Some issuing houses had recognized their responsibility to the holders of bonds issued through them as early as the 1850's, but this was not universally the case. By the 1880's, however, it was a fairly well-established practice. J. S. Morgan was already acting in this manner in the 1870's, as was Barings.

supporting the Reading against the Pennsylvania,[48] had begun constructing a line called the South Pennsylvania designed to parallel the Pennsylvania and cut into its traffic.[49] At the same time, the New York, Ontario and Western had been constructing a road called the New York, West Shore and Buffalo for the specific purpose of cutting into the profits of the New York Central. There were also rumors that the Pennsylvania was supporting the West Shore, but there is no concrete evidence of this.[50] At this juncture, J. P. Morgan invited three guests, Chauncey Depew of the New York Central and George B. Roberts and Frank Thomson of the Pennsylvania, for a day's outing at sea.

None of the four participants ever made a statement concerning the discussions held that day about the West Shore.[51] The official report released did not even mention the company. It only announced that a controlling interest in the South Pennsylvania would be transferred to the Pennsylvania.[52] Nevertheless, the next day newspapers emblazoned the report that the Pennsylvania had sold the West Shore to the New York Central and had received in return the South Pennsylvania.[53] These negotiations have gone down in railway history as the West Shore "deal."

[48] William H. Vanderbilt had bought a substantial block of shares in the Reading during the McCalmont-Gowen struggle.

[49] The first instance of a line's being built specifically to cut into the profits of another line occurred in the early 1850's. The line whose track was being paralleled was the Chicago and Galena, which was forced to purchase its upstart rival just as the New York Central was later forced to purchase the New York, Chicago and St. Louis (the Nickel Plate) and the West Shore. There is no doubt that the West Shore's purpose was to parallel the New York Central; a statement to this effect appeared in the public press credited to friends of Woerischoffer, Villard, Pullman and Porter, members of the board of directors of the West Shore. The remark attributed to this group was that if the West Shore could get one-fourth of the traffic of the New York Central it would be able to pay a 7 percent dividend. *Commercial and Financial Chronicle*, XXXIII (July 2, 1881); 24. It is not clear whether the statement refers to traffic diverted from the New York Central or to new traffic, but the implication of direct competition is clear.

[50] In June 1885 there were reports that the Pennsylvania was trying to get control of the West Shore. *Economist*, XLIII (June 20, 1885), 754–55. Indeed it would be odd if the Pennsylvania had not considered this means of protecting itself.

[51] Burgess and Kennedy, 411.

[52] The full report stated that:

1. J. P. Morgan would obtain the consent of the owners of 60 percent of the interest in the South Pennsylvania syndicate to sell such interest to the Pennsylvania Railroad, for which the Pennsylvania would give in payment $5.6 million in 3 percent bonds of the Bedford and Bridgeport Railroad Company, which it would guarantee.

2. The Pennsylvania (through the Northern Central) would gain control of the Beech Creek on appropriate terms.

Incidentally neither the Reading nor Andrew Carnegie, both backers of the South Pennsylvania, were consulted about the sale. Carnegie was in Britain when the sale was announced and was reportedly indignant.

[53] *Economist*, XLIII (July 25, 1885), 907.

All the stories about these negotiations ignore one important interested party, the British investor. There is considerable evidence to support the contention that the reason no announcement was ever made that the Pennsylvania had sold the West Shore was because in fact it was not the Pennsylvania's to sell. It was Morgan himself who sold the West Shore, and in doing so he had the support of the British holders of the New York, Ontario and Western, who, as will be noted, were in a key position.[54]

The New York, Ontario and Western, a reorganization of the New York and Oswego Midland, had been formed in 1880. It had issued $48 million of common stock and $2 million of preferred stock, and had virtually no funded debt.[55] Shortly after the formation of the Ontario, it reached a three-way agreement with the North River Construction Company and the New York, West Shore and Buffalo.[56] Shareholders in the Ontario were given the right to purchase shares in the North River Construction Company.[57] The latter was to take over and complete the West Shore, receiving payment in the railway's bonds and shares.[58] Additional funds for building

[54] Both William Henry Vanderbilt and J. P. Morgan were in London in June 1885, immediately preceding the *Corsair* negotiations.

[55] There was in fact a small funded debt of $200,000.

[56] The West Shore itself had been struggling through a long receivership in the 1870's. It had tried to negotiate bonds in Amsterdam in 1873, but it was not very successful; in 1878, of $7 million of bonds outstanding, $3 million was held by former Governor Page, the president of the construction company. *Commercial and Financial Chronicle*, XXVII (Oct. 5, 1878), 358. The West Shore was then sold at foreclosure, and it was announced that a new company would be set up. This plan never came to fruition, presumably because alternative arrangements were concluded. Thus, in the spring of 1880 the purchasing committee offered the West Shore for sale, just as the committee received the road from the court. *Ibid.*, XXX (June 26, 1880), 675. The three-way contract between the two railways and the construction company was announced at the beginning of 1881.

[57] Each ten shares held in the Ontario entitled the holder to purchase one share in the North River Construction Co. It was further announced that a syndicate would take all shares not taken up by Ontario shareholders. *Ibid.*, XXXII (Feb. 12, 1881), 183–84. In fact, it is doubtful whether British shareholders of the Ontario acquired many shares of the North River Construction, since the right to purchase was accorded to the registered and not the actual owners of the shares of the Ontario.

[58] In addition, the Ontario advanced $10 million in cash, receiving in return $10 million in 5 percent bonds of the West Shore and a bonus of 25 percent in stock. *Ibid.*, XXXIII (Oct. 1, 1881), 358. In 1882 part of these bonds were offered to shareholders of the Ontario at $500 each. *Ibid.*, XXXV (July 29, 1882), 132. Again, few of these bonds appear to have gone in the first instance to the British shareholders of the Ontario. According to a pamphlet issued by the English Association of American Bond and Share Holders in 1888, *American Railway Share Certificates*: "In 1882, the New York, Ontario, and Western Railway Company had in its treasury $10,000,000 Bonds of the West Shore Railway, which had been paid to them for the construction of the Weehawken and Middletown section of that railway. Notice was suddenly given by the then Board of the Company in New York, that these Bonds would be sold to

the West Shore were obtained by the negotiation of a large amount of the railway's bonds with a syndicate of foreign and American bankers.[59]

By the end of 1883 both the Ontario and the West Shore were in serious financial difficulties. Negotiations were opened for a lease of these lines to the Grand Trunk; the expedient of a lease seems to have been the first idea to occur to the managers of largely British-owned roads whenever financial difficulties were encountered.[60] In this case the plan never materialized.

At the beginning of 1884 British shareholders of the Ontario mobilized for action. A meeting was held, a committee was appointed, and shareholders were asked to deposit their shares. Indeed, deposit was virtually obligatory; the principal dealers in the American market in London had agreed that, from February 28, 1884, they would deal only in the London Committee's certificates for the Ontario and not in the shares themselves.[61] When the shares were deposited, it was revealed that at least $17.5 million of the common stock of this road was held by British and Dutch investors.[62]

Because the Ontario was in desperate need of financial assistance, the representatives of the London Committee [63] were able to exact a number of concessions from the railway's management. In return for the London Committee's authorization for the issue of $4 million of first-mortgage bonds, five places on the line's board were immediately accorded to representatives of foreign shareholders.[64] Most important, the London Commit-

---

stockholders of record, at fifty cents on the dollar. The natural result was, that the real owners in this country knew nothing about it, as only a fortnight's notice was given in New York, consequently registered stockholders having no right to the option obtained at least 95 percent of these Bonds, with the accompanying benefit of the large advance at which they were saleable very soon afterwards."

[59] The total of this mortgage on the West Shore was $50 million, of which $10 million in bonds was issued to the Ontario. The remainder was issued gradually, the final $5 million being taken in late 1883. *Commercial and Financial Chronicle,* XXXIII (Oct. 1, 1881), 358, and XXXVII (Dec. 22, 1883), 695.

[60] *Ibid.,* XXXVII (Nov. 17, 1883), 534. This plan of making some arrangement between the Ontario and the Grand Trunk had been considered as early as 1880. When the Ontario was first formed, it was announced that it would seek connections with the Grand Trunk and with the Atlantic and Great Western. *Ibid.,* XXXI (Dec. 4, 1880), 589.

[61] *Economist,* XLII (Feb. 16, 1884), 207.

[62] This is the amount of the certificates of shares registered with the London and Amsterdam Committees of the Ontario admitted to quotation in London on June 23, 1884. *Burdett's Official Intelligence* (1885).

[63] Joseph Price and Charles Russell (of E. F. Satterthwaite and Co.) were the delegates sent to New York by the London Committee for the Ontario. R. van Ress was the delegate of the Dutch holders.

[64] These places on the Ontario's board were filled by Thomas Powell Fowler, Richard Irvin, Jr., Charles Canda, Joseph Price, and Thomas Swinyard. *Com-*

tee's delegates contrived to purchase a controlling majority of the preferred shares; this type of stock carried the right to elect eight of the thirteen members of the board of directors.[65] The board therefore now became completely foreign and largely British controlled.

Meanwhile, the fight over the West Shore continued throughout the spring of 1885. William H. Vanderbilt was obviously an interested party, and there were rumors that he had purchased a large quantity of West Shore bonds as early as March 1885.[66] It was in the summer of this year that the famous *Corsair* cruise took place.

It has already been pointed out that there was no mention of the West Shore in the announcement made to the public after the *Corsair* cruise. Nevertheless, a few weeks later Drexel, Morgan and Company announced a new plan of reorganization for this line.[67] Under this plan, to which the West Shore and the New York Central had agreed, E. D. Adams of Winslow, Lanier and Company exercised his option to purchase $1,250,000 of the preferred shares of the Ontario.[68] This could not have been accomplished without the cooperation of the London Committee of the Ontario, since it held $1,002,000 of the $2 million of preferred shares of the line.

The *Investor's Monthly Manual* reported that these shares of the Ontario had been purchased by W. H. Vanderbilt from a London syndicate without

---

mercial and Financial Chronicle, XXXIX (July 5, 1884), 22, and (Aug. 16, 1884), 182. Canda was the appointee of the Dutch holders. Fowler was an American lawyer who became president of the line after it came under British control.

[65] According to a report of a meeting of the London Committee for the Ontario, these shares were purchased "at a fair price." In addition, the London Committee agreed to take $1.8 million of the new first-mortgage issue. Indeed, subscription to first-mortgage bonds appears to have been the *quid pro quo* by which the preferred shares were acquired. The $1,002,000 of preferred shares and the $1.8 million of first-mortgage bonds were held in trust by the London Committee which issued against them $2.5 million of collateral certificates. *Ibid.*, XL (April 18, 1885), 481. These collateral certificates were offered to the ordinary shareholders of the Ontario, who do not appear to have taken them. Indeed, at this point in the story matters become less clear.

[66] In March 1885 it was reported that W. H. Vanderbilt had purchased a very large quantity of West Shore bonds to relieve a New York banking house that was in financial difficulties. At the time, very few credited this report because it was believed that no one house held the quantity of bonds that Vanderbilt was stated to have purchased. *Economist*, XLIII (March 14, 1885), 321. Nevertheless, the report appears to have been correct in substance, for the banking house of Winslow, Lanier, which had been deeply involved in West Shore affairs, was somehow won over to absorption of this road by the New York Central about this time. Indeed, it was E. D. Adams of Winslow, Lanier who managed the actual transfer to the New York Central.

[67] *Commercial and Financial Chronicle*, XLI (Aug. 1, 1885), 112, 133.

[68] *Ibid.* (Aug. 29, 1885), 242.

agreement of the London shareholders.[69] It might be possible to credit this statement were it not for the fact that the control of the Ontario was returned to the London Committee after the reorganization of the West Shore and its absorption by the New York Central had been accomplished.[70] On the contrary, the London Committee could have been privy to Morgan's plans. Certainly its members were overjoyed at the outcome of the *Corsair* cruise, and it was the optimism generated in London by these arrangements that is said to have begun the new boom in American railway shares in the summer of 1885.[71] [In the United States the depressed conditions of the mid-1880's had given way to a period of railway expansion.]

Looking ahead, it is interesting to note that the Ontario, like the Denver and Rio Grande, fared well under management from London. Although both were inherently weak lines, neither caused any difficulty even in the long depression of the 1890's. The Ontario now became the New York connection for the Canadian Pacific.

For a time Sir Henry Tyler of the Grand Trunk nourished hope of rivaling J. P. Morgan as the savior of American railways. Thus, in the autumn of 1886 a memorial was circulated for signature among American railway shareholders asking Sir Henry Tyler to convene a public meeting to discuss the ruinous competition in which these railways had been indulging since the beginning of 1884.[72] Tyler was too late. The West Shore negotiations had already established J. P. Morgan in this position.[73]

The second example of the use of British capital to force a railway to curb its competitive policy also involved the Morgan family. The Chicago, Milwaukee and St. Paul falls into the classification of railways that en-

[69] In Sept. 1885 the *Investor's Monthly Manual* stated that Vanderbilt had bought the preferred shares from a syndicate and added: "The Ontario ordinary shareholders were advised to buy these shares themselves, but having failed to do so, they will have to pay the cost." P. 427.

[70] These preferred shares of the Ontario were called in and paid off by certificates issued by Drexel, Morgan and Co. The certificates were exchangeable for new West Shore 4 percent bonds guaranteed by the New York Central. Control of the road then reverted to the ordinary shareholders, that is to say, to the London Committee. *Ibid.* This may have been part of the settlement of the Ontario's claims against the West Shore. It was because of these claims that Vanderbilt and Morgan needed the cooperation of the Ontario in reorganizing the West Shore. If Vanderbilt now held a large quantity of West Shore bonds, he could conceivably have foreclosed without the consent of the Ontario, but this would have involved a struggle. Since the *Corsair* negotiations were for the making of peace, Vanderbilt and Morgan naturally wished to avoid a struggle.

[71] All parties concerned seem to have profited from the arrangements made on the *Corsair*. There seem to have been no losers.

[72] *Economist*, XLIII (Sept. 26, 1885), 1169.

[73] London now looked to W. H. Vanderbilt and J. P. Morgan to control ruinous competition, and when Vanderbilt died in late 1885 the City was reported to be more alarmed than Wall Street. *Ibid.* (Dec. 26, 1885), 1577.

joyed for many years a close relationship with British financial institutions. This association undoubtedly stemmed in part from the fact that its president, Alexander Mitchell, was a Scot and a protégé of George Smith.[74] As early as 1869 this road had been receiving support from the City of Glasgow Bank,[75] and in 1872 the first public issue of bonds of the antecedent Milwaukee and St. Paul had been made in London.[76] Some of the shares of this line had also found their way to London by the late 1870's.[77] Like the Norfolk and Western, it was considered a "cliqued" road, and the fact that its securities were never popular in New York is additional evidence of its close association with London finance.[78]

However, it would appear that unlike the Norfolk and Western, whose financial connections in London were all with the same group, the Milwaukee had a number of strings to its bow.[79] Perhaps it was this that enabled Mitchell to pursue a fairly independent policy, a policy of aggressive expansion that brought the line into conflict with the Chicago and North Western and other roads fanning out west of Chicago through wheat-growing country.

[A succession of events followed the expansive building policy of the Milwaukee and the depressed middle 1880's.] In 1887 Alexander Mitchell died.[80] The following June, George Magoun of Kidder, Peabody was elected to the board of directors.[81] Then, in the autumn of 1888 the Milwaukee passed its dividend. Immediately, an announcement appeared in the London press stating that J. S. Morgan and Company was prepared to receive shares of the Milwaukee for registration in the name of Morgan and

[74] See above, p. 179 ff.

[75] The City of Glasgow Bank in 1869 took all the bonds of a subsidiary line, the Western Union Railroad, whose shares were divided between the City of Glasgow Bank and the Milwaukee in the proportions of 49 to 51 percent. After the collapse of the City of Glasgow Bank in 1878, the Milwaukee repurchased all these bonds ($3.5 million), the shares being thrown in as a bonus. *Commercial and Financial Chronicle*, XXX (April 17, 1880), 406.

[76] An early name of the road was the Milwaukee and St. Paul. It became the Chicago, Milwaukee and St. Paul in 1874. The bonds of the Milwaukee and St. Paul were issued through Morton, Rose. The amount was £800,000 of which £200,000 was reserved for Amsterdam.

[77] Dividends on both the common and preferred shares of the Milwaukee and St. Paul were regularly announced in the *Times* in the late 1870's.

[78] *Economist*, XXVI (Sept. 29, 1888), 1224.

[79] Besides having connections in Scotland, the Milwaukee floated loans through Morton, Rose in the 1870's and through Borthwick, Wark and Co., Speyer Brothers, and Blake Brothers in the 1880's.

[80] After Mitchell's death it was expected that Frank Bond, who was then vice-president of the Milwaukee, would become president. However, he was passed over for Roswell Miller, the railroad's general manager. [See Arthur M. Borak, "The Financial History of the Chicago, Milwaukee and St. Paul Railway Company" (unpublished doctoral thesis, University of Minnesota, 1929).]

[81] *Commercial and Financial Chronicle*, XLIV (June 11, 1887), 751.

Company.[82] A short time later this proposal was again put to the shareholders at a meeting sponsored jointly by J. S. Morgan and Company and by the English Association of American Bond and Share Holders. No shareholders' committee was appointed; instead matters were entrusted directly to Morgan. The response, moreover, was immediate and overwhelming. Within a week over $20 million of shares had been deposited.[83]

The Milwaukee was now firmly in hand. Its expansionist policy was for the time stopped, and the way was paved for the formation of the Western Traffic Association. This association for the control of railway rates was, in fact, short-lived.[84] It was not, however, the Milwaukee that brought about its downfall. A few months after the agreement, the Chicago, Burlington and Northern cut rates by a third. Other Granger roads were forced to follow suit.[85]

Another new development in the protection of British investment in American railways, originating in the 1880's, was the establishment of a number of almost completely British lines. Of these the Chicago Great Western is the outstanding example. In general these companies were usually unlike the Alabama Great Southern in that they were neither British incorporated nor British managed.[86] They were also unlike the Illinois Central, although similar to that line in having bypassed the New York money market and having obtained virtually all their finances from London. In the case of the Illinois Central, British investors intervened

[82] In noting this announcement about the Milwaukee's shares, the *Economist* remarked that although British investors were said to hold three quarters of the shares of this line, a few wealthy men headed by Philip Armour had so far had matters all their own way. XLVI (Sept. 22, 1888), 1189.

[83] *Ibid.* (Oct. 6, 1888), 1256.

[84] The original proposal was for an American Railway Association, a proposal put forward by Morgans; Barings; and Brown, Shipley jointly at the beginning of 1889. Furthermore, the proposed association was said to have the support of the following railways, in most of which British interest was strong: Atchison, Topeka and Santa Fe; Chicago, Burlington and Quincy; Chicago and North Western; Chicago, Rock Island and Pacific; Chicago, Milwaukee and St. Paul; Missouri Pacific; St. Louis and Santa Fe; Chicago, St. Paul and Kansas City (later the Chicago Great Western); Wabash Western; Pennsylvania; New York Central; Erie; Delaware, Lackawanna and Western; Baltimore and Ohio; and Lehigh Valley. However, within a few months hopes for the accomplishment of this plan for an American Railway Association were fading. Both the Illinois Central and the Chicago, Burlington and Northern held aloof. The position of the Chicago and Alton was also in doubt. Nevertheless, negotiations over this plan continued through 1889, and finally a measure of success was attained with the formation of the Western Traffic Association. *Economist*, XLVII (Jan. 26, 1889), 107; (Feb. 23, 1889), 240; (July 20, 1889), 925; and XLVIII (Jan. 11, 1890), 43.

[85] The Chicago, Burlington and Northern was a line [from Chicago to Saint Paul] built by persons influential in the Chicago, Burlington and Quincy. *Ibid.*, XLVIII (March 1, 1890), 275.

[86] The Alabama Great Southern soon began to employ Americans in management.

only when financial difficulties were encountered and were content, once
the line had become a solid dividend-paying concern, to have their interest
in that railway become purely rentier in character.[87] The closest analogy is
with the Philadelphia and Reading, but even here the analogy is not
complete. For one thing, there seems to have been more active British
participation in roads like the Chicago Great Western. For another, the
relationship between the British fiscal agents and the various American
railways in the 1880's seems to have been more on a basis of equality than
was the case with the Reading. The relationship between McCalmont
Brothers and the Reading may originally have been of this nature and
then, over the course of time, have been transformed into a more purely
proprietary relationship, as it became necessary to place in control of the
line [88] men with whom McCalmonts had never had a close relationship.

The idea for the formation of the Chicago Great Western,[89] which
belonged to the Granger group, reportedly originated in London in the
middle 1880's.[90] Unfortunately, the new railway did not get onto its feet
before the advent of the Baring crisis and the depression of the 1890's. It
was therefore forced to reorganize in 1892, a reorganization that earned it
the enmity of a small but extremely vocal group of bondholders.[91] Perhaps
the articles attacking this company and the group of London houses
associated with it [92] were in part responsible for a scandal that forced the
resignation of the chief cashier of the Bank of England in 1894. The
cashier was accused of having persuaded private customers of the bank to

[87] Nevertheless, it should be noted that the man who was responsible for
British interest in the Chicago Great Western was Robert Benson, the son of the
Robert Benson who had for many years been the agent of the Illinois Central in
London.

[88] When John Cryder first intervened in the Reading, the relationship between
him and McCalmont Brothers may very well have been of this sort.

[89] British interest in the Chicago Great Western resulted from an original
interest in the Minnesota and Northwestern. A companion road, the Chicago, St.
Paul and Kansas City, was formed in 1886, partly out of already existing short
lines. In 1888 the two lines, which although technically independent had been
operated by the same group, were amalgamated under the name Chicago, St.
Paul and Kansas City. In 1889 the company asked bondholders to fund coupons
for three years, and in 1892 the line was reorganized as the Chicago Great
Western.

[90] *Investor's Review* (1893), 637–46.

[91] S. F. Van Oss was one of the most vocal of this group. He contended that
the first-mortgage bondholders of the two constituent lines, who got for each
$1,000 bond one $500 debenture bond and $600 in 5 percent preferred A stock,
had been sacrificed to the general mortgage bondholders who received dollar for
dollar in 4 percent preferred B stock. However, Van Oss seems to have been an
admirer of the American president of the Chicago Great Western, A. B. Stickney. Van Oss, *American Railroads as Investments*, 23–27 and 533–34.

[92] The houses connected with this line were Robert Benson, J. K. Gilliat, and
Rathbone Brothers. A member of each of the last two houses was then on the
board of governors of the Bank of England.

invest in the Chicago Great Western, sometimes with money borrowed from the bank.[93]

In connection with the Chicago Great Western, a line running south from Kansas City to the Gulf of Mexico must be mentioned, for it also falls into this category of British lines. This was the Kansas City, Pittsburg and Gulf.[94] A number of companies in the South should also be included, in particular a group that eventually became part of the Atlantic Coast Line.

Another point should be made in connection with this group of railways. British investors had at last found a group of Americans with whom they could cooperate. This group neither ignored them, as the Pennsylvania was accused of doing, nor cheated them, as Jay Gould reportedly was intent on doing.

In a sense this is not entirely a development of the 1880's. There had always been a group of American lawyers and bankers on whom the British investor could rely; indeed, J. P. Morgan himself probably belongs in this category. The British investors had found Americans on whom they could depend in the Erie troubles. David A. Wells had worked with the British investors on the Alabama and Chattanooga.

However, there is a difference. In the 1880's British houses built up a group of operating railway men whom they could trust. New England–born Frank Bond was one of the earliest recruits to these ranks, and it is interesting to watch his progress from one largely British-controlled road to another. The first of these companies on which he served was the Reading. Then, after a short time on the Texas-Pacific, he moved to the Erlanger system and next to the Milwaukee. Thomas Fowler, who was for a long time the president of the Ontario, also belongs in this group. So, too, does Alpheus Beede Stickney of the Chicago Great Western.[95]

[93] According to Clapham: "Rumours were soon abroad in the City, which spread later to the country. The Bank [of England] had been mixed up in 'shady transactions;' 'one or two directors might have to resign;' and so forth." *Bank of England*, II, 359. Subsequently at the General Court held in Nov. 1894, charges were made that a number of the bank's old customers had been advised by the chief cashier, who had recently been forced to resign, to invest in "rubbish," specifically securities of the Chicago Great Western Railway and that some of these investments had been with funds borrowed from the bank. Edward Clark asked that a committee be appointed to go into the relations between the late chief cashier and the bank's customers, but the governor wanted the matter dropped, and the motion was not seconded. *Economist*, LII (Sept. 15, 1894), 1140.

[94] The Pittsburg referred to in the title of this railway is not in Pennsylvania but in Kansas; the road is a beeline to the Gulf of Mexico.

[95] Stickney is remarkable in two respects. First, he aligned himself with Richard T. Ely against rate discrimination. Second, he testified before the Interstate Commerce Commission that much of the wheat carried on the Chicago Great Western was in fact owned by the railway before it left the farm so that the rate charged was irrelevant: "I organised the Iowa Development Company, which took over the surplus land of the Great Western. The Anglo-American Provision Company bought wheat for this Corporation on a commis-

But British investors did not leave all practical matters to Americans. When it came to reorganizations, the representatives of the British investor were, as already noted, now taking a very active part in the formulation of plans. Again, this is not entirely a new development. But in earlier periods the British had usually relied on Americans like Samuel Tilden or Pierre Chouteau to carry their wishes into effect. In the 1880's default was no sooner announced than British representatives were on their way to the United States.

---

sion. Every dollar of stock of the Iowa Development Company is owned by the railroad." Quotation in *Investor's Review*, XLIV (Dec. 1896), 371. For this statement, he is said to have earned the enmity of the other Granger roads.

IX

Conclusion

ALTHOUGH this chapter is mainly a recapitulation, there are a few points that have either been glossed over or omitted entirely from the preceding chapters and therefore merit further consideration. Specifically, these are: the various areas that attracted British investment as the American railway system developed; the types of investment into which British capital flowed in the three periods considered; and the extent of British entrepreneurship, in the sense of active participation in the affairs of a railway.

In the 1830's the American railways that floated issues in London under their own names [1] were of two types. Some were constituent parts of a great north-south chain of lines along the Atlantic seaboard.[2] Others were lines clustered about Philadelphia or New York. British capital was made available for the construction of ambitious lines to the West that men in the various seaboard cities were planning if the states concerned were willing to underwrite these ventures. The reasons are obvious. A north-south chain in the area of major settlement was considered to be certain of success. Lines near Philadelphia and New York, the two largest cities of the United States, could also count on substantial traffic.[3] Lines to the West involved more risk; additional guarantees were required. Moreover, the financial institutions through which these securities found their way to

[1] This does not refer to railways that obtained British capital through the sale of state securities.

[2] Starting at New York this chain was made up of the Camden and Amboy, the Philadelphia, Wilmington and Baltimore, the Washington branch of Baltimore and Ohio, the Richmond, Fredericksburg and Potomac, the Richmond and Petersburg, and the Wilmington and Raleigh (Wilmington and Weldon). From Wilmington it was necessary to go by steamer to Charleston where the route turned west toward New Orleans. Except for the South Carolina, most of the remainder of this route had to be covered by stage and steamer in the 1840's.

[3] The Harrisburg and Lancaster ran west from Philadelphia but traversed territory that was already well populated and therefore can also be considered to be a tributary road of Philadelphia.

London were usually New York or Philadelphia concerns like the Second Bank of the United States or the Morris and Essex Banking Corporation.[4]

In the 1850's British investors continued to display a preference for the securities of well-situated trunk lines. Except for such roads, the British investor was not interested in the railways of Ohio and Indiana, nor in the municipal securities of these states issued in aid of railways. Yet these became great favorites on the Continent. Illinois, however, was a different matter. After the introduction of the land grant bonds of the Illinois Central, the securities of other Illinois roads came onto the London market one after another in quick succession. This was the first manifestation of an interest that was to persist throughout the nineteenth century, not merely in railways, but in land for the settlement of European emigrants and for the growing of food for Europe.

The British investor in the post–Civil War period avoided investment in the new western lines that began to build as soon as hostilities ceased. In particular, the transcontinental lines did not attract much British capital at first,[5] in spite of the enormous publicity attending the triumphal opening of the Union Pacific–Central Pacific line in 1869. The St. Paul and Pacific (later the Great Northern Railway Company)[6] and the Kansas Pacific became Dutch favorites, and the Northern Pacific[7] and the Oregon Railway and Transportation Company[8] became German favorites.

The senior securities floated in London after 1871 to tempt the "immensely rich, but extremely conservative"[9] class of British investors, who had earlier eschewed American railway securities, were not confined to those of the railways of any single area. On the whole, these securities were of old established lines in the East and the Old Northwest. Newer lines, or lines in areas whose future was more problematical, also found

[4] Even some of the southern issues probably found their way to London via Philadelphia. Thus, the Richmond and Petersburg very early referred to bonds of the Philadelphia list.

[5] There was some investment in the Oregon and California in the 1870's. By the end of the 1880's there was substantial British investment in other transcontinental lines.

[6] [The St. Paul and Pacific depended on Dutch bondholders, but the succeeding company had a more diversified group of nationalities among its investors.]

[7] German investment in this line did not become important until the 1880's. However, by 1898, German investment in the Northern Pacific was estimated to account for $20–$25 million of total German investment, which was estimated at $150–$200 million. Bacon, 270–71. Henry Villard, having served as receiver for the Kansas Pacific, became the representative of the German bondholders of this line. Hence his subsequent interest in the Northern Pacific.

[8] In 1898 German investors were estimated to hold $15 to $17 million in the Southern Pacific and $12 to $15 million in the Central Pacific. The only other roads in which they had substantial interests were the Chicago, Milwaukee and St. Paul ($7 to $8 million) and the Illinois Central ($7 to $8 million). *Ibid.*

[9] Hon. George S. Boutwell, "An Historic Sale of United States Bonds in England, 1871–72," *McClure's Magazine,* XV (May and Sept., 1900).

favor when they carried the guarantee of a road like the Pennsylvania, or the endorsement of a house like Morton, Rose.

But the British entrepreneur, as distinct from the rentier, was looking mainly to the growing areas in the South and Southwest.[10] His interest was not confined to railways. The ranches of Texas were more attractive to the British emigrant than the pioneer wheat farms of the Dakotas. Nevertheless, wheat continued to be important to the British investor in spite of the spectacular burst of investment in cattle ranches that began in the late 1870's and reached such large proportions in the 1880's.[11] The Iowa Land and Mortgage Company was also started in the late 1870's.[12] The other area that attracted British entrepreneurs after the Civil War was the South, where British investment in railways was often connected with interest in coal and iron.

Interest in the South and Southwest, displayed by venturesome British investors in the 1870's, became more general and more important in the 1880's. British entrepreneurs were convinced that this area would soon grow; they were active in establishing a foothold there before the boom began. Almost every railway company of any importance had connections with London;[13] as a result Southerners were able to obtain funds for

[10] There had been a slight British interest in Texas even before it became a part of the United States, and indeed Texas had unsuccessfully attempted to attract British emigrants during the 1830's. However, the first Texas railway that sought European capital in the late 1850's tried to issue bonds in Paris. This issue, for the Galveston, Houston and Henderson, was eventually brought out in London. *Economist*, XVI (March 13, 1858), 292. Incidentally, Texas never accepted the Confederate currency but remained on specie throughout the Civil War. This may well have prejudiced British investors in its favor. Compare, for example, the attitude of the state of Pennsylvania, which in 1868 paid off an issue (of which British investors held $15,068,000 out of a total of $27,176,000) in greenbacks but refunded in sterling. *Times*, Feb. 24, 1868, p. 10, and March 27, 1868, p. 5.

[11] It was Scottish investment that predominated in cattle ranching. The annual statistics on these companies were compiled and published not in the City but in Dundee. The most famous and probably the first of these cattle companies was the Prairie Land Co. of Edinburgh. [See Jackson, chaps. 3 and 5.] Just as the coal and iron lands in which the British invested were sometimes purchased from railways that had received the land in the form of land grants, much of the land purchased for ranches was also obtained in this way. Thus, in the Texas-Pacific reorganization, the income bondholders took the land in part payment of their claim against the railway. Similarly, in 1884, the St. Louis and San Francisco sold a large tract of land, 168,534 acres, to a Scottish company. *Commercial and Financial Chronicle*, XXXVIII (March 15, 1884), 330.

[12] Robert Benson and Co. were particularly active in Iowa land companies.

[13] In 1882, Colonel Buford, president of the Richmond and Danville, said: "We have not negotiated any foreign acceptance since 1873; we have no need to do so, for we can borrow all the money that we want at home." The implication was that most southern railways were dependent on short-term funds. However, it must be added that Buford may have been using the term foreign to include Yankees. *Commercial and Financial Chronicle*, XXXV (Oct. 21, 1882), 457.

expansion. Railway mileage in the South, which had increased little in the 1870's,[14] almost doubled in the 1880's.[15]

The second-string syndicate (Fleming, Vivian, Gray, *et al.*) and the various investment trusts were particularly active in the South and Southwest.[16] The great houses continued their interest in the older lines of the East and established new contacts with two or three large-scale projects such as the Northern Pacific.[17] By what was probably a tacitly agreed division of labor, the newer projects in the South that involved more risk but required less capital were frequently left to the attention of the lesser houses. However, in constructing the Chicago Great Western, the smaller houses participated in financing the Granger group.[18]

By the end of the 1880's not only was some British capital invested in almost every first-class railway in the United States, but it had also been attracted to the connections of American railways with Canada to the north and Mexico to the south. In the nineteenth century, the main economic strength of Canada lay in Upper Canada (Ontario). Lower Canada and the Maritime Provinces were poor.[19] Their soil and climate were even more inhospitable than those of New England; they had not

[14] One other area, New England, also did little railway building during this period. This, however, was because its railway system was already far advanced.

[15] The following table clearly brings out the fact that the south Atlantic, east south central, and west south central regions experienced their greatest railway expansion in the 1880's:

Railroad Mileage of the United States, 1860–1900

	1860	1870	1880	1890	1900
New England	3,660	4,494	5,982	6,721	7,521
Middle Atlantic	5,840	9,709	13,832	18,161	20,708
So. Atlantic	5,976	7,349	9,789	18,270	23,362
East South Central	3,392	4,656	6,343	11,144	13,343
East North Central	9,583	14,701	25,109	36,923	41,007
West North Central	1,472	8,046	19,094	38,354	42,988
West South Central	680	1,417	5,044	13,782	18,221
Mountain	—	1,466	5,082	12,676	15,809
Pacific	23	1,084	2,992	7,567	10,388
Total	30,626	52,922	93,268	163,598	193,347

This table has been compiled from various editions of the *Statistical Abstract of the United States.*

[16] Baring Brothers shared an interest in the Atchison with Kidder, Peabody and an interest in the Louisville and Nashville with Rothchilds.

[17] A large tract of Northern Pacific land was sold in the 1880's to a syndicate including British bankers.

[18] The Atchison built into Chicago in the 1880's and a number of the Granger roads were still building farther west. The configuration in Minnesota, the Dakotas, and Montana was not set until later.

[19] Lower Canada included Montreal and Quebec. The Maritime Provinces are Nova Scotia, New Brunswick, and Prince Edward Island.

developed industries to compensate for these natural disadvantages as New England had done.[20] The important wheat-growing provinces of Manitoba and Saskatchewan were still pioneering country. As a generalization, in their early years, Canadian roads derived much of their traffic from the American Midwest. They sought outlets to the seaboard at New York, since that route from Ontario to the sea is much shorter than via lower Canada.

The eagerness with which the Grand Trunk sought American connections has been noted several times.[21] Not only did this line depend on connections in the United States for a year-round ice-free port on the Atlantic, it also depended on the United States for the bulk of its traffic from the west. This road, although primarily serving Canada, is usually grouped with the New York Central, the Pennsylvania, and the Baltimore and Ohio as one of the great east-west trunk lines.[22]

On the other hand, the Great Western of Canada and its ally, the Detroit and Milwaukee,[23] were for many years largely connections for an American road, the New York Central. Even after the construction in the 1870's of the Canada Southern, a direct competitor for the Great Western and still more closely allied to the New York Central, the Great Western refused to unite with the Grand Trunk.[24] The latter therefore sought other connections to the United States and eventually built its own line, the Chicago and Grand Trunk Railway Company, into Chicago.

[20] Maine, similar to Canada and Vermont, with good farming land, did not participate in the industrial growth of the rest of the New England states.

[21] One connection of the Grand Trunk that has not so far been noted is that with the Wabash. The main line of the Grand Trunk traversed lower Canada and reached seaboard by a connecting line to Portland, Maine. This road was built before the American Midwest had become so important.

[22] The Grand Trunk, as the weakest of the trunk lines, was reputedly a consistent rate cutter. Even after the establishment of the United States Interstate Commerce Commission, it was possible to control the rates of the Grand Trunk only on those portions of the line lying within the United States. The total charges of the Grand Trunk to the seaboard could not be controlled because it could charge what it wished on those portions lying across the border in Canada.

[23] The Detroit and Milwaukee was constructed in the 1850's with British capital by George Wythes, who, according to the Report of the Investigating Committee, did nothing except lend his name. In addition, Wythes was reported to have had a secret contract with Sir Samuel Laing, one of the trustees, to share the profit or loss. Others involved in this road were W. J. Chaplin, Charles DeVaux, H. J. Enthoven, A. L. Gower, G. Hudson, J. Masterman, Jr., and Matthew Uzielli. Many of these men were originally connected with the flotation of the Illinois Central securities in London. However, Robert Benson and Co. had, by this time, become the agent of the Illinois Central. *Daily News,* Feb. 21, 1861, p. 6.

[24] The Great Western was reported to be unwilling to amalgamate with the Grand Trunk for fear that the New York Central would retaliate by withdrawing the traffic that the Canadian line had been receiving from the Michigan Central, by this time a subsidiary of the New York Central.

The Canadian Pacific, a relative newcomer, was like the Grand Trunk primarily a Canadian line that in its early days relied on the United States both for its seaboard port and for the bulk of its traffic. It reached New York in the East by way of the Rome and Watertown [25] and the New York, Ontario and Western. In the West [its first connection to St. Paul was the St. Paul, Minneapolis and Manitoba (Great Northern), and later] it could also use the Minneapolis, Sault Ste. Marie and Atlantic. The latter connected at Minneapolis with the Minneapolis and Pacific.[26] These two lines were amalgamated in 1888, and in addition a direct link between Minneapolis and St. Louis was constructed.[27]

The railway interconnections, both geographic and financial, of the United States and Canada were complex. However, with the exception of the Canada Southern and a few earlier short lines around Buffalo, most of the lines making up the Canadian systems, even those that ran within the United States, obtained most of their funds from London. American lines constructed by Canadian interests, like the Detroit and Milwaukee, the Minneapolis Sault Ste. Marie and Atlantic, and the Chicago and Grand Trunk, are omitted from this estimate of British investment in the United States. However, included is investment in lines like the Ontario or the Wabash, which became connections of Canadian roads after their construction was completed.

The railway connections between the United States and Mexico present fewer complexities than those with Canada. Of the two principal lines, the Mexican Central was the more completely British; it was not only British-financed but British-incorporated and managed. The Mexican National was incorporated in the United States, and its officials were Americans. Nevertheless, it also derived most of its financial support from Britain.[28]

The types of British investment varied over time. In the 1850's, virtually all British investment in American railways was growth investment. American railway securities were of little interest to the rentier investor who was able to get 6 percent on federal securities. Since communication between New York and London was still slow, there was little British interest in the type of speculation associated with the name of Jacob Little,

[25] An issue of $2 million of the bonds of the Rome, Watertown and Ogdensburg was negotiated through J. S. Kennedy and Co.; one-half was to go to London. (Kennedy was the correspondent of the Scottish American Investment Trust). *Commercial and Financial Chronicle,* XIX (Aug. 15, 1874), 169.

[26] The Minneapolis, Sault Ste. Marie and Atlantic, and the Minneapolis and Pacific had the same president, Hon. W. D. Washburn, and the same secretary, W. P. Hawkins. However, each had its own treasurer.

[27] This line eventually became the Minneapolis and St. Louis.

[28] The Panama Railroad, an American enterprise in which the British invested large amounts, is perhaps the first of these joint Anglo-American ventures in Latin America. It was a short line across the isthmus, designed to facilitate communication with California. This road was brilliantly successful. Its dividends in the period from 1862 to 1867 ranged from 15 to 24 percent and included a 40 percent stock dividend in 1865.

the man who until the advent of Daniel Drew and Jay Gould was undoubtedly the foremost stock exchange speculator of the United States. However, the City was already interested in speculation over the course of the business cycle, and British holdings of a number of American railway securities were increased substantially in the crisis of 1857.

Because the British investor in this period was interested in growth investment, it is natural that the type of bond that found the most response in London was the convertible bond. These bonds offered security during the period when the railway was being built and earnings were uncertain; they could, moreover, be converted into shares when the railway had become an established dividend-paying line. After the success of the Illinois Central, land-grant bonds, particularly when offered in connection with shares, were even more sought after. However, only a few of the railways of the Old Northwest, the area which at this time was developing its railway system most rapidly, could offer this type of bond. Land-grant bonds became common only when railways began to move across the more sparsely settled areas of the trans-Mississippi West. When this happened, these bonds were able to displace convertible bonds in the foreign investor's favor.[29]

The Atlantic cable was laid in 1866; Wall Street and Throgmorton Street in London were now in immediate communication. As soon as the City had begun to recover from the panic of 1866, a panic with which one American railway had been intimately connected, the City embarked on its first in-and-out speculative venture in American rails. Undoubtedly some of the speculators suffered losses.[30] Profits probably at least balanced these losses. Nevertheless, speculative interest did not spread beyond the Erie shares until after 1879.

Meanwhile, British and more especially Continental investors had been making large capital gains on the federal government bonds and railway securities purchased immediately after the Civil War, when the United States currency stood at a substantial discount.

When panic struck on the Continent in the spring of 1873, London was ready to make bargain purchases from Frankfort and other Continental cities. After the Jay Cooke crisis in the autumn it became almost impossible to float railway issues in New York, and a large amount of the senior securities of American railways were therefore offered in London at prices calculated to yield large capital gains.

With securities of this caliber to offer, issuing houses like Morton, Rose and J. S. Morgan made a serious effort to attract the rentier investor and

[29] Jay Gould's manipulations also helped to discredit convertible bonds. However, some bonds of this type continued to be issued in the 1870's.

[30] Heath and Co., of which Robert Heath of the Erie Protective Committee was a member, finally failed in the mid-1880's. It supported a client who, rushing in where Cornelius Vanderbilt had more discreetly trodden, was trying to break Jay Gould.

thus to widen the market for American railway securities.[31] Because the United States still had not resumed specie payment, many of these securities were made payable in gold or in sterling. Endorsement by the issuing house further protected investors against loss due to a possible deterioration in the position of the United States currency. In addition, endorsement implied that, in case of default, interest would be paid by the issuing house.

Since American railway bonds are bearer bonds, it is difficult to say to what extent the rentier investor did purchase American railway bonds in the 1870's. But by the 1880's, through the fact that most of these securities proved both safe and profitable, it had become an established principle that any large portfolio should contain some first-class American railway bonds because they paid better than, and were practically as safe as, home railway debentures.

A second method by which the City attempted to widen the market for American railway bonds was the establishment of a number of investment trust companies specifically formed for investment in American rails. Since these companies were designed to spread risk, it is perhaps natural that a portion of their portfolios appears to have been made up of more speculative securities.

The steady increase of British investment in "good" (the term used by the *Economist* for senior securities) American railway bonds was, at least quantitatively, the most significant development of the 1880's.[32] The burst of speculative interest in shares with which this last period opened in 1879 died away in 1881. It revived in the middle of 1885 and died away again in 1887. Moreover, the more speculative American railway securities were partly displaced from favor by the rising interest in South Africa in the late 1880's.

However, there was no pause, until the Baring crisis, in the flow of British capital into senior obligations of American railways. As a result, the prices of many bonds rose above par. The fact that American railway bonds were terminable, a feature originally considered to be one of their advantages, now began to be a disadvantage.[33] Moreover, established American railways now started to issue bonds bearing lower rates of interest. The Chicago, Burlington and Quincy was able to float bonds

[31] The United States Treasury was also anxious at this time to widen the market for federal securities by attracting this type of investor. Boutwell, 417–23.

[32] Throughout this period the *Economist* regularly ran articles warning against investment in American railway shares or the bonds of new American railways that usually ended with a paragraph saying that investment in "good" American railway bonds was quite a different matter and perfectly safe.

[33] The fact that American railway bonds were terminable meant that, as long as these securities were issued below par, which was usually the case up to the 1880's, the holder could look forward to a substantial capital gain within ten, fifteen, or twenty years.

bearing only 5 percent as early as 1877, although only at an issue price of 89½ percent. In 1883, both the Pennsylvania and the Baltimore and Ohio floated bonds paying 4½ percent, the former at 97½ and the latter at par. And by 1886 the Illinois Central was able to market bonds bearing only 3½ percent at par. By the late 1880's even a new line like the Chicago, St. Paul and Kansas City floated at 98 bonds paying 5 percent. Indeed, by this date only the smaller southern lines were offering securities bearing 6 percent, usually around 95.

While it cannot be compared with investment of the rentier type in magnitude, the movement of venture capital into projects closely related to the export of food to Europe is a most significant extension of British interests in United States railways. Investments grew in the Chicago Great Western, in grain elevators and flour mills, and in slaughtering and meat packing. British investment in southern railways connected with coal and iron lands is a parallel development. Although some of these projects took on a speculative appearance, there was genuine investment in these areas.

The question is the extent of British participation in various American railways and, thus, the extent of the British contribution. [Estimates of the total investment have been analyzed in earlier chapters.]

The overwhelming British contribution is, of course, the railway itself. Many of the major inventions connected with railways until late in the nineteenth century were British. In this early period the major American technical contribution was building cheap and building fast; its importance, particularly with reference to American conditions, should not be underestimated. The Stevens rail, a rail designed to be spiked directly to the sleepers and to dispense with chairs, is a good example. But even some inventions long claimed to be of American origin prove, on further examination, to have been at least partly British. For example, the bogie, the wheeled undercarriage by which American locomotives and wagons were able to negotiate sharp curves safely, appears to have been suggested to its American inventor by Dr. George Stephenson, an Englishman. This claim is supported by the fact that the word *bogie* is from a dialect peculiar to Newcastle.[34]

Moreover, the American railway system could not have expanded at

---

[34] *Engineering*, X (Nov. 11, 1870), 347, printed a letter from W. W. Evans of New York which reported that Robert Stephenson had said in 1853 that the use of the bogie had been suggested to American engineers by his father, George Stephenson, and that if George Stephenson had lived, the bogie would have come into use in Britain also. This letter concluded: "The bogie was adopted in this country [United States]. It had an English origin but, here is its home; here it has been petted, and nursed, and twisted, and turned, and made to do all manner of things, in running around corners of streets, and making itself feel at home everywhere on 50,000 miles of track, good track (if you will allow we have such a thing) and bad track; rough track and smooth track; up hill and down hill; over the mud of spring and the frost of winter. . . . We claim the bogie as ours, we love it, place our faith in it, and defy any other people to make it do more for them than it has done for us."

such a rapid rate in the 1850's and in the 1870's [35] without imports of British rails. Railway mileage in the United States grew from 5,598 miles in 1847 to 9,021 miles in 1850, 30,626 miles in 1860, 52,922 in 1870, and 93,267 in 1880. Many of the British bond purchases in the 1850's were tied to sales of iron. Even when American railways were able to sell large quantities of bonds on the Continent, as in the late 1860's and early 1870's, the greater part of the rails purchased with the proceeds still came from Britain.

Americans also adopted many railway financing devices from Britain. For example, convertible securities, known in Britain in the 1840's, were later used by Americans. There are also claims that British accountants, sent to the United States to go over the books of American railways, introduced modern accounting methods.[36] This is a subject in itself.

The main purpose here is to consider the extent of active British participation in the affairs of those American railways in which they invested largely. Active participation ranged from almost 100 percent [37] in the case of the Alabama Great Southern to virtually zero in the case of railways like the Pennsylvania or the New York Central.[38] The Alabama Great Southern was the most completely British railway in the United States. Other railways, like the Chicago Great Western, although partly the conception of British entrepreneurs and largely British financed, were never British managed. Most of these roads came under British control at some period. The Denver and Rio Grande, a line in which British subjects participated from the beginning and which eventually came under the control of a London Committee, also belongs in this category.

There appears, however, to have been little British participation in the Ontario in its earliest days;[39] it was therefore controlled by the British less than the Denver and Rio Grande, although it was also managed by a London Committee for a long time. The Philadelphia and Reading also belongs to the group of roads that were controlled from London, although it never came under the control of a London Committee.

Active British participation was less direct in railways like the Norfolk and Western than in the lines that came under the control of a London Committee. Nevertheless, British influence was strong in this line. The Atchison, the Louisville and Nashville, and perhaps the Chicago, Milwaukee and St. Paul belong to the group of lines where British influence,

[35] For the mileage after 1880, see p. 193, n. 15.

[36] These trips to the United States were begun very early. Almost every delegation of bondholders or shareholders to an American railway in financial difficulties included a member of one of the large accountancy firms, in the early days usually of Turquand, Young and Co. or Quilter, Ball and Co.

[37] Even in the case of the Alabama, Great Southern, the road was not entirely British, for part had been constructed before the British bondholders took over, and Americans became more and more important in the management.

[38] There was also substantial British investment in the Delaware, Lackawanna and Western, the Delaware and Hudson, and a number of other roads.

[39] Pierce, 7.

although indirect, was a factor that the American managers could never ignore.

Still lower in this descending scale are the lines in which British influence seems to have been kept to a minimum except in periods of financial difficulties. Included as active participation are the trouble-shooting excursions of Robert Fleming in connection with lines like the Texas Pacific or the East Tennessee.[40]

What form of control did the London Committees and London banking houses actually take? First, the British were able to determine the amount of expansion of the American railways under their control by advancing or refusing capital for building by the railway itself and by buying up control of subsidiary lines that the parent roads desired to use as extensions.[41] Second, and one of the most striking features of British control, was the fact that the American railways often worked together with Canadian lines. Finally, pressure was exerted through various banking houses, especially Morgan's, to control competitive building and to stop rate wars. However, the British did not ordinarily intervene in the day-to-day running of the railways in which they invested. This they felt could be better left to Americans.

Needless to say, the control exercised by London Committees and banking houses was most extensive in financial matters. These included reorganizations, issuance of new securities, and dividend policy.

The 1890's marked the end of an era. The men who had been young in the 1850's when a substantial number of American railway securities first came onto the London market were now dying off. W. H. Vanderbilt died in 1885 and Hugh McCalmont in 1887. J. S. Morgan and August Belmont died in 1890. Thomas Baring died in 1891, soon after the Baring crash, while Jay Gould died in 1892. Levi Morton lived to be well over ninety, but he had, by the end of the period of this study, ceased to be active in the banking business and was devoting his attention to political and social affairs. Sir Samuel Laing also retired from the Railway Share Investment Company in the early 1890's.

Much more important, the international economic position of the United States was changing. America was beginning to export capital on a significant scale. Writing of America at the end of the century, Nathaniel T. Bacon stated of the new financial giant with great prescience: "Already we are reaching a point where we are becoming so powerful financially that we are beginning to compete in European financial affairs instead of being dependent on them for support." [42]

---

[40] When the East Tennessee threatened at one time to default, a British delegation immediately went to the United States and succeeded in persuading the railway not to do so.

[41] [The British money market had great influence but on occasion important alternative sources of funds were tapped.]

[42] P. 284.

APPENDIXES
BIBLIOGRAPHY
INDEX

American Railway Securities
Issued Publicly in London, 1865-80

Company	Firm marketing security	Type of security [a]	Amount	Issue price
		Issued in 1865		
Philadelphia and Erie	T. Wiggin	6% 1st mortgage convertible, sterling (guarantor: the Pennsylvania)	£ 1,000,000	73%
Erie	J. S. Morgan	6% sterling	£ 1,000,000	75%
Atlantic and Great Western	Joshua Hutchinson; E. F. Satterthwaite; and Lawrence Son and Pearce, brokers	7% sterling	£ 2,771,000	78¼%
		Issued in 1866		
St. Paul and Pacific	Robert Benson	7% consolidated	£ 780,000	70%
Pennsylvania	Glenn and Co.	2-year 6%, sterling		90%
St. Croix and Lake Superior	Company's London office	7% 1st mortgage, sterling	£ 1,300,000	62½%
		Issued in 1867		
Pennsylvania	London Asiatic and American Co.; Foster and Braithwaite	6% general mortgage, sterling	£ 200,000	82%
		Issued in 1868		
West Wisconsin	Miller and Co. (company's banker: London and County Bank)	7% convertible, sterling	£ 800,000	70%
Chesapeake and Ohio	Lewis Haslewood (company's banker: London and County Bank)	7% 1st mortgage, sterling	£ 400,000	75%

[a] Throughout sterling and gold bonds are treated as equivalent. This was the practice at the time.

Company	Firm marketing security	Type of security [a]	Amount	Issue price
Indiana Southern	Lewis Haslewood (offered; later withdrawn)	7% sterling	£ 2,000,000	80%
		Issued in 1869		
Ohio and Mississippi	Frank H. Evans (company's London agent)	6% sterling	£ 200,000	75%
St. Paul and Pacific	Robert Benson	7% sterling	£ 1,200,000	70%
United Canal and Railroad of New Jersey	J. S. Morgan	6% sterling (guarantors: three railway companies)	£ 369,000	86%
Alabama and Chattanooga	J. H. Schroeder	8% 1st mortgage, sterling	£ 600,000	81%
		Issued in 1870		
Danville, Urbana, Bloomington & Pekin	Huggins and Rowsell	7% 1st mortgage	$ 400,000	£167 per $1,000
Denver Pacific	Huggins and Rowsell	1st mortgage, land grant	$ 1,500,000	£156 per $1,000
East Tennessee, Virginia & Georgia	Joshua Hutchinson (company's banker: Union Bank of London)	6% sterling	£ 780,000	82½%
Indianapolis, Bloomington & Western		7% 1st mortgage, convertible	$ 3,000,000	£168 per $1,000
Illinois and St. Louis Bridge	J. S. Morgan	7% 1st mortgage, sterling	£ 800,000	90%
Alabama State (in aid of Alabama and Chattanooga Railroad)	J. H. Schroeder	8% gold	£ 450,000	94%
Des Moines Valley	Chadwick, Adamson Collier and Co. (company's banker: John Stuart of Manchester)	8% 1st mortgage	$ 1,300,000	£178.2.6 per $1,000
Chicago, Danville and Vincennes	Huggins and Rowsell; W. Bailey Lang, merchants	7% 1st mortgage	$ 1,500,000	£155 per $1,000
Grand Rapids and Indiana	Speyer Brothers	7% 1st mortgage (guarantor: the Pennsylvania as lessee)	$ 4,000,000	87½%
Baltimore and Ohio	Baring Brothers	6% sterling	£ 800,000	
		Issued in 1871		
Oregon and California	London and San Francisco Bank	7% 1st mortgage	$ 3,000,000	65⅞%

Company	Firm marketing security	Type of security [a]	Amount	Issue price
Camden and Amboy	J. S. Morgan	6% sterling	£ 500,000	92%
Lake Shore and Michigan Southern		7% consolidated	$ 2,000,000	
Omaha Bridge	London and San Francisco Bank	8% gold (guarantor: Union Pacific)	£ 500,000	93½%
St. Paul and Pacific Extension	Robert Benson	7% 1st mortgage	£ 3,000,000	74%
Memphis and Ohio	Baring Brothers	7% 1st mortgage (guarantor: Louisville and Nashville)	£ 700,000	
Atlantic, Mississippi and Ohio	Union Bank of London	7% mortgage	$ 6,000,000	
U.S. Rolling Stock	Bischoffsheim and Goldschmidt	£20 shares	£ 1,000,000	
Philadelphia and Erie	J. S. Morgan	6% general mortgage, sterling (guarantor: the Pennsylvania)	£ 1,000,000	87½%
		Issued in 1872		
Northern Pacific	Jay Cooke, McCulloch	7³⁄₁₀% 1st mortgage, sterling (Each £100 bond carried the right to 250 acres of land; this issue failed.)	£4,000,000	85%
Gilman, Clinton and Springfield	Morton, Rose	7% 1st mortgage, sterling (guaranteed by traffic agreement with Illinois Central and Pennsylvania)	£ 400,000	90%
Baltimore and Potomac Railroad	Speyer Brothers	6% tunnel bonds, sterling (guarantors: the Pennsylvania and Northern Central Railroad)	£ 300,000	89½%
Atlantic and Great Western	Bischoffsheim and Goldschmidt	Leased lines rental trust, sterling	£ 760,000	83%
Cairo and Vincennes	J. S. Morgan	7% 1st mortgage, sterling (guaranteed by traffic agreement the Pennsylvania)	£ 700,000	87½%
Elk and McKean (a coal road of Pennsylvania)	Govett, Pease and Co.; Bernard Cracroft	7% 1st mortgage	$ 1,500,000	85%
Arkansas (in aid of Arkansas Central Railroad)	Lombard Syndicate	7%	$ 2,165,000	65%

Company	Firm marketing security	Type of security [a]	Amount	Issue price
Plymouth, Kankakee and Pacific	Blyth and Co.; National Bank of Scotland	7% 1st mortgage, sterling (guaranteed by traffic agreement with the Pennsylvania)	£ 400,000	83%
Atlantic and Great Western	Bischoffsheim and Goldschmidt	1st mortgage (remainder)	$ 1,750,000	£180 per $1,000
Atlantic and Great Western	Bischoffsheim and Goldschmidt	2nd mortgage (remainder)	$ 2,000,000	£162 per $1,000
Baltimore and Potomac	Jay Cooke, McCulloch and Co.	Tunnel bonds, second tranche	$ 3,000,000	91⅔%
Atlantic and Great Western	Bischoffsheim and Goldschmidt	Leased lines rental trust	£ 340,000	88%
Milwaukee and St. Paul	Morton, Rose	7% 1st mortgage, sterling	£ 600,000	93%
Arkansas Central	Credit Foncier of England	8% 1st mortgage, sterling	£ 240,000	
Philadelphia and Reading	McCalmont Brothers; P. Cazenove and Co.	6% general consolidated mortgage, sterling	£ 600,000 (£800,000 actually issued in May 1871)	94%
Erie	Bischoffsheim and Goldschmidt	7% consolidated bonds, sterling	£ 1,289,200	92%
Louisville and Nashville	Baring Brothers	6% sterling	£ 500,000	88%
Canada, Michigan and Chicago (a connection for the Grand Trunk)	Sutton Miller and Co. (company's banker: Anglo-Hungarian)	7% 1st mortgage	$ 2,750,000	£157 per $1,000
Philadelphia and Reading	McCalmont Brothers	7% currency bonds (offered pro rata to shareholders of the line)	$10,000,000	
Allegheny Valley	J. S. Morgan	7% 1st mortage (6% if in sterling) (guarantor: the Pennsylvania, Mahoning Extension)	$ 6,000,000	88%
Baltimore and Ohio	Baring Brothers	6% sterling	£ 1,000,000	97%
Paris and Decatur	Grant and Co.	7% 1st mortgage, sterling	£ 240,000	78%
United States Rolling Stock	Bischoffsheim and Goldschmidt	£20 shares	£ 1,000,000	par
Burlington, Cedar Rapids and Minnesota	Clews Habicht and Co.	7% convertible, sterling	£ 440,000	83%

Company	Firm marketing security	Type of security [a]	Amount	Issue price
		Issued in 1873		
Atlantic and Great Western	Bischoffsheim and Goldschmidt	Leased lines rental trust	£ 200,000	89%
United Canal and Railroad of New Jersey (This company was leased to the Pennsylvania.)	J. S. Morgan	6% sterling	£ 300,000	96½%
Erie	Bischoffsheim and Goldschmidt	7% convertible, sterling	£2,000,000	82%
Massachusetts (in aid of railways)	Baring Brothers	5% sterling	£ 413,200	
Baltimore and Ohio	Heseltine and Powell; Foster and Braithwaite	6% sterling debentures	£ 200,000	99½% .
Central Pacific	Speyer Brothers	6% sterling Oregon and California Division	£ 400,000	79½%
Galveston, Harrisburg and San Antonio	Sutton, Miller and Co.; Credit Foncier of England	6% 1st mortgage, sterling	£ 240,000	83%
New York, Boston and Montreal	Bischoffsheim and Goldschmidt	6% 1st mortgage	$ 6,250,000	80%
Eastern of Massachusetts	Baring Brothers	6% sterling	£ 200,000	93%
New York Central and Hudson River	R. Raphael and the Union Bank of London	6% sterling	£2,000,000	95½%
United Canal and Railroad of New Jersey	J. S. Morgan and Co.	6% sterling, second tranche	£ 300,000	97%
Perkiomen	McCalmont Brothers	6% consolidated, sterling (guarantor: Philadelphia and Reading)	£ 240,000	90%
Louisville and Nashville	Baring Brothers	6% sterling (secured on mortgage on North and South Alabama Railroad)	£1,100,000	87%
Atlantic and Great Western	Bischoffsheim and Goldschmidt	8% Western Extension certificates	£1,520,000	94%
Chicago and Paducah	Huggins and Co.	7% 1st mortgage, sterling	£ 115,200	78%
New Orleans, Jackson and Great Northern	Illinois Central Office in London	7% consolidated, sterling	£ 600,000	87%
Mississippi Central	Illinois Central Office in London	7% consolidated, sterling	£ 600,000	87%
Illinois, Missouri and Texas	Blyth and Co. (company's banker: National Bank of Scotland)	7% 1st mortgage	£ 300,000	87½%

Company	Firm marketing security	Type of security [a]	Amount	Issue price
West Wisconsin	Jay and Co.	7% 1st mortgage, Southern Extension	£ 100,000	87½%
Illinois and St. Louis Bridge	J. S. Morgan	7% 2nd mortgage	£ 400,000	80%
Pennsylvania	London, Asiatic and American Co.	6% consolidated, sterling	£2,000,000	90%
Chicago and Alton	J. S. Morgan	6% consolidated, sterling	£ 300,000	91%
Baltimore and Ohio	Baring Brothers	6% sterling	£1,000,000	96½%
Arkansas Central	Jay Cooke, McCulloch and Co.	8% 1st mortgage	$ 500,000	90%
		Issued in 1874		
Baltimore and Ohio	J. S. Morgan	6% sterling	£2,000,000	96½%
Illinois Central	Morton, Rose	5% sterling	£1,000,000	90%
Lehigh Valley	J. S. Morgan	6% convertible, sterling	£1,000,000	90%
Atlantic and Great Western	London Baking Association, Ltd.	7% Western Extension bonds	£ 480,000	85%
Erie	London Banking Association, Ltd.	7% 2nd consolidated	£3,000,000	78%
Chicago and Northwestern	Railway Share Investment Trust Co., Ltd.	7% consolidated, sterling	£ 500,000	94%
Pittsburgh, Fort Wayne and Chicago	Railway Share Investment Trust Co., Ltd.	8% equipment bonds	$ 1,000,000	97½%
Eastern of Massachusetts	Baring Brothers	6% sterling	£ 400,000	92½%
Lehigh and Wilkes-Barre Coal Co.	Thomson Bonar	6% sterling (guarantor: Central of New Jersey)	£2,000,000	90%
Northern Central (of Pennsylvania)	McCalmont Brothers	6% consolidated, sterling	£ 400,000	87½%
Geneva and Ithaca	Martin and Co.	6% 1st mortgage, sterling	£ 160,000	87½%
Philadelphia and Reading	McCalmont Brothers	6% general mortgage, sterling	£2,000,000	90%
Iowa Pacific	Blyth and Co.	7% 1st mortgage, sterling (guaranteed by traffic agreement with Chicago, Burlington and Quincy)	£ 570,000	87½%
Saint Louis Tunnel	J. S. Morgan	9% 1st mortgage, sterling	£ 250,000	par
Delaware and Hudson	Baring Brothers	6% 1st mortgage, sterling	£ 800,000	92½%
Cleveland, Columbus, Cincinnati and Indianapolis	J. S. Morgan	6% consolidated, sterling	£ 500,000	88%

Company	Firm marketing security	Type of security [a]	Amount	Issue price
Little Rock Bridge	George Burnard	7% sterling	£ 200,000	87½%
Issued in 1875				
Baltimore and Ohio	Frederick Banbury and Naylor Benzon	2-year promissory notes	£ 200,000	
Pennsylvania	London, Asiatic and American Co.; Foster and Braithwaite; Heseltine and Powell	6% sterling, second tranche	£2,000,000	90%
Central of New Jersey	Brown, Shipley	7% currency	$3,000,000	95%
Chicago and Alton	J. S. Morgan	6% sterling	£ 200,000	96½%
Lehigh Valley	J. S. Morgan	6% consolidated	$3,000,000	88%
Delaware and Hudson	Morton, Rose	7% currency	$2,000,000	95%
United Canal and Railroad, New Jersey	J. S. Morgan	6% general mortgage, sterling	£ 460,000	par
Massachusetts (in aid of Troy and Greenfield Railroad)	Baring Brothers	5% sterling	£ 309,500	98%
Northern Central	McCalmont Brothers	6% consolidated, sterling	£ 200,000	87½%
Keokuk and Kansas City	Co-operative Credit Bank	7% 1st mortgage, sterling (bonus of 20% in fully paid-up shares offered)	£ 500,000	
Pittsburg and Connellsville (This line was leased to the Baltimore and Ohio.)	J. S. Morgan	6% consolidated, sterling	£1,300,000	97%
Utica, Ithaca and Elmira	Henry S. King and Co.	1st mortgage	£ 300,000	
Issued in 1876				
Utica, Ithaca and Elmira	Henry S. King and Co.	1st mortgage, second tranche	£ 150,000	92½%
Philadelphia and Reading	McCalmont Brothers	6% general mortgage, sterling	£2,000,000	
Pennsylvania	Foster and Braithwaite; Heseltine and Powell	6% consolidated mortgage, sterling	£ 600,000	90%
Albany and Susquehanna	Scottish American Investment Trust	7% consolidated, sterling	£ 200,000	
City of Cincinnati (to complete Cincinnati Southern Railroad)	Alliance Bank Ltd.	6% sterling	£ 300,000	
Illinois Central	Morton, Rose	5% sterling	£ 200,000	96%

Company	Firm marketing security	Type of security [a]	Amount	Issue price
		Issued in 1877		
Chicago, Burlington and Quincy	Morton, Rose	5%	$ 1,500,000	89½%
Baltimore and Ohio	J. S. Morgan	5% sterling	£ 1,600,000	88½%
		Issued in 1878		
Syracuse, Binghamton and New York	Morton, Rose	7% 1st mortgage, sterling (guarantor: Delaware and Hudson)	£ 350,000	par
Alabama Great Southern	Directors of the company	6% 1st mortgage	$ 815,000	£180 per $1,000
		Issued in 1879		
		Issued in 1880		
New York Central	J. S. Morgan	Shares	$25,000,000	137¾%
Southern Pacific	Speyer Brothers	6% 1st mortgage	$10,000,000	92½%
Chicago, Milwaukee and St. Paul	Morton, Rose	5% 1st mortgage (LaCrosse and Davenport Division)	$ 1,500,000	93½%
Chicago and Tomah	L. Cohen	6% 1st mortgage (guarantor: Chicago and North Western)	$ 1,528,000	110%
Alabama Great Southern	The company	£10 preferred shares	£ 193,400	

SOURCE: Compiled from various contemporary periodicals.

Appendix II

Nonlisted American Railway Securities Known in London in 1886

Railway	Issue	Interest	Price	
Atlantic and Pacific	Western Div. 1st	6	84¼	85
Baltimore and Ohio	Parkersburg 1st	6	126	—
" " "	Connellsville (gen. mort.)	5	—	—
Canada Southern	2nd	5	92¼	92½
Central Iowa	1st	7	—	109
" "	Eastern Div. 1st	6	72	—
" "	Illinois Div. 1st	6	70	75
Central of New Jersey	American Dock Co.	5	101	101½
" " " "	Lehigh and Wilkes Barre consol.	7	—	111
Central Pacific	San Joaquin Valley 1st s. f.	6	114	—
" "	Northern Railway 1st	6	—	—
Chesapeake and Ohio	"B"	6	76½	77
Chicago and Alton	1st	7	116½	118
Chicago, Burlington and Quincy	Consol.	7	132⅝	133
" " " "	Debentures	5	106¾	107¼
" " " "	Iowa Division sinking fund	5	113½	—
" " " "	" " " "	4	101¾	—
" " " "	Denver Extension s. f.	4	—	99
" " " "	Southwest Div. s. f.	4	—	—
Chicago and E. Illinois	Consol.	6	112½	113
Chicago and Northwestern	Consol. s. f.	7	—	141⅞
" " "	General consol.	7	132⅝	—
" " "	Collateral trust s. f.	6	118	120
" " "	" " " "	5	109	—
" " "	Debentures	5	107	108
Chicago, Rock Island and Pacific	1st	6	136½	137½
Chicago, St. Louis and Pacific	Consol.	5	98	101
Chicago, St. Paul, Minneapolis and Omaha	Consol.	6	123½	127
Columbus, Hocking Valley & Toledo	Consol.	5	84⅞	85
Delaware, Lackawanna and Western	Consol.	7	136	—
" " " "	Morris & Essex consol.	7	143½	—
" " " "	New York, Lackawanna & Western 1st	6	128	—

Railway	Issue	Interest	Price	
Denver and Rio Grande	1st	6	120½	—
Denver and Rio Grande Western	1st	6	82	82½
East Tennessee, Virginia & Georgia	1st consol.	5	102	104
" " " " "	Income	6	—	—
Evansville & Terre Haute	Consol.	6	116½	—
Forth Worth & Denver City	1st	6	84¾	85
Galveston, Harrisburg and San Antonio	Western Div. 1st	5	100¼	—
Gulf, Colorado and Santa Fe	1st	7	123	124½
Houston and Texas Central	Main Line land grant s. f.	7	110¾	111
" " " "	Western Div. land grant 1st	7	—	105
" " " "	Main Line & Western Div. consol.	8	80	90
" " " "	General mortgage	6	—	67
Indiana, Bloomington and Western	Mortgage deferred	6	—	—
" " " "	Eastern Div. 1st	6	90	93
Kentucky Central	General mortgage (reduced)	4	66	69
Lake Shore	1st consol. s. f.	7	—	130
" "	2nd consol.	7	124	—
Louisville and Nashville	1st consol.	7	120	—
" " "	Collateral trust 3rd	6	103¼	103½
" " "	Henderson Bridge 1st	6	—	—
Louisville, New Orleans & Texas	1st	5	90	—
Metropolitan Elevated	1st	6	117	118
Mexican Central	1st	7	41	42
Michigan Central	Consol.	7	130	—
" "	"	5	108	—
Milwaukee, Lake Shore & West, Canada	Consol.	6	—	—
Missouri Pacific	Consol.	6	115⅜	115½
" "	St. Louis and Iron Mountain 1st	7	110½	—
" "	General 2nd	7	116	—
" "	General consol.	5	96	96½
" "	Cairo & Fulton Division 1st	7	108	110
" "	Mo., Kan., & Texas Div. gen. consolidated	6	96	96¼
" "	International and Great Northern 1st	6	—	118
" "	2nd mortgage	6	87	89
Mobile and Ohio	1st	6	—	—
Morgan's Louisiana and Texas	1st	7	—	—
New York Elevated	1st	7	125½	126
New York, Lake Erie and Western	1st lien	6	—	—
" " " " " "	Collateral trust	6	—	107
" " " " " "	Long Dock 1st	7	117	—
" " " " " "	Gold bonds of 1935	6	—	123¼
New York and New England	1st	6	118	121
New York, Ontario & Western	1st	6	—	105
Norfolk and Western	New River Div. 1st	6	—	112
Oregon Railway and Navigation	1st	6	110½	111½
" " " "	Consol.	5	105⅝	106

Railway	Issue	Interest	Price	
Oregon-Transcontinental	Collateral trust	6	102	102¼
Philadelphia, Wilmington & Baltimore	Collateral trust	4	—	—
Pittsburg, C. & St. Louis	Consol.	7	—	—
Pittsburgh, Fort Wayne & Chicago	1st	7	140	—
" " " " "	2nd	7	—	139½
Richmond and Danville	General	6	—	—
St. Louis and San Francisco	General	6	108½	109¾
St. Paul, Minneapolis & Manitoba	1st	7	112	114½
" " " " "	2nd	6	118	—
" " " " "	Dakota Division 1st	6	120½	—
" " " " "	Consol.	6	—	119½
Shenandoah Valley	1st	7	77	78
" "	General	6	36¾	—
South Carolina	1st consol.	6	—	109
Texas & Pacific	Consol.	6	—	—
" " "	Rio Grande Div. ex.	6	60	67¼
" " "	Income and land grant	7	53	53¾
" " "	New Orleans Div. 1st	6	—	—
" " "	General and Terminal	6	58	59
Union Pacific	Collateral trust	6	—	—
" "	Kansas Pacific 1st	5	95¼	—
" "	Consol.	6	110½	—
" "	Oregon Short Line 1st	6	106¾	107
Wabash, St. Louis and Pacific	Chicago Division	5	89½	90
" " " " "	Detroit Division 1st	6	—	85
" " " " "	Toledo & Wabash Extension 1st	7	111¼	113
" " " " "	Northern Missouri 1st	7	115½	—

SOURCE: *Economist*, XLIV (Oct. 2, 1886), 1246

Appendix III

Directors and Founders of
Three Anglo-American Investment Trusts

A. London and New York Investment Corporation (1889)

The London directors were:

Dillwyn Parrish, *English & Scottish Investment Co., Ltd.*
H. Pollock
Henry P. Sturges, *London & Westminster Bank*

The New York directors were:

H. W. Cannon, *Chase National Bank*
J. Greenough, *Poor and Greenough*
John G. Moore

The founders in London were:

John Bathurst Akroyd, *stockbroker; Cazenove & Akroyd*
Arthur Anderson, *stockbroker*
Hon. Evelyn Ashley, *Railway Passenger Assurance*
Netterville J. Barron, *merchant; Flack, Chandler & Co.*
Stanley Carr Boulton, *Guardian Investment Co.*
Alexander Hargreaves Brown, M.P.
Clarence Carey, *attorney; New York*
Fred Chalmers
W. H. Chesebrough, *Chesebrough Manufacturing Co.*
A. D. Clarke, *Bankers Investment Trust*
Thomas Coleman, *stockbroker*
John S. Collmann, *merchant; Frederick Huth & Co.*
Granville Farquhar, *stockbroker; Steer Lawson & Co.*
F. H. Forth, *Trustees, Executors & Securities Insurance Co.*
A. Bower Forwood, M.P.
Sir William B. Forwood, *Bank of Liverpool*
P. du P. Grenfell, *merchant*
Lord Claud J. Hamilton, *G. E. Railway*
Hon. C. N. Lawrence, *Trustees, Executors & Securities Insurance Co.*

Hon. H. A. Lawrence, *merchant*
Ernest O. Lloyd, *stockbroker; Lloyd & Hardy*
N. Story Maskelyne, M.P.
Frank Boyd May, *stockbroker*
Ernest Noel, *Mercantile Investment Trust*
Sir Thomas Paine
Edgar J. Payne, *solicitor*
Charles Palgrave, *shipowner; Palgrave, Murphy & Co.*
Dillwyn Parrish, *English & Scottish American Mortgage and Investment*
Sir John Pender, *Direct U.S. Cable*
J. Denison Pender, *Eastern Telegraph*
H. Pollock
Sir John H. Puleston, M.P.
Ernest Ruffer
Leopold Salomons
Edward Fowler Satterthwaite, *stockbroker*
J. Carr Saunders, *underwriter*
Rt. Hon. Sir Henry Selwin-Ibbetson, M.P.
J. Fisher Smith, *New York Life Insurance Co., London*
Lindsay Eric Smith, *banker*
J. A. Stirling, *banker*
Rt. Hon. Lord Sudeley, *P and O*
Arthur Tate
G. A. Touch, *Industrial & General Trust, Ltd.*
B. Tritton, *stockbroker*
William Trotter, *50 Throgmorton*
Samuel Untermeyer, *attorney; New York*

The founders in New York were:

Edward D. Adams, *Winslow, Lanier & Co.*
John Crosby Brown, *Brown Brothers*
Henry W. Cannon, *Chase National Bank*
Alfred C. Chapin, *mayor of Brooklyn*
George Coppell, *Maitland, Phelps & Co.*
Charles D. Dickey, *Brown Brothers*
F. O. French, *Manhattan Trust Co.*
William A. French, *Massachusetts National Bank*
F. A. Gans, *merchant*
James E. Grammis, *Georgia Midland*
John Greenough, *Poor & Greenough*
G. P. Hawes, *solicitor*
L. von Hoffmann, *banker*
Richard Irvin, *banker*
Adrian Iselin, *banker*
C. E. Kessel, *Kessel & Co.*
Thomas Maitland, *Maitland, Phelps & Co.*
Arnold Marcus, *Louisville and Nashville*
John G. Moore, *Moore & Schley*
F. P. Olcott, *Central Trust Co., New York*
Oliver H. Payne, *Standard Oil*
Henry W. Poor
James A. Roosevelt, *Chemical National Bank*

C. H. Sanford, *Samuel B. Hale and Co.*
Jacob H. Schiff, *Kuhn, Loeb and Co.*
G. B. Schley, *Moore & Schley*
Samuel Thomas, *East Tennessee, Virginia and Georgia*
Edward Tuck, *Munroe and Co.*
M. van Rennselaer, *Wheeling and Lake Erie*
William C. Whitney, *former Secretary of the Navy*
F. W. Whitridge, *solicitor*
A. Wolff, *Kuhn, Loeb and Co.*

B. UNITED STATES TRUST AND GUARANTEE CORPORATION, LTD. (1890)

The directors were:

*Archibald Balfour, *I. Thomson, T. Bonar and Co.*
*Bernard T. Bosanquet, *Lloyds Bank*
*Alfred H. Huth, *Union Bank of Spain and England*
  C. Fraser Mackintosh, M.P., *Anglo-American Land Mortgage and Agency Co.,
    Ltd.*
  Hildebrand Ramsden, *Ramsden and Austin*

The members of the Advisory Board in the United States were:

Charles S. Fairchild, *New York Security and Trust, former Secretary of the
    Treasury*
James L. Lombard, *First National Bank of Kansas City*
B. Lombard, *Lombard Investment Co., Boston*
William A. Lombard
Thomas Miller, *Sawyer, Wallace and Co., merchants of New York and London*
Henry W. Munroe, *John Munroe and Co., bankers*
James Stillman, *Woodward & Stillman, cotton merchants*

The manager was James Lombard.

The founders in New York were:

Edward A. Abbott, *Abbott Dawney and Co.*
Marshall Ayres, *Lombard, Ayres and Co.*
Bangs, Stetson, Tracy & Macveagh
William Barbour, *Barbour Brothers, linen thread*
August Belmont, Jr.
Simon Borg, *Simon Borg and Co., bankers*
Henry W. Cannon, *Chase National Bank*
James A. Chapman, *solicitor*
George C. Clark, *Clark, Dodge and Co.*
R. I. Cross, *Morton, Bliss*
* These men were also directors of the Imperial and Foreign Investment and Agency
Corporation, Ltd.

Charles S. Fairchild, *New York Security and Trust*
Charles R. Flint, *New York Commercial Rubber Co.*
Thomas P. Fowler, *New York, Ontario and Western*
Joel F. Freeman, *Standard Oil*
F. O. French, *Manhattan Trust Co.*
William H. Fuller, *Fuller, Lang, paper manufacturer*
Wendell Goodwin
George Hotchkiss, *Hammond Dressed Beef Co.*
Richard Irvin
Edgar M. Johnson, *Hoadley, Lauterbach and Johnson*
John Jay Knox, *National Bank of the Republic*
Daniel S. Lamont, *John Munroe and Co., bankers*
Edgar Lockwood, *John Munroe and Co., bankers*
Josiah Lombard, *Tide Water Oil Co.*
W. A. Lombard
Thomas Miller, *Sawyer, Wallace and Co.*
Moore and Schley
Henry W. Munroe, *John Munroe and Co., bankers*
R. F. Oakes, *Northern Pacific Railroad*
Francis A. Palmer, *National Broadway Bank*
Oliver H. Payne
Charles H. Pine, *Ansonia National Bank*
William Rockefeller
James Stillman
J. and W. Seligman
H. K. Thurber, *Thurber, Wayland and Co.*
Edward Tuck, *John Munroe and Co.*
J. I. Waterbury, *Manhattan Trust Co.*
William C. Whitney, *former Secretary of the Navy*

The founders in Boston were:

Frederick L. Ames, *Union Pacific*
William H. Goodwin, *Elliot National Bank*
Benjamin Lombard
Asa P. Potter, *Maverick National Bank*
Nathaniel Thayer

The founders in Philadelphia were:

George Burnham, *Baldwin Locomotive Co.*
S. A. Caldwell, *Fidelity Trust, Insurance and Safe Deposit Co.*
J. L. Erringer, *Philadelphia Trust and Safe Deposit*
Wayne Macveagh, *solicitor, former Attorney General*
George S. Pepper
Doctor William Pepper, *Provost, University of Pennsylvania*

The founders in South and West were:

Alexander Brown, *Alexander Brown and Sons, Baltimore*
George S. Brown, *Alexander Brown and Sons, Baltimore*

John Gill, *Mercantile Trust & Safe Deposit, Baltimore*
Henry James, *Citizens' National Bank, Baltimore*
Henry James, *E. Pratt and Bros., Baltimore*
James L. Lombard, *First National Bank, Kansas City*
R. E. Pairo, *solicitor, Washington, D.C.*
E. Pratt, *George Peabody Institute*
W. W. Pence, *Mercantile Trust, Baltimore*
Francis White, *Johns Hopkins University*
William Winchester, *broker, Baltimore*

The founders in Great Britain were:

E. D. Appert
Atlas Investment Co.
Archibald Balfour
R. D. Balfour, *5 & 6 Throgmorton*
Barrow, Wade, Guthrie and Co., *Manchester and New York*
J. F. Bennett, *Anglo-American Land, etc.*
Lt. Col. A. H. Bircham, *32 Carlyle Square*
B. T. Bosanquet
J. H. Buckingham, *Central Bank of London*
George Clay, *Manchester*
H. K. Day
Alfred James Emberson
Howard Gilliat
Spencer W. Gore
W. H. Gramshaw
Alexander Gray
Lord Greville
William Hudson
George Breedon Hulme, *Alfred Kimbe and Co., N.Y.*
A. H. Huth
Imperial and Foreign Investment and Agency Corp., Ltd.
Sir Henry E. Knight, *Mortgage Insurance Corp., Ltd.*
Herman Lescher
London Trust Co., Ltd.
Charles Fraser Mackintosh
Manchester Trust, Ltd.
R. B. Martin
W. Mendel, *Andre Mendel and Co.*
Joseph Moseley, *Manchester*
Joseph Wright Morgan
Thomas H. Norman
H. T. Norton, *Norton, Rose and Norton, solicitors*
H. Ramsden, *Ramsden and Austin, solicitors*
Edmund Robertson, M.P.
G. A. St. C. Rose, *Norton, Rose, Norton & Co., solicitors*
Sir Philip Rose, *Norton, Rose, Norton & Co., solicitors*
Godfrey Samuel Saunders
L. W. Sawyer, *Sawyer and Wallace*
T. Y. Strachan, *Mortgage Insurance Corp., Ltd.*
Thomas, Wade, Guthrie and Co., *Manchester*

The founders in Scotland were:

Rev. John Baird, *Edinburgh*
A. W. Davidson, *Edinburgh*
Henry Knox Dick, *Glasgow*
Rev. James Dodds, D.D., *Edinburgh*
James Grahame, *Glasgow*
C. Macpherson Grant, *Drumduon Forres, N.B.*
Henry Moncrieff Horsbrugh, C.A., *Edinburgh*
Kenneth Macdonald, *Inverness*
Realisation and Debenture Corporation of Scotland, Ltd., *Edinburgh*
Duncan Shaw, *Inverness*
William Sime, S.S.C., *Edinburgh*
Nathaniel Spens, *Grahame, Spens and Spens*
Trustee Assets and Investment Insurance Co., Ltd., *Glasgow*
James Thompson Wilson, *Edinburgh*

C. LONDON SCOTTISH AMERICAN TRUST, LTD. (1889)

The London directors were:

Alexander Hargreaves Brown, M.P., *Brown, Shipley*
Rt. Hon. Lord Hamilton of Dalzell
Thomas Fickus, *Melville, Evans and Co.*
William John Menzies, *Scottish Am. Invest. Co., Ltd., Edinburgh*
Hon. H. Oliver Northcote, *J. Kennedy Tod and Co., N.Y.*
Nathaniel Spens, *Grahame, Crum and Spens, C.A., Glasgow*

The New York directors were:

John Crosby Brown, *Brown Brothers and Co.*
Thomas Denny
James A. Roosevelt, *Roosevelt and Sons*
J. Kennedy Tod, *J. Kennedy Tod and Co.*

Reorganization Plans of the Texas-Pacific and Missouri, Kansas and Texas Railroads

A. THE TEXAS-PACIFIC RAILROAD

1. LIABILITIES PRECEDING RECEIVERSHIP

Type of liability	Amount
Shares	$32,161,900
First mortgage (Eastern Division)	3,874,000
Consolidated mortgage (Eastern Division)	9,316,000
First mortgage (Rio Grande Division)	13,028,000
First mortgage (New Orleans and Pacific)	6,720,000
Income and land-grant bonds	8,862,000
Old land-grant bonds	6,000
General and terminal mortgage	1,624,000
Texas School Fund loan	165,965
Script on income and land-grant bonds	2,709,760
Convertible coupon scrip	77,760
Sundry scrip	26,037
Interest due and accrued	916,360
Sundry	13,725
Bills payable	1,130,873
Land department	2,106,513
Total	$82,651,595 [a]

[a] The correct figure is $82,738,893. The mistake in addition appears in the source.

2. PLAN OF REORGANIZATION

Type of security in old company	Participation in new company
Texas State lien	Undisturbed
First mortgage (Eastern Division)	Undisturbed
Consolidated mortgage (Eastern Division)	112% in 5% 1st mort. bonds
Income and land mortgage (Eastern Division)	The land grant and 40% in 2nd mort.
First mortgage (Rio Grande Division)	40% in 5% 1st mort. and 80% in 2nd mort.

First mortgage (New Orleans and Pacific)	60% in 5% 1st mort. and 60% in 2nd mort.
General and terminal mortgages	25% in 5% 1st mort. and 95% in 2nd mort.
Assessment of shareholders	Dollar for dollar in 2nd mortgage

3. CAPITAL STRUCTURE AFTER REORGANIZATION

Type of security	Amount
First mortgage	$23,815,620
Second mortgage	21,632,560
Common	40,000,000

B. THE MISSOURI, KANSAS AND TEXAS RAILROAD

1. LIABILITIES PRECEDING RECEIVERSHIP

Type of liability	Amount
Ordinary shares	$46,405,000
Preferred shares	5,157
Funded indebtedness	46,630,460
Interest due	886,115
Net proceeds, land department	1,126,235
Total	$95,052,967

2. PLAN OF REORGANIZATION

Old security	Amount	First	Second	Preferred
		Participation in new company		
6% general consolidated mort.	$1,000	$ 640	$550	$275
5% general consolidated mort.	1,000	550	500	200
Income bonds	each	550	500	—
Assessment of $10 on shares	10	—	10	—
Cash subscription by bondholders	400	500	—	120
Cash subscription by holders of 100 shares	1,600	2,000	—	480

3. CAPITAL STRUCTURE AFTER REORGANIZATION

Type of security	Amount
First 4% mortgage	$ 39,466,000
Second 4% mortgage	20,000,000
4% preferred shares	13,000,000
Common	47,000,000
Total	$119,466,000

SOURCES: A, 1: *Commercial and Financial Chronicle*, XL (March 7, 1885), 302; A, 1 and 2: *Burdett's Official Intelligence* (1887), 499; B, 1: *Commercial and Financial Chronicle*, XLVI (March 24, 1888), 380; B, 2 and 3: *Burdett's Official Intelligence* (1890), 490.

Bibliography

UNPUBLISHED MATERIAL AND OFFICIAL PUBLICATIONS

The Bute Papers (Sir W. F. Lewis). Dock Statistics No. 1. Bute XI, 56. Cardiff Public Library, Cardiff, Wales.

Council of Foreign Bondholders. *First Report of the Alabama and Chattanooga Railroad, "First Mortgage Indorsed Bonds of 1869," and 8% State Gold Bonds of 1870.* London, July 1875.

———. *Final Report of the Committee Appointed to Act in Conjunction with the Council of Foreign Bondholders, Alabama and Chattanooga "First Mortgage Bonds of 1869."* London, 1875.

The Dowlais Iron Company. Letter Books (Main Series, 1830–36; London Series [House], 1837–56). Glamorgan Public Archives, Cardiff, Wales.

English Association of American Bond and Shareholders. "Memorandum on the Formation of the Company (1887)." Files of English Association of American Bond and Shareholders, London.

———. Annual Reports, 1888–1900. Files of English Association of American Bond and Shareholders, London.

———. *American Railway Certificates.* Pamphlet.

English Committee of the Alabama 8 percent Gold State Bonds of 1870. *The Hill Country of Alabama, U.S.A.* London: E. & F. N. Spon, 1878.

Fleming, Major Philip. Personal letter to the author, Jan. 29, 1958.

Great Britain. *Parliamentary Papers (Accounts and Papers),* Commercial Reports 1873–79 by H. M. Consuls in Baltimore, Galveston, Mobile, New York, Richmond, etc.

———. *Parliamentary Papers,* LXV (*Accounts and Papers,* Commercial No. 18, 1874), "Report by Mr. Harriss-Gastrell on the Iron and Steel Industries of the United States," H.M.S.O., London, 1875.

———. *Parliamentary Papers,* XXI (no. 4715, 1886, Minutes of Evidence and Appendix [C-4715], Appendix A, Part I), "Second Report of the Royal Commission Appointed to Inquire into the Depression of Trade and Industry, 1886."

———. *Parliamentary Papers,* XIII (*Accounts and Papers,* no. 212, 1919), "Report of the Dollar Committee," H.M.S.O., London, 1920.

———. *Statistical Abstract of the United Kingdom, 1855–1885.* H.M.S.O., London.

Satterthwaite Family. Personal letters to the author, 1957.

Times Librarian. Personal communication to the author, 1957.

United States. Department of Commerce, Bureau of the Census. *Historical Statistics of the United States, 1789–1945.* Washington, D.C., 1949.

——. Congress. *House Report 296.* 27th Cong., 3d sess., 1842.

——. Congress. *Senate Executive Document 42.* 33d Cong., 1st sess., "Report of the Secretary of the U.S. Treasury Dept. in answer to a resolution calling for the amount of Foreign securities held in Europe and other foreign countries on the 30th June, 1853," 1853–54.

——. Department of the Interior. *Tenth Census of the United States.* VII, 1884.

——. *Statistical Abstract of the United States.* Washington, D.C., 1884–.

——. Congress, National Monetary Commission. *Senate Document 579.* 61st Cong., 2d sess., 1910.

PERIODICALS

American Law Review. 1872.

American Railroad Journal. New York, 1832–72.

Bankers' Magazine. London, 1850–90.

Bankers' Magazine. New York, 1854–90.

Blackwood's Edinburgh Magazine. 1866–82.

Bullionist. London, 1866.

Circular to Bankers. London, 1845–46.

Commercial and Financial Chronicle. New York, 1873–96.

Commercial History and Review of 1866, Supplement to the *Economist* (March 9, 1867).

Commercial and History Review of 1879.

City Press. London, 1857, 1880–90.

Daily News. London, 1852–62.

De Bow's Review. Nashville, Tennessee, 1866–68.

Economist. London, 1845–1900.

Engineering. London, 1866–76.

Financier. New York, 1870.

Glamorgan, Monmouthshire and Brecon Gazette, Cardiff Advertiser and Merthyr Guardian. Cardiff, 1845–50.

Herapath's Railway and Commercial Journal. London, 1835–70.

Hunt's Merchants' Magazine. New York, 1859–60.

Investor's Monthly Manual. London, 1883–87.

Investor's Review. London, 1892–97.

Journal of Commerce. London, 1841–55.

Journal of the Institute of Bankers. London, 1879–95.

Morning Chronicle and London Advertiser. London, 1838–42.

North American Review. Boston, 1865–85.

Quarterly Review. London, 1877–82.

Railroad and Engineering Journal. New York, 1887.

Railway Age. New York, 1887.

Railway Times. London, 1847–56.

Statist. London, 1895–1900.

Times. London, 1850–90.

ANNUALS AND WORKS OF REFERENCE

The Banking Almanac, Directory, Yearbook and Diary for 1845(–1919). Ed. by
R. H. I. Palgrave. London: Waterhouse, 1880–96.

Bradshaw's Railway Manual, Shareholder's Guide. Manchester, 1890–92.

Burdett's Official Intelligence. London: Effingham Wilson, 1882–1900.

Dictionary of American Biography. London: Oxford University Press.

Dictionary of National Biography. London: Smith, Elder.

Directory of Directors. London: T. Skinner, 1880–90.

Fenn, Charlie. *Compendium of the English and Foreign Funds.* Ed. by P. L.
Simmons. 8th edition. London: Effingham Wilson, 1860.

——. *Compendium of the English and Foreign Funds.* Ed. by R. L. Nash. 9th,
12th, 13th, 14th, and 15th editions. London: Effingham Wilson, 1867, 1874,
1883, 1889, and 1893.

Gore's Directory of Liverpool. Liverpool: J. Mawdley, 1849, 1859.

Post Office Directory of London (later Kelly's). London: W. Kelly & Co.

Merchant Shippers of London. London, 1867.

National Cyclopaedia of American Biography. New York: J. T. White, 1893.

Poor's Directory of Railway Officials. New York, London, 1891–93.

SECONDARY WORKS

Adams, Charles Francis, Jr. "A Chapter of Erie" and "An Erie Raid," *in* Frederick C. Hicks (ed.), *High Finance in the Sixties.* New Haven: Yale University Press, 1929.

——. "The State and the Railroads," *Atlantic Monthly,* XXXVIII (July 1876),
72–85.

Addis, John P. *The Crawshay Dynasty.* Cardiff: University of Wales Press, 1957.

Albion, Robert Greenhalgh. *The Rise of New York Port [1815–1860].* New York:
Charles Scribner's Sons, 1939.

Ambler, Charles Henry. *A History of Transportation in the Ohio Valley.* Glen-
dale, Calif.: Arthur H. Clark Co., 1932.

Anderson, George L. *General William J. Palmer: A Decade of Colorado Railroad
Building.* Colorado College Publication, General Series no. 209, Study Series
no. 22. Colorado Springs, 1936.

An Anglo-American. *American Securities.* London: Mann, 1860.

Arnold, Percy. *The Bankers of London.* London: Hogarth Press, 1938.

Bacon, Nathaniel T. "American International Indebtedness," *Yale Review,*
Nov. 1900, pp. 265–85.

Baring, Alexander. *An Inquiry into the Causes and Consequences of the Orders
in Council and an Examination of the Conduct of Great-Britain towards the
Neutral Commerce of America.* London: J. M. Richardson, 1808.

Belcher, Wyatt Winton. *The Economic Rivalry between St. Louis and Chicago,
1850–1880.* New York: Columbia University Press, 1947.

Bell, I. Lowthian. "Notes of a Visit to Coal- and Iron-Mines and Ironworks in the United States," *Journal of the Iron and Steel Institute,* 1875.

Bell, William A. *New Tracks in North America.* 2 vols. London: Chapman and Hall, 1869.

Benson, Lee. *Merchants, Farmers & Railroads: Railroad Regulation and New York Politics, 1850–1887.* Cambridge, Mass.: Harvard University Press, 1955.

Berthoff, Rowland T. "Southern Attitudes towards Immigration, 1865–1900," *Journal of Southern History,* XVII (August 1951), 328–36.

Bessborough, Earl of (ed.). *Lady Charlotte Guest: Extracts from Her Journal, 1833–1852.* London: John Murray, 1950.

Blake, Nelson Morehouse. *William Mahone of Virginia.* Richmond: Garrett & Massie, 1935.

Bogart, Ernest Ludlow. *Financial History of Ohio.* University of Illinois Studies in the Social Sciences, I, nos. 1-2. Urbana: University of Illinois Press, 1912.

Bogen, Jules I. *The Anthracite Railroads.* New York: Ronald Press, 1927.

Boutwell, Hon. George S. "An Historic Sale of United States Bonds in England, 1871–72" *McClure's Magazine,* XV (May and Sept., 1900), 417–23.

Brayer, Herbert O. "The Influence of British Capital on the Western Range-Cattle Industry," *Journal of Economic History,* Supplement IX (1949), 85–98.

Brownson, Howard Gray. *History of the Illinois Central Railroad to 1870.* University of Illinois Studies in the Social Sciences, IV, nos. 3–4. Urbana: University of Illinois, 1915.

Bruce, Kathleen. *Virginia Iron Manufacture in the Slave Era.* London: Century Co., 1931.

Buck, Norman Sydney. *The Development of the Organisation of Anglo-American Trade, 1800–1850.* New Haven: Yale University Press, 1925.

Bullock, Charles J. *Historical Sketch of the Finances and Financial Policy of Massachusetts from 1780 to 1905.* New York: Macmillan, 1907.

Bullock, Charles J., John H. Williams, and Rufus S. Tucker. "The Balance of Trade of the United States," *Review of Economic Statistics,* Preliminary Vol. I (1919), 215–53.

Burgess, George H., and Miles C. Kennedy. *Centennial History of the Pennsylvania Railroad Company, 1846–1946.* Philadelphia: Pennsylvania Railroad Co., 1949.

Caird, Sir James. *English Agriculture in 1850–51.* London: Longmans, Brown, Green, and Longmans, 1852.

Cairncross, A. K. *Home and Foreign Investment, 1870–1913.* Cambridge: Cambridge University Press, 1953.

Campbell, R. H. "Edinburgh Bankers and the Western Bank of Scotland," *Scottish Journal of Political Economy,* II (June 1955), 133–48.

Carlson, Theodore L. *The Illinois Military Tract.* University of Illinois Studies in the Social Sciences, XXXII, no. 2. Urbana: University of Illinois Press, 1951.

Casey, Robert J., and W. A. S. Douglas. *Pioneer Railroad: The Story of the Chicago and North Western System.* New York: Whittlesey House, McGraw-Hill, 1948.

Cawley, Elizabeth Hoon (ed.). *The American Diaries of Richard Cobden.* Princeton: Princeton University Press, 1952.

Chandler, Alfred D., Jr. *Henry Varnum Poor: Business Editor, Analyst, and Reformer.* Cambridge, Mass.: Harvard University Press, 1956.

Chandler, Alfred D., Jr. "Patterns of American Railroad Finance, 1830–1850," *Review of Business History*, XXVIII (Sept. 1954), 248–63.

Chevalier, Michel. *Society, Manners, and Politics in the United States: Being a Series of Letters on North America.* (Translated from the 3d Paris edition.) Boston: Weeks Jordan and Company, 1839.

Clapham, J. H. *An Economic History of Modern Britain.* 3 vols. Cambridge: Cambridge University Press, 1926, 1938, 1952.

Clapham, Sir John. *The Bank of England.* 2 vols. Cambridge: Cambridge University Press, 1944.

Clark, Thomas D. *A Pioneer Southern Railroad from New Orleans to Cairo.* Chapel Hill: University of North Carolina Press, 1936.

Clark, Victor S. *History of Manufactures in the United States.* Vol. I. New York: McGraw-Hill, 1929.

Clements, Roger V. "British-Controlled Enterprise in the West between 1870 and 1900 and Some Agrarian Reactions," *Agricultural History*, XXVII (Oct. 1953), 132–39.

——. "British Investment and American Legislative Restrictions in the Trans-Mississippi West, 1880–1900," *Mississippi Valley Historical Review*, XLII (Sept. 1955), 207–28.

Clews, Henry. *Twenty Eight Years in Wall Street.* New York: Irving Publishing Co., 1887.

——. *The Wall Street Point of View.* New York: Silver, Burdett & Co., 1900.

Cochran, Thomas C. *Railroad Leaders, 1845–1890.* Cambridge, Mass.: Harvard University Press, 1953.

Corliss, Carlton J. *Main Line of Mid-America.* New York: Creative Age Press, 1950.

Crick, W. F., and J. E. Wadsworth. *A Hundred Years of Joint Stock Banking.* London: Hodder & Stoughton, 1936.

Currie, A. W. *The Grand Trunk Railway of Canada.* Toronto: University of Toronto Press, 1957.

Curtis, B. R. "Debts of the States," *North American Review*, LVIII (Jan. 1844), 109–57.

Daggett, Stuart. *Railroad Reorganization.* New York: Houghton, Mifflin and Company, 1908.

Dorfman, Joseph. "A Note on the Interpenetration of Anglo-American Finance, 1837–1841," *Journal of Economic History*, XI (1951), 140–47.

Dowrie, George William. *The Development of Banking in Illinois, 1817–1863.* University of Illinois Studies in the Social Sciences, II, no. 4. Urbana: University of Illinois, 1913.

Dozier, Howard Douglas. *A History of the Atlantic Coast Line Railroad.* Boston: Houghton Mifflin Company, 1920.

Eckel, Edwin C. *Coal Iron and War.* London: George G. Harrap & Co., 1920.

Egleston, N. H. "The Story of the Hoosac Tunnel," *Atlantic Monthly*, XLIX (March 1882), 289–304.

Feis, Herbert. *Europe the World's Banker, 1870–1914.* Council of Foreign Relations. New Haven: Yale University Press, 1931.

Felton, Paul. "The History of the Atlantic and Great Western Railroad Company." Unpublished doctoral dissertation, University of Pittsburgh, 1943.

Fisher, John S. *A Builder of the West: The Life of General William Jackson Palmer.* Caldwell, Idaho: Caxton Printers, 1939.

Fite, Emerson D. *Social and Industrial Conditions in the North during the Civil War*. New York: Macmillan Company, 1910.

Fleming, Howard. *Narrow Gauge Railways in America*. Lancaster, Pa.: Inquirer Printing and Publishing Company, 1875.

Francis, John. *Chronicles and Characters of the Stock Exchange*. London: Willoughby, 1849.

Fulford, Roger. *Glyn's 1753–1953*. London: Macmillan & Co., 1953.

Gates, Paul Wallace. *The Illinois Central Railroad and Its Colonization Work*. Cambridge, Mass.: Harvard University Press, 1934.

Giffin, Sir Robert. *American Railways as Investments*. London: Edward Stanford, 1873.

——. *Essays in Finance*. 2d ser. London: Bell & Sons, 1886.

——. *The Growth of Capital*. London: G. Bell & Sons, 1889.

——. "On Recent Accumulations of Capital in the United Kingdom," *Journal of the Statistical Society*, 1878.

Gilbert, John C. *A History of Investment Trusts in Dundee*. London: P. S. King, 1939.

Goodrich, Carter. "Public Aid to Railways in the Reconstruction South," *Political Science Quarterly*, LXXI (Sept. 1956), 407–42.

Grayson, Theodore J. *Investment Trusts*. New York: J. Wiley & Sons, 1928.

Gregory, T. E. *The Westminster Bank through a Century*. 2 vols. London: Oxford University Press, 1936.

Hacker, Louis M. *The Triumph of American Capitalism*. New York: Simon and Schuster, 1940.

Hacker, Louis M., and Benjamin B. Kendrick. *The United States since 1865*. New York: F. S. Crofts & Co., 1934.

Haney, Lewis H. *A Congressional History of Railways in the United States to 1850*. Bulletin of the University of Wisconsin, no. 211. Madison, Wis., 1908.

Hanna, Hugh Sisson. *A Financial History of Maryland (1789–1858)*. Baltimore: Johns Hopkins Press, 1907.

Hardcastle, Daniel, Jr. *Banks and Bankers*. London: Whittaker and Co., 1842.

Healy, Kent T. "Transportation as a Factor in Economic Growth," *Journal of Economic History*, Supplement VII (1947), 72–88.

Henderson, W. O. "The American Chamber of Commerce for the Port of Liverpool, 1801–1908," *Transactions of the Historical Society of Lancashire and Cheshire for 1933*, LXXXV. Liverpool: printed for the Society, 1935.

——. *The Lancashire Cotton Famine, 1861–1865*. Manchester University Press, 1934.

Hicks, Frederick C. (ed.). *High Finance in the Sixties*. New Haven: Yale University Press, 1929.

Hidy, Muriel. "George Peabody, Merchant and Financier, 1829–1854." Unpublished doctoral thesis, Radcliffe College, 1939.

Hidy, Ralph W. *The House of Baring in American Trade and Finance, 1763–1861*. Cambridge, Mass.: Harvard University Press, 1949.

——. "A Leaf from Investment History," *Harvard Business Review*, XX (Autumn 1941), 65–74.

Hellman, Geoffrey T. "Sorting Out the Seligmans," *New Yorker*, Oct. 30, 1954, pp. 34–65.

Hobson, C. K. *The Export of Capital*. London: Constable, 1914.

Hughes, Thomas. *Rugby, Tennessee*. London: Macmillan and Co., 1881.

Hungerford, Edward. *Men and Iron: The History of the New York Central*. New York: Thomas Y. Crowell Company, 1938.

——. *The Story of the Baltimore and Ohio Railroad*. New York: G. P. Putnam's Sons, 1928.

Hunt, Freeman. *Lives of American Merchants*. New York: Derby and Jackson, 1858.

Imlah, Albert. "British Balance of Payments and Export of Capital, 1816– 1913," *Economic History Review*, 2d ser., V (1952), 208–39.

Jenks, Leland H. "Britain and American Railway Development," *Journal of Economic History*, XI (Fall 1951), 375–88.

——. *The Migration of British Capital to 1875*. New York: Alfred A. Knopf, 1927.

John, A. H. *The Industrial Development of South Wales, 1750–1850*. Cardiff: University of Wales Press, 1950.

Knapp, John. "Capital Exports and Growth," *Economic Journal*, LXVII (Sept. 1957), 432–44.

Kuznets, Simon. "Long Term Changes in the National Income of the United States of America since 1870," in Simon Kuznets (ed.), *Income and Wealth of the United States: Trends and Structure*. International Association for Research in Income and Wealth. Income and Wealth Series 2. Cambridge: Bowes and Bowes, 1952.

Lambie, Joseph T. *From Mine to Market: The History of Coal Transportation on the Norfolk and Western Railway*. New York: New York University Press, 1954.

Lance, William. *Review of the Commerce of Chicago in 1855*. Pamphlet. Chicago: Chicago, St. Paul and Fond du Lac Railroad Co., 1856.

Lardner, Dionysius. *Railway Economy*. London: Taylor, Walton and Maberley, 1850.

Lavington, F. *The English Capital Market*. London: Methuen & Co., 1921.

Lehfeldt, R. A. "The Rate of Interest on British and Foreign Investment," *Journal of the Royal Statistical Society*, 1913.

Lewis, Cleona. *America's Stake in International Investments*. Washington, D.C.: Brookings Institution, 1938.

Lidstone, James Torrington Spencer. *The Londoniad*. London: Reed and Barton, 1856.

Lyell, Sir Charles. *A Second Visit to the United States*. 2 vols. London: John Murray, 1849.

MacCallum, E. D. *The Iron and Steel Industry in the United States*. London: P. S. King & Co., 1931.

McCulloch, J. R. *A Dictionary, Practical, Theoretical, and Historical, of Commerce and Commercial Navigation*. London, 1834.

McGrane, Reginald C. *Foreign Bondholders and American State Debts*. New York: Macmillan Company, 1935.

Martin, Sidney Walter. *Florida during the Territorial Days*. Athens, Ga.: University of Georgia Press, 1944.

Martin, William Elejius. *Internal Improvements in Alabama*. Baltimore: Johns Hopkins Press, 1902.

Medbery, James K. *Men and Mysteries of Wall Street*. Boston: Fields, Osgood & Co., 1870.

Mercier, Francis, and Arthur Strettell. *A Manual of American Railroad Securities.* London, 1876.

Meyer, B. H. (ed.). *History of Transportation in the United States before 1860.* Washington, D.C.: Carnegie Institution of Washington, 1917.

Moody, John. *The Railroad Builders.* New Haven: Yale University Press, 1919.

Morley, John. *The Life of Richard Cobden.* London: T. Fisher Unwin, 1896.

Mott, Edward Harold. *Between the Ocean and the Lakes: The Story of Erie.* New York: John S. Collins, 1899.

Myers, Gustavus. *History of the Great American Fortunes.* Revised edition. New York: Random House, 1936.

Myers, Margaret G. *The New York Money Market.* 2 vols. New York: Columbia University Press, 1931.

Nash, R. L. *A Short Inquiry into the Profitable Nature of Our Investments.* 2d and 3d editions. London: Effingham Wilson, 1881.

Nevins, Allen. *Fremont, Pathmarker of the West.* New York: Appleton-Century Company, 1939.

Nevins, Allen (ed.). *Selected Writings of Abram S. Hewitt.* New York: Columbia University Press, 1937.

Oberholtzer, Ellis Paxson. *Jay Cooke, Financier of the Civil War.* Philadelphia: George W. Jacobs & Co., 1907.

Overton, Richard C. *Burlington West.* Cambridge, Mass.: Harvard University Press, 1941.

———. *Gulf to Rockies: The Heritage of the Fort Worth and Denver-Colorado and Southern Railways.* Austin: University of Texas Press, 1953.

Paish, Sir George. "Great Britain's Capital Investments in Individual Colonial and Foreign Countries," *Journal of the Royal Statistical Society,* LXXIV, pt. II (Jan. 1911), 167–201.

———. "Great Britain's Capital Investments in Other Lands," *Journal of the Royal Statistical Society,* LXXII, pt. III (Sept. 30, 1909), 464–95.

———. *The Trade Balance of the United States.* National Monetary Commission, 61st Cong., 2d sess., Senate Document no. 579. Washington, D.C., 1910.

———. *Statist Supplement,* Feb. 1914.

Palmer, William J. *The Westward Current of Population in the United States.* London: W. A. Bell, 1874.

Paxson, Frederick L. *History of the American Frontier, 1763–1893.* Boston: Houghton Mifflin Company, 1924.

Perkins, J. R. *Trails, Rails and War.* Indianapolis: Bobbs-Merrill Company, 1929.

Perry, Bliss. *Life and Letters of Henry Lee Higginson.* Boston: Atlantic Monthly Press, 1921.

Peto, Sir Samuel Morton. *The Resources and Prospects of America.* London: Alexander Strahan, 1866.

Pierce, Harry H. *Railroads of New York: A Study of Government Aid, 1826–1875.* Cambridge, Mass.: Harvard University Press, 1953.

Potts, Charles S. *Railroad Transportation in Texas.* Bulletin of the University of Texas no. 119. Humanistic Series, no. 7. Austin: University of Texas Press, 1909.

Pratt, Sereno S. *The Work of Wall Street.* New York: D. Appleton and Company, 1912.

Ramsay, G. D. *English Overseas Trade during the Centuries of Emergence.* London: Macmillan & Co., 1957.

Ratchford, B. U. *American State Debts.* Durham, N.C.: Duke University Press, 1941.

Raymond, R. W. "The American Iron-Master's Work," *Atlantic Monthly,* XL (Nov. 1877), 525–36.

Riegel, Robert E. *The Story of the Western Railroads.* New York: Macmillan Company, 1926.

Ripley, William Z. *Railroads: Finance and Organization.* London: Longmans, Green and Co., 1915.

Robinson, Ralph M. *Coutts!* London: John Murray, 1929.

Sanborn, John Bell. *Congressional Grants of Land in Aid of Railways.* Bulletin of the University of Wisconsin no. 30. Economics, Political Science, and History Series, II, no. 3. Madison, Wis.: University of Wisconsin, 1899.

Smithers, Henry. *Liverpool: Its Commerce, Statistics, and Institutions.* Liverpool: Thomas Kaye, 1825.

Snyder, Carl. *American Railways as Investment.* New York: Moody Corporation, 1907.

Stickney, Albert K. "The Erie Railway and the English Stock," *American Law Review,* VI (Jan. 1872), 230–54.

Stover, John F. *The Railroads of the South, 1865–1900.* Chapel Hill: University of North Carolina Press, 1955.

Swank, James M. *History of the Manufacture of Iron in All Ages.* Philadelphia: American Iron and Steel Association, 1892.

Taylor, G. R. *The Transportation Revolution.* New York: Rinehart, 1951.

Thomlinson, William (ed.). *Thomas Whitwell.* Unpublished extracts made available to the author by Mrs. Amelia Eliza Wallis, Darlington. [Published by the "Gazette" Office, Middlesbrough and Stocton, 1879.]

Trotter, Alexander. *Observations on the Financial Position and Credit of Such of the States of the North American Union as Have Contracted Public Debts.* London: Longman, Orme, Browne, Green and Longman, 1839.

Trottman, Nelson. *History of the Union Pacific.* New York: Ronald Press Company, 1923.

Truptil, R. J. *British Banks and the London Money Market.* London: Jonathan Cape, 1936.

Van Oss, S. F. *American Railroads and British Investors.* London: Effingham Wilson and Co., 1893.

——. *American Railroads as Investments.* London: Effingham Wilson and Co., 1893.

Vernon, Edward. *American Railroad Manual.* London, 1874.

Villiers, Brougham, and W. H. Chesson. *Anglo-American Relations, 1861–1865.* London: T. Fisher Unwin, 1919.

Waters, L. L. *Steel Rails to Santa Fe.* Lawrence, Kansas: University of Kansas Press, 1950.

Watkin, Edward. *A Trip to the United States and Canada.* London: W. H. Smith, 1852.

Way, W. W., Jr. *The Clinchfield Railroad.* Chapel Hill: University of North Carolina Press, 1931.

EDITOR'S ADDITIONS TO THE BIBLIOGRAPHY

Athearn, Robert G. *Rebel of the Rockies.* New Haven: Yale University Press, 1962.

Borak, Arthur M. "The Financial History of the Chicago, Milwaukee and St. Paul Railway Company." Unpublished doctoral thesis, University of Minnesota, 1929.

Bosch, Kornelis Douwe. *De Nederlandse Beleggingen in de Verenigde Staten.* Amsterdam: Uitgeversmaatschappij Elsevier, 1948.

Dew, Charles B. *Ironmaker to the Confederacy: Joseph R. Anderson and the Tredegar Iron Works.* New Haven: Yale University Press, 1966.

Eddy, Harry L. (comp.). "Railroads 100 Years Old, 1945–1955." Mimeographed. Washington, D.C.: Association of American Railroads, 1948.

Fogel, Robert W. *The Union Pacific Railroad: A Case in Premature Enterprise.* Baltimore: Johns Hopkins University Press, 1960.

Goodrich, Carter. *Government Promotion of American Canals and Railroads, 1800–1890.* New York: Columbia University Press, 1960.

Grodinsky, Julius. *Jay Gould, His Business Career, 1867–1892.* Philadelphia: University of Pennsylvania Press, 1957.

Harlow, Alvin F. *The Road of the Century.* New York: Creative Age Press, 1947.

Hidy, Muriel. "The Capital Markets, 1789–1865," *in* Harold F. Williamson (ed.), *The Growth of the American Economy.* 2d ed. Englewood Cliffs, N.J.: Prentice-Hall, 1951, 256–78.

Hidy, Ralph W. "The Organization and Functions of Anglo-American Merchant Bankers, 1815–1860," *The Tasks of Economic History, Journal of Economic History,* I (Dec. 1941), 53–66.

Hidy, Ralph W., and Muriel E. Hidy. "Anglo-American Merchant Bankers and the Railroads of the Old Northwest, 1848–1860." *Business History Review,* XXXIV (Summer 1960), 150–69.

Jackson, W. Turrentine. *The Enterprising Scot: Investors in the American West after 1873.* Edinburgh: Edinburgh University Press, 1968.

Johnson, Arthur M., and Barry E. Supple. *Boston Capitalists and Western Railroads.* Cambridge, Mass.: Harvard University Press, 1967.

King, Wilfred Thomas Cousins. *History of the London Discount Market.* London: George Routledge & Sons, 1936.

Kirkland, Edward Chase. *Men, Cities, and Transportation: A Study in New England History, 1820–1900.* 2 vols. Cambridge, Mass.: Harvard University Press, 1948.

Lane, Wheaton J. *Commodore Vanderbilt: An Epic of the Steam Age.* New York: Alfred A. Knopf, 1942.

Lanier, J. F. D. *Sketch of the Life of J. F. D. Lanier.* New York, 1870.

Larson, Henrietta. *Jay Cooke, Private Banker.* Cambridge, Mass.: Harvard University Press, 1936.

McGrane, Reginald Charles. *The Panic of 1837.* Chicago: University of Chicago Press, 1924.

Neu, Irene. *Erastus Corning, Merchant and Financier, 1794–1872.* Ithaca, N.Y.: Cornell University Press, 1960.

Pierce, Harry H. "Foreign Investment in American Enterprise," *in* David T. Gilchrist and W. David Lewis (eds.), *Economic Change in the Civil War Era.* Greenville, Del.: Eleutherian Mills–Hagley Foundation, 1965. Pp. 41–61.

Redlich, Fritz. *The Molding of American Banking Men and Ideas.* History of American Business Leaders, II. 2 pts. New York: Hafner Publishing Co., 1951.

Salsbury, Stephen. *The State, the Investor, and the Railroad: The Boston and Albany, 1825–1867.* Cambridge, Mass.: Harvard University Press, 1967.

Smith, Alice E. *George Smith's Money: A Scottish Investor in America.* Madison, Wis.: State Historical Society of Wisconsin, 1966.

Stevens, Frank Walker. *The Beginnings of the New York Central Railroad: A History.* New York: G. P. Putnam's Sons, 1926.

Supple, Barry E. "A Business Elite: German-Jewish Financiers in Nineteenth-Century New York," *Business History Review,* XXXI (Summer 1957), 143–78.

Index